Economics of Agricultural Commodities SERIES

Tobacco and Other Small Crops

Guar and Guar Gum
Hops, Lac and Cadbury

Economics of Agricultural Commodities

Other Volumes in the Series

Spices and Medicinal Plants

Plantation Crops

Sugar

Vegetables

Fruits and Nuts

Fiber, Cotton and Jute

Oil Seeds

Cereals

Pulses

Economics of Agricultural Commodities SERIES

Tobacco and Other Small Crops

PC Bansil PhD

Director
Techno Economic Research Institute
New Delhi

CBS Publishers & Distributors Pvt Ltd

New Delhi • Bengaluru • Chennai • Kochi • Mumbai • Pune
Hyderabad • Kolkata • Nagpur • Patna • Vijayawada

Disclaimer

Science and technology are constantly changing fields. New research and experience broaden the scope of information and knowledge. The author has tried his best in giving information available to him while preparing the material for this book. Although, all efforts have been made to ensure optimum accuracy of the material, yet it is quite possible some errors might have been left uncorrected. The publisher, the printer and the author will not be held responsible for any inadvertent errors, or inaccuracies.

Economics of Agricultural Commodities SERIES

Tobacco

ISBN: 978-81-239-2621-6

First Edition: 2015

Published by Satish Kumar Jain and produced by Varun Jain for
CBS Publishers & Distributors Pvt Ltd
4819/XI Prahlad Street, 24 Ansari Road, Daryaganj, New Delhi 110 002, India.
Ph: 23289259, 23266861, 23266867 Website: www.cbspd.com
Fax: 011-23243014 e-mail: delhi@cbspd.com; cbspubs@airtelmail.in.
Corporate Office: 204 FIE, Industrial Area, Patparganj, Delhi 110 092
Ph: 4934 4934 Fax: 4934 4935 e-mail: publishing@cbspd.com; publicity@cbspd.com

Branches

- **Bengaluru:** Seema House 2975, 17th Cross, K.R. Road, Banasankari 2nd Stage, Bengaluru 560 070, Karnataka
  Ph: +91-80-26771678/79 Fax: +91-80-26771680 e-mail: bangalore@cbspd.com
- **Chennai:** 7, Subbaraya Street, Shenoy Nagar, Chennai 600 030, Tamil Nadu
  Ph: +91-44-26260666, 26208620 Fax: +91-44-42032115 e-mail: chennai@cbspd.com
- **Kochi:** Ashana House, No. 39/1904, A.M. Thomas Road, Valanjambalam, Ernakulam 682016, Kochi, Kerala
  Ph: +91-484-4059061-65, 67 Fax: +91-484-4059065 e-mail: kochi@cbspd.com
- **Mumbai:** 83-C, Dr E Moses Road, Worli, Mumbai-400018, Maharashtra
  Ph: +91-22-24902340/41 Fax: +91-22-24902342 e-mail: mumbai@cbspd.com
- **Pune:** Bhuruk Prestige, Sr. No. 52/12/2+1+3/2 Narhe, Haveli (Near Katraj-Dehu Road Bypass), Pune 411 041, Maharashtra
  Ph: +91-20-64704058, 64704059, 32392277 Fax: +91-20-24300160 e-mail: pune@cbspd.com

Representatives

- **Hyderabad** 0-9885175004
- **Kolkata** 0-9831437309, 0-9051152362
- **Nagpur** 0-9021734563
- **Patna** 0-9334159340
- **Vijayawada** 0-9000660880

Printed at: India Binding House, Noida, UP

to

my father

Late L. Radha Ram, a landlord, held the titles of Rais, Kursi Nashin, Honorary Magistrate and Assessor. These titles, which need an explanation for those born after independence, were bestowed upon him by the British Government, even though he was educated only to Class 8. Rais meant a respectable person. As a Rais, he was expected to entertain any official visiting the village. For this purpose, he had constructed a small bunglow called Kothi at the corner of the village Garden. As to the tile of a Kursi Nashin, only individuals holding this title were offered a chair to sit when visiting senior officials, those without the title had to stand. Once my father took me with him to the office of a Deputy Commissioner and gave a four anna coin to the peon who opened the door. When I enquired about the reason, my father told me that otherwise the peon will not bring him a chair to sit even though he is officially allowed to sit in a chair. Finally, the title of an Assessor indicated that he was a member of the Board, responsible for final ruling on death sentences. I think he was invited four or five times to serve on such a proceeding. In each case, without giving any detailed reason, he voted against the death sentence.

My father went to Delhi to attend the Coronation of King George. After my graduation, when I was leaving for Delhi, he warned me to be very careful, saying that Delhi is a big town. I write all this to give the present generation a glimpse into the workings of the British Raj. My father's blessings have stood by me throughout my life. May God give peace to his soul. I am honored to dedicate this book in his wonderful memory.

Preface

The book *Tobacco and Other Small Crops* is one of the volumes in the Series of Economics of Agricultural Commodities. The book consists of 5 chapters •Tobacco, •Hops, •Lac, •Cadbury, and •Guar and Guar Gum.

Each chapter deals in depth of the topic concerned. Starting with a historical approach, each chapter covers in details the various economic aspects along with the benefits and other relevant issues. Then in the final situation world issues are discussed in detail. Each chapter covers national and international aspects of the tobacco economy.

The entire work depends on secondary sources including the net. Although every possible source has been studied to provide data, there are a number of difficulties one faces. For example, the FAO and the USDA are primary sources for international production and trade. But both of these sources provide widely different data. We have provided the original data from all possible sources since we have no way to screen this vast source.

During the course of our studies, we observed that information available on various aspects of tobacco is scattered. It is difficult at present to lay one's hand at a specific publication which supplies relevant information. We thought to fill this gap, hence this series.

Although Cadbury is a company and not a commodity, it has been included in this volume because it produces chocolates and other products which are important commodities utilizing the agricultural produce from different region of the country.

The study is the result of innumerable sources—published/unpublished, quite a large number of daily newspapers, journals, magazines and books. The final presentation, however, is in a specific order so as to give the reader the required information at one place. We are grateful to a large number of authors whose work/research formed the base of this study. Thanks are due to Dr ML Srivastava and Mr Ravi Shankar without whose contribution the book would not have been able to see the light of the day. Our faculty members, Dr PN Radhakrishnan and Dr SR Mohnot, were always available to guide and contribute their bit. Last but not the least is the major contribution of our staff members Mrs Vasantha Krishnan and Mrs Ajitha Ganagadharan who never got tired to type and retype the material.

I do hope that the book in its updated form will prove useful to the students of agricultural economics, researchers, educated farmers, administrators, policymakers and bankers alike. I shall very much welcome any comments for further improvement of the volume.

PC Bansil

Contents

2 Cadbury 157

3 Guar and Guar Gum 179

4 Hops 199

5 Lac 227

1

Tobacco

Tobacco is an agricultural product processed from the leaves of plants in the genus *Nicotiana*. It can be consumed, used as an organic pesticide, and, in the form of nicotine tartrate, it is also used in some medicines. In consumption it most commonly appears in the forms of smoking, chewing, snuffing, or dipping tobacco or snus. Tobacco has long been in use as an entheogen in the Americas. However, upon the arrival of Europeans in North America, it quickly became popular as a trade item and as a recreational drug. This popularization led to the development of the Southern economy of the United States until it gave way to cotton. Following the American Civil War, a change in demand and a change in labor force allowed for the development of the cigarette. This new product quickly led to the growth of tobacco companies, until the scientific controversy of the mid-1900s.

There are many species of tobacco, which are all encompassed by the plant genus *Nicotiana*. The word *nicotiana* (as well as *nicotine*) was named in honor of Jean Nicot, French ambassador to Portugal, who in 1559 sent it as a medicine to the court of Catherine de Medici. It can also be chewed or inhaled (as with powdered snuff).

Because of the addictive properties of nicotine, tolerance and dependence develops. Absorption quantity, frequency, and speed of tobacco consumption are believed to be directly related to biological strength of nicotine dependence, addiction and tolerance. The usage of tobacco is an activity that is practiced by some 1.1 billion people, and up to one-third of the adult population. The World Health Organization (WHO) reports it to be the leading preventable cause of death worldwide and estimates that it currently causes 5.4 million deaths per year. Rates of smoking have leveled off or declined in developed countries; however, they continue to rise in developing countries.

Botanically, the tobacco plant belongs to the family *Solanacea* and the genus *Nicotiana*. The genus embraces over 60 species of which two alone are cultivated. India grows both *Nicotiana tabacum* and *Nicotiana rustica*. The largest area is under *Nicotiana tabacum*, which is grown all over the country, while *Nicotiana rustica* is confined to the Northern and Northeastern states, i.e. Uttar Pradesh, Bihar, West Bengal and Assam. The cultivation of *Nicotiana tabacum* accounts for more than 80% of the foreign exchange earnings.

Tobacco is cultivated more or less just like other agricultural products. Seeds are sown in cold frames or hotbeds to prevent attacks from insects, and then transplanted into the fields. Tobacco is an annual crop, which is usually harvested by a large single-piece farm equipment. After harvest, tobacco is stored for curing, which allows for the slow oxidation and degradation of carotenoids. This allows for the agricultural product to take on properties that are usually attributed to the "smoothness" of the smoke. Following this, tobacco is packed into its various forms of consumption, which include smoking, chewing, sniffing, and so on.

HISTORY

The Spanish word *"tabaco"* is thought to have its origin in Arawakan language, particularly, in the Taino language of the Caribbean. In Taino, it was said to refer either to a roll of tobacco leaves (according to Bartolome de Las Casas, 1552), or to the *tabago*, a kind of Y-shaped pipe for sniffing tobacco smoke (according to Oviedo; with the leaves themselves being referred to as *cohiba*).

However, similar words in Spanish and Italian were commonly used from 1410 to define medicinal herbs, originating from the Arabic *tabbaq*, a word reportedly dating to the 9th century, as the name of various herbs.

Tobacco had already been used for long in the Americas when European settlers arrived and introduced the practice to Europe, where it became popular. At high doses, tobacco can become hallucinogenic accordingly native Americans never used the drug recreationally. Instead, it was often consumed as an entheogen; among some tribes, this was done only by experienced shamans or medicine men. Eastern North American tribes would carry large amounts of tobacco in pouches as a readily accepted trade item, and would often smoke it in pipes, either in defined ceremonies that were considered sacred, or to seal a bargain, and they would smoke it at such occasions in all stages of life, even in childhood. It was believed that tobacco was a gift from the Creator and that the exhaled tobacco smoke was capable of carrying one's thoughts and prayers to heaven.

"In ancient times, when the land was barren and the people were starving, the Great Spirit sent forth a woman to save humanity. As she traveled over the world everywhere her right hand touched the soil, there grew potatoes. And everywhere her left hand touched the soil, there grew corn. And in the place where she had sat, there grew tobacco" Huron Indian myth.

"The Spaniards upon their journey met with great multitudes of people, men and women with firebrands in their hands and herbs to smoke after their custom". Christopher Columbus' journal, **6 November 1492.**

"Smoking is a custom loathsome to the eye, hateful to the nose, harmful to the brain, dangerous to the lungs, and in the black, stinking fume thereof nearest resembling the horrible Stygian smoke of the pit that is bottomless". **James I of England** *A Counterblaste to Tobacco* **1604.**

"I say, if you can't send money, send tobacco". First US President George Washington's request to help finance **the American Civil War, 1776.**

Within 150 years of Columbus's finding "strange leaves" in the New World, tobacco was being used around the globe. Its rapid spread and widespread acceptance characterize the addiction to the plant *Nicotina tobacum*. Only the mode of delivery has changed. In the 18th century, snuff held sway; the 19th century was the age of the cigar; the 20th century saw the rise of the manufactured cigarette and with it a greatly increased number of smokers. At the beginning of the 21st century

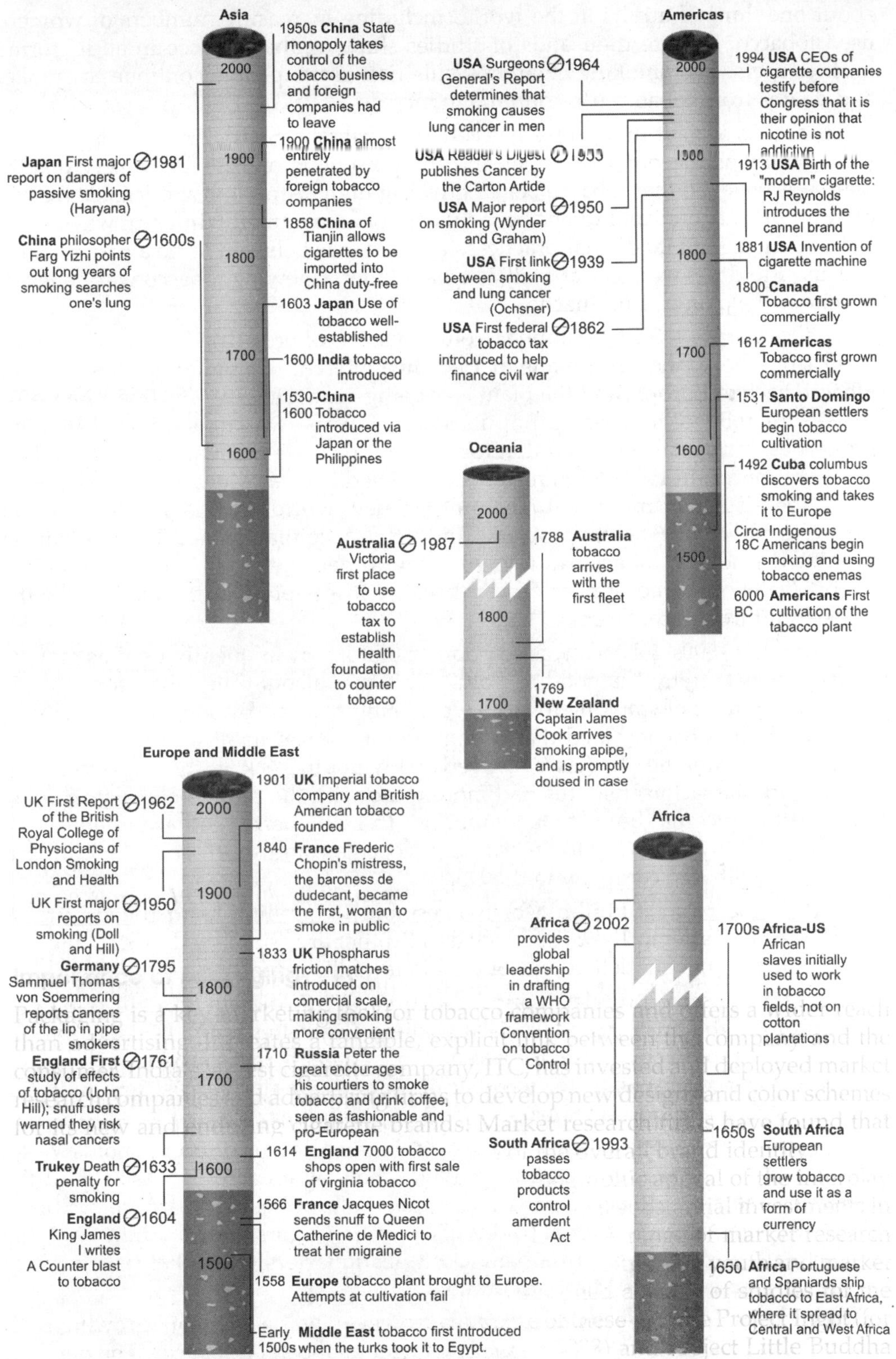

Asia
2000
1900
1800
1700
1600
1950s China State monopoly takes control of the tobacco business and foreign companies had to leave
1900 China almost entirely penetrated by foreign tobacco companies
1858 China of Tianjin allows cigarettes to be imported into China duty-free
1603 Japan Use of tobacco well-established
1600 India tobacco introduced
1530-China
1600 Tobacco introduced via Japan or the Philippines
Japan First major 1981 report on dangers of passive smoking (Haryana)
China philosopher 1600s Farg Yizhi points out long years of smoking searches one's lung
Americas
2000
1900
1800
1700
1600
1500
USA Surgeons 1964 General's Report determines that smoking causes lung cancer in men
USA Reader's Digest 1953 publishes Cancer by the Carton Artide
USA Major report 1950 on smoking (Wynder and Graham)
USA First link 1939 between smoking and lung cancer (Ochsner)
USA First federal 1862 tobacco tax introduced to help finance civil war
1994 USA CEOs of cigarette companies testify before Congress that it is their opinion that nicotine is not addictive
1913 USA Birth of the "modern" cigarette: RJ Reynolds introduces the cannel brand
1881 USA Invention of cigarette machine
1800 Canada Tobacco first grown commercially
1612 Americas Tobacco first grown commercially
1531 Santo Domingo European settlers begin tobacco cultivation
1492 Cuba columbus discovers tobacco smoking and takes it to Europe
Circa 18C Indigenous Americans begin smoking and using tobacco enemas
6000 BC Americans First cultivation of the tabacco plant
Oceania
2000
1800
1700
Australia 1987 Victoria first place to use tobacco tax to establish health foundation to counter tobacco
1788 Australia tobacco arrives with the first fleet
1769 New Zealand Captain James Cook arrives smoking apipe, and is promptly doused in case
Europe and Middle East
2000
1900
1800
1700
1600
1500
UK First Report 1962 of the British Royal College of Physiocians of London Smoking and Health
UK First major 1950 reports on smoking (Doll and Hill)
Germany 1795 Sammuel Thomas von Soemmering reports cancers of the lip in pipe smokers
England First 1761 study of effects of tobacco (John Hill); snuff users warned they risk nasal cancers
Trukey Death 1633 penalty for smoking
England 1604 King James I writes A Counter blast to tobacco
1901 UK Imperial tobacco company and British American tobacco founded
1840 France Frederic Chopin's mistress, the baroness de dudecant, became the first, woman to smoke in public
1833 UK Phospharus friction matches introduced on comercial scale, making smoking more convenient
1710 Russia Peter the great encourages his courtiers to smoke tobacco and drink coffee, seen as fashionable and pro-European
1614 England 7000 tobacco shops open with first sale of virginia tobacco
1566 France Jacques Nicot sends snuff to Queen Catherine de Medici to treat her migraine
1558 Europe tobacco plant brought to Europe. Attempts at cultivation fail
Early 1500s Middle East tobacco first introduced when the turks took it to Egypt.
Africa
Africa 2002 provides global leadership in drafting a WHO framework Convention on tobacco Control
South Africa 1993 passes tobacco products control amerdent Act
1700s Africa-US African slaves initially used to work in tobacco fields, not on cotton plantations
1650s South Africa European settlers grow tobacco and use it as a form of currency
1650 Africa Portuguese and Spaniards ship tobacco to East Africa, where it spread to Central and West Africa

about one-third of adults in the world, including increasing numbers of women, used tobacco. Despite thousands of studies showing that tobacco in all its forms kills its users, and smoking cigarettes kills non-users, people continue to smoke, and deaths from tobacco use continue to increase.

Tobacco is a plant that grows natively in North and South America. It is in the same family as the potato, pepper and the poisonous nightshade, a very deadly plan. It is believed that tobacco began growing in the Americas about 6,000 BC. As early as 1 BC, American Indians began using tobacco in many different ways, such as in religious and medicinal practices. Tobacco was believed to be a cure-all, and was used to dress wounds, as well as a pain killer. Chewing tobacco was believed to relieve the pain of a toothache.

On October 15, 1492, Christopher Columbus was offered dried tobacco leaves as a gift from the American Indians that he encountered. Soon after, sailors brought tobacco back to Europe, and the plant was being grown all over Europe. The major reason for tobacco's growing popularity in Europe was its supposed healing properties. Europeans believed that tobacco could cure almost anything, from bad breath to cancer. In 1571, A Spanish doctor named Nicolas Monardes wrote a book about the history of medicinal plants of the new world. In this, he claimed that tobacco could cure 36 health problems. In 1588, A Virginian named Thomas Harriet promoted smoking tobacco as a viable way to get one's daily dose of tobacco. Unfortunately, he died of nose cancer (because it was popular then to breathe the smoke out through the nose).

During the 1600s, tobacco was so popular that it was frequently used as money! Tobacco was literally "as good as gold"! This was also a time when some of the dangerous effects of smoking tobacco were being realized by some individuals. In 1610, Sir Francis Bacon noted that trying to quit the bad habit was really hard! In 1632, 12 years after the Mayflower arrived on Plymouth Rock, it was illegal to smoke publicly in Massachusetts! This had more to do with the moral beliefs of the day, than health concerns about smoking tobacco. In 1760, Pierre Lorillard establishes a company in New York City to process tobacco, cigars and snuff. Today, P Lorillard is the oldest tobacco company in the US.

In 1847, the famous Phillip Morris is established, selling hand rolled Turkish cigarettes. Soon after in 1849, JE Liggett and Brother are established in St. Louis, Mo (The company that has settled out of the big lawsuits recently).

Cigarettes became popular around this time when soldiers brought it back to England from the Russian and Turkish soldiers. Cigarettes in the US were mainly made from scraps left over after the production of other tobacco products, especially chewing tobacco. Chewing tobacco became quite popular at this time with the "cowboys" of the American west.

In 1875, RJ Reynolds Tobacco Company (better known for its Reynolds Wrap Aluminum Foil) was established to produce chewing tobacco. It wasn't until the 1900s that the cigarette became the major tobacco product made and sold. Still in 1901, 3.5 billion cigarettes were sold while 6 billion cigars were sold. In 1902, the British Phillip Morris sets up a New York headquarters to market its cigarettes including a now famous Marlboro brand.

Along with the popularity of cigarettes, however, was a small but growing anti-tobacco campaign with some states proposing a total ban on tobacco. The demand for cigarettes grew however, and in 1913 RJ Reynolds began to market a cigarette brand called Camel.

"The use of cigarette exploded during World War I (1914–1918), where cigarettes were called the soldier's smoke". By 1923, Camel controls 45% of the US market! In 1924, Phillip Morris begins to market Marlboro as a woman's cigarette that is a "Mild as May"! To battle this, American Tobacco Company, maker of the Lucky Strike brand, begins to market its cigarette to women and gains 38% of the market. Smoking rates among female teenagers soon triple during the years between 1925 and 1935!

In 1939, American Tobacco Company introduces a new brand, Pall Mall, which allows American to become the largest tobacco company in the US! During World War II (1939–1945), cigarette sales are at an all time high. Cigarettes were included in a soldier's C-Rations (like food!). Tobacco companies sent millions of cigarettes to the soldiers for free, and when these soldiers came home, the companies had a steady stream of loyal customers.

During the 1950s, more and more evidence was surfacing that smoking was linked to lung cancer. Although the tobacco industry denied such health hazards, they promoted new products which were "safer", such as those with lower tar and filtered cigarettes. In 1952, P Lorillard markets its Kent brand with the "micronite" filter, which contained asbestos! This was fortunately discontinued in 1956. In 1953, Dr Ernst L Wynders finds that putting cigarette tar on the backs of mice causes tumors! In 1954, RJ Reynolds introduces the filtered Winston brand. In 1956, Reynolds introduces the Salem brand, which is the first filter-tipped menthol cigarette.

In 1964, the Surgeon General's report on "Smoking and Health" came out. This report assisted in allowing the government to regulate the advertisement and sales of cigarettes. The 1960s in general was a time when much of the health hazards of smoking were reported.

In 1965, television cigarette ads are taken off the air in Great Britain.

In 1966, those health warnings on cigarette packs begin popping up.

In 1968, Bravo, a non-tobacco cigarette brand was marketed. Made primarily of lettuce, it failed miserably!

Because of the negative press about tobacco, the major tobacco companies begin to diversify their products. Phillip Morris begins to buy into the Miller Brewing Company, makers of Miller Beer, Miller Lite, and Red Dog Beer. RJ Reynolds Tobacco Company drops the "Tobacco Company" in its name, and becomes RJ Reynolds Industries. It also begins to buy into other products, such as aluminum. American Tobacco Company also drops "Tobacco" from its name, becoming American Brands, Inc.

In 1971, television ads for cigarettes are finally taken off the air in the US Cigarettes, however, are still the most heavily advertised product second to automobiles!

In 1977, the first national Great American Smoke out takes place. In 1979, the Surgeon General reports on the Health Consequences of Smoking for Women. This is in light to the increasing number of women who are taking up the bad habit. Some attribute it to the slick ad campaign of the Virginia Slims brand, "You've Come a Long Way Baby"!

During the 1980s, there were many lawsuits filed against the tobacco industry because of the harmful effects of its products. Smoking becomes politically incorrect, with more public places forbidding smoking.

In 1982, the Surgeon General reports that second hand smoke may cause lung cancer. Smoking in public areas is soon restricted especially at the workplace.

In 1985, lung cancer became the 1 killer of women, beating out breast cancer!

Phillip Morris continues to diversify into other products, buying into General Foods Corporation and Kraft Inc in 1985. R Reynolds, also diversifies, buying Nabisco (of Oreo fame) and becoming RJR/Nabisco.

In 1987, Congress bands smoking on all domestic flights lasting less than 2 hours. In 1990, Smoking is banned on all domestic flights, except to Alaska and Hawaii.

In 1990, Ben & Jerry's (of icecream fame) boycotts RJR/Nabisco, and drops Oreos from its icecream products.

During the 80s and 90s, the tobacco industry starts marketing heavily in areas outside the US, especially developing countries in Asia. Marlboro is considered the world number 1 most valuable brand of any product with a value over $30 billion! Over this period, there is a battle between Coca Cola and Marlboro as the No. 1 brand in the world!

In recent, years, there is growing evidence that the tobacco industry has known all along that cigarettes are harmful, but continued to market and sell them. There is also evidence that they knew that nicotine was addictive and exploited this hidden knowledge to get millions of people hooked on this dangerous habit!

Popularization

Following the arrival of the Europeans, tobacco became increasingly popular as a trade item. It fostered the economy for the Southern United States until it was replaced by cotton. Following the American civil war, a change in demand and a change in labor force allowed inventor James Bonsack to create a machine which automated cigarette production. This increase in production allowed tremendous growth in the tobacco industry until the scientific revelations of the mid-1900s.

Contemporary Facts

Following the scientific revelations of the mid-1900s, tobacco became condemned as a health hazard, and eventually became encompassed as a cause for cancer, as well as other respiratory and circulatory diseases. This led to the Tobacco Master Settlement Agreement (MSA) which settled the lawsuit in exchange for a combination of yearly payments to the States and voluntary restrictions on advertising and marketing of tobacco products.

In the 1970s, Brown & Williamson cross-bred a strain of tobacco to produce Y1. This strain of tobacco contained an unusually high amount of nicotine, nearly doubling its content from 3.2–3.5% to 6.5%. In the 1990s, this prompted the Food and Drug Administration (FDA) to use this strain as evidence that tobacco companies were intentionally manipulating the nicotine content of cigarettes.

In 2003, in response to growth of tobacco use in developing countries, the WHO successfully rallied 168 countries to sign the Framework Convention on Tobacco Control (FCTC). The Convention is designed to push for effective legislation and its enforcement in all countries to reduce the harmful effects of tobacco. This led to the development of tobacco cessation products.

TOBACCO VARIETIES

Types of Tobacco

There are a number of types of tobacco as detailed below:

- **Aromatic fire-cured** is cured by smoke from open fires. In the United States, it is grown in northern middle Tennessee, central Kentucky and in Virginia. Fire-cured tobacco grown in Kentucky and Tennessee are used in some chewing tobaccos, moist snuff, some cigarettes, and as a condiment in pipe tobacco blends. Another fire-cured tobacco is Latakia, which is produced from oriental varieties of *N. tabacum*. The leaves are cured and smoked over smoldering fires of local hardwoods and aromatic shrubs in Cyprus and Syria.
- **Bright leaf tobacco** is commonly known as "Virginia tobacco", often regardless of the state in which they are planted. Prior to the American Civil War, most tobacco grown in the US was fire-cured dark-leaf. This type of tobacco was planted in fertile lowlands, used a robust variety of leaf, and was either fire cured or air cured. Most Canadian cigarettes are made from 100% pure Virginia tobacco.
- **Burley tobacco** is an air-cured tobacco used primarily for cigarette production. In the US, burley tobacco plants are started from palletized seeds placed in polystyrene trays floated on a bed of fertilized water in March or April.
- **Cavendish** is more a process of curing and a method of cutting tobacco than a type. The processing and the cut are used to bring out the natural sweet taste in the tobacco. Cavendish can be produced from any tobacco type, but is usually one of, or a blend of Kentucky, Virginia, and Burley, and is most commonly used for pipe tobacco and cigars.
- **Criollo tobacco** is a type of tobacco, primarily used in the making of cigars. It was, by most accounts, one of the original Cuban tobaccos that emerged around the time of Columbus.
- **Dokham** is a tobacco originally grown in Iran, mixed with leaves, bark, and herbs for smoking in a midwakh.
- **Turkish tobacco** is a sun-cured, highly aromatic, small-leafed variety (*Nicotiana tabacum*) that is grown in Turkey, Greece, Bulgaria, and Macedonia. Originally grown in regions historically part of the Ottoman Empire, it is also known as "oriental". Many of the early brands of cigarettes were made mostly or entirely of Turkish tobacco; today, its main use is in blends of pipe and especially cigarette tobacco (a typical American cigarette is a blend of Bright Virginia, Burley and Turkish).
- **Perique**, a farmer called Pierre Chenet is credited with first turning this local tobacco into the Perique in 1824 through the technique of pressure-fermentation. Considered the truffle of pipe tobaccos, it is used as a component in many blended pipe tobaccos, but is too strong to be smoked pure. At one time, the freshly moist Perique was also chewed, but none is now sold for this purpose. It is typically blended with pure Virginia to lend spice, strength, and coolness to the blend.
- **Shade tobacco** is cultivated in Connecticut and Massachusetts. Early Connecticut colonists acquired from the Native Americans the habit of smoking tobacco in pipes, and began cultivating the plant commercially, even though

the Puritans referred to it as the "evil weed". The industry has weathered some major catastrophes, including a devastating hailstorm in 1929, and an epidemic of brown spot fungus in 2000, but is now in danger of disappearing altogether, given the value of the land to real estate speculators.

- **White burley**, in 1865, George Webb of Brown County, Ohio planted red burley seeds he had purchased, and found that a few of the seedlings had a whitish, sickly look. The air-cured leaf was found to be more mild than other types of tobacco.
- **Wild tobacco** is native to the southwestern United States, Mexico, and parts of South America. Its botanical name is *Nicotiana rustica*.
- **Y1** is a strain of tobacco cross-bred by Brown & Williamson in the 1970s to obtain an unusually high nicotine content. In the 1990s, the United States FDA used it as evidence that tobacco companies were intentionally manipulating the nicotine content of cigarettes.

Manufactured cigarettes consist of shredded or reconstituted tobacco processed with hundreds of chemicals. Often with a filter, they are manufactured by a machine, and are the predominant form of tobacco used worldwide.

Bidis consist of a small amount of tobacco, hand-wrapped in dried temburni leaf and tied with string. Despite their small size, their tar and carbon monoxide deliveries can be higher than manufactured cigarettes because of the need to puff harder to keep bidis lit. Bidis are found throughout Southeast Asia, and are India's most used type of tobacco.

Cigars are made of air-cured and fermented tobaccos with a tobacco wrapper, and come in many shapes and sizes, from cigarette sized cigarillos, double coronas, cheroots, stumpen, chuttas and dhumtis. In reverse chutta and dhumti smoking, the ignited end of the cigar is placed inside the mouth. There was a revival of cigar smoking at the end of the 20th century among both men and women.

Kreteks are clove-flavored cigarettes. They contain a wide range of exotic flavorings and eugenol, which has an anesthetizing effect, allowing for deeper smoke inhalation. Kreteks are clove flavored cigarettes widely smoked in Indonesia.

Pipes are made of briar, slate, clay or other substance—tobacco is placed in the bowl and inhaled through the stem, sometimes through water. Sticks are made from sun-cured tobacco known as brus and wrapped in cigarette paper.

Cigarettes are available throughout the world. Filter-tipped cigarettes are usually more popular than unfiltered cigarettes. Hand-rolled cigarettes are also widely smoked in many countries.

Cigars are smoked throughout the world. Regional variations include cheroots and stumpen (Western and Central Europe) and dhumtis (conical cheroots) used in India.

Tobacco is used orally throughout the world, but principally in Southeast Asia. In Mumbai, India, 56% of women chew tobacco.

Other Tobacco

Chewing tobacco is also known as plug, loose-leaf and twist. Pan masala, or betel quid consists of tobacco, areca nuts and staked lime wrapped in a betel leaf. They can also contain other sweetenings and flavoring agents. Varieties of pan include kaddipudi, hogesoppu, gundi, kadapam, zarda, pattiwala, kiwam, mishri and pills.

Moist snuff is taken orally. A small amount of ground tobacco is held in the mouth between the cheek and the gum. Increasingly, manufacturers are prepackaging moist snuff into small paper or cloth packets, to make the product easier to use. Other products include khaini, shammaah and nass or naswa.

Dry snuff is powdered tobacco that is inhaled through the nose or taken by mouth. Once widespread, its use is now in decline.

Curing

Curing and subsequent aging allow for the slow oxidation and degradation of carotenoids in tobacco leaf. This produces certain compounds in the tobacco leaves, and gives a sweet hay, tea, rose oil, or fruity aromatic flavor that contributes to the "smoothness" of the smoke. Starch is converted to sugar, which glycates protein, and is oxidized into advanced glycation end-products (AGEs), a caramelization process that also adds flavor. Inhalation of these AGEs in tobacco smoke contributes to atherosclerosis and cancer. Levels of AGEs are dependent on the curing method used.

Tobacco can be cured through several methods which include but are not limited to:

- **Air-cured** tobacco is hung in well-ventilated barns and allowed to dry over a period of 4–8 weeks. Air-cured tobacco is low in sugar, which gives the tobacco smoke a light, sweet flavor, and high in nicotine. Cigar and burley tobaccos are air cured.
- **Fire-cured** tobacco is hung in large barns where fires of hardwoods are kept on continuous or intermittent low smoulder and takes between 3 days and 10 weeks, depending on the process and the tobacco. Fire curing produces a tobacco low in sugar and high in nicotine. Pipe tobacco, chewing tobacco, and snuff are fire cured.
- **Flue-cured** tobacco was originally strung onto tobacco sticks, which were hung from tier-poles in curing barns (Aus: kilns, also traditionally called Oasts). These barns have flues which run from externally fed fire boxes, heat-curing the tobacco without exposing it to smoke, slowly raising the temperature over the course of the curing. The process will generally take about a week. This method produces cigarette tobacco that is high in sugar and has medium to high levels of nicotine.
- **Sun-cured** tobacco dries uncovered in the sun. This method is used in Turkey, Greece and other Mediterranean countries to produce oriental tobacco. Sun-cured tobacco is low in sugar and nicotine and is used in cigarettes.

CIGARETTE TOBACCO

Virginia Flue-Cured Tobacco

Cigarettes are a product consumed through the inhalation of smoke and manufactured from cured and finely cut tobacco leaves and reconstituted tobacco, often combined with other additives, then rolled or stuffed into a paper-wrapped cylinder. Virginia Tobacco used in cigarettes is the most important commercial variety and is an export-oriented crop this accounts for about 21% of Indias total production of tobacco. About 40% of the total Virginia tobacco production is used for domestic cigarette industry while the rest is exported to markets all over the world. Virginia tobacco is grown mostly in the States of Andhra Pradesh and Karnataka. In Andhra Pradesh, the cultivation of Virginia tobacco is concentrated in the coastal districts of Prakasam, Guntur, Krishna, East and West Godavari and Nellore and in Khammam, Karimnagar and Warangal Districts of Telangana. Traditional Virginia tobacco used to be cultivated in black soil areas. In view of the changing tastes in the consumers preference for light bodied leaf with less nicotine/ tar content in the international market, the cultivation of Virginia Flue cured Tobacco has been extended to the light soil areas also.

Natu Tobacco

Andhra Pradesh also produces about 30 million kg of sim cured country or natu tobacco which is used in the manufacture of cigarettes and tobacco mixtures for pipes. This type is mainly grown in the districts of Kurnool, Guntur, East and West Godavari and Krishna.

Burely Tobacco

Burely Tobacco which is also a cigarette type is grown to a small extent in East Godavari, Guntur, Visakhapatnam and Telangana areas of Andhra Pradesh.

BIDI TOBACCO

Beedi are thin, often flavored, South Asian cigarettes made of tobacco wrapped in a tendu leaf, and secured with colored thread at one end. Bidi Tobacco is the most important Non-Virginia tobacco produced in the country. More than 85% of the world bidi production is accounted for by India. Bidi tobacco occupies 30–35% of the total area under tobacco in the country whereas in terms of production its share is around 35–40%. Gujarat, Karnataka and Maharashtra are the main bidi tobacco producing States. In Gujarat, bidi tobacco is grown in Charotar area comprising Anand, Borsad, Petlad and Nadiad Taluks of Kaira District and Baroda district. It is mostly grown under irrigated conditions. In Karnataka, bidi tobacco is mainly grown in Nipani area of Belgaum District on the banks of River Krishna and its tributaries. Kolhapur and Sangli are the two important districts for cultivation of bidi tobacco in Maharashtra. Bidi tobacco grown in Nipani area of Karnataka is considered to be superior in quality. Yield-wise it is low only about 100 kg/ha in Karnataka as against 1800 kg/ha in Gujarat State.

Chewing Tobacco

Chewing tobacco is one of the oldest ways of consuming tobacco leaves. It is consumed orally, in two forms: through sweetened strands, or in a shredded form. When consuming the long sweetened strands, the tobacco is lightly chewed and compacted into a ball. When consuming the shredded tobacco, small amounts are placed at the bottom lip, between the gum and the teeth, where it is gently compacted, thus it can oftentimes be called *dipping tobacco*. Both methods stimulate the saliva glands, which led to the development of the spittoon.

Chewing tobacco is mostly grown is the States of Tamil Nadu, Uttar Pradesh, Bihar, West Bengal and Orissa. Coimbatore and Periyar in Tamil Nadu, Farrukhbad in Uttar Pradesh, Vaisali and Samastipur in Bihar, Cooch Behar in West Bengal, Koraput in Orissa are the important chewing tobacco growing districts.

Maharashtra to Ban Chewing Tobacco in Public Places

The Maharashtra Government is working on a law to ban chewing of tobacco in public places. Once the law comes into effect, chewing of tobacco products like maava, zarda, khaini, etc in offices, gardens, hospitals, airports, restaurants and public areas will be prohibited. At present, only smoking of cigarettes and bidis are prohibited in the above areas. "The provisions of the Cigarette and Other Tobacco Products Act (COTPA) will be expanded to bring in smokeless tobacco products within its ambit", Saunik told reporters here.

Cigar Tobacco

Cigars are tightly rolled bundle of dried and fermented tobacco which is ignited so that its smoke may be drawn into the smoker's mouth.

There are three distinct types of tobacco used in the manufacture of cigar viz. filler, binder and wrapper. In India, good quality filler tobacco is also used as a binder. Wrapper tobacco of good quality is mainly grown in Cooch Behar district of West Bengal. Cigar filler tobacco is mainly grown in Dindigul and Trichy districts of Tamil Nadu.

Expensive Cigars

According to Businessinsider.com, Gurkha Black Dragon is the world's most expensive cigar, retailing at $1,150 apiece. Here is a list of the top 10.

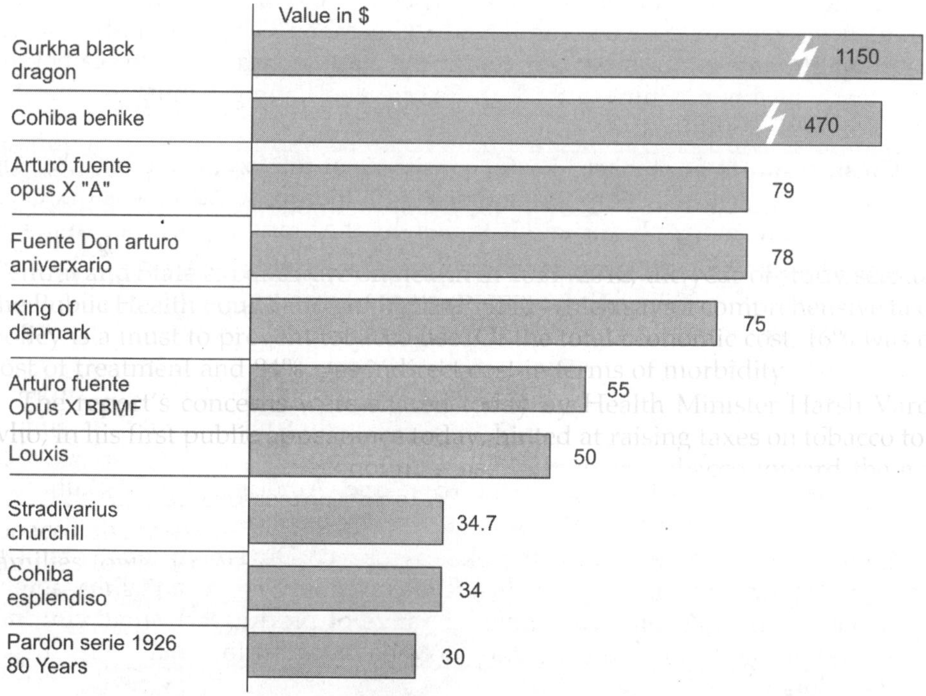

Cheroot Tobacco

This type of tobacco is mainly grown in Andhra Pradesh and Tamil Nadu. Lanka tobacco is grown in the Godavari river belt is also used for the manufacture of cheroots. In Saled, Trichy and Dindigul districts of Tamil Nadu cheroot tobacco is grown. Natu tobacco grown in Guntur, Kurnool and Godavari areas of Andhra Pradesh is also used in the manufacture of cheroots.

Hookah Tobacco

The tobacco which is used in smoking through the hookah or hubble-bubble is called Hookah tobacco. Hookah tobacco is mostly *N. rustica* type and it is grown in cold climate. Hookah is a single or multi-stemmed (often glass-based) water pipe for smoking. Originally from India, the hookah has gained immense popularity, especially in the Middle East. A hookah operates by water filtration and indirect heat. It can be used for smoking herbal fruits or cannabis.

This type of tobacco is cultivated in Uttar Pradesh, West Bengal and Orissa and it is locally known as Calcutta, Vilayati and Motihari. The major districts cultivation hookah tobacco are Purnea in Bihar, Cooch Behar and Jalpaiguri in West Bengal, Kaira and Ahmedabad in Gujarat and Farrukhabad and Etah districts in Uttar Pradesh.

Snuff Tobacco

Tobacco used for snuff is grown in Andhra Pradesh, Kerala, West Bengal, Uttar Pradesh and Gujarat. There is no special variety grown exclusively for snuff tobacco in the country. Generally, the tobacco varieties used for snuff manufacture are mainly consumed in a number of forms viz. hookah, chewing and bidi. The important snuff manufacturing states in India are Tamil Nadu, Gujarat and Uttar Pradesh. Chennai in Tamil Nadu State is an important center for manufacture of snuff. Generally, tobacco leaf which is medium to thick in texture and having a pungent aroma is selected for snuff manufacture.

1. **Creamy snuffs** are tobacco paste, consisting of tobacco, clove oil, glycerin, spearmint, menthol, camphor, and sold in a toothpaste tube. It is marketed mainly to women in India, and is known by the brand names Ipco (made by Asha Industries), Denobac, Tona, Ganesh. It is locally known as "mishri" in some parts of Maharashtra.

   Snuff is a generic term for fine-ground smokeless tobacco products. Originally, the term referred only to dry snuff, a fine tan dust popular mainly in the 18th century. Snuff powder originated in the UK town of Great Harwood, and was famously ground in the town's monument prior to local distribution and transport further up north to Scotland. There are two major varieties which include European (dry) and American (moist); although American snuff is often referred to as dipping tobacco.

2. **Dipping tobaccos** are a form of smokeless tobacco. Dip is occasionally referred to as "chew", and because of this, it is commonly confused with chewing tobacco, which encompasses a wider range of products. A small clump of dip is "pinched" out of the tin and placed between the lower or upper lip and the gums.

3. **Electronic cigarette** is an alternative to tobacco smoking although no tobacco is consumed. It is a battery-powered device that provides inhaled doses of nicotine by delivering a vaporized propylene glycol/nicotine solution.
4. **Gutka** is a preparation of crushed betel nut, tobacco, and sweet or savory flavorings. It is manufactured in India and exported to a few other countries. A mild stimulant, it is sold across India in small, individual-size packets.
5. **Kreteks** are cigarettes made with a complex blend of tobacco, cloves and a flavoring "sauce". It was first introduced in the 1880s in Kudus, Java, to deliver the medicinal eugenol of cloves to the lungs.
6. **Roll-Your-Own**, often called rollies or roll ups, are very popular, particularly in European countries. These are prepared from loose tobacco, cigarette papers and filters all bought separately. They are usually much cheaper to make.
7. **Pipe smoking** typically consists of a small chamber (the bowl) for the combustion of the tobacco to be smoked and a thin stem (shank) that ends in a mouthpiece (the bit). Shredded pieces of tobacco are placed into the chamber and ignited.
8. **Snus** is steam-cured moist powder tobacco product that is not fermented, and does not induce salivation. It is consumed by placing it in the mouth against the gums for an extended period of time. It is a form of snuff that is used in a manner similar to American dipping tobacco, but does not require regular spitting.
9. **Topical tobacco paste** is sometimes recommended as a treatment for wasp, hornet, fire ant, scorpion, and bee stings. An amount equivalent to the contents of a cigarette is mashed in a cup with about a 0.5 to 1 teaspoon of water to make a paste that is then applied to the affected area.
10. **Tobacco water** is a traditional organic insecticide used in domestic gardening. Tobacco dust can be used similarly. It is produced by boiling strong tobacco in water, or by steeping the tobacco in water for a longer period. When cooled, the mixture can be applied as a spray, or "painted" on to the leaves of garden plants, where it will prove deadly to insects.

From early times man has developed various types of tobacco for various uses. There are about 65 valid species of tobacco but among these only two species viz, *Nicotiana tabacum* and *Nicotiana rustica* are cultivated extensively. India grows both these species, but, by far, the largest area is under *Nicotiana tabacum* which is grown all over the country. *Nicotiana rustica* requires cooler climate. Its cultivation is confined mainly to the Northern and Northeastern region.

Cigarette, bidi, chewing, hookah, cigar, cheroot, snuff, natu, burley, etc are the various types of tobacco grown in different parts of the country. The plant characteristics, soil and climatic requirements, agronomic practices, harvesting and curing techniques and the chemistry of end-products are all different in different types of tobacco grown in different zones. The area of concentration of the various types of tobacco is indicated below and is also depicted in the Tobacco Map of India. Tobacco is consumed in many forms and through a number of different methods. Below are examples including, but not limited to, such forms and usage.

Tobacco Consumption in China

One of the world's largest tobacco producing and consuming countries, China manufactures about 100 billion packs of cigarettes each year. The country now has a smoker population of 350 million a third of the world's total. Each year, about 1 million Chinese did from lung cancer and cardiovascular diseases, according to statistics from the Chinese Association of Tobacco Control (CATC). Under the WHO-FCTC, which China rectified in 2005, the country will ban all types of tobacco advertisement and prevention by 2011. However, tobacco industries use other surrogate forms, such as outdoor activities, to promote their products. However, an anti-smoking law world inevitably affects the tobacco industry which has long been considered a major source of government tax revenues.

Tobacco in India

The history of global tobacco trade is integrally linked with the history of India. It was to discover a sea route to this fabled land, reputed for its spices, silk and gems, that Cristopher Columbus set sail in 1492. His wayward journey took him instead to America. This "discovery" of the "New World" was accompanied by the discovery of tobacco by Portuguese sailors. This plant, treasured by the American "Indians" for its presumed medicinal and obvious stimulant properties, was eagerly embraced by the Portuguese who then moved it to the "Old World of Europe". Even though their quest for easy access to Indian spices was delayed by some years, the Europeans did not fail to recognize the commercial value of this new botanical acquisition.

When the Portuguese eventually did land on India's shores, they brought in tobacco. They introduced it initially in the royal courts where it soon found favor. It became a valuable commodity of barter trade, being used by the Portuguese for purchasing Indian textiles. The taste for tobacco, first acquired by the Indian royals, soon spread to the commoners and, in the 17th century, tobacco began to take firm roots in India. Thus, tobacco traveled to the real. Indians from their curiously named American cousins through the medium of European mariners and merchants who sailed the seas and spanned the continents in search of new markets and colonies.

It was with the establishment of British colonial rule, however, that the commercial dimensions of India's tobacco production and consumption grew to be greatly magnified. Initially, the British traders imported American tobacco into India to finance the purchase of Indian commodities. When the American colonies declared independence in 1776, the British East India Company began growing tobacco in India as a cash crop. Attempts were made, under the colonial rule, both to increase the land under tobacco cultivation and to enhance the quality of the leaves produced. The British East India Company and its successor, the British Raj, used tobacco as an important cash crop, both for domestic consumption and foreign trade. The manufacturing industry was, however, not established till much later, as the British believed in exporting the leaf to Britain and re-importing cigarettes to India, with considerable value addition in the process. As domestic consumption of cigarettes rose, the Imperial Tobacco Company commenced production within India, retaining control and repatriating the profits.

In the late 19th century, the beedi industry began to grow in India. The oldest beedi manufacturing firm was established around 1887 and by 1930 the beedi industry had spread across the country. The price differential from cigarettes favored the use of beedis by the working classes and this domestic product soon supplanted cigarettes as the major form of tobacco consumption. The tax policies adopted by the Indian Government after Independence also favored the beedi in comparison to cigarettes. This further fostered a growth in beedi consumption.

While tobacco chewing was practiced for many centuries, commercial production and marketing have been markedly upscaled recently, with the introduction of the gutka. The rate of growth of consumption of gutka has overtaken that of smoking forms of tobacco. As a result, oral tobacco consumption has opened a new and broader front in the battle between commercial tobacco and public health in India.

The economics of tobacco, which introduced it into India and entrenched it during the colonial rule, also provided a compelling reason for continued state patronage to the tobacco trade, even in free India. The ready revenues that bolster the annual budgets, the ability to export to a tobacco-hungry world market and the employment opportunities offered to millions provided the rationale for encouraging tobacco, both as a crop and as an industry.

While economics may have been the principal force propelling the seemingly inexorable advance of tobacco in India, there are also a multitude of social and cultural factors which need to be recognized, so that the variations in its use across social, religious and ethnic subgroups can be comprehended. Such factors have operated since the time tobacco entered India, although the nature of the socio-cultural determinants that influence individual and community responses to tobacco may have varied over time, region, religious denomination and social class. It is this tapestry of international linkages, powerful economic factors and distinctive cultural influences which make the history of tobacco in India a fascinating study.

Presently, tobacco is one of the important commercial crops of India. It is cultivated over an area of 400,000 hectares. Production is around 700 million kg. The production of flue-cured Virgina (FCV) tobacco is around 250 million kg from an area of 200 thousand hectares. India produces almost all types of tobacco. FCV and burley tobacco are the main exportable types. Tobacco provides employment to 38 million people including 6 million farmers. India occupies third place in area and production after China and Brazil. It accounts for 10% of world's area and 9% of tobacco production. Endowed with varied agroclimatic condition, India has the capacity to produce different types of tobacco, ranging from colory neutral filler to flavorful leaf, catering to the needs of a wide variety of customers globally. Also, production and processing costs of tobacco are quite low in India. It thus enjoys the advantage of competitive pricing.

India has an edge over other tobacco producing countries due to low production cost, average farm price and average export price. However, Zimbabwe and Brazil are producing better quality leaf with higher productivity levels. Farmers there have full support of the governments. Tobacco is used in India mainly for manufacturing bidi and chewing tobacco (like gutkha). Gujarat supplies 80% of the tobacco for manufacturing these products.

Tobacco occupies a prime place in the Indian economy on account of its considerable contribution to the agricultural, industrial and export sectors. India is currently the world's second largest producer of tobacco next to China, and the fourth largest exporter of unprocessed tobacco in the world. It is the third largest contributor to the national excise kitty after petroleum and textiles and provides direct/indirect employment to 35 million people. Six million farmers are engaged in tobacco cultivation. The *beedi* industry, which provides employment to around

44 lakh essentially unskilled rural folk, and mostly women, is partly responsible for arresting the migration of rural labor to urban centers.

It is the third largest contributor to the national excise kitty after petroleum and textiles and provides direct/indirect employment to 35 million people. Six million farmers are engaged in tobacco cultivation. India is perhaps the only tobacco producing country where the states decide exactly how much tobacco should be grown where. There is no such arrangement eve in China. Other leading producers like the US, Brazil, and Malawi also have a system of contract farming so as to facilitate linkages between the trade, the industry, and the growers.

In New Report, List of Smoking-Related Illnesses Grows

In a broad review of scientific literature, the US top doctor has concluded that cigarette smoking—long known to cause lung cancer and heart disease—also causes diabetes, colorectal and liver cancers, erectile dysfunction and ectopic pregnancy.

In a report, the acting surgeon general, Dr Boris D Lushniak, significantly expanded the list of illnesses that cigarette smoking has been scientifically proved to cause. The other health problems the report names are vision loss, tuberculosis, rheumatoid arthritis, impaired immune function and cleft palates in children of women who smoke. Smoking has been known to be associated with these illnesses, but the report was the first time the federal government concluded that smoking causes them.

The finding does not mean that smoking causes all cases of the health problems and diseases listed in the report, but that some of the cases would not have happened without smoking. The surgeon general has added to the list of smoking-related diseases before. Bladder cancer was added in 1990 and cervical cancer in 2004.

The report is not legally binding, but is broadly held as a standard for scientific evidence among researchers and policy makers.

"I thought the science was very well done and up to date", said Dr Robert Wallace, a professor of epidemiology and internal medicine at the University of Iowa, who helped review the report. The report comes 50 years after the pivotal 1964 surgeon general's report in which the government concluded for the first time that smoking caused lung cancer. That report was credited with starting to change public attitudes toward smoking, which has declined sharply. In 1965, about 43% of adults were smokers; in 2012, about 18% were.

But that decline has slowed in recent years, and the new report calls for stronger action in combating smoking. The report concluded that the evidence was insufficient to say that smoking caused prostate cancer. The evidence was suggestive, but not definite, that smoking causes breast cancer smokers.

While smoking causes most cases of lung cancer, it causes only a small fraction of liver and colorectal cancers. A current smoker is 25 times as likely to develop lung cancer as someone who has never smoked, but only about 1.5 times as likely to develop liver cancer. "It is a fairly modest association, but because so many people smoke, it is still an important cause of these cancers", said Neal Freedman, an epidemiologist at the National Cancer Institute. He pointed out that the surgeon general last looked at the effect of smoking on liver cancer in 2004, and found the evidence only suggestive. Since then, 90 new studies have been published allowing the surgeon general to conclude smoking is a cause.

The report also finds that the risks of lung cancer are far higher today than in past decades, even though smokers today consume fewer cigarettes. In 1959, women who smoked were 2.7 times as likely as women who never smoked to develop lung cancer, and by 2010, the additional risk had jumped nearly tenfold. For men, the risk doubled over the same period. The report said changes in cigarettes, design, namely to the filter, contributed to the increased deadliness.

Health Gained, Happiness Lost

Rarely has the concept of happiness caused so much consternation in public health circles. Buried deep in the federal government's voluminous new tobacco regulations is a little-known cost-benefit calculation that public health experts see as potentially poisonous: the happiness quotient. It assumes that the benefits from reducing smoking—fewer early deaths and diseases of the lungs and heart—have to be discounted by 70% to offset the loss in pleasure that smokers suffer when they give up their habit.

Experts say that calculation wipes out most of the economic benefits from the regulations and could make them far more vulnerable to legal challenges from the tobacco industry. And it could have a perverse effect. The more successful regulators are at reducing smoking, the more it hurts them in the final economic accounting.

"This threatens the FDAs ability to take strong actions against tobacco", Frank J Chaloupka, an economist at the University of Illinois at Chicago, said of the FDA. "If they can't demonstrate that there is a significant economic benefit to doing it, then it makes their job much harder". The group said the happiness quotient was way too high and should be changed before the regulations take effect.

"There's reason to believe that number is much too big", The idea of lost happiness is new for health regulation. But, it has surfaced as part of a long standing requirement—first codified under President Bill Clinton—that every set of federal regulations with more than a $100 million effect on the economy needs an analysis to prevent the adoption of regulations with high costs and low benefits.

The cost-benefit analysis is embedded in a proposal from April that would extend the FDAs authority, for the first time, to electronic cigarettes and other tobacco products such as cigars and pipe tobacco, with potentially large consequences for the multibillion-dollar tobacco industry.

The FDA released a statement on Wednesday detailing the economics behind its analysis, but the explanation did not address the central assertion made by the economists. An FDA spokeswoman, Jennifer Haliski, said that there was "still a great deal of uncertainty" surrounding the calculation.

If the formula for assessing costs and benefits remains unchanged in the final version of the regulations, it could set a dangerous precedent that would constrain public-policy making for years to come, experts and advocates warned.

This approach to cost-benefit analysis could also have broader implications for regulations of the food and beverage industries, which could likewise point to lost pleasure from consumption of sugar, salt or other substances regulators seek to limit.

The economists' assessment of the agency's approach is part of a flood of public comments—more than 69,000 as of Wednesday—submitted to the FDA on the tobacco regulations. The rules are supposed to become final by next summer, and experts anticipate that legal challenges will soon follow.

Economists speaking out on Wednesday said a basic assumption consistent with traditional economic theory lay at the heart of the federal government's miscalculation on the costs and benefits of the regulations: that most people were rational, well-informed market participants making decisions they would not later regret.

But smokers, they said, were different. A vast majority began smoking before age 18, when judgment is impaired. And many want to quit, but are addicted, and forgo the long-term satisfaction of better health for short-term pleasure.

"It would be ridiculous to suggest that a 16-year-old who has no idea what addiction means and feels immortal is a rational decision-maker when it comes to smoking", said Kenneth E Warner, one of the paper's authors and a professor of public health at the University of Michigan.

Pleasure was not the only problem with the FDAs economic analysis, the economists said. For example, it did not count the benefits to non-smokers of less secondhand smoke, or of reductions in infant mortality were fewer pregnant women to smoke, they said.

The only previous application of the happiness loss by the FDA—to the proposal of graphic warning labels on cigarette packaging—went largely unnoticed, but the current one is drawing attention because of how much the lost happiness counts.

Now "Paan" from India may be Banned by European Union

Betel or "paan" leaves from India may be the next item to be banned by the European Union (EU), which has already imposed an import ban on Alphonso mangoes over claims of a fruit fly infestation. The EUs Rapid Alert System for Food and Feed (RASFF) warned in its annual report this week that there have been consistent reports of Salmonella contamination of betel leaves from the country. The EU had already issued a ban on the import of paan leaves from Bangladesh earlier this year, effective until at least end July.

"The continuing reason since 2011 for the high number of reports on Salmonella is paan leaves. The continuous reports notified by the UK prompted the adoption of a safeguard measure suspending temporarily imports of paan leaves from Bangladesh and setting up reinforced checks for paan leaves from India and Thailand", the RASFF 2013.

In War on Tobacco, Government may Scrub Brand name off packs.

The Narendra Modi-led NDA government has virtually declared war on tobacco. After raising taxes on cigarettes and calling for a countrywide ban on sale of tobacco products, the center is now planning to introduce tougher provisions under law to curb tobacco consumption in the country.

From banning branding on cigarette packets to raising the age limit on tobacco consumption to 25 years from 18, to substantively increasing penalties for smoking in public, the Union Health Ministry is considering a host of amendments to the anti-tobacco law.

Health Minister Harsh Vardhan constituted a committee of experts headed by Delhi government's former principal secretary, health, Ramesh Chandra, last month to review and suggest changes to the Cigarettes and Other Tobacco Products Act (COTPA), 2003 and it is expected to submit its report by the end of this month.

"The idea is to make our law more compliant with WHO-FCTC", said a top ministry official, who did not wish to be identified. The FCTC is a treaty which lays down a set of universal standards to limit the use of tobacco worldwide. India ratified the FCTC in 2004, a year after passing its own anti-tobacco legislation.

"We have asked the experts to broadly look at the feasibility of raising the age limit for tobacco consumption to 25 years from 18, banning advertisement at the point of sale, and plain packaging of cigarette packs, among other things, and also review the best practices around the world to reduce tobacco consumption", the official added.

Currently, tobacco companies in India can advertise their products at the "point of sale", that is at stores and kiosks. That apart, cigarette packets carry brand names and are usually glossy in their looks, a factor activists claim is responsible for getting youngsters hooked into smoking. Although the packets also carry a warning on one side, the committee of experts is also looking at increasing the surface areas of the warning and having it on either sides of the packet. Governments across the world are now giving more teeth to their anti-tobacco laws.

Reaching a Fag End?

Health Ministry considering Amendments to Anti-tobacco Law.

- **Banning** branding on cigarette packets
- **Raising** age limit on tobacco consumption to 25 years from 18
- **Increasing** penalties for smoking in public
- Banning advertisement at the point of sale.

Increasing surface area of warning on pack.

HARMFUL EFFECTS OF TOBACCO

Gender Bias of Unsafe Sex

- In Africa, 1 million women die every year due to sexually transmitted infections like HIV and the human papillomavirus.
- Cervical cancer is the leading cause of cancer deaths in Africa
- Eleven percent of cancer deaths worldwide are due to cervical cancer.

A Breakup of the Big Risks

The major factors that can be addressed.

Ergonomics of a Brave New World

- Occupational hazards can be as simple as backache—more than a third of backaches are related to the work.
- Occupational noise causes 16% of hearing loss in adults.

What the Report Offers

- In the absence of these risks, life expectancy would have been at least a decade longer in 2004. Poor countries have the most to gain from prevention.
- The way out is timely policy action. As health improves, gains multiply.
- Lower disease burden could raise income levels which, in turn, will further help to reduce health inequalities.

Tobacco and Polluted Air

Three in four lung cancer cases can be attributed to tobacco smoking and air pollution or both. Any effective measures to control these two would bring a dramatic improvement. This is the reason tobacco advertising is such a controversial issue.

An Investment Tip

The returns on improving health are palpable and measurable.

Tobacco will Kill a Billion This Century: WHO

Tobacco is a silent killer and the single largest cause of preventable disease including cancer, heart attacks, chronic obstructive lung disease and asthma. According to WHO, tobacco killed 100 million people in the 20th century and will kill a billion people (ten times more) in the 21st century. Deaths due to tobacco in India are expected to rise from 1.4% in 1990 to 13.3% in 2020. A survey carried out by the Indian Council of Medical Research revealed that one in every five male deaths and one in every 20 deaths are caused by tobacco smoking. A review of literature shows that India loses 54.8 lakh precious lives because of tobacco.

Dharamshila Hospital and Research Center (DHRC) consultant surgical oncologist Dr Anshuman Kumar says: "Sixty percent of the patients reporting at DHRC are found suffering from cancers of the mouth (gum, tongue, cheek, and nasopharynx), larynx (voice box) esophagus and lungs. Out of the 60,000 cancer patients reported at DHRC, 40% are beedi smokers, 40% tobacco chewers, 16% cigarette smokers and 4% passive smokers. Eighty percent of the cancer patients reporting to DHRC are inoperable. However, patients reporting in early stages are being operated and have a very high probability of disease-free survival. The hospital's proactive initiatives on cancer awareness, early cancer detection, tobacco cessation clinics have helped it to downstage the cancer as well as help people quit smoking".

Cigarettes contain cancer-causing tumor initiators and toxic agents such as arsenic, tar, ammonia, carbon monoxide, hydrogen cyanide, lead, DDT and acetaldehydes. Ninety percent of lung cancers are tobacco-related.

"India has a high burden of submucous fibrosis and oral cancer accounting for one-third of the world burden. The rate of growth of *gutka* chewing has overtaken that of smoking forms of tobacco. Also the falling rates of lung cancer in the US and Europe are proof of the effective control methods used for tobacco consumption in these countries because of the awareness and cooperation of the citizenry. Quitting tobacco has major and immediate health benefits for all ages", says DHRC physician Dr Biswajit Sanyal. "Mass education and dissemination of information on the harmful effects of tobacco is the only way to ensure that tobacco abuse is stopped".

Smokeless Tobacco has 28 Carcinogens

Smokeless tobacco products being marketed in India contain 3,095 chemical components with serious implications for human health. About 28 of these components are proven carcinogens, areca nut the most commonly used of all. What's more—the latest studies demonstrate the presence of heavy metals including lead, cadmium, chromium, arsenic and nickel in these products, with one recent research reporting that 30% gutkha brand samples freely available in tea-stalls, bus stops, railway stations and several public places in the country, exceed the permissible levels of lead and copper when compared to the provisional tolerable intake limits determined by the WHO and the Food and Agriculture Office (FAO).

These startling revelations were made today by the Health Ministry officials who led the debate with the stakeholders on the need to regulate the availability and use of smokeless tobacco in India. The Global Adult Tobacco Survey 2010 has put the overall tobacco users in India at 34.6%; of these, 25.9% are using smokeless tobacco (as against 14% smokers). Alarmed by the rising oral cancer burden in the country and the fact that there's no regulation on smokeless tobacco, the Health Ministry today shared shocking findings of studies that show abundant presence of tobacco-specific N-nitrosamines (TSNA) harmful chemicals and even radioactive polonium in smokeless forms. "No safe level of TSNAs has been ascribed so far. Other carcinogens in smokeless tobaccos include volatile N-nitrosamines, certain lactones, metals and radioactive polonium," Dr Jagjit Kaur, Chief Medical Officer, Directorate of Health Services, today told TNS, admitting that easy and cheap availability of such forms and low taxes on them make their production lucrative.

Studies have further indicated an increased risk of all-cancer mortality in smokeless tobacco users compared to nonusers and the increased risk was specifically visible in female users. "There is also evidence of increased risk of drying from cardiovascular diseases among these users", Kaur said at the national consultation on ways to regulate smokeless tobacco, which began here today.

The Government has elicited these findings for submission to the Supreme Court, currently hearing the Ankur Gutkha versus Indian Asthma Care Society case in which it earlier banned the sale of smokeless tobacco in plastic sachets.

Surrogate ads by tobacco majors

Concerned over indiscriminate surrogate advertising by tobacco majors, especially pan masala companies, the Health Ministry has decided to take up the issue with the Information and Broadcasting Ministry. A meeting will be held on Wednesday. The government has documented several recent cases of violations by tobacco majors who have, in contravention of Section 5 of the Cigarettes and Other Tobacco products Act, 2003, gone ahead advertising their products clandestinely to advance their business interests. Among the alleged violators are Godfrey Philips, ITC and Pan Parag.

The need for regulation of smokeless tobacco further arises from the rising use of these forms by youngsters and women. Worryingly, a lot of these users are daily users. Out of the 25.9% current smokeless tobacco consumers in India, for example, 21.4 are daily users. Out of these 27.4% are males and 14.9% are females.

While males prefer khaini (18% usage), women prefer tobaccos for oral application (6.3% usage). Overall, khaini tops the smokeless tobacco usage charts with 11.6 per cent consumers by Gutkha at 8.2, betel quid (paan) with tobacco at 6.2 and tobacco-laced dentrifices at 4.7% users.

Passive Smoking Kills 1 in 100

Percentage exposed to second-hand smoke in 2004

Children	40%
Non-smoking women	35%
Non-smoking men	33%

This exposure was estimated to have caused:

- 379,000 deaths from heart disease
- 165,000 from lower respiratory infections
- 36,900 from asthma
- 21,400 from lung cancer.

Around one in a hundred deaths worldwide is due to passive smoking. An estimate of 600,000 people a year.

WORLD ANTI-SMOKING LAWS

In first, study of its kind, the WHO said on Friday, that the approximately 603,000 deaths from secondhand smoking should be added to the 5.1 million deaths that smoking itself causes every year. The lowest rates of exposure were in the Americas, the Eastern Mediterranean and Africa. Researchers found the highest number of people exposed to second-hand smoke are in Europe and Asia.

The study which analyzed data from 2004 for 192 countries, found that children are more heavily exposed to second-hand smoke than any other age-group. Children whose parents smoke have a higher risk of sudden infant death syndrome, ear infections, pneumonia, bronchitis and asthma. In many parts of the world, women are at least 50% more likely to be exposed to secondhand smoke than men.

If Tobacco Kills – Kill it

Clinical epidemiology centre, Trivandrum, KB Leena, KT Shenoy (until 2005). Dept. of Community medicine, Gujarat Medical college, Ahmedabad: DV Bala, P Seth, KN Trivedi Dept. of Community Medicine, Kolkata Medical College, Kolkata: SK Roy Dept of Community Medicine, Osmania Medical College, Hyderabad, P Bhatia, Dept. of Community medicine, Regional Institute of Medical Sciences. Imphal: L Usharani Dept. of Community Medicine, SCB Medical College, Cuttack, Orissa: B Mohapatra, Dept. of Community Medicine, SMS Medical College. Jaipur. AK Bharadwaj, R Gupta Epidemiological Rsearch Center, Chennai: V Gajalakshmi, CV Kanimozhi, Gandhi Medical College, Bhopal: RP Dikshit, S Sorangi, Healis Seskarhia Institute of Public Health, Mumbai: PC Gupta, MS Pednekar, S Sreevidya, Institute of Health System Research, Hyderabad: M Mahapatra (until 2004). St. Johns Research Institute, St. Johns Academy of Health Sciences, Bangalore: A Kurpad, P Mony. Training Center Ministry of Health, Government of India, New Delhi N Dhingra (until 2008), National Institute of Mental Health and Neurosciences, Bangalore G Gujarat (until 2004), North Eastern India Gandhi Regional Institute of Health and Medical Sciences, Shillong: FU Ahmed (until 2005), DK Parida, Regional Medical Research Centre ICMR, Bhubaneshwar. AS Karketta, SK Dar School of Preventative Oncology, Patna: DN Sinha, School of Public Health, Post Graduate Institute of Medical Education and Research, Chandigarh: N Kaur, R Kumar, JS Thakur, Tata Memorial Hospital, Mumbai, RP Dikshit.

Lead Partners

Office of the Registrar-General of India (RGI), New Delhi, India: C, Chandramouli (RGI since March 2009). DK Sikri (RGI since Sept. 2004), RC Sethi, S Jain, DK Dey, AK Saxena, J Sudhir, MK Thapa, JK Banthia (RGI until Sept. 2004) Million Death

Study Coordinating Center, Center for Global Health Research, SL Michael's Hospital, University of Toronto, Canada: DG Bassani, DJ Corsi, P Jha, R Jotkar, D Kam, R Kamadod, P Mony, S Rao-Seshadri, J Sudhir, W Suraweera.

Affiliated Partners

Clinical Trial Service Unit and Epidemiological Studies Unit (CTSU), University of Oxford, England: J Boreha, Z Che, R Collins, J Godwin, R Peto, Indian Council of Medical Research (Dept. of health Research), New Delhi, India, VM Katoch (Director General), NK Ganguly (Director-General until 2008), L Kani, SK Bhattacharya (Acting Director-General from 2008) School of Population Health. The University of Queensi and Australia: AD Lepez, C Rao World Health Organization, Geneva and New Delhi. T Boema, T Evans. A Fric, S Habayeb (WHO Representative – India), S Kharum, CD Mathers, K Shibuya, N Singh, P Singh Deputy Regional Director), DN Sinha.

What is common in names mentioned above?

They all are Million Death Study Collaborators.

Smoking and Death in India

- India: 1 million (10 lakh) smoking deaths per year during 2010s
- Smoking causes 10% of the 10 million (1 crore) deaths per year from all fatal disease
- 70% of smoking deaths are in middle age (30–69): 700,000; 600,000 men and 100,000 women
- 20% of all adult male deaths and 5% of all adult female earths in middle age
- Over 50% of smoking deaths are in illiterate adults.

Female Smokers in India Die 8 Years Earlier than Non-smokers

Indian women are among the worst in the world when it comes to smoking. According to the latest Tobacco Atlas, the country ranks third in the top 20 females smoking populations across the globe. Only the US with 2.3 crore female smokers and China with 1.3 crore women smokers are worse off than India in this chart. However, as far as percentage of women smoking is concerned, it is below 20% for India. Among India's immediate neighbors, only Pakistan figures this infamous list, but right at the bottom at 20th with around 30 lakh female smokers.

According to the Atlas, about 250 million women in the world are daily smokers – 22% being from high resource countries and 9% from low and middle resource countries. Realizing the potential of this growing market, the Atlas said the tobacco industry has been marketing cigarettes to women using seductive but false images of vitality, emancipation, slimness, sophistication and sexual allure.

Tobacco consumption reduced birth weight of the fetus, decreased their gestational age leading to premature babies, increased the risk of still births and chances of anemia among adult pregnant women. The government is not focusing on anti-tobacco campaign that specially targets women. Smoking is increasing in young college going women showing that the tobacco industry is targeting then very strongly. The Atlas said tobacco killed some 6 million people each year more than a third of whom will die from cancer and drained $500 billion annually from global economies. As 25% of smokers die and many more become ill during their most productive years. Income loss devastates families and communities. In 2010, 72% of those who die from tobacco-related illness would be in low and middle

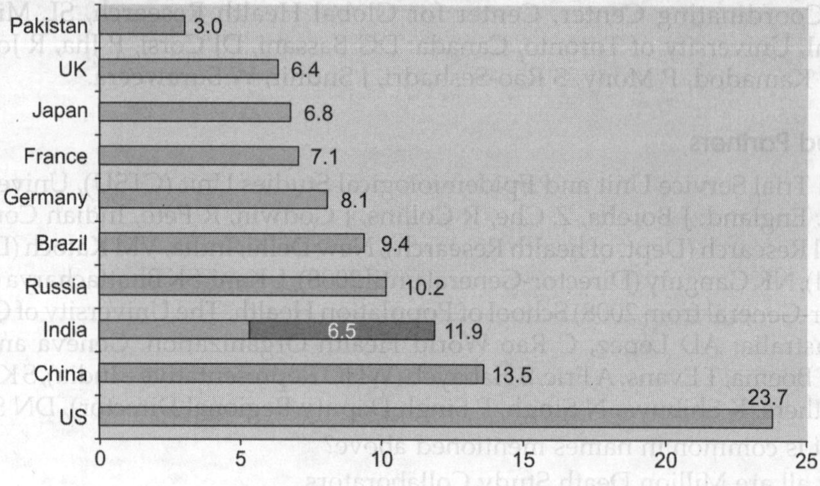

Top female smoking poputations

Figures in million for 2008 (estimates)
* Oral tobacco users.

income countries. By 2030, 83% of these deaths will occur in low and middle-income countries occurrence.

A Terrorist Called Tobacco

Tobacco is a leading cause of preventable death, and is estimated to kill more than five million people each year worldwide. The gap in deaths between the low and middle income countries and the high income countries is expected to widen further over the next several decades if we do nothing. If the current trends persist, tobacco will kill more than 8 million people worldwide each year by 2030, with 80% of these premature deaths in the low and middle income countries.

By the end of this century, tobacco may kill a billion people or more unless urgent action is taken. Within the next 2 years, around 10 lakh people will die of smoking in India, says one of the most comprehensive studies. India is on the threshold of a tobacco-unleashed epidemic. Smoking increases the level of poisonous carbon monoxide in the lungs. It gets quickly absorbed in the blood, affecting its capacity to carry oxygen. It strains the smoker even more as the heart has to work harder. High levels of carbon monoxide in the blood can impair vision, perception of time and coordination. Smokers are more likely to develop respiratory ailments, thickening of the arteries, blood clots, and cancers of the lung, cervix, larynx, mouth, esophagus, bladder, pancreas and kidneys. It could also lead to impotence.

Environmental tobacco smoke (also called passive smoke or second-hand smoke) affects people who are frequently around smokers. Second-hand smoking can cause chronic respiratory conditions, cancer and heart disease. It is estimated that around 35,000 non-smokers die of heart diseases each year as a result of exposure to environmental tobacco smoke.

Tobacco consumption is a leading cause of death among Indians aged 30–69 and 1 million Indians die of smoking-related diseases each year; among all women, 11%

(over 54 million women) use some form of tobacco; approximately one in 20 (or 90,000) deaths among women of 35–69 years can be attributed to smoking.

Tobacco products are the only legally available products that can kill up to one half of their regular users if consumed as recommended by the manufacturer.

People, non-governmental organizations and governments unite on World No Tobacco Day (May 31) to draw attention to the health problems that tobacco use can cause. The theme for this year is: "Ban tobacco advertising, promotion and sponsorship".

The tobacco industry operates as a global force and uses a wide range of methods to buy influence and power, and penetrate markets. Such strategies include direct and indirect political lobbying and campaign contributions, financing of research, attempts to affect the course of the regulatory and policy machinery and engaging in social responsibility initiatives as part of public relations campaigns.

As more and more countries move to fully meet their obligations under the WHO-FCTC, the industry's attempts to undermine the treaty become more aggressive. These include weakening public health efforts to ban tobacco advertising, promotion and sponsorship.

There should be an effective surveillance system which should collect information on the prevalence of tobacco use, tobacco-related morbidity and mortality, and policy and program interventions. It will enhance government capacity to find out the relation between the tobacco and the health status of the population. Hence, it will assist in setting public health priorities. There is an urgent need to strengthen research to deal with tobacco control.

Say no to smoking worldwide

2013	*2030*	*2100*
Million deaths worldwide with a high percentage from low and middle income countries	Million deaths worldwide with 80% from low and middle income countries	Billion or more deaths are estimated worldwide by the end of this century

35,000 non-smokers die from heart disease as a result of exposure each year

90 or 1 in 20 women's deaths between ages 35 and 69 attributed to smoking	1 is an estimated number of deaths as result of smoking

The following activities are recommended for addressing the tobacco industry's interference in public health policies:

- Raise awareness of the addictive and harmful nature of tobacco products and of the interference of tobacco industry and ensure transparency in those interactions.
- Establish measures to limit interactions with the industry and ensure transparency in those interactions.
- Avoid conflicts of interest for government officials and employees.
- Make information provided by the tobacco industry transparent and accurate
- Denormalize and, to the extent possible, regulate activities described as socially responsible by the tobacco industry including but not limited to activities described as "corporate social responsibility".
- Do not give preferential treatment to the tobacco industry.

TOBACCO – A MAJOR KILLER

19 biggest reasons for sickness...

Time in the sick bay is time lost in a life. 2004 figures split into income groups

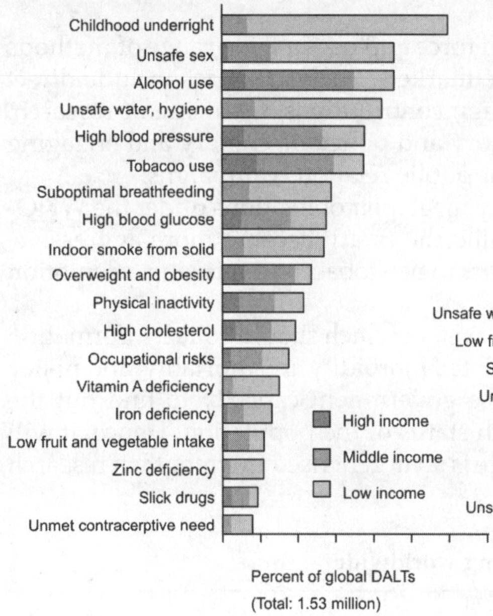

and the top 19 reasons for death

The biggest killers breach the class divide. They kill the rich as well as the poor

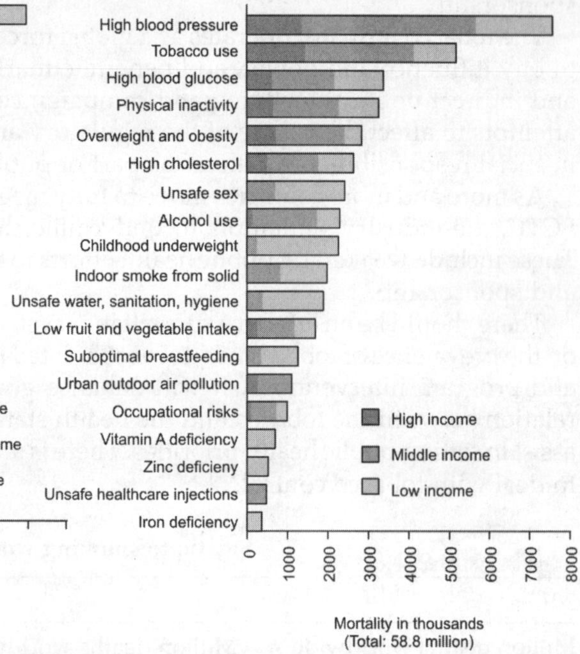

Kills in Excess, Moderates Smile

- Alcohol abuse contributes to 60 types of diseases and injuries.
- Strangely, the habit could save you from coronary heart disease, stroke and diabetes as long as you do not binge.
- Twenty percent of all motor vehicle accidents are linked to alcohol.
    - o Tobacco smoking alone causes 71% of lung cancer deaths worldwide. Air pollution contributes.
    - o This overlap represents about three-fourths of lung cancer deaths in 2004 that could have been averted if either tobacco exposure or urban air pollution had been lower.
    - o Of all the childhood deaths due to infections and parasites, 34% can be attributed to low body weight, 26% to unsafe drinking water, and 15% to smoke from indoor use of solid fuels.

Adipose Risk

- For the first time in human history, excess body weight and obesity cause more deaths than being underweight.
- Obesity epidemic (a combination of lack of physical activity and gluttony) is comparable to the HIV/AIDS crisis in poor and middle income countries.

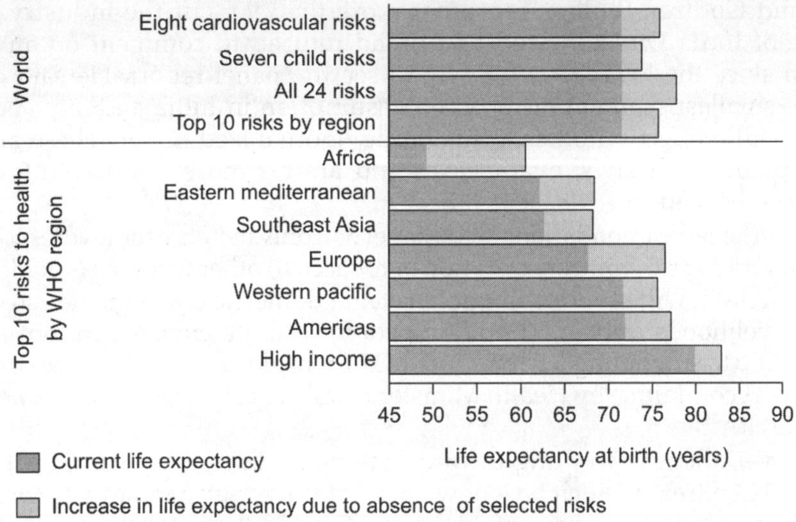

Teri's source: Down to earth

Smokers Likely to Face Heavy Stick for Puffing in Public

Tougher Norms Fine for public smoking may jump to Rs 20,000, loose sale to be banned, minimum age may rise to 25 and size of warnings on packs to double.

The government is considering a proposal to ban the sale of loose cigarettes, a move that will hit ITC and other cigarette makers hard as 70% of retail takes place in this form. This is one of the many measures proposed by an expert panel setup by the health ministry. Other suggestions include raising the age limit for consumption and increasing the fine for smoking in public spaces to Rs 20,000 from Rs 200, apart from making this a cognizable offence.

If accepted, these suggestions on curbing tobacco consumption could soon be part of tougher legislation being drafted by the Modi government, which it wants to introduce in the winter session of Parliament as it looks to curb the damage caused by the habit in the form of cancers, cardiovascular diseases and other health issues. Headed by the Delhi government's former principal secretary Ramesh Chandra, the expert panel submitted its report to the Health Ministry last week. The expert panel also wants the government to impose a harsher penalty of Rs 50,000, up from Rs 5,000 now, on manufacturers for violating the provision on carrying pictorial warning signs on cigarette packets. Members of the committee, who spoke to ET on condition of anonymity, said the panel also recommended raising the age limit for tobacco consumption to 25 years from 18 years, banning advertisements at the point of sale, and increasing the size of health warnings to cover almost 80% of packaging. Currently, they cover 40% of the pack front. Discouraging tobacco consumption appears to be high on the government's agenda. Just 5 days after being sworn in as Prime Minister, Modi had tweeted: "On World No Tobacco Day, let us pledge to spread awareness on the risks of tobacco consumption and work to reduce tobacco consumption in India."This seems to have had an impact on stocks. Since Modi came to power on May 26, only ITC has moved up (3.7%) while rival stocks have fallen. Godfrey Phillips India (GPI) has lost 6.4%, Vasir Sultan Tobacco (VST) Industries 8.5% and Golden Tobacco 30%. In contrast, the Sensex has gained more than 10% in the same period.

ITC and Godfrey Phillips represent more than 90% of the industry. Tobacco Institute of India Director Syed M Ahmad refused to comment on any specific proposal since the lobby group is yet to see the panel report. He said cigarettes form the smallest segment of tobacco consumption in India and any such moves will have little effect on other forms in the unorganized sector. These are largely noncompliant with laws, evade taxes and are far more affordable for tobacco consumers, he said.

"Hence, the recommendations of the panel will only increase the level of contraband and illegal trade and shift consumption of tobacco to other forms as is evident today. In the process, it will severely impact the legal domestic cigarette industry in India and the livelihoods of over 38 million people who are engaged in tobacco whilst giving a fillip to smuggling", Ahmad said. ET reported last month on the constitution of the expert committee by Health Minister Harsh Vardhan to propose amendments to the COTPA.

The government is working toward making its laws more compliant with the WHO-FCTC, a treaty which lays down a set of universal standards to limit the use of tobacco worldwide. India ratified the FCTC in 2004, a year after enacting its own anti-tobacco legislation. The government is currently preparing a Cabinet note based on the recommendations of the panel. According to officials, the Health Minister has accepted the report but not all of the committee's suggestions might find a place in the Cabinet note. "Some of the amendments suggested are too radical. Like, for instance, the government is in favor of increasing the fine on smoking in public places but what's been suggested by the panel is too much. It will not be as high as Rs 20,000", said a ministry official, who didn't want to be named as he is not authorized to speak to the media.

According to analysts, the impact on volumes could be anywhere between 10% and 20% as only some consumers will be able to afford the shift to packets.

Some fund managers told ET that this will create an overhang on the stocks of cigarette companies such as ITC and Godfrey Phillips which until now have been shielded from the slowdown in consumption due to the inelastic nature of cigarette demand. In the year to date, ITC has gained 11% while Godfrey Philips' stock has risen 17%. To be sure, ITC has embarked on a strategy of diversification into other businesses away from tobacco over the past few years.

Any decline in sales, however, will cut both ways as the cigarette industry generates more than Rs 25,000 crore in tax revenue. Putting such steps into effect will be difficult. "It needs to be seen how the government will be able to implement this, as there are lakhs of pan shops and selling points and implementing this could be a challenge. In the past also, the government has come out with several norms related to smoking in public", said Abneesh Roy, consumer analyst, Edelweiss Securities. "However, it has not been able to execute them entirely". Tobacco Institute's Ahmad said such recommendations will neither serve the government's tobacco control aim nor maximize revenue from the sector. According to the grouping, India has a unique pattern of tobacco consumption with legal cigarettes accounting for just 12%. The remaining 88% is represented by illegal cigarettes and a host of traditional products such as bidis, chewing tobacco and khaini. It estimates that illegal trade in cigarettes leads to a loss of Rs 6,000 crore to the Indian exchequer. "As a result, while tobacco consumption in the cigarette form has declined from 21% in 1981–1982 to 12% currently, overall tobacco consumption has increased by

42%, making tobacco control policies in the country counter-productive. The government is considering a ban on the sale of electronic cigarettes, a vapor device that delivers a nicotine hit minus the smoke, ET reported last month. An expert panel on e-cigarettes constituted by the Health Ministry has recommended a blanket ban on the product, saying its safety has not been established.

Fag end for smoking

Jumping signal/using mobiles while driving first offence Rs 100, subsequent offence up to Rs 300	Municipal Corporation of Delhi (MCD) sanitation laws prohibit spitting defecating and bathing public places Rs 50 (new Stricter law in the works).
	Dogs defecating in public NDMC areas Rs 500 fine on owners.
North Delhi Municipal Corp has decided to penalize citizens throwing trash/ splitting urinating in public places Rs 100–500	Smoking banned in public places in 2003 Fine up to Rs 200 As per '08 rules, public places exclude parking space, road open markets, parks and homes
	At present, Chandigarh is the only smoke free city in India.

Big amendments suggested by expert panel

No sale of loose cigs. tobacco	Ban on ads for products at kiosks	Public smoking to be cognizable offence
Rs 20,000 fine on public smoking		Higher fine on cost over pictorial signs

Soon, Rs 20,000 Fine for Smoking in Public

A fine of 20,000 for smoking in public, banning the sale of loose cigarettes and increasing age limit for tobacco consumption from 18 to 25: these are some of the recommendations of the expert panel appointed by Health Ministry to review and suggest changes to the COTPA, 2003. Other suggestions include making public smoking a cognizable offence.

If accepted, these suggestions could soon be a part of amendments the government is planning to introduce in the winter session of parliament to curb tobacco consumption. Tobacco use accounts of 40% of all cancers in India. It is also associated with higher morbidity and mortality caused due to respiratory problems, heart diseases and tuberculosis (TB) among others.

"This is the first time we have seen any government which is so aggressive about tobacco-control measures. We are hopeful that they will consider the changes suggested", said Dr G K Rath, one of the experts appointed by the Health Ministry.

Tobacco use Accounts for 40% of all Cancers

- Tobacco use accounts for 40% of all cancers in India. It is also associated with higher morbidity and mortality caused due to respiratory problems, heart diseases and TB.

- About 275 million Indians 35% of adult population and 14% of children aged 13–15 years). Are tobacco users mainly smokeless tobacco?
- Total economic costs attributable to tobacco use from all diseases in India in 2011 amounted to Rs 1.04 lakh crore – 12% more than the combined State and Central Government expenditure on healthcare in the same year.

He said the existing anti-tobacco law has many loopholes and the manufacturers of tobacco-products are using them to market it to the vulnerable population. On implementation of the changes proposed, Dr Rath said the government needs to push for bigger changes only then it can achieve the minimum. Ten years ago, who would have thought that people will stop smoking in offices or at airports? It has happened. Similarly, we can reduce tobacco sale by introducing stringent measures like this.

Health minister Harsh Vardhan, senior officials in the ministry said, is on a visit to Bangladesh and he will return on Friday. "The minister has taken up the curbing tobacco consumption issue on campaign basis. The recommendations of the expert panel will be reviewed by him for further action and deliberations before it is included in the draft of amendments", the official said. About 275 million Indians (35% of adult population and 14.1% of children aged 13–15 years) are tobacco users, mainly smokeless tobacco.

According to a recent report prepared by the Public Health Foundation of India, total economic costs attributable to tobacco use from all diseases in India in the year 2011 amounted to a staggering Rs 1,04,500 crores - 12% more than the combined State and Central Government expenditure on healthcare in the same year.

Cigarette Butts to Make Steel Rust - Free

Chemical extracts from cigarette butts so toxic they kill fish can be used to protect steel pipes from rusting, a study in China has found. In a paper published in the American Chemical Society's journal industrial and Engineering Chemistry Research, the scientists in China said they identified nine chemicals after immersing cigarette butts in water. They applied the extracts to N80, a type of steel used in oil pipes, and found that they protected the steel from rusting. The metal surface can be protected and the Iron atom's further dissolution can be prevented. The chemicals, including nicotine, appear to be responsible fo this anti-corrosion effect, they added. The research was led by Jun Zhao at Xi an Jiaotong University's School of Energy and Power Engineering and funded by China's State oil firm China National Petroleum Corporation. Corrosion of steel pipes used by the oil industry costs oil producers million of dollars annually to repair or replace. According to the paper, 4.5 trillion cigarette butts find their way into the environment each year.

Enormous Odds: the Tobacco Epidemic Confronting

By the 1990s, the tobacco epidemic was a public health problem of epic proportions. It was a leading cause of premature death. The escalation of smoking and other forms of tobacco use worldwide had resulted in the loss of at least 3.5 million human lives in 1998 and was expected at that time to cause at least 10 million deaths a year by 2030 if the pandemic was not controlled, with 70% of these deaths occurring in developing countries.

Past efforts to stem the global tobacco epidemic had proved ineffective, Propelled by a multinational industry driven by the extremely profitable nature of tobacco manufacture and trade and fostered by the addictiveness of nicotine, the epidemic spread rapidly from the developed to the developing world. Globalization enfeebled the efforts of individual country to control tobacco use. Active promotion of tobacco use by the industry rendered the approach of the medical model inadequate. The traditional public health methods for reducing tobacco use were no match for the tobacco industry's power transnational reach and formidable resources.

Successful control of the tobacco epidemic seemed close to impossible. In the face of these enormous odds, it was time to change the rules of the game.

The future of the WHO-FCTC: health-over-trade

Dr Hatai Chitamondh (Thailand, President. Conference of the Parties—2007–2008) said:

"My fight for the health-over-trade issue dated back to 1989. I was a delegate of Thailand to the Forty-second World Health Assembly and our group drew up a resolution advocating that trade sanctions should not used to force a country to accept imported tobacco products. When our delegates went around explaining the issue, asking for support from delegates of other countries, our friends would not agree and said we are here to discuss health, not trade. However, I intervened in Committee A to address the issue. This was the first time WHO officially recognized the potential menace from trade on tobacco control. It remains a critical area that will require much attention from the conference of the parties".

Five Years in Force

The WHO-FCTC marked substantial progress after its entry into force in February 2005.

- The principal treaty bodies, the Conference of the Parties and the Permanent Secretariat were established and are fully functional
- Several key tools for implementation, such as the first protocol and several guidelines covering more than 10 Articles of the Convention have been adopted or are in an advanced stage of development.
- The treaty reporting system is established, and more than 80% of the reports expected from Parties have been received and analyzed.
- Support to Parties in meeting their obligations is gradually being put and place by the dissemination of guidelines, convening of needs assessments, support in developing legislation, the transfer of expertise and facilitation of access to internationally available resources.

The absolute majority of States have now ratified the WHO-FCTC, making it one of the most widely embraced treaties in the history of the United Nations. This is increased its appeal partners, and several more international organizations have been accredited as observers to the Conference of the Parties, resulting in greater technical cooperation.

WHO-FCTC and the Future of Public Health

The Framework Convention represents a new approach to International Health Cooperation, with a legal framework to shape the future of health for all people. It provides a model for a powerful, effective global response to the negative effects of globalization on health with potentially other similar applications in public health.

Role of the treaty in prompting international action

Dr Margaret Chan (WHO Director-General), The WHO-FCTC is the first modern treaty to tackle an individual public health threat directly. The sheer power of being first, and of being so successful, has changed the way that we think about global public health, the tools that we have to combat multifaceted health problems, and the capacity that we have when the global community works together on health. Beyond the political impact of the WHO-FCTC, I also believe that the treaty demonstrates very practically the need for concerted horizontal, multilateral action to solve difficult multisectoral health problems. This horizontalism needs to happen at local, national and international level, with practitioners speaking to each other, ministrics working together, and countries sharing their expertise and experience. The WHO-FCTC provides a roadmap for that kind of work and serves at the same time as a living example of the success of this king of joint action.

The WHO-FCTC has given rise to noteworthy changes in public health, both in countries and within WHO. By necessity, the conventional brought together diverse ministries (some of which had never engaged closely with each other and civil society to work on a single public health issue, under the auspices of WHO and alter the Conference of the Parties. Thus, it led to the creation of mechanisms for multisectoral coordination, which were eventually carried over into tobacco control work in many countries, within WHO, international treaty work, which had never previously been undertaken by the Organization, became an integral component of the work of the office of the Legal Counsel. For Member States, negotiation of the WHO-FCTC showed that effective engagement and agreement are possible despite widely divergent views.

A model for other areas of public health

Dr Javed Al-Lawati (Oman): Public health is about saving people's lives and that is what the treaty does. In the addition, it sets a precedent – that any risk factor can be regulated and public. Mr Steve Tamplin (former TFI Regional focal point, WHO Regional office for the Western (Pacific). The FCTC process has been the single most successful health promotion capacity building initiative ever undertaken by WHO. Among other things. It has required the health sector to substantially engage and work with other public sectors, the private sector and civil society. The success of the FCTC process can be should inform the development and use of effective mechanisms for resolving other complex multi-sector public health problems.

Improving the way we work

Dr Abdullah MA I – Bedah (Saudi Arabia): Te FCTC process is a unique example of continuous education and capacity building in all aspects of tobacco control. No. public health process has been as successful in bringing people from different sectors and interests under the leadership of the public health sector, and in accelerating global interest and action to control tobacco use. Dr Bill Kean (WHO headquarters, former INB secretary), one major impact of the WHO-FCTC not related to tobacco is that WHO Member States have more confidence in each other and are more able to listen to each other perspectives. Subsequent intergovernmental processes (under WHO an auspices) demonstrated a heightened degree of respect and trust". Mr Gian Luca Burci (legal Counsel, WHO): the negotiation and then the implementation of the FCTC made WHO fully appreciate. Probably for the first time, the importance of international law and of treaties in particular, as a toll for the pursuit of erucial public health goals. Dr Derek Yach (South Africa, Former WHO Executive Director): The WHO-FCTC set the scene for WHO to take a more multisectoral and regulated approach to global health. Tobacco became legitimized as a major global issue at a time when pressures were shrinking the scope of global health toward AIDS, malaria and TB. It opens the door to addressing chronic diseases.

Moving Further with the WHO-FCTC

For the next phase of the WHO-FCTC, the focus is different, and many of the players are new. The legacy of the early days remains valuable, even as the urgency of the tobacco epidemic remains us of the need for speedy, effective action at national and local levels. The Death Clock is truly in exorable. But today, the rules of the game have shifted. And because we now have the WHO-FCTC, the odds are no longer insurmountable.

Already, tangible benefits have occured from the WHO-FCTC. Numerous countries have passed or are renewing and strengthening national legislation and policies to conform to the evidence-based interventions set forth in the Framework Convention. Tobacco control is now acknowledged almost universally as a significant public health priority, and donor support is growing. The global tobacco control community has expanded, and tobacco control capacity continuous to improve at various levels.

The global public health community cannot, however relax its vigilance. The tobacco industry continues to thrive and continues to fuel the conflict between profit and health. Nicotine's addictiveness persists to enslave over one-third of the world's adult population, and globalization continues to facilitate the spread of the tobacco epidemic thorough trade, travel and communication.

While the WHO-FCTC represents a pivotal step in controlling the tobacco epidemic, it remains a tool. Its success, or failure, depends on how it is used by countries and how well it is explained and implemented at national and community level. The political theorist John Schaar said.

The future is not a result of choices among alternative paths offered by the present, but a place that is created—created first in the mind and will, created next in activity. The future is not some place we are going to but one we are creating. The paths are not to be found, but the activity of making them, changes both maker and the destination.

The WHO-FCTC represents a future that is being created by committed men and women who believe that all people deserve a healthy tobacco—free world these men and women have the vision and the courage to tackle a global health challenge with a powerful, innovative and radical experiment in global public health, one that has literally changed the rules of tobacco control.

If there is one lesson to be learnt from the history of the WHO-FCTCs early days, it is that the determinants of its success in tobacco control were the leadership, commitment, political will, integrity, vision and courage of the people, organizations and governments entrusted by the countries to turn the framework convention into reality. Now that the rules have changed the commitment of all the players will make the difference.

World Health Assembly Resolution WHA54.18 on transparency in tobacco control process, citing the findings of the Committee of Experts on Tobacco Industry Documents, states that the tobacco industry has operated for years with the express intension of subverting the role of governments and of WHO in implementing public health polices to combat the tobacco epidemic".

Use of the guidelines for implementation of Article 5.3 of the convention will have an overarching impacting on countries tobacco control policies and on implementation of the convention, because the guidelines recognize that tobacco industry interference, including that from the State-owned tobacco industry, cuts across a number of tobacco control policy areas, as stated in the Preamble of the Convention, articles referring to specific tobacco control policies and the Rules of Procedure of the Conference of the Parties to the WHO-FCTC.

There is a fundamental and irreconcilable conflict between the tobacco industry's interests and public health policy interests. The tobacco industry produces and promotes a product that has been proven scientifically to be addictive, to cause disease and death and to give rise to a variety of social ill, including increased poverty. Therefore, parties should protect the formulation and implementation of public health policies for tobacco control from the tobacco industry to the greatest extent possible.

Recommendations

The following important activities are recommended for addressing tobacco industry interference in public health policies.

1. Raise awareness about the addictive and harmful nature of tobacco products and about tobacco industry and ensure the transparency of those interactions that occur.
2. Establish measures to limit interactions with the tobacco industry and ensure the transparency of those interactions that occur.
3. Reject partnerships and non-binding or non-enforceable agreements with the tobacco industry.
4. Avoid conflicts of interest for government officials and employees.
5. Require that information provided by the tobacco industry be transparent and accurate.
6. Denormalize and, to the extent possible, regulate activities described as socially responsible by the tobacco industry, including but not limited to activities described as corporate social responsibility.
7. Do not give preferential treatment to the tobacco industry.
8. Treat State-owned tobacco industry in the same way as any other tobacco industry.

Plain Packaging of Cigarettes

An Idea Whose Time has Come

In December 2012, Australia became the rst country in the world to introduce legislation mandating plain packaging for tobacco products. Plain packaging legislation prohibits the use of logos, colors, brand images or promotional information on the packaging of tobacco products. However, brand and product names are allowed in a prescribed, standardized color and style, in addition to pictorial health warnings. Our contention is that the Government of India (GOI) must seriously consider introducing this legislation to stem the preventable deaths of more than 1.2 million Indians annually due to tobacco use. Tobacco's active ingredient is nicotine, an addictive substance. But, contributing to the persistence of the addiction is the status associated with the attractiveness of the package in which the substance itself is marketed and sold. The manner in which tobacco packaging serves the purpose of staining this addiction in its current users and converting new ones to it is well researched and has been perfected by the tobacco industry.

Tobacco packaging has served India's tobacco companies in multiple ways. This goes well beyond assisting in product differentiation and is commonly termed "selling from the shelf". It includes, but is not limited to brand identication, brand navigation and nally, brand s election. The pack is an important component of an overarching strategy to not only create a brand but also a future cohort of addicts. One may even argue that as part of the branding exercise, packaging assists in developing brand loyalty. Packaging is used to promote the product by using the same strategies employed by other consumer goods rms: specically, packaging innovation, design and value packaging.

Packaging is a key marketing tool for tobacco companies and offers a wider reach than advertising. Plain packaging legislation prohibits the use of logos, colors, brand images or promotional information on the packaging of tobacco products. In countries where it has been introduced, a large number of smokers were shown to be more likely to give quitting smoking a higher priority in their lives.

Importance of Packaging

Packaging is a key marketing tool for tobacco companies and offers a wider reach than advertising. It creates a tangible, explicit link between the company and the consumer. India's largest cigarette company, ITC, has invested and deployed market research companies and advertising firms to develop new designs and color schemes for its new and enduring cigarette brands. Market research firms have found that the color of the pack is an important attribute of the overall brand identity.

The tobacco industry is well aware of the psychographic appeal of the interplay of color and design. Tobacco industry documents reveal substantial investments in packaging design research from as early as the 1950s. A range of market research methods has been deployed including the use of focus groups with youth and market surveys in colleges and office areas. ITC commissioned a series of studies for the launch and the re-engineering of its brands. Some of these include Project Ingot (for the re-launch of Benson and Hedges cigarettes in 1998) and Project Little Buddha (for the global launch of State Express 555). In May and June 1988, ITCs main rival, GPI conducted focus—group discussions to understand the role of its brands, their packaging and image and how these could be improved.

Budget allocations to read the minds of potential and existing smokers have never posed a monetary constraint for the cigarette industry. In 1991–1992, ITC spent $700,000 annually on market research alone. In 1983, VST Company spent $3,000,000 on the market research and launch of its new brand Charms. The advertising firm which was given the mandate put most of its efforts into product packaging with a breakthrough of the new denim look, which signified a low price but fashionable cigarettes.

In May 1993, ITC conducted an ambitious market study called Project Barracuda to launch global brands in India with both international and locally—relevant packaging. Taking advantage of access to these materials reveals much about the role of packaging as a subset of the marketing strategies of key Indian companies. For example, surveys done by ITC and GPI conclude that urban consumers (and increasingly tier-2 cities and rural pockets) have become so accustomed to this use of color and design that their responses to these cues are automatic.

Elements of the packaging bouquet have been used by cigarette companies to strengthen brand image and bring in gender acceptability (in the case of Wills by ITC and Charms by GPI) and color is one variable of this targeted approach. But, there is more cigarettes have even been positioned in terms of a product with an exclusive "male" positioning, conveying a sense of strength and dominance (for example, India Kings). Market studies have also found that changing the packaging for cigarette packs can alter taste perceptions. Thus, even traditional cigarette brands need to reinvent themselves with new fonts, pack designs and color schemes.

The depth and range of research that tobacco companies have engaged in with respect to ne-tuning the design element on the package serves one fundamental purpose: to initiate and retain users. Analyzes of the target market converge on the fact that most smokers begin smoking when they are young. Further, a large majority of these young adults who smoke are also brand conscious. In fact, teenage smokers smoke the most heavily-advertised brands.

In 2003, India instituted the COTPA and Regulation of Trade and Commerce, Production, Supply and Distribution Act. This effectively eliminated public advertising and event sponsorships as a key avenue of marketing and brand building. However, attractive cigarette packaging continues to remain a vital tool in retaining users despite the many useful provisions of COTPA.

Effectiveness of Plain Packaging

This raises the obvious question: what if cigarette packaging were made unattractive, Through a mix of unattractive or nonexistent brand imagery, unattractive colors and enhanced pictorial warnings? Would cigarette use decline? Various studies from the mid-1990s have explored these causal factors and the main finding is that unattractive cigarette packages are in fact associated with reduced initiation of smoking, greater cessation-seeking behavior amongst smokers, better quit rates and also strengthening recall of health and pictorial warnings. A brief survey of a few key findings will suffice.

When New Zealand introduced textual health warnings on cigarette packages in 1990, a group of young people (the average age was 13) was surveyed in an examination of branding and plain packaging. The key finding was that if brand imagery was reduced, there was higher recall of health warnings. In December 2011, the British Heart Foundation commissioned a study and found that 80% young Scots thought that selling cigarettes in plain packages without colorful branding or logos and with larger health warnings would make it easier for people to smoke less or to quit.

India-specific data from the Global Adult Tobacco Survey (GATS) assessing the effects of cigarette package health warnings on interest in quitting smoking documented the following. Of the Indian smokers who observed the package warning, over 50% thought about quitting. In 2008, an experimental study examined the hypothesis that smokers would "rate an original branded pack more positively than their plain pack counterparts, and that plain packs with progressively fewer brand-associated elements (would) be rated more negatively".

This study found that of the various kinds of plain packages that cigarettes were presented in, those "packs with increasingly fewer brand design elements (were) perceived increasingly unfavorably in terms of the smokers' appraisals of the packs, the smokers who might smoke such packs, and the inferred experience of smoking a cigarette from these packs". Not surprisingly, the policy conclusion from this experiment was simple: the removal of as many brand design elements from the cigarette package as possible would be favorable for tobacco control efforts. Many more such studies can be cited. As Wakefield suggests, and this is consistent with market research applicable to other products, tobacco package branding and labeling does modify the subjective experience of products when they are consumed.

Further studies in India conducted in 2012 also suggest that regardless of socioeconomic status, individuals perceive the "badge value" of attractively packaged tobacco products as a way to flaunt one's wealth and, conversely, the fact that if the packaging of tobacco products were mandatorily made far less attractive, consumers would shift to more attractively packaged products. Further, in terms of the ranking of the elements on the package that were noticed rst, over 50% of the respondents noticed the brand name, the color and the package design and only after that, did they Notice the pictorial health warnings.

Plain packaging is likely to meet active resistance from the tobacco industry. It will affect the use of trademarks and other intellectual property. The tobacco industry is likely to oppose plain packaging on grounds of trademark and property rights violations. Provisions under bilateral investment treaties and International investment agreements also are likely to be presented as being hostile to plain packaging provisions. However, a closer legal analysis and reading of legal texts will demonstrate that sovereign states are well within their rights to introduce plain packaging legislation. Plain packaging legislation as a public health measure is compatible with the overriding public health interests that it seeks to enshrine.

Conclusions

A cigarette package is not a neutral physical space—it is used by tobacco companies to express cognitive cues to retain existing users and even attract new users. As a tobacco company executive put it:

> If you smoke, a cigarette pack is one of the few things you use regularly that makes a statement about you. A cigarette pack is the only thing you take out of your pocket 20 times a day and lay out for everyone to see. That's a lot different than buying your soap powder in generic packaging.

Plain packaging is effective. Recent evidence before the introduction of the legislation and evidence after the introduction of the legislation from Australia supports this fact. In fact, a recent study on the impact of plain packaging in Australia demonstrates that smokers who used plain-packaged cigarettes were 66% more likely to view their cigarettes as being of a poorer quality than 1 year ago and 81% of these were more likely to have thought about quitting at least once a day during the previous week, and many were more likely to view and give quitting smoking a higher priority in their lives. To paraphrase the words of Victor Hugo, plain packaging legislation in India may well be an idea whose time has now come.

International Collaboration and Updated and Revision of the Guidelines

International cooperation is essential for making progress in preventing interference by the tobacco industry with the formulation of public health policies on tobacco control. Article 20.4 of the Convention provides the basis for collecting and exchanging knowledge and experience with respect to tobacco industry practices, taking into account and addressing the special needs of developing country Parties and Parties with economies in transition.

Efforts have already been made to coordinate the collection and dissemination of national and international experience with regard to the strategies and tactics used by the tobacco industry and to the monitoring of tobacco industry activities. Parties would benefit from sharing legal and strategic expertise for countering tobacco industry strategies. Article 21.4 of the Convention provides that information exchange should be subject to national laws regarding confidentially and privacy.

The WHO-FCTC draft guidelines and recommendations (November 12-17, 2012) have been strongly criticized by tobacco farmers. The draft guidelines aim to cap tobacco arming production, restrict the available land for tobacco farming, deny farmers their political and commercial rights, and ban contractual relations between farmers and their buyers. It is said that the guidelines were based on the wrong assumption that the tobacco growing countries could shift tobacco farmers to alternative crops or livelihoods. Experts feel that there are no alternatives for the tobacco growing regions around the globe because tobacco is grown on soils with low fertility and arid climates, and such land is not suitable for growing other crops.

According to the original goals of the FCTC, tobacco growers and workers were to be involved in decision-making and ought to have been given adequate channels to voice their needs and concerns. But, so far, tobacco farmers have been totally excluded from the debate.

The Tobacco Board is urging the Central Government to request the FCTC working group to revise its draft policy recommendations and incorporate the views of tobacco farmers' organizations. There should be specific, detailed and credible options for the farmers to diversify to alternative crops.

WORLD NO TOBACCO DAY

May 31 is observed as "World no tobacco day". Worldwide, more than 1 billion people—about one-third of the world's population that's older than 15—smokes. Tobacco kills around half of its users. In cigarette smoke, there are more than 4,000 toxic chemical compounds and over 40 cancer causing chemicals. Very early on, in a short span of time, users develop a strong addiction to the nicotine in tobacco. It is as powerful an addictive substance as cocaine or heroin.

Almost half the country's tobacco using population wants to give up the fatal habit but does not know what to do or where to go to reduce their dependence on tobacco. The habit kills 1 million annually. Yet, for the 275 million users of smoking and smokeless tobacco products, the country has just 19 Tobacco Cessation Clinics (TCCs), where trained medics provide nicotine replacement therapy to help clients kick the butt. Most such centers are in urban areas of 17 states, leaving a vast chunk of rural India uncovered.

This, at a time when the country's first scientific study on the results of clinically aided cessation among tobacco users threw up an encouraging quit rate of 22%. The global quit rate average with the best cessation facilities is about 33%.

The first cessation clinic was established in 2001 National Center for Asthma Allergy and Immunology, Vallabhbhai Patel Chest Institute, where, a study by the institute that their study on 500 clients revealed a quit rate of 22% at the end of a year of therapy. The study also revealed the benefits of cessation with counseling. "Though the quit rate at 1 year among clients who received both counseling and medication was higher at 52%, it was as high as 15% even among those who didn't receive drugs and were only counseled. This makes a case for upscaling of cessation services. Counseling alone can also make a huge difference", Kumar said.

The India Tobacco report released last November provided ample evidence of current smokers and smokeless tobacco users wanting to quit. Whereas 46.6% smokers said they were interested in quitting and 38.4% tried quitting, 45.2% smokeless tobacco users admitted to an urge to quit and 35.4% said they tried. Health Ministry's own data from the National Anti-tobacco Helpline (1800110456) also shows that out of 10,722 calls received over the last year, 1,500 related to cessation facilities alone. That explains the massive urge among people to reduce nicotine dependence. A survey by The Tribune Today on the use of anti-smoking gums available in the market firmed up the evidence of the need for Nicotine Replacement Therapy, which the government now plans to subsidize. Currently, a strip of 10 gum costs between Rs 50 and Rs 65.

CESSATION FACTS

- Most smokers desire to quit; 30% try annually and 5% succeed. Unaided cessation not very successful.
- The body starts repairing itself within 24 hours of quitting.
- Among quitters, heart disease death rate halves in a year; lung cancer risk drops by half in 10 years.
- In 2001, India was among the first Southeast Asian countries to offer cessation with WHOs help.

WHO-FCTC. During 2011–2012, the tobacco crop output declined in India because of incessant rains caused by the Nilam cyclone, leading to production of low-grade leaf in Andhra Pradesh, except in Northern light soils (NLS) where quality is reported to be good. Decline in production in Andhra Pradesh amounted to about 5 million kg. The NLS of Andhra Pradesh is known to produce the best quality FCV tobacco in the country, which secured a maximum price of Rs 150 a kg in 2011–2012.

The Tobacco Board launched an e-auctioning platform at Periyapatna in Mysore district in November 2012. It is planning to introduce a similar facility in all the 11 auction platforms in Karnataka. This will be extended to Andhra Pradesh in 2013.

The government is keen on reducing tobacco output as India is a signatory of the FCTC of WHO. It wants to come up with a package for farmers. It aims to identify viable alternative crops to be grown in place of tobacco, and fix the remuneration to be given to farmers. This will be done in coordination with the Central Tobacco Research Institute (CTRI) and the ministry of Health and Family Welfare—the nodal ministry for tobacco production control. The government's objective is to bring down the total area under tobacco cultivation from 450,000 hectares to 200,000 hectares by 2020, in a phased manner. This is expected to bring down tobacco production from 750 million kg to 250 million kg.

Punjab has lowest tobacco use, Northeast highest. Indian women more addicted to nicotine than men.

India's obsession with tobacco continues despite laws to tell the users of its lethal consequences. Though 64% of all adults believe tobacco leads to heart attacks, 35% (one-third) continue to consume tobacco in some form or the other. An average Indian starts tobacco use at 17.8 years, the initiation age being the lowest, 14.9 in Chhattisgarh and the highest 20.4 years in Himachal. Over 60% daily tobacco users are so addicted that they want tobacco within half an hour of waking up, concludes the 2009–2010 GATS for India, conducted on 99.9% of India's population in 29 States, Union Territories (UTs) of Chandigarh and Puducherry.

The survey findings, released by Health Minister Ghulam Nabi Azad today, state that India houses 274.9 million tobacco users; 84% (231.9 million) of these are daily users-that's the population of Indonesia. While 14% adults are smokers, 25.9% use smokeless forms, the highest (12%) use being of a tobacco-lime mixture (khaini), followed by 8% use of areca nut. Nine percent of all smokers use bidis, 6% use cigarettes, 1% hookahs. Though overall tobacco prevalence is lesser in females (20.3%) as against males (47.9) so is overall cigarette use (2.9% females smoke as against 24.3% men), the fair sex is much more nicotine dependent than men. Cigarettes smoked a day, which is an indicator of nicotine addiction, is much higher for females who consume 7 cigarettes a day while men smoke 6.2. Urban male smokers smoke a higher number of cigarettes (6.4) than their rural counterparts (6), but female cigarette smokers in rural areas beat urban females by consuming 7.2 cigarettes a day against 5.8 sticks a day in cities.

Tobacco India report: highlights

- 52% adults exposed to second hand smoke at home, highest in J&K (68%), lowest in Chandigarh (15%); 29% exposed in public places
- Cigarette smokers' monthly expense Rs 400 as against Rs 94 for bidi smokers.

- Monthly cigarette expenditure highest in Arunachal (Rs 1,265), lowest in Jharkhand (Rs 181.70)
- Mizoram has highest tobacco use (67%), while Goa (9%), Punjab (12%), Chandigarh (14%) have lowest
- Mizo women most addicted (62% use tobacco) as against least addicted in Punjab (under 1%), Chandigarh, Himachal and Goa (under 5%)
- Most tobacco use in East (45%), Northeast (44%), lowest in North (19%)

In cigarette smoking, women beat males by age too: Boys aged 15–24 smoke 4.8 cigarettes a day; girls puff 9 a day. Men aged 25–44 smoke 6 cigarettes a day while women that age consume 8.4 sticks a day. Even beyond 65 years, males are smoking 6.3 cigarettes a day but women want 7.9 a day. Further, working males (government/private sectors) smoke lesser cigarettes a day (6.3) than their female counterparts (7.6). By regions, the Northeast leads the cigarette-smoking pack, consuming 8.5 cigarettes a day (Meghalaya is the smokiest Indian city and puffs 14.8 cigarettes a day). The North seems more interested in bidis than cigarettes. So where Uttarakhand and Haryana have the lowest cigarette smoking frequency in India at 4.3 and 4.9 cigarettes a day, respectively, they consume 10.7 and 11.1 bidi sticks a day, respectively. Daily cigarettes smoked in Chandigarh are also less – 6.4, Punjab 7.7; Himachal 4.8 and Jammu and Kashmir 7.6 but respective bidi consumption in these areas is 12.8, 10.7, 9.5, 10.7 a day.

GATS (conducted by Health Ministry and Indian Institute of Population Sciences, Mumbai) shows the mean frequency of bidi smoking (10.9 sticks a day) in North is higher than cigarette smoking (6.8). South India consumes the most bidis (13.4 sticks a day), with Karnataka leading the pack at 16.5 bidis smoked per day.

Government Hike Cigarette Prices to Deter Smokers

Terming the health and social costs of smoking a menace, Union Health Minister Dr Harsh Vardhan wrote to Finance Minister Arun Jaitely proposing a step hike in the costs of cigarettes in the Union budget.

A per his proposal, the price of a cigarette should be raised from Rs 2 to Rs 3.5. I propose to reform tobacco taxes in the 2014 budget implement a large but feasible tax hike in the budget on cigarettes to Rs 3.5 per stick. The tax would be applied to all lengths to prevent the industry shifting production and marketing of lower length cigarettes, the letter. His move opposes the current practice of raising taxes based on the length of a cigarette—the longer the cigarettes, the more it costs. Tobacco products like cigarettes, bidis and gutka are a source of many diseases. It is a menace said Dr Vardhan. In his proposal, Dr Vardhan has stated that raising the proportion of specific tax of cigarettes as a percentage of their retial price, that is from 45% to 60% of the retail price will make nearly three million smokers quit. It will discourage nearly 3 million first time—smokers form picking up the habit. He added that this should save the lives of 4 million people.

There will also be an attempt to regulate the largely unregulated bidi industry. There is a urgent need to remove the exemption on tan given to bidi manufactures producing less than 2 million bidis, and to redefine taxation points in the bidi tax policy to ensure collection of revenue and prevent tax evasion in the long run.

The letter also emphasized on the need for stringent action at the State level, in the form of additional VAT, mass awareness campaigns, etc.

Tobacco, smoking cigarettes and bidis causes about 1 million deaths in the country annually. The number of male smokers has gone up from 83 million 106 million over the last decade and cigarettes are displacing bidis in popularity. Tobacco use id forcing more than 15 million Indians into poverty from ill health every year. The more expensive they become, the better it is for all of us. Their price should be hiked. They should become rare.

Up, Up and Away

Brand	*Current rate (Pack of 10)*	*Proposed rate*	4 mn
Marlboro	Rs 85	Rs 120	The number of lives the proposed move is expected to save, according to Dr Vardhan
Benson and Hedges	Rs 170	Rs 240	
Navy Cut	Rs 69	Rs 104	
Gold Flake	Rs 85	Rs 120	

Smoking is no Reason to Give Health Insurance a Miss

Do some individuals avoid buying a health insurance cover due to certain unhealthy habits or ailments that they have? Do they conceal them as they feel that their application will be rejected otherwise by the insurance companies? According to a new survey, nearly one-third of the respondents said that they decided against buying a policy as they feared that their application would be turned down by insurance firms. Over half of those participating in the survey also said that they had not disclosed their smoking habit while buying health insurance policies. The survey was conducted by ICICI Lombard on the occasion of World Tobacco Day.

"Smokers fear that insurers will attribute ailments that may arise in future to their habit and reject the application or claims. However, such concerns are unfounded", says Sanjay Datta, chief, underwriting and claims, ICICI Lombard.

You Can Still Get Covered

Smoking or pre-existing ailments don't automatically disqualify you from getting a health cover. Companies take a more nuanced position while examining such applications. "It is a myth that if the proposer is a smoker, the application for policy purchase will be rejected outright. In India, smoking, by itself, does not result in premium loading or rejection of policy applications", says Datta. "However, if smoking has resulted in health complications at the time of making the proposal, it can impact the insurer's decision to issue you a policy".

Cover for All

- 56% haven't disclosed their smoking or tobacco consumption habit
- 71% don't mind paying a higher premium if the policy covers tobacco consumption related ailments.
- 30% fear rejection while applying for health cover
- 60% feel tobacco users or smokers could face difficulties in their claim settlement.

Most insurers do not charge higher premiums to smokers, but some do factor it in while issuing policies. However, that decision depends on the individual's declaration, medical reports and the company's stance. "The impact of declaration of daily cigarette smoking is considered by us on a case-to-case basis. We usually ask additional questions to habitual smokers while underwriting their policy request", says Antony Jacob, CEO, Apollo Munich. The decision will depend on the frequency of smoking. "For regular smokers, we may load or exclude certain health conditions depending on the health status of the proposer", he adds. The company usually rejects proposals if the seeker smokes more than 40 cigarettes a day.

As for pre-existing lifestyle diseases like diabetes and hypertension, the severity of the condition would determine the fate of your application. Those under the age of 45 are typically issued policies on the basis of declaration of good health. However, if you happen to be a smoker or suffer from lifestyle diseases, you will have to undergo medical tests. "Premiums will be determined on the basis of your state of health. For instance, if you suffer from type-II diabetes, most insurers will refuse to issue policies. Even if they do, they could issue specialized policies and the premium could be four to five times higher", says Yashish Dahiya, CEO, Policybazaar.com.

According to Deepak Yohannan, CEO, myinsuranceclub.com, an insurance aggregator portal, many companies refuse to extend policies when you declare pre-existing lifestyle diseases. "Even if some companies agree to issue policies, they will come with premium loading".

Full Disclosure is a Must

However, this does not mean that one should conceal a health condition or personal habits to obtain a cover. The cover won't be worth anything if you develop complications later. The insurance firm will be within its rights to reject such claims.

India Loses More to Tobacco than it Spends on Health, Reveals Study

India is annually losing more in terms of economic costs of tobacco use than it is spending on health. A new research on the financial consequences of tobacco use has revealed that economic costs of tobacco use, which causes serious diseases, was Rs 104,500 crore in 2011 for users aged 35–69 years.

This burden translates into 1.16% of the GDP—0.12% more than the combined Central and State expenditure on health in 2011–2012, the year of study selected by the Public Health Foundation of India (PHFI), which says a comprehensive taxation policy is a must to prevent tobacco use. Of the total economic cost, 16% was direct cost of treatment and 84% was indirect cost in terms of morbidity.

The report's concerns were shared today by Health Minister Harsh Vardhan, who, in his first public appearance today, hinted at raising taxes on tobacco to curb its use. "It makes perfect economic sense to regulate tobacco toward the goal of noncommunicable disease control in India. Unless we come together to fight tobacco, the financial burden of tobacco-attributable diseases will continue to push families toward poverty and decelerate our economic growth. We must not let it happen", he said, making the report public on the eve of World No Tobacco Day on May 31.

The noncommunicable diseases (NCDs) account for 53% of all deaths in India and over 80% NCD deaths are attributed to four diseases—cardiovascular diseases

(CVDs), cancers, chronic respiratory diseases and diabetes. Tobacco consumption is a major risk factor for all these NCDs.

The PHFI found that CVDs shared the highest burden (Rs 3,600 crore) on account of tobacco use, followed by respiratory diseases (Rs 2,800 crore), TB (Rs 2,300 crore) and cancers (Rs 1,400 crore). The direct medical costs of hospital care and treatment of tobacco attributable diseases amounted to Rs 16,800 crore and associated indirect morbidity cost came to Rs 14,700 crore. The study shows that men are major contributors to economic burden related to tobacco, sharing 91% of the cost. The women's contribution was higher (29%) for smokeless tobacco.

The Research Says

- The economic cost of tobacco use was Rs 104,500 crore in 2011 for users aged 35–69
- It translates into 1.16% of the GDP – 0.12% more than the combined central and state expenditure on health in 2011–2012.
- Men share 91% of the economic burden, while women's contribution is higher (29%) for smokeless tobacco.

Production

Tobacco is an important commercial crop cultivated in an area of 0.4 million hectare producing annually around 700 million kg of cured leaf out of which 260 Mkg is FCV tobacco (cigarette type). India is the 3rd largest producer of tobacco in the world after China and Brazil. Majority of the states in the Indian union territory grow one type or the other to a greater or lesser extent, significantly influencing the economy and prosperity of the farming community. FCV, *Bidi,* Hookah and Chewing, Cigar filler, Cigar Wrapper, *Cheroot,* Burley, Oriental, HDBRG, *Lanka,* etc are the different types of tobacco grown in the country. Tobacco is consumed in the form of cigarettes, cigars, cheroots, *bidis,* pipe and hookah. It is chewed in the form of *Surti, Zarda, Qiwamquid, Masheri, Kharamasala.* Also, tobacco is inhaled in the form of snuff. The crop provides employment to about 36 million people directly or indirectly including 6 million farmers in the country. India ranks 5th largest exporter of tobacco in the world after Brazil, USA, Malawi and Turkey. The crop fetches annually around Rs 1,713 crores as foreign exchange through exports and over Rs 9,100 crores as excise revenue. An estimated ~250 million people in the country use tobacco in different forms.

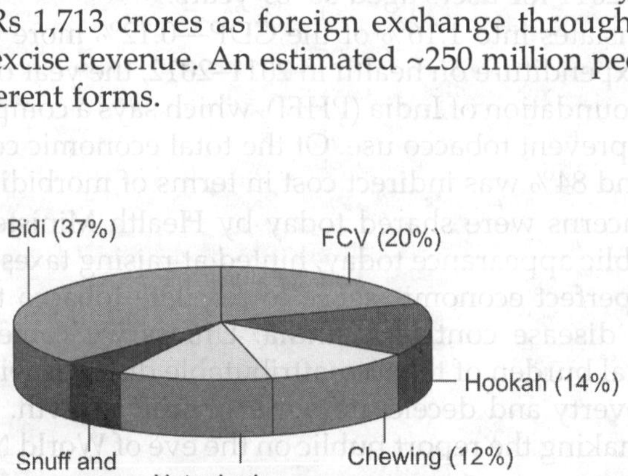

Types of tobacco produced in India

India is a small player with less than 10% share in the world production of tobacco. During 1950–1951, area was just 360 thousand hectare and production 260 thousand tons. Productivity levels were also low-only 731 kg/hectare. With minor fluctuations from year to year, there has been hardly any change—370 thousand hectares in 2005–2006 and 440 thousand hectare in 2009-10. With Productivity and the share of irrigated area nearly doubling up, production also increased to 550 thousand tons in 1989–1990 and 740 thousand tones. In 1998–1999 (Table 1.1). All India compound growth rate of area, production and yield for different periods from 1949–1950 shows that despite decrease in area, production has gone up due to yield increase (Table 1.1A). Distribution of area and production variety wise shows that by and large bidi variety has been at the top followed by Virginia in area and production. Snuff tobacco has had the smallest area of a few thousand hectare (Table 1.1B). Distribution of production of different types follows more or less the same as area, but for the fact that bidi has been at the top throughout (Table 1.1C). Area planted and registered under FCV shows that recorded area and production has invariably been higher (Table 1.1D). According to the WHOs vision document, India should aim to achieve at least a 30% reduction in tobacco consumption by 2020 and 25% reduction in tobacco related mortality by 2050. Area production and yield of tobacco in major tobacco producing states coverage under irrigation is Table 1.1E.

Table 1.1: All India area, production and yield of tobacco along with percentage coverage under irrigation

(Area - million hectares; Production - million tons; Yield - Kg/hectare)

Year	Area	Production	Yield	Coverage under irrigation (%)
1	2	3	4	5
1940-41	40.0	31.5	788	–
1941-42	52.6	37.2	707	–
1942-43	31.9	25.5	799	–
1943-44	37.2	29.8	801	–
1944-45	40.5	32.8	810	–
1945-46	49.0	35.9	733	–
1946-47	51.4	36.8	716	–
1947-48	55.4	39.2	708	–
1948-49	54.2	39.6	731	–
1950-51	0.36	0.26	731	NA
1951-52	0.29	0.21	723	NA
1952-53	0.36	0.25	675	9.7
1953-54	0.37	0.27	737	9.7
1954-55	0.35	0.26	737	10.8
1955-56	0.41	0.30	739	16.9
1956-57	0.42	0.31	728	20.4

(Contd.)

Table 1.1: All India area, production and yield of tobacco along with percentage coverage under irrigation

Area - million hectares; Production - million tons; Yield - Kg/hectare)

Year	*Area*	*Production*	*Yield*	*Coverage under irrigation (%)*
1	*2*	*3*	*4*	*5*
1957-58	0.36	0.24	669	22.5
1958-59	0.38	0.32	836	21.0
1959-60	0.41	0.29	716	22.4
1960-61	0.40	0.31	766	21.9
1961-62	0.42	0.34	811	17.9
1962-63	0.41	0.34	842	18.2
1963-64	0.44	0.36	817	15.4
1964-65	0.41	0.36	876	17.0
1965-66	0.38	0.29	778	16.9
1966-67	0.42	0.35	834	17.1
1967-68	0.42	0.37	871	17.4
1968-69	0.44	0.36	821	20.4
1969-70	0.44	0.34	770	19.5
1970-71	0.45	0.36	810	23.7
1971-72	0.46	0.42	914	24.5
1972-73	0.45	0.37	837	26.3
1973-74	0.46	0.46	1001	24.2
1974-75	0.38	0.36	954	21.0
1975-76	0.37	0.35	950	29.8
1976-77	0.43	0.42	969	30.2
1977-78	0.50	0.49	979	23.3
1978-79	0.41	0.45	1109	31.5
1979-80	0.43	0.44	1031	32.6
1980-81	0.45	0.48	1065	33.7
1981-82	0.44	0.52	1172	33.9
1982-83	0.50	0.58	1157	29.6
1983-84	0.44	0.49	1120	34.0
1984-85	0.44	0.49	1113	37.7
1985-86	0.40	0.44	1111	39.9
1986-87	0.39	0.46	1187	40.7
1987-88	0.32	0.37	1155	45.9
1988-89	0.38	0.49	1307	42.4
1989-90	0.41	0.55	1335	43.2
1990-91	0.41	0.56	1353	43.2

Table 1.1: All India area, production and yield of tobacco along with percentage coverage under irrigation *(Contd.)*

(Area - million hectares; Production - million tons; Yield - Kg/hectare)

Year	*Area*	*Production*	*Yield*	*Coverage under irrigation (%)*
1	2	3	4	5
1991-92	0.43	0.58	1369	39.0
1992-93	0.42	0.60	1425	40.4
1993-94	0.38	0.56	1463	43.7
1994-95	0.38	0.57	1486	45.3
1995-96	0.39	0.54	1356	46.5
1996-97	0.43	0.62	1444	43.8
1997-98	0.46	0.64	1394	39.8
1998-99	0.51	0.74	1451	43.1
1999-00	0.43	0.52	1211	46.0
2000-01	0.26	0.34	1318	52.8
2001-02	0.35	0.55	1565	43.6
2002-03	0.33	0.49	1506	46.2
2003-04	0.37	0.55	1486	49.9
2004-05	0.37	0.55	1498	42.3
2005-06	0.37	0.55	1481	40.9
2006-07	0.37	0.52	1409	40.6
2007-08	0.35	0.49	1417	52.6
2008-09	0.39	0.62	1590	NA
2009-10	044	069	1559	—

NA, Non-available.

Source: Directorate of Economics and Statistics, Department of Agriculture and Cooperation.

Table 1.1A: All India compound growth rate of area, production and yield of tobacco

[Base T.E 1981-82 = 100 (% per annum)]

Period	*A*	*P*	*Y*
1949-50 to 1997-98	0.07	1.94	1.68
1949-50 to 1964-65	1.66	2.79	1.10
1964-65 to 1967-68	– 0.08	2.22	2.23
1967-68 to 1977-78	– 0.31	1.77	2.08
1980-81 to 1997-98	– 0.44	1.45	1.09

A = Growth rate of area
P = Growth rate of production
Y = Growth rate of yield

Table 1.1B: All India estimates of area and production of tobacco (variety wise) from 1987-88 to 2002-03 (derived estimates)

Area: thousand ha, production:million kg.

Variety		*1987-88*	*88-89*	*89-90*	*90-91*	*91-92*	*92-93*	*93-94*	*94-95*	*95-96*	*96-97*	*97-98*	*99-99*	*99-00*	*2000 -01*	*01-02*	*02-03*
Virginia	Area	80.6	106.3	110.0	118.9	158.6	155.2	133.2	120.8	125.6	149.2	181.0	183.0	220.8	82.6	174.4	180.1
	Prodn.	56.7	104.6	105.1	112.9	164.7	165.8	123.8	113.4	117.7	138.2	152.4	187.2	193.8	63.4	182.9	173.2
Natu	Area	30.8	40.0	53.6	50.0	50.0	38.1	38.2	30.0	33.4	40.0	44.7	42.8	32.4	27.4	26.7	22.4
	Prodn.	35.7	59.0	74.4	58.2	72.8	62.2	60.1	45.0	48.2	50.0	52.5	61.0	44.3	37.7	48.6	42.7
Bidi	Area	103.0	117.9	138.7	128.3	113.3	123.8	118.6	130.9	138.5	139.1	137.2	140.2	95.9	81.0	78.8	66.3
	Prodn.	138.5	167.2	192.7	197.1	167.1	188.3	188.2	218.8	205.2	211.4	190.7	127.9	126.8	108.0	139.2	122.3
Cigar & Cheroot	Area	10.2	13.5	12.9	13.7	13.0	11.7	11.9	14.6	12.6	12.0	10.9	10.6	8.9	7.5	7.3	6.1
	Prodn.	9.9	14.1	15.0	14.4	14.1	16.8	16.0	17.6	17.3	13.0	9.8	23.9	11.4	9.7	12.5	11.0
Hookah	Area	22.9	25.9	26.4	32.9	29.3	31.5	29.3	15.2	13.1	16.4	18.3	69.5	25.5	21.5	20.9	17.6
	Prodn.	31.9	46.2	34.3	82.7	72.3	78.9	97.3	21.9	17.0	35.9	42.9	165.6	53.1	45.2	58.3	51.2
Chewing	Area	63.7	66.4	69.5	58.5	54.7	52.2	48.5	62.3	65.4	64.3	63.6	52.4	43.3	36.6	35.6	30.0
	Prodn.	88.4	92.8	129.5	78.8	79.0	71.2	65.7	138.3	118.8	159.6	188.0	150.4	88.0	75.0	96.7	84.9
Snuff	Area	6.8	7.0	10.0	8.5	8.1	6.0	5.1	7.6	6.0	7.0	7.8	9.6	5.8	5.0	4.7	4.1
	Prodn.	6.1	8.9	13.4	11.8	14.4	13.3	11.8	11.7	11.0	9.8	9.7	20.2	6.6	8.0	7.3	6.4
Total	**Area**	**318.0**	**377.0**	**413.1**	**410.8**	**427.0**	**418.5**	**384.8**	**381.4**	**394.6**	**432.3**	**436.5**	**508.1**	**432.6**	**261.5**	**348.5**	**326.6**
	Prodn.	**367.2**	**492.8**	**551.6**	**555.9**	**584.4**	**596.5**	**562.9**	**566.7**	**535.2**	**599.1**	**646.0**	**736.2**	**524.0**	**344.7**	**545.5**	**491.7**

Source: Directorate of Tobacco Development, Government of India, Ministry of Agriculture, (Deptt. of Agri .& Coopn.),Chennai-600 006.

Table 1.1C: Distribution (percentage) of production of different types of tobacco in India.

Year	*Percentage distribution of production of different tobacco types*							*Total harvest ('000 ton)*
	FCV	*Natu*	*Bidi*	*Cigar*	*Hookah*	*Cheroot*	*Snuff*	
1975/76	27.7	10.9	31.4	4.3	7.1	17.2	1.4	349.8
1980/81	26.1	10.6	36.5	2.8	7.7	14.8	1.5	520.1
1985/86	18.0	13.8	39.3	4.0	6.8	17.0	1.8	441.2
1986/87	23.7	9.5	40.0	2.4	6.1	16.9	1.4	461.8
1987/88	15.4	9.8	37.6	2.7	8.7	24.1	1.7	367.4
1988/89	21.2	12.2	33.9	2.9	9.4	18.8	2.1	492.8
1989/90	18.8	12.9	33.4	2.8	6.2	23.5	2.4	551.6
1990/91	20.3	10.5	35.5	2.6	14.1	14.9	2.1	558.4
1991/92	28.2	12.3	28.6	2.4	12.4	13.5	2.6	584.4
1992/93	27.8	10.4	31.6	2.8	13.3	11.9	2.2	596.5
1993/94	22.0	10.7	33.4	2.8	17.3	11.7	2.1	562.9
1994/95	20.0	7.9	38.6	3.1	3.9	24.4	2.1	566.7
1995/96	22.0	9.0	38.3	3.2	3.2	22.2	2.1	535.2
1996/97	23.4	8.1	34.2	2.1	5.8	25.8	1.6	617.9
1997/98	23.6	8.1	29.5	1.5	6.6	29.1	1.5	646.0

Source: Directorate of Tobacco Development, Ministry of Agriculture, Chennai.

Table 1.1D: Area registered and planted to FCV tobacco cultivars, and production

Year	*Area ('000 ha)*			*Production ('000 tone)*			*Change in price (%)*
	Recorded	*Planted*	*Difference [(3) - (2)]*	*Expected*	*Actual*	*Difference [(6) - (5)]*	
(1)	*(2)*	*(3)*	*(4)*	*(5)*	*(6)*	*(7)*	*(8)*
1986/87	111.20	104.871	–6.33	110.20	132.73	3.07	21.37
1987/88	83.20	68.31	–14.89	83.20	59.34	–23.77	–34.18
1988/89	92.08	105.52	13.44	100.00	116.21	16.21	98.66
1989/90	88.58	105.32	16.74	93.00	100.82	7.82	1.59
1990/91	103.52	122.40	18.88	105.00	109.48	4.48	–11.45
1991/92	122.26	153.55	31.29	144.83	159.19	14.36	–13.37
1992/93	113.56	140.71	27.15	124.06	158.86	34.80	–18.37
1993/94	86.11	122.84	36.73	92.64	125.50	32.86	1.68
1994/95	81.69	106.39	24.70	86.27	96.34	10.07	10.00
1995/96	94.28	124.14	29.86	99.67	114.40	14.73	26.32
1996/97	100.54	152.72	52.18	112.76	168.21	55.45	24.38
1997/98	105.38	154.03	48.65	141.81	177.09	35.28	37.61
1998/99	118.23	183.47	65.24	139.26	204.49	65.23	n.a.
1999/00	120.73	178.93	58.20	132.28	190.00	57.72	n.a.

Source: Tobacco Board (various issues). Annual Administrative Report.

Table 1.1E: Area, production and yield of tobacco in major tobacco producing states along with coverage under Irrigation

(Area - '000 hectares; Production - '000 tons; Yield - Kg/ hectare)

State	*2008-09*					*2007-08*					*Area under irrigation during 2007-08*(%)*
	Area	*% to all-India*	*Production*	*% to all-India*	*Yield*	*Area*	*% to all-India*	*Production*	*% to all-India*	*Yield*	
1	2	3	4	5	6	2	3	4	5		
Andhra Pradesh	171.00	43.83	314.00	50.54	1836	120.00	34.47	175.00	35.48		
Uttar Pradesh	23.12	5.93	135.55	21.82	5863	25.50	7.33	140.80	28.54	5522	100.0
Gujarat	49.20	12.61	70.10	11.28	1425	46.00	13.21	79.00	16.02	1717	91.5
Karnataka	108.00	27.68	52.00	8.37	481	113.00	32.46	46.00	9.33	407	14.9
Bihar	9.90	2.54	12.90	2.08	1303	13.50	3.88	15.50	3.14	1148	78.1
Tamil Nadu	5.38	1.38	8.21	1.32	1526	5.90	1.69	9.10	1.84	1542	100.0
Maharashtra	5.00	1.28	7.00	1.13	1400	6.00	1.72	7.00	1.42	1167	16.4
Others	18.55	4.75	21.49	3.46	@	18.20	5.23	20.86	4.23	@	–
All India	**390.15**	**100.00**	**621.25**	**100.00**	**1592**	**348.10**	**100.00**	**493.26**	**100.00**	**1417**	**52.6**

@ Since Area/Production is low, yield rate is not worked out.
* Provisional.
Note: States have been arranged in descending order of percentage share of production during 2008-09.

Even though the cultivation of tobacco is spread all over the country, it is concentrated in states like Andhra Pradesh, Karnataka, Gujarat, Maharashtra, Bihar, Tamil Nadu and West Bengal, etc [Table 1.2 is shown in annexure at the end of chapter and 1.2A]. Cigarette tobacco is mostly cultivated in Andhra and Karnataka, whereas *beedi* tobacco is grown in Tamil Nadu, Andhra Pradesh and West Bengal, and chewing tobacco is grown in Tamil Nadu, Gujarat, Bihar, West Bengal and UP. Hookah tobacco is grown in UP and West Bengal.

Andhra Pradesh accounts for around 35% of production, covering the same percentage of area. Although Karnataka is number 2 in area (over 27%), it produces only around 11% of the crop—UP comes number 2 in production with its share of over 20% . VFC variety tobacco—most important from all the varieties—is primarily restricted to Andhra Pradesh, Maharashtra and Karnataka. Basic data for area and production in these three states shows wide fluctuations in Table 1.2B. Productivity of FCV tobacco in India is low (1,519 kg/hectare) when compared with Zimbabwe (2,645 kg/hectare), the US (2,238 kg/hectare), and China (1,770 kg/hectare). Indian FCV tobacco is generally branded as filler, being substitute rather than component of blends in major international cigarette brands.

Out of the total production, only 9% goes into the manufacturing of cigarettes, whereas 81% is consumed for chewing, making *beedi*, snuff, gutkha paste, jarda, hookah paste, etc. India is perhaps the only tobacco producing country where the states decide exactly how much tobacco should be grown and where. There is no such arrangement even in China. Other leading producers like the US, Brazil and Malawi also have a system of contract farming so as to facilitate linkages between the trade, the industry and the growers.

Table 1.2A: Area, production and yield of tobacco during 2007-08 to 2009-10 in major producing states along with coverage under irrigation

(Area - '000 hectares; Production - '000 tons; Yield - Kg/hectare)

State	*2007-08*			*2008-09*			*2009-10**			*Area under irrigation % (2008-09*)*
	Area	*Produ.*	*Yield*	*Area*	*Produ.*	*Yield*	*Area*	*Produ.*	*Yield*	
Andhra Pradesh	120.00	175.00	1458	171.00	314.00	1836	199.00	360.00	1809	27.3
Gujarat	46.00	79.00	1717	49.20	70.10	1425	62.00	101.00	1629	86.4
Karnataka	113.00	46.00	407	108.00	52.00	481	118.00	91.00	771	12.8
Uttar Pradesh	25.50	140.80	5522	23.69	82.76	3493	23.39	79.76	3410	100.0
Bihar	13.50	15.50	1148	9.90	12.90	1303	9.24	17.25	1867	82.0
Tamil Nadu	5.90	9.10	1542	5.40	8.20	1519	7.05	10.74	1523	99.8
Maharashtra	6.00	7.00	1167	5.00	7.00	1400	5.00	7.00	1400	16.4
Others	18.20	20.86	@	18.50	21.70	1173	20.60	25.74	1250	-
All India	**348.10**	**493.26**	**1417**	**390.69**	**568.66**	**1456**	**444.28**	**692.49**	**1559**	**46.0**

@ Since Area/ Production is low, yield rate is not worked out.
* Provisional.
Note: States have been arranged in descending order of percentage share of production during 2009-10.
Source: Directorate of Economics and Statistics, Department of Agriculture and Cooperation.

Table 1.2B: Estimates of area and quantity marketed of VFC tobacco from 1986-87 to 1998-99

(Area: Hectare; Quantity: Million kg)

Year	*State*	*Area*	*Quantity*
1986-87	Andhra Pradesh & Maharashtra	88816	97.51
	Karnataka	17219	16.22
	Total	106035	113.73
1987-88	Andhra Pradesh & Maharashtra	52995	47.67
	Karnataka	15380	11.67
	Total	68375	59.34
1988-89	Andhra Pradesh & Maharashtra	89401	105.63
	Karnataka	15817	10.58
	Total	105218	116.21
1989-90	Andhra Pradesh & Maharashtra	85921	85.47
	Karnataka	19404	15.38
	Total	105325	100.85
1990-91	Andhra Pradesh & Maharashtra	103378	89.17
	Karnataka	19059	20.32
	Total	122437	109.49
1991-92	Andhra Pradesh & Maharashtra	127994	132.78
	Karnataka	25580	26.41
	Total	153574	159.19
1992-93	Andhra Pradesh & Maharashtra	110078	125.62
	Karnataka	30675	33.24
	Total	140753	158.86
1993-94	Andhra Pradesh & Maharashtra	87696	76.63
	Karnataka	35136	32.93
	Total	122832	109.56
1994-95	Andhra Pradesh & Maharashtra	76786	74.15
	Karnataka	29601	22.19
	Total	106387	96.34
1995-96	Andhra Pradesh & Maharashtra	96410	90.10
	Karnataka	27729	24.30
	Total	124139	114.40
1996-97	Andhra Pradesh & Maharashtra	119813	111.41
	Karnataka	32910	31.81
	Total	152723	143.22
1997-98	Andhra Pradesh & Maharashtra	113040	130.69
	Karnataka	40988	45.64
	Total	154028	176.33
1998-99	Andhra Pradesh & Maharashtra	129197	147.18
	Karnataka	54235	54.69
	Total	183432	201.87

Source: Tobacco Board, Guntur.

As for as quality is concerned, it is the Karnataka Light Soil (KLS) tobacco that stands first. Karnataka is known for FCV tobacco that has an export potential. Around 20,000 registered growers and an equal number of unregistered growers cultivate FCV tobacco crop in an area of 40,000 to 50,000 hectares in the KLS zone extending from South of Mysore district up to Shimoga district. Regarding the consumption pattern of tobacco, bidis account for 48%, cigarettes 14%, and chewing and other 38%.

In 2001, the tobacco farmers in Karnataka had to pay Rs 150 million in penalties to the Tobacco Board at the rate of 5% on the sale value of tobacco for growing crop in excess of the stipulated quantity. The Tobacco board imposes Rs 500 as penalty on tobacco growers who build unauthorized barns and 15% penalty on unauthorized crop.

Tobacco farmers have been able to show considerable improvement in yield through better cultivation practices notwithstanding the drought. By adapting to laboratory to land' programs, one farmer from Andhra Pradesh has produced a record yield of 2,827 kg per hectare. Another farmer from Karnataka has produced 2,091 kg per hectare for the variety—one of the highest yields in Mysore. Some farmers have adopted energy conservation techniques while curing to cut down production costs.

The tobacco farmers face stiff competition from Brazil and China, which are offering tobacco at a lower price than India. Indian farmers face this problem even though Indian tobacco contains less nicotine. So far, Indian tobacco had been exported to Russia and the UK. With the disintegration of Russia and the UK opting for flavored tobacco, India tobacco export is bound to dip in the coming years.

It is said that tobacco growers in Andhra Pradesh are suffering a loss of Rs 1 billion a year because of unauthorized cultivation in Karnataka. The crop comes to auction in Andhra Pradesh 4–5 months after it is up in the market in Karnataka. As per the planning of the Board, the auction platforms in Karnataka should close by December. But, because of unauthorized cultivation, transaction takes place till June-July. Karnataka has 26,064 authorized curing barns and 23,274 unauthorized barns.

The Tobacco Industry: An Overview

The tobacco industry in India contributes in a unique manner to several important facets of the Indian economy, covering revenue, export, employment, and *gross domestic product* (GDP) growth. It mainly involves the manufacture of cigarettes, beedis, cigars and cheroots, hookahs, snuff and other chewing tobacco like zarda, gutkha and paan masala. The cigarette industry in India is essentially capital intensive in nature. The growth of this industry, both in India and abroad, represents a big revenue opportunity for the economy.

The beedi industry is one of the foremost cottage industries in India. Around 37% of the tobacco produced in India goes into beedi making as per an Indian Market Research Bureau (IMRB) report in 1996. The social significance of the beedi industry is that it generates more employment compared to the cigarette industry. From the beginning of the 17th century, tobacco has been playing an important role in international trade. Recently, there has been a worldwide anti-tobacco campaign, which resulted in modest drop in the area under cultivation and in the production of tobacco. But, consumption of tobacco in the world has remained more or less stable.

Illegal tobacco Farming in India

Crop year	*Registered acreage*	*Illegal cultivation*
2006–07	73490	78162
2007–08	73470	85755
2008–09	79407	90427
2009–10	79607	106601
2010–11*	80000	116000-121000

* Board estimate
Source: Tobacco Board, acreage in hectares

> **Worldwide limitation A**
>
> Creage cannot go up as India is a signatory to a WHO agreement aimed at limiting tobacco crop.

The tobacco board is projecting a big jump in the area in which the crop is cultivated illegally in Karnataka for 2010–2011. Although the registered area in Karnataka has not seen much growth, Tobacco Board officials estimate the quantum of illegal acreage to be around 10,000–15,000 hectares more than the previous crop year. The registered area for tobacco in Karnataka stands at 80,000 hectares. Acreage cannot be increased as India is a signatory to a WHO-backed global agreement aimed at limiting tobacco production. Karnataka produced 115 million kg of tobacco on nearly 1.06 lakh hectares in crop year 2009–2010 while its authorized crop size is pegged at 100 million kg. Tobacco farmers who spoke to ET said the rise in acreage has partly to do with the rise in average realization which have risen from Rs 87 per kg in 2007–2008 to Rs 110 per kg in 2008–2009.

Flue-cured Virginia tobacco: is grown in Andhra Pradesh, FCV tobacco is grown in an area of 125,000 hectares in East Godavari, West Godavari, Khammam, Krishna, Guntur, Prakasam, Nellore, Karim Nagar and warangal districts with a total production of 170 million kg of leaf. While in Karnataka, FCV tobacco is cultivated in 85,000 hectare of area with a production of 87 million kg leaf. It is also grown in a smaller area in the states of Maharashtra and Orissa. FCV tobacco production in India is declining for the last three years after a peak of 323.25 million kg in 2009–2010. In 2012–2013 it is estimated at 270.51 million kg as compared to last year production of 266.99 million kg. Unfavorable weather—prolonged drought in Karnataka and unseasonal rains in Andhra Pradesh is the main reason for this decline. Year wise and statewise production of FCV tobacco in India is given in Table 1.3. The recommended production technologies for FCV tobacco cultivation in Andhra Pradesh and Karnataka are presented in Tables 1.3 and 1.3A.

Table 1.3: Year-wise/statewise FCV production trends in India

(Quantity in million kg)

Years	*Andhra Pradesh*	*Karnataka*	*Total*
1997–1998	130.69	45.64	176.33
1998–1999	147.12	54.69	201.81
1999–2000	131.63	45.21	176.84
2000–2001	Crop Holiday	41.98	41.98
2001–2002	120.04	57.68	177.72
2002–2003	127.67	63.26	190.93
2003–2004	147.97	73.69	221.66
2004–2005	153.00	90.34	243.34
2005–2006	145.36	82.91	228.27
2006–2007	171.95	96.98	268.93
2007–2008	165.32	87.66	252.98
2008–2009	203.94	113.99	317.93
2009–2010	207.58	115.67	323.25
2010–2011	173.24	127.85	301.09
2011–2012	162.70	104.29	266.99
2012–2013	176.65*	93.86	270.51

* Estimated Qty.

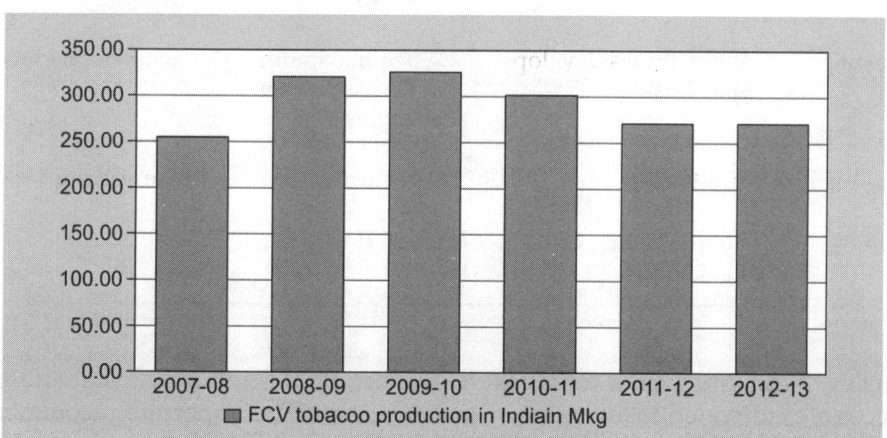

Table 1.3A: Recommended production technologies

Cultural practice	*Andhra Pradesh*		*Karnataka*	
	Traditional black soils	*Northern light soils*	*Southern light soils*	*Karnataka light soils*
Variety	Gauthami, Hema VT-1158, Hemadri and Siri	Kanchan	Gauthami, Hema, VT-1158 and Kanthi	Kanchan, Thrupthi, Rathna Swarna, Bhavya
Harvesting	Priming mature leaves	Priming mature leaves	Priming mature leaves	Priming mature leaves
Curing method	Flue-curing	Flue-curing	Flue-curing	Flue-curing
Grading	Farm grading	Plant position grading	Farm grading	Plant position grading

Bidi and pikka tobacco: *Bidi* tobacco is cultivated in Gujarat and Karnataka in 1.15 lakh hectare area *Pikka* tobacco is an important tobacco cultivated in Orissa for chewing and cheroot purposes. Important production technologies recommended for *Bidi* tobacco cultivation in Gujarat and Karnataka and for *Pikka* tobacco in Orissa are furnished in the below Table.

Cultural practice	*Bidi tobacco*		*Pikka tobacco Orissa*
	Gujarat	*Karnataka*	
Variety	Anand 119, Anand 2, GT-4, GT-5, GT-7, GT-9, GTH-1, GTH-1 (MR)	A-119, NPN 190, Spoorthy Bhavya Sree NBD-43	Pyruvithanam, JP 1, NG-74, II-1327
Harvesting	When leaves develop spangles	When maximum no. of leaves develop Spangles	Stalk cut method
Curing method	Sun-curing	Sun-curing	Sun-curing
Grading	Bukha, Geran, Galia, Lankada	I sort, II sort, etc.	–

Burley, *Natu* and *Lanka* tobaccos: In Andhra Pradesh, Burley, *Natu* and *Lanka* tobaccos are cultivated to an extent of 45,000 hectare. The important recommended production technologies for these tobaccos are given at the next page.

Cultural Practice	*Burley*	*Irrigated Natu*	*Rainfed Natu*	*Lanka*
Variety	Burley-21 and Banket A1	Kommugudem, Peddavithanam, Pyruvithanam, Rangapuram	Tokaku, Viswanath, Natu Spl., Prabhat, WAF, Bhairavi	Lanka Spl.
Harvesting	Priming	Stalk cut (katta) or priming (Thoranam method)	Priming	Stalk cut
Curing method	Air-curing	Air-curing	Air-curing	Air-curing
Grading	Flyings, bottom, middle and top	Melmi and Gulla	Bright, brown, dark brown, green and perished leaf	Kotaku, Baraku Mattasam and Gulla

Cigar and cheroot, chewing, hookah and HDBRG tobaccos: Chewing, cigar and cheroot tobaccos are the major types grown in Tamil Nadu. Chewing tobacco is mainly grown in West Bengal, Bihar, UP and Assam, while hookah tobacco is cultivated in UP.

Bihar, Gujarat, Haryana and Assam, HDBRG (*Harvel de Baixo Rio Grande)* tobacco is mainly cultivated in black soils of Guntur district in Andhra Pradesh with 3–4 irrigations which is used in cigarette blending.

Cultural practice	*Cigar and cheroot Tamil Nadu*	*Chewing: Bihar, Tamil Nadu and West Bengal*	*Hookah: West Bengal*	*HDBRG: Andhra Pradesh*
Variety	O-K 1, Bhavani Spl., Olor-10, I-737, Sangami	Bihar: Vaishali Spl., Sona, PT-76, Lichchavi West Bengal: Podali, Chama Tamil Nadu: Bhagyalakshmi, Meenakshi, Abirami, Kaviri, Meenakshi (CR)	DD-437 and Dharla Sonar-Motihari, Manasi	HDBRG
Harvesting	Stalk-cut	Stalk-cut	Priming	Priming
Curing method	Sun-curing	Sun-curing	Air-curing	Sun-curing
Grading	Plant position (*Rasi* and *Kruz*)	Bihar: 1st, 2nd, 3rd and 4th grades T.N: *Rasi and Kruz*	*Panpatta* No. 1, *Niras* And *Jalapatta*	Bottom, middle and top primings

West Bengal, Bihar, UP and Assam, while hookah tobacco is cultivated in UP.

Bihar, Gujarat, Haryana and Assam, HDBRG (*Harvel de Baixo Rio Grande*) tobacco is mainly cultivated in black soils of Guntur district in Andhra Pradesh with 3–4 irrigations which is used in cigarette blending.

KARNATAKA – 2012–2013 CROP SEASON (2012 CROP)

Production Policy and Crop Size

The Board fixed a crop size of 98 million kg for 2012–2013 Karnataka crop season covering 58,429 target barns. The Registration Committee for growers and others laid down the criteria for registering commercial nurserymen, growers and barn operators. The area accorded for registration, quantity authorized per a licensed barn and maximum number of barns permitted for grant of license per individual grower during 2012–2013 was as follows:

Particulars	*Simplex barn*	*Duplex barn*
Area to be registered	1.30 hectare	2.60 hectare
Authorized quantity	1,720 kg	3,440 kg
Maximum no. of barns allowed per individual	4	2

Initially the per barn quota was fixed at 1,675 kg considering 58,429 target barns but at the end of the season, taking in to account the barns actually registered and listed in pending eligible category (57,082 barns) the quota was enhanced to 1,720 kg.

Nursery

During 2012–2013 crop season, an area of 1,001 hectare nursery was raised by growers as against 1130.80 hectare of nursery sown in 2011–2012 crop season. The area under variety "Kanchan" was 943.70 while the balance 57.30 hectare of area was sown with other varieties.

During 2012–2013 crop season, an area of 93,974 hectare was planted under FCV tobacco in Karnataka as against 104,393 hectare under cultivation during 2011–2012 crop season. An area of 60,454 hectare was under early plantation, 8,484 hectare under middle plantation and balance 25,036 hectare was planted as late crop. Majority of the area—about 89,367 hectare was covered under cultivation of "Kanchan" variety and rarest 4,607 hectare was planted with other varieties.

Crop Prospects, 2012–2013

The area under plantation during 2012–2013 crop season is less than the previous season by 10% due to drought during plantation period. Farmers were unable to plant tobacco in some areas due to prolonged drought. The early planted crop initially has suffered from this drought, which resulted in stunted growth with narrow leaves. The middle and late planted crop has recovered well after receipt of

Damage to Tobacco Crop in Karnataka Due to Drought During 2012–2013

The tobacco crop in Mysore and Hassan districts suffered this year due to severe drought during the late planting and grand growth periods of the crop, i.e. June and July resulting in deterioration in both quality and quantity of leaf. As per Central Tobacco Research Institute report, there is a reduction in productivity from 1,100 kg to 1,200 kg to 800 to 850 kg per hectare. However, with receipt of late rains the crop had recovered to some extent.

Tobacco Board had discussed the issue of providing compensation to the drought affected farmers in 134th Board meeting held at Hyderabad and resolved to send proposals to Government of India seeking sanction for payment of compensation Rs 6,000 per hectare and Rs 4,000 per hectare respectively for fully and partially affected crop. As per grower-wise enumeration of crop damage taken up by field staff, tobacco crop in about 16,080.36 hectares was partially damaged. Accordingly, Tobacco Board had sent proposals to the Ministry of Commerce for sanction for payment of compensation.

Production Policy and Crop Size

The Board in its 134th Board meeting held on 26/08/12 at Hyderabad fixed a crop size of 170 million kg in Andhra Pradesh, Maharashtra and Odisha for 2012–2013 crop season as against the 162 million kg crop size fixed during previous year. The Registration Committee met on 13/09/2012 at Guntur and laid down the criteria for registering commercial nurserymen, tobacco growers and licensing barn operators for 2012–2013. The area accorded for registration, quantity authorized per barn and maximum number of barns permitted for registration per grower for 2012–2013 was as follows:

Soil region	*Crop size fixed (million kg)*	*Area to be regd. per grower with curing facility*	*Quantity authorized per barn (in kg)*	*Maximum area to be regd. per grower (in hectare)*	*Maximum no. of curing units permitted per grower*
Northern Light Soils/ Eastern Light Soils	53.31	2.00	4400	8.00	4
Southern Light Soils.	58.19	4.40	4400	17.60	4
Southern Black Soils	45.88	2.20	3950	8.80	4
Northern Black Soils	6.08	1.90	3325	7.60	4
Central Black Soils	6.47	1.90	3325	7.60	4

Andhra Pradesh Crop Prospects During 2012–2013

Nursery

During 2012–2013 crop season in Andhra Pradesh, tobacco nursery was raised in an area of 922.18 hectare. Of this, 591.29 hectare was raised by registered growers for their own use and 330.89 hectare was under commercial nursery. 657 commercial nurserymen were registered with Board for the season. "SIRI" was the main variety sown in black soils and southern light soils regions followed by G11 (Hema) and V-1158. "Kanchan" is the major variety sown in NLS region. Area under hybrid variety LV-6 in NLS had also increased significantly.

Main Crop

During 2012–2013 crop season an area of 120,105 hectares was under FCV tobacco cultivation covering all the soil zones in Andhra Pradesh and Odisha. The growers in Maharashtra have not taken up cultivation of FCV this year, as they have opted for going out of tobacco cultivation by selling away their barns under shifting policy of the Board. During this season, the crop growth was optimum with proper leaf expansion and elongation in early and middle plantation crop. In late plantation, the crop growth is not up to the mark because of moisture stress. The area under cultivation and over all crop condition under different soil zones during the season is as under.

Production Regulation Campaign

The Board had undertaken various measures to regulate production and to prevent excess/unauthorized production of FCV tobacco. The following production regulation measures were taken up by the Board during 2012–2013 crop season.

- Campaign in the villages on crop regulation.
- Playing audio cassettes on crop regulation in the villages.
- Supplying pamphlets to each farmer advising on the international/domestic market situation, on alternative crops, with request to refrain from excess and unauthorized crop production.
- Ad- campaign in press requesting farmers to refrain from excess/unauthorized production.
- Village level meetings in tobacco growing areas involving local growers/people representatives to increase awareness of growers on the ill effects of excess production.
- Appeals in Press statements by the field executives and grower leaders advising farmers to refrain from production of excess and unauthorized tobacco.
- Conducting Mahazars and issuing notices in respect of unauthorized construction of barns.

Soil and Water Analysis

The Board every year extends the services of analyzing soil and water samples collected from growers' fields to advise growers on suitability of soil and irrigation water used for tobacco cultivation and thereby avoiding cultivation in soils with high chloride contents. Based on the soil sample analysis, the growers were recommended on required dosages of fertilizers to be applied to produce quality leaf and improve yields and thereby obtain remunerative returns. 2117 soil samples and 610 water samples were analyzed during 2012–2013 at the Board's Soil Testing Laboratories at Ongole in Andhra Pradesh. In Karnataka, 5450 samples were got analyzed utilizing the services of Rashtriya Chemicals and Fertilizers Limited, soil testing laboratory at Hassan.

Credit Facilities to Growers

The Board arranges every year crop/ input / barn repair loans to the tobacco farmers at lower rate of interest through various commercial banks for raising the crop to procure various inputs, i.e. seed, fertilizers, pesticides, etc. and to meet expenses for operation of barns. Details of various types of loans advanced by banks in Andhra Pradesh and Karnataka for 2012–2013 crop season are as below:

	Andhra Pradesh		*Karnataka*	
Type of loan	*No. of beneficiaries*	*Amount (Rs in lakh)*	*No. of beneficiaries*	*Amount (Rs in lakh)*
Crop loans	*42,424*	*1,06,007.69*	*37,398*	*42,630.16*
Barn repair loans	–	1,793.62		4,216.73
Input loans	–	7,775.10		8,440.07

The Board makes the payment of auction sale proceeds of the loanee growers through their respective banks to enable prompt recovery of the loans advanced during the season.

Minimum Support Prices (MSP)

Government of India has not announced Minimum Support Price for FCV tobacco for 2012- 13 crop season.

Barn and Stock Insurance for FCV Tobacco Growers

The Board is facilitating insurance coverage of barns, stocks and allied structures associated with curing and storage during the crop season through Standard Fire and Allied Perils policy since 2003. Registered tobacco growers are also being covered under Group Personal Accident Policy (GPA) every year. During 2012–2013 crop season, The Oriental Insurance Company Limited, Guntur provided a cover of Rs 2,472 crore for 45,104 growers and 37,436.74 barns in Andhra Pradesh. The details are as follows:

Particulars	*GPA policy*	*Barns, stocks and allied structures policy*	*Total premium (Rs)*
Sum assured	1.00 lakh	5.40 lakh	
Premium per grower in Rs. in Zone-III	68	823	891
Premium per grower in Rs. in Zone-IV	68	774	842

The premium amount paid during 2012 Rs 2013 season is Rs 32,678,026. As on 31/03/2013, 104 claims worth Rs 3,120,294 are settled.

Penalties on Sale of Excess Unauthorized Production

As per the direction of Government of India, vide notification No. SO1694 (E) and SO1695 (E), dated 25th July, 2012 (for Andhra Pradesh) and notification no. 352 (E) and 353 (E) Date 11/02/2013 (for Karnataka) the excess tobacco produced by registered growers and unauthorized tobacco produced by unregistered growers in Andhra Pradesh (during 2011–2012) and Karnataka (during 2012–2013) was allowed for sale by levying penalties as follows:

a. An amount of Rs 2 per kg and 7.5% (including a normal service charges of 1% of proceeds payable by growers) of the proceeds of the sale for the excess FCV tobacco produced by every registered grower.
b. An amount of Rs 2 per kg and 15% (including a normal service charges of 1% of proceeds payable by growers) of the proceeds of the sale for the FCV tobacco produced by every unregistered grower.

The Schemes and their Coverage

Farm Mechanization

The Indian tobacco farmer requires to strive hard to improve quality, yield and cut costs to make Indian tobacco cost competitive, more attractive and sustainable in the light of increasing competition and changing preferences in the Global Market. Nowadays, tobacco farmers are finding labor shortages in many areas of operation. It is, therefore, proposed to help the farmers of Andhra Pradesh and Karnataka in certain areas of operation by popularizing implements like bullock drawn ridges, Tyne cultivators, weighing scales, Knapsack sprayers and PVC pipes for irrigation.

To achieve the stated objective, the tobacco farmers in Andhra Pradesh and Karnataka were supplied with the farm implements, as given hereunder during the year under report.

Bullock drawn ridgers	242 Nos.
Tyne cultivators	1973 Nos.
Weighing scales	358 Nos.
PVC pipes	41771 Nos.
Taiwan sprayers	151 Nos.

Integrated Nutrient Management (INM)

To achieve the balanced fertilization, Tobacco Board is supplying the fertilizers to the growers every year in Andhra Pradesh and Karnataka. During 2012–2013, we have organized supply of 31,892.45 tons of fertilizers in Andhra Pradesh and 32,464.9 tons in Karnataka.

Improving Yield and Quality of Tobacco

Integrated Pest Management (IPM)

The importers nowadays are more stringent about the quality and pesticide residues. The Board, therefore, in its continuous pursuit, is promoting the practice of integrated pest management thereby reducing the use of agrochemicals and their residues in leaf tobacco, besides protecting the environment and soil microflora and fauna.

Under the scheme, a combination of all pest control methods, i.e. biological, cultural, mechanical and botanical in addition to chemical methods were implemented for pest control. During the year 2012–2013, an area of about 1,500 hectares was covered by providing 30,016 pheromone traps and lures to 1,161 growers. The Board had spent Rs 3.33 lakh toward subsidy.

Under this scheme, the farmers were encouraged to adopt traditional and eco-friendly IPM methods such as rising of trap crops, barrier crops, installation of bird perches Rs 96,200 yellow sticky traps at free of cost and application of neem products. The Board has supplied castor seed to help raise trap crop for controlling caterpillars.

Further, pheromone traps and lures of two most important insect pests viz. *S. litura* and *H. armigera* were supplied to the farmers to monitor pest population *vis-à-vis* threshold limits and take pest control measures as and when needed. That apart, the Board conducted training programs on IPM for the benefit of farmers and extension personnel with the help of scientists of CTRI and ITC Ltd – ILTD division.

Control and Monitoring of Agrochemical Residues

In an effort to reduce and further eliminate agro-chemical residues in leaf tobacco, the Board adopted a three pronged strategy to deal with the problem viz. (1) education of growers continuously on the use of recommended agrochemicals as per recommended dosages and schedules so as to produce safer and cleaner tobacco and boost exports, (2) implementation of integrated pest management practices and (3) analysis of leaf samples for determining the levels of agrochemical residues in leaf tobacco every year and to take corrective action accordingly.

The Board had made Rs 10.27 lakh payment to CTRI toward analysis charges of pesticide residues in 127 samples of Flue-Cured tobacco pertaining to Andhra Pradesh collected during 2010–2011 crop season and Rs 5.53 lakh toward chemical analysis charges of 299 samples for nicotine, reducing sugars and chlorides (10 Nos. of 2012–2013 Karnataka crop season and 289 Nos. of 2011–2012 Andhra Pradesh crop season). By and large, the residues were found at zero or within the Guidance Residue Levels (GRL).

Karnataka Auctions, 2011-2012

The auction for sale of 2011–2012 crop of Karnataka was spread in two financial years, i.e. 2011–2012 (from 15/9/2011 to 31/03/2012) and 2012–2013 (from 1/04/2012 to 11/04/2013). During 2012–2013 financial year, a total of 1.57 million kg of tobacco was marketed at an average price of Rs 77.64 per kg. The auction platform wise quantities of tobacco marketed and average price realized from 1/4/12 to 11/04/12 is given at page No. 201.

Karnataka Auctions, 2012-2013

Crop Size-Fixed and Estimated Production

The production is estimated at 89.71 million kg as against the target crop size of 98.00 million kg fixed by the Board. The estimated percentage grade out turn of the crop in terms of bright, medium and low grades is 37:40:23 as against 21:50:29 during 2011–2012 crop season.

Commencement of Auction Sales

Auction sales commenced on 26/09/2012 at all the 11 auction platforms which were operated during 2011–2012 auction season.

Market Trends

The highest price recorded on the starting day of auctions is Rs 140 per kg and during the season the highest price recorded is Rs 160 per kg which is the highest price recorded ever in the Karnataka FCV tobacco auctions. Graph depicting highest bids recorded in Karnataka auctions since 2002 is given below:

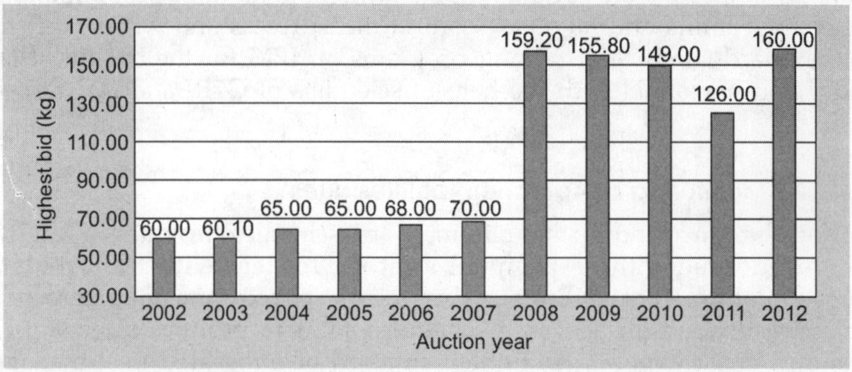

Highest bid recorded for FCV tobacco in Karntaka

As on 31/03/2013, a total quantity of 88.29 million kg of tobacco was marketed at an average price of Rs 118.11 per kg leaving a balance quantity of 1.42 million kg for marketing. The auction sales except at Hunsur-I and Hunsur-III auction platforms were concluded as on 23/03/2013 and the auction sales at the remaining 9 Nos. Auction platforms is expected to close by 10th April 2013.

The grade out turn of the tobacco marketed in terms of bright, medium and low grades as on 31/03/2013 are as follows:

S. No.	*Grade*	*Qty. marketed (million kg)*	*Share (%)*	*Average price (Rs/kg)*
1	Bright	20.37	23.07	144.20
2	Medium	42.46	48.09	128.83
3	Low	25.46	28.84	79.35
	Total	**88.29**	**100.00**	**118.11**

The prices of bright, medium and low-grade tobaccos were more are less consistent throughout the auction season u to 31/03/2013.

Graph depicting average prices realized in Karnataka auctions since 2001 is given at the next page.

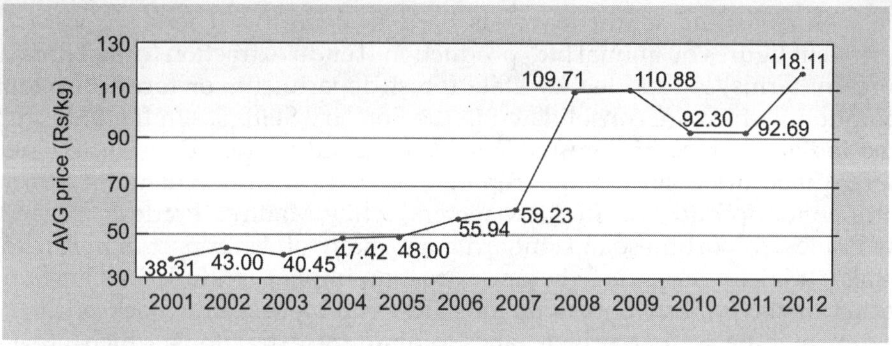

Average price raised for FCV tobacco Karnataka auctions

Note: Information furnished is as on 31/03/2013.

Permission to Growers to Sell Excess Crop and Unauthorized Crop

Government of India vide notifications No. SO 352 (E) and SO 353 (E), dated 15th February 2013 permitted the sale of excess quantity of tobacco produced by the registered growers and unauthorized tobacco produced by the unregistered growers in Karnataka subject to payment of 7.5% service charges and extra fee of Rs 2.00 per kg for sale excess tobacco produced by registered growers and upon payment of 15% service charges and extra fee of Rs 2.00 per kg for sale of unauthorized tobacco produced by the unregistered growers.

The particulars of excess quantity of tobacco sold by the registered growers and the unauthorized tobacco sold by the unregistered growers as on 31/03/2013 are as follows:

S. No.	*Category of the growers*	*No. of growers*	*Qty. marketed (million kg)*	*Avg. price (Rs/kg)*
1	Registered growers	18068	8.99	106.18
2	Unregistered growers	21820	4.46	84.89

The Perverse Economics of the Bidi and Tendu Trade

The tendu (leaf) and bidi trade is dominated by a handful of traders, who have gained political clout and economic concessions under the guise of providing employment and livelihood. Bidis are smoked by over 73 million adults, mostly rural men (GOI and IIPS, 2010). Tendu leaf plucking generates about 6 weeks employment for about 7.5 million people (Arnold, 1995) while rolling bidis engages nearly 4.4 million women and children (Ministry of Labor various years), and their collective efforts result in 600 billion to 1 trillion bidis being produced every year, making bidis perhaps the most produced commodity in India. They are also the single largest cause of preventable premature death among adults in India. Despite these staggering numbers of employment, production and early deaths, there are no national estimates of the numbers of bidis made or tendu leaves plucked, and the revenues realized or forgone.

Data on bidis and tendu leaves is hard to come by. There are virtually no government figures on annual bidi production. Tendu extraction (called production in forestry terms) is reported by state forest departments or forest development corporations, which are consolidated in the Forestry Statistics India (FSI) prepared by the Indian Council of Forestry Research and Education, Dehradun. However, these are inaccurate since states report their data in different units (Karnataka reports annual production in cubic meters, while Madhya Pradesh, Gujarat and Uttar Pradesh report these in standard bags, many others report in metric tons or quintals). It is also not clear whether extraction implies tendu leaves auctioned or collected or the total inventory or the sales. The biggest drawback of the (State) government data is that private and community extractions which are legally permitted are not recorded or reported. Much of this is also illicit extraction which benefits corrupt traders, local politicians and even insurgent groups. The States also chose to ignore reporting in the standard unit prescribed (the standard bag, which contains 1,000 bundles of 50 sun-dried leaves each in a sack which weighs about 40 kilos (FAO, 2005)). In Maharashtra, the measure of a standard bag is also different. If viewed objectively, the FSI data is grossly inaccurate. According to FSI's cumulative data (as reproduced from the Ministry of Statistics and Program Implementation (MoSPI)) in 2002–2003, India produced 592,853 metric tons of tendu capable of making 740 billion bidis. This increased to 7,10,109 million tons (or 880 billion bidis) in 2003–04 which declined drastically to 312,660 million tons and 268,464 million tons in subsequent years. Tobacco industry reports do not suggest any staggering decline in the bidi trade or show massive migration of bidi smokers shifting their preference to cigarettes. How does the FSI explain such a decline? Officially, how much tendu leaf is extracted in India, is a question that remains unsubstantiated.

Illicit tendu trade: Using back-of-the-envelope methods could help us arrive at the magnitude if not precise numbers of tendu leaves plucked and bidis rolled. To begin with, since every bidi contains on an average 0.2 gram of tobacco (Gupta and Asma, 2008), dividing the bidi tobacco produced (Directorate of Tobacco Development, 2010) provides an estimation of the total bidis produced annually. Export of bidi tobacco as a proportion of total production is too small (0.14% in 1996–1997 and 0.08% in 2006–2007) and can therefore be ignored. From 1975, bidi production grew from 0.55 trillion to nearly 1 trillion by 1990. By the mid-1990s, more than 1 trillion were produced, but it started to decline after 1998.

For simplicity of calculation, for production factors (like quality of leaves, skill of labor which can reduce wastage, damage to leaves during the entire production cycle, etc). It is assumed that every tendu leaf produces just one bidi which is the acceptable norm. To estimate the national tendu leaf production, auction data from Madhya Pradesh (MP), the largest tendu leaf producing state only can be used. This data is consistently reported and publicly available in their annual reports. Prior to 2000, MP produced nearly 41–45% of the total tendu. After its bifurcation to create a separate State—Chhattisgarh the proportion has been reduced to about 25% since 2001. As a conservative estimate, 45% is used as MP's share of the national production prior to 2000. To test whether these ratios are effective, national, and state level data from MP from 1975 to 1998 from two other studies are compared and only minor variations (±3 to ±5%) are observed. The difference between the total number of bidis produced (using bidi tobacco production data) and the national tendu leaf production provides an estimate of the size of the private, unregulated and illicit tendu market. Between 2000 and 2003, new States like Jharkhand and Chhattisgarh took time to create their auction systems, and this is corrected in the estimation as shown in Fig. 1.1.

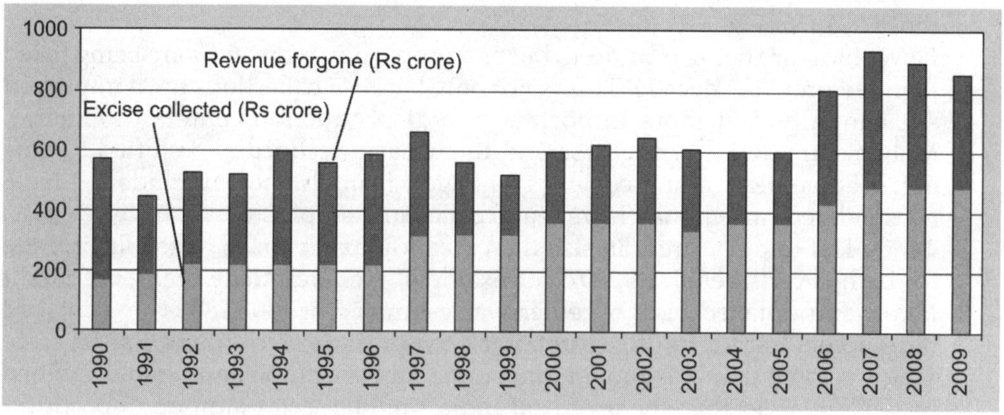

Fig. 1.1: Estimated tax revenue forgone for bidis

As these states quickly organised their auction system, tendu leaf extraction has intensified in Chhattisgarh and Jharkhand. In some states especially Bihar, Rajasthan, Gujarat and Maharashtra there has been a steady decline in the extraction since 2003. Since Jharkhand has more tendu leaf producing districts, Bihar's Forest Department has little incentive to focus on tendu leaf plucking. With the removal of food subsidy to tendu leaf pluckers in 2001, there has been a sharp decline of tendu through forest department in Eastern Uttar Pradesh. Rajasthan has a very variable tendu leaf trade. According to Rajasthan extracted just 1.57 lakh standard bags in 2005, which rose to 5.27 in 2007. In Maharashtra, it has become a major drain for the forest department as Naxalites allegedly claim most of the benefits of the harvest, and since 2007 restrictions on over-extraction are being put in place as result of which there is a decline in the extraction.

States like Jharkhand and Chhattisgarh are extracting more tendu while offering a higher price each year. There have been concerns about over-extraction and deciding on the optimum harvest size for tendu and many of these forests are irreparably damaged. These estimates for bidi correspond well with tendu leaves auctioned those claimed by the bidi industry lobby the All India Bidi Industry Federation of around 550 billion pieces during this period. The current level of bidis produced 650-720 billion (605 billion in 2007–2008) estimated here is considerably less than more recent estimate of 1 to 1.2 trillion bidis. The difference between estimated tendu leaves produced versus total bidis made is nearly 40–50% and is met through illicitly or privately traded tendu. In 2007–2008, only 310 billion tendu leaves were legally available but nearly 605 billion bidis were made—which implies that about 49% tendu leaves were acquired illegally by bidi manufacturers. The GATS suggests that nearly 553 billion bidis were consumed in India in 2008–2009 (GOI and IIPS, 2010).

Three lessons emerge from this:

1. The most important factor in the bidi trade is the tendu leaf. It is the critical ingredient that makes bidis cheap and is available in abundance. Its production is subsidized by state governments and the states determine prices arbitrarily Tendu leaf prices are variable each year but have not increased over the past 20 years. In Madhya Pradesh, for example prices in 2006 were the same as those in 1976 (Fig. 1.2).
2. Fewer bidis are being produced, but as a proportion more bidis are being taxed than the previous decade. This is not only because collections have improved substantially, but more importantly, bidi production centers in Gujarat, Maharashtra, Rajasthan, Orissa and Bihar have declined and shifted to new areas. Some bidi rolling centers like Sagar, Damoh and Murshidabad have consolidated, which may have made collection simpler.
3. Tendu leaf trade is larger in size than the bidi tax revenues, when illicit trade for both is considered. In 2007, for example, the illicit trade market of tendu leaves and untaxed bidis together was estimated at Rs 1,288 crore (untaxed bidis accounted for Rs 381 crore), illicit tendu trade was around Rs 907 crore which is more than the budget for routine immunization and polio combined in 2007 or larger than the profits of India's public sector aluminum producer National Aluminum Company.

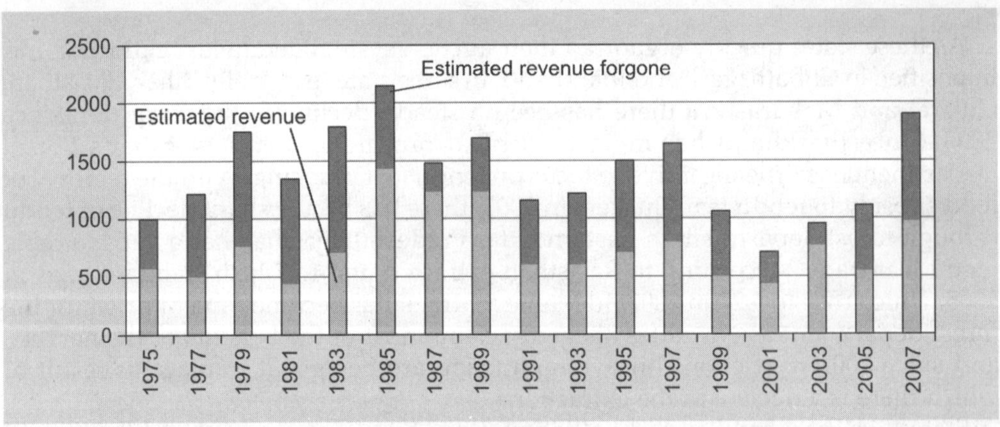

Fig. 1.2: Estimated revenue forgone in tendu trade (Rs crore)

Other Factors Considered

Unlike flue-cured tobacco (used for making cigarettes) which is regulated though the Tobacco Board of India, bidi tobacco cultivation is not regulated, and its price is set by a handful of tobacco traders. Only bidi tobacco prices have been rising in the past decades, but remain largely affordable. In effect, when bidi tobacco prices are favorable the margins can absorb any price or tax increase since the other two inputs (labor and tendu) are abysmally low. Bidi rolling wages are determined by the states and are set for 1,000 pieces rolled, although states like Karnataka, Orissa and Uttar Pradesh have minimum wages per day. The wages have been low and seldom revised. Even if revisions take place, the wages are controlled by middlemen who exploit vulnerable women, children and old men who depend solely on bidi rolling.

The notion that bidi rolling supplements family incomes is delusional for those who accept this; indeed families that roll bidis depend on it for their only real income.

TOBACCO CONSUMPTION

Production of cigarettes in India was 62,400 million prices in 1974–1975. Production has been moving up and down from year to year, the highest number produced was 94,086 million in 20011–2012 and 50,000 million in 2003–2004.

Over 27% of Indians smoke tobacco in one form or the other (beedi, cigarette, etc), says the third edition of Tobacco Atlas. Published by the World Lung Foundation and the American Cancer Society, the Atlas portrays a comprehensive volume of research on tobacco. According to the Atlas, tobacco drains $500 billion from global economy each year.

Cigarettes are the world's most widely smuggled legal consumer product. In 2006, about 600 billion smuggled cigarettes made it to the market, representing an enormous missed tax opportunity for governments, as well as a missed opportunity to prevent many people from starting to smoke and encourage others to quit. A 10% increase in cigarette prices reduces demand by up to 5% among adults, with even better results among young smokers. Tobacco replaces potential food production on almost four million hectares of the world's agricultural land, equal to all of the world's orange groves or banana plantations. In developing countries, smokers spend great amount of money in proportion to their incomes that could otherwise be spent on food, healthcare and other necessities.

It is estimated that in 2010, tobacco will kill six million people worldwide annually, 72% of whom will be in low and middle-income countries. Since 1960, global tobacco production has increased 300% in low and middle-resource countries, while dropping more than 50% in high-resource countries. In Bangladesh alone, if the average household buys food with the money normally spent on tobacco, more than 10 million people would no longer suffer from malnutrition and 350 children under the age of 5 would be saved each day.

Cigarette consumption is likely to fall on account of health warnings. It is also feared that health warning may spur the demand for smuggled cigarettes that have a large market in India because of high taxes on domestic cigarettes. Unlike the rest of the world where, on an average, cigarettes account for as much as 90% of the tobacco consumed, in India cigarettes represent only 15% of total tobacco consumption. The balance 85% is fragmented amongst a host of traditional tobacco products like bidis, chewing khani and gutkha. Of course, these are sold in unbranded and unpacked (loose) form and may not carry the pictorial health warnings.

Of the total expenditure, the share on paan, tobacco and Sunday intoxicants shows that Andhra tops the list in rural areas and Assam in urban India (Table 1.3B). Domestic consumption of tobacco (all types) is estimated in 1999 as 478 million kg which went upto 488 million kg in 2003.

Prevalence of smoking and chewing tobacco in the age group 15–30 was for males and females 2004 was 28.3 and 2.7% corresponding figures for urban India was 20.6 and 1.5%. For those above 30, the level was 39 and 3.5% for rural and 28.9/1.9 for urban. Corresponding chewing levels during the same period were much lower for males, but higher for females (Table 1.3C). With regard to chewing Bihar and

Table 1.3B: Total expenditure, the share on paan, tobacco and Sunday intoxicants shows that Andhra Pradesh tops the list in rural areas and Assam in urban India

	Rural (%)	*Urban (%)*
Andhra Pradesh	4.3	2.11
Chhattisgarh	4.25	2.65
Assam	4.13	2.99
Madhya Pradesh	4.07	1.94
Rajasthan	3.66	1.68
Jharkhand	3.77	1.28
Karnataka	3.29	1.11
Gujarat	2.87	1.08
West Bengal	2.85	2.01
Kerala	2.84	2.03
Tamil Nadu	2.84	1.29
Odisha	2.67	1.77
Haryana	2.47	1.25
Uttar Pradesh	2.29	1.39
Maharashtra	2.24	1.18
Bihar	2.08	1.11
Punjab	1.88	1.77
India	2.95	1.54

Source: NSSO 2009–2010.

Table 1.3C: Domestic and global consumption of tobacco

Year	*Domestic consumption (million kg)*	
	All tobaccos	*FCV*
1999	478	60
2000	474	61
2001	472	60
2002	481	64
2003	488	70
2004 (E)	486	70

Year	*Global consumption (tons)*
1999	6435,029
2000	5136,087
2001	6411,165
2002	5992,135
2003	5883,502
2004 (E)	5724,505

Source: USDA (E) Estimate.

Jharkhand males are at the top and females in rural Chhatishgarh with 10% in the age group 15 plus and 12.2% in the 30+ categories were the highest consumers. Kerala and Tamil Nadu are the two States with lowest levels of chewing (Table 1.3D).

Paan, Tobacco and Sundry Intoxicants

Rural Andhra spends 4.4% of monthly expenses on stuff that the virtuous frown upon Chandigarh and Assam are just behind. Here is a scan.

The total consumption of tobacco products is increasing globally although it is decreasing in some developed countries. More than 80% of the world's one billion smokers live in the Third World.

In India, around 2,500 people die every day due to tobacco used. By recent counts, there are about 94 million smokers in India. Of these, about 14 million are ill with chronic obstructive pulmonary disease (COPD). In India, almost 5% of women and a third of all men aged between 30 and 69 smoke. They smoke bidis, apart from conventional cigarettes. Bidi smoking has been found to be even more harmful than cigarettes, shortening the life span of men by 6 years and women by 8 years, compared to non-smokers. Smoking cigarettes causes death 10 years sooner. The government is keen on curbing smoking central budget 2013–2014 has increased the specific excise duty on cigarettes by about 18%. Similar increases are proposed on cigars, cheroots and cigarillos.

Soon, Legal Age to Buy Tobacco may Go upto 25

If the Union Health Ministry has its way, then the legal age for buying and using tobacco products will increase from 18 years to 25 years. "Since the age of selling tobacco varies from one State to another, we will write to each State Government to increase the age for buying tobacco to 25", Union health secretary Luv Verma said at the release of "An Empirical Study of India's Fiscal Policies against Tobacco: a State Level Analysis"—a study by the Public Health Foundation of India.

He added that State governments will be responsible for implementing the move. The study reported that a 10% increase in cigarette prices will lead to almost a 3% decrease in consumption, increasing the government revenue by 7%. "Based on the recommendations, we will make a strong case for increasing taxation on tobacco", said Verma.

He also slammed the tobacco promotion board and said that better coordination is required between ministries. "The commerce ministry's tobacco promotion board is a ridiculous thing. While we are condemning the use of tobacco products, how can they promote it? I will speak to my counterpart in the Commerce Ministry and see what can be done about it".

Government to Tax Tobacco more to Reduce Consumption

Union Health Minister Harsh Vardhan is for levying increased taxes on tobacco and tobacco-related products to discourage its consumption. Releasing a report on the economic burden of tobacco related diseases in India on Thursday, the Minister said he will be writing to the Finance Ministry soon seeking necessary action on the issue.

"It makes perfect economic sense to regulate the use of tobacco in order to achieve the goal of controlling noncommunicable disease in India. Tobacco use is a

Table 1.3D: Prevalence of smoking, chewing tobacco and drinking alcohol in India, 2004

(Percent)

States	*Age group*	*Rural/ urban*	*Smoking*		*Chewing*		*Drinking alcohol*	
			Male	*Female*	*Male*	*Female*	*Male*	*Female*
India	15+	Rural	28.3	2.7	12.7	3.7	21.0	3.8
		Urban	20.6	1.5	7.9	1.3	16.2	1.8
	30+	Rural	39.0	3.5	15 .8	4.8	28.2	4.3
		Urban	28.9	1.9	9.9	1.7	22.2	2.0
Andhra Pradesh	15+	Rural	26.7	2.3	2.8	2.1	21.5	2.9
		Urban	19.2	1.2	1.1	0.1	19.8	1.5
	30+	Rural	38.4	3.3	3.7	2.9	30.3	3.7
		Urban	28.3	1.8	1.2	0.1	28.3	2.0
Assam	15+	Rural	38.8	6.1	13.0	3.5	26.2	14.4
		Urban	31.8	2.6	12. 6	1.6	20.0	4.0
	30+	Rural	50.5	7.6	14.3	3.9	33.4	17.8
		Urban	41 .9	3.2	14.5	1.7	26.0	4.6
Bihar	15+	Rural	25.1	3.3	40.4	2.3	24.3	2.8
		Urban	17.4	1.8	24.6	1.8	17.7	1.8
	30+	Rural	33.1	4.2	55.0	2.9	31.8	3.1
		Urban	25.7	2.6	34.7	2.4	25.2	2.1
Chhattisgarh	15+	Rural	28.2	5.7	25.0	10.0	41.2	18.7
		Urban	15.1	0.8	12.3	2.4	26.4	2.8
	30+	Rural	37.4	6.3	31.5	12.7	52.6	23.4
		Urban	22.6	1.1	16.9	3.4	36.9	3.9
Delhi	15+	Rural	25.0	1.9	4.1	0.1	14.2	0.7
		Urban	20.8	1.5	5.4	0.3	19.3	1.7
	30+	Rural	38.1	2.8	4.4	0.2	21.0	0.6
		Urban	29.4	2.0	6.1	0.5	27.1	1.7
Gujarat	15+	Rural	28.4	1.5	12.6	0.8	9.9	1.7
		Urban	13.7	0.6	15.5	0.9	4.7	0.8
	30+	Rural	40.7	1.9	11.9	0.7	12.4	1.9
		Urban	20.1	0.8	17.2	1.0	6.0	0.8
Haryana	15+	Rural	41.6	2.8	2.0	0.2	20.9	1.4
		Urban	22.9	1.2	1.7	0.1	18.0	1.0
	30+	Rural	58.7	3.9	2.6	0.3	29.3	1.5
		Urban	32.0	1.7	2.2	0.1	24.7	1.1
Jammu & Kashmir	15+	Rural	29.9	2.4	6.8	0.7	14.3	1.1
		Urban	24.9	1.7	3.7	0.3	8.6	1.2
	30+	Rural	43.7	3.5	9.7	1.0	20.3	1.1
		Urban	35.9	2.2	5.3	0.5	12.4	1.4
Jharkhand	15+	Rural	24.0	4.7	41.7	6.2	34.1	14.2
		Rural	15.6	1.9	23.7	1.9	17.2	3.4
	30+	Urban	32.3	6.0	55.7	8.1	43.2	16.9
		Rural	22.4	2.3	33.0	2.5	23.8	3.8

Table 1.3D: Prevalence of smoking, chewing tobacco and drinking alcohol in India, 2004 *(Contd.)*

(Percent)

States	*Age group*	*Rural/ urban*	*Smoking*		*Chewing*		*Drinking alcohol*	
			Male	*Female*	*Male*	*Female*	*Male*	*Female*
Karnataka	15+	Urban	23.1	1.2	2.0	1.6	19.6	1.9
		Rural	18.0	0.8	1.6	0.3	13.8	0.7
	30+	Urban	33.8	1.7	2.6	2.4	28.7	2.7
		Rural	25.5	1.0	1.8	0.5	19.6	0.9
Kerala	15+	Urban	32.3	1.0	0.8	0.4	28.7	1.6
		Rural	21.1	0.6	0.1	0.1	21.1	0.8
	30+	Urban	44.1	1.2	1.0	0.6	38.3	1.7
		Rural	29.0	0.7	0.1	0.1	29.0	0.9
Madhya Pradesh	15+	Urban	31.1	2.0	23.6	6.2	21.2	3.0
		Rural	16.7	0.8	12.8	2.9	13.1	1.0
	30+	Urban	41.5	2.4	30.4	8.3	27.6	3.2
		Rural	25.5	1.1	16.6	4.3	18.6	1.0
Maharashtra	15+	Urban	9.7	0.5	27.3	9.7	14.7	1.3
		Rural	10.0	0.5	11.8	2.2	12.1	0.8
	30+	Urban	14.7	0.6	35.7	12.9	20.9	1.5
		Rural	14.3	0.5	15.7	3.2	17.3	0.9
Orissa	15+	Urban	25.8	3.5	24.8	20.9	22.9	8.6
		Rural	20.3	2.4	9.3	5.6	17.0	3.2
	30+	Urban	34.1	3.8	29.9	26.4	28.6	10.0
		Rural	28.4	3.3	11.8	8.0	22.7	4.3
Punjab	15+	Urban	9.7	0.5	6.6	0.3	28.2	1.8
		Rural	13.5	0.6	5.0	0.1	23.4	1.3
	30+	Urban	13.1	0.6	8.4	0.3	35.8	1.8
		Rural	18.3	0.7	5.4	0.1	32.5	1.4
Rajasthan	15+	Urban	41.2	4.2	14.0	1.5	24.1	3.7
		Rural	16.5	1.4	8.4	1.1	11.4	1.2
	30+	Urban	54.5	5.5	15.7	1.5	29.7	3.9
		Rural	24.9	2.0	11.0	1.5	15.7	1.1
Tamil Nadu	15+	Rural	16.6	1.5	0.9	0.7	16.3	3.2
		Urban	15.1	0.6	0.2	0.2	11.0	0.9
	30+	Rural	23.5	2.0	1.2	0.9	22.7	3.5
		Urban	20.7	0.7	0.2	0.2	15.3	0.9
Uttar Pradesh	15+	Rural	31.3	2.5	18.6	2.9	15.5	1.8
		Urban	19.3	1.3	8.3	1.2	12.4	1.5
	30+	Rural	43.7	3.2	25.0	4.1	21.3	1.8
		Urban	28.5	1.8	11.3	1.8	18.0	1.5
West Bengal	15+	Rural	42.0	4.0	11.5	3.6	15.5	5.0
		Urban	34.5	1.3	8.4	0.9	10.3	1.1
	30+	Rural	55.9	5.3	14.4	4.6	19.5	5.9
		Urban	45.0	1.5	10.2	1.2	13.0	1.1

preventable risk factor for major diseases and the resultant economic consequences", Vardhan said, releasing the report, compiled by PHFI and supported by WHO.

WHO representative to India Nata Menabde said raising taxes is one of the strongest weapons to fight out tobacco and this is what the WHO-FCTC mandates.

Deadly puff

Economic costs due to diseases caused by tobacco use in India is Rs 104,500 crore. (1.2% of GDP and 12% more than the combined Central and State Government expenditure on healthcare. Medical cost is Rs 16,800 crore, associated indirect morbidity cost is Rs 14,700 crore, cost from premature mortality is Rs 73,000 crore, cardiovascular diseases shared the highest burden, Rs 600 crore and followed by respiratory diseases (Rs 2,800 crore), tuberculosis is (Rs 2,300 crore) and cancer (Rs 1,400 crore).

Tripling of Tobacco Taxes may Prevent 200 million Deaths'

Tripling tobacco tax globally would reduce smoking by a third and prevent 200 million premature deaths from lung cancer and other diseases this century, researchers including an Indian-origin scientist, say.

Such a large tax increase would double the street price of cigarettes in some countries and narrow the price gap between the cheapest and the most expensive cigarettes, which would encourage people to stop smoking rather than switch to a cheaper brand and help young not to start, researchers said.

This would be especially effective in low and middle income countries where the cheapest cigarettes are relatively affordable and where smoking rates continue to rise, said Dr Prabhat Jha, director of the Center for Global Health Research of St. Michael's Hospital. But, it would also be effective in rich countries, said Jha, who is also a professor in the Dalla Lana School of Public Health at the University of Toronto.

"A higher tax on tobacco is the single most effective intervention to lower smoking rates and to deter future smokers".

"Worldwide, around a half-billion children and adults under the age of 35 are already—or soon will be—smokers and on current patterns few will quit", said Professor Sir Richard Peto of the University of Oxford, the coauthor. "This study demonstrates that tobacco taxes are a hugely powerful lever and potentially a triple win—reducing the numbers of people who smoke and who die from their addiction, reducing premature deaths from smoking and yet, at the same time, increasing government income", researchers wrote in the review published in the New England Journal of Medicine.

CIGARETTE

Cigarette (from the French word *cigarette* meaning "small cigar") is a small cylinder of finely cut tobacco leaves rolled in thin paper for smoking. The cigarette is ignited at one end and allowed to smouler; its smoke is inhaled from the other end, which is held in or to the mouth and in some cases a cigarette holder may be used as well.

Most modern manufactured cigarettes are filtered and include reconstituted tobacco and other additives.

The term cigarette, as commonly used, refers to a tobacco cigarette but can apply to similar devices containing other herbs, such as cloves or cannabis. A cigarette is distinguished from a cigar by its smaller size, use of processed leaf, and paper wrapping, which is normally white, although other colors are occasionally available. Cigars are typically composed entirely of whole-leaf tobacco.

Rates of cigarette smoking vary widely, and have changed considerably over the course of history—since cigarettes were first widely used in the mid-20th century. While rates of smoking have over time leveled off or declined in the developed world, they continue to rise in developing nations.

Cigarettes carry serious health effects with them, which are more prevalent than in other tobacco products. Nicotine, the primary psychoactive chemical in tobacco and therefore cigarettes, is addictive.

About half of cigarette smokers die of tobacco-related disease and lose on average 14 years of life. Cigarette use by pregnant women has also been shown to cause birth defects including low birth weight, fetal abnormalities, and premature birth. Second-hand smoke from cigarettes has been shown to be injurious to by-standers, which has led to legislation that has prohibited smoking in many workplaces and public areas. Cigarettes are a frequent source of fires leading to loss of lives in private homes, which has prompted the European Union and the United States to ban cigarettes that are not fire standard compliant by 2011.

The earliest forms of cigarettes were similar to their predecessor, the cigar. Cigarettes appear to have had antecedents in Mexico and Central America around the 9th century in the form of reeds and smoking tubes. The Maya, and later the Aztecs, smoked tobacco and various psychoactive drugs in religious rituals and frequently depicted priests and deities smoking on pottery and temple engravings. The cigarette and the cigar were the most common methods of smoking in the Caribbean, Mexico and Central and South America until recent times.

The North American, Central American and South American cigarette used various plant wrappers; when it was brought back to Spain, maize wrappers were introduced, and by the 17th century, fine paper. The resulting product was called *papelate* and is documented in Goya's paintings *La Cometa, La Merienda en el Manzanares*, and *El juego de la pelota a pala* (18th century). **By 1830, the cigarette had crossed into France, where it received the name *cigarette*;** and in 1845, the French State tobacco monopoly began manufacturing them.

Tobacco is grown in over 125 countries, on over 4 million hectares of land, a third of which is in China alone. The global tobacco crop is worth approximately, US$20 billion, a small fraction of the total amount generated from the sale of manufactured tobacco products. Tobacco is grown on less than 1% of the world's agricultural land, and a wide variety of soils and climates. Since the 1960s, the bulk of production has moved from the Americas to Africa and Asia: land devoted to tobacco growing has been halved in the USA, Canada and Mexico, but has almost doubled in China, Malawi and United Republic of Tanzania.

The production of tobacco leaves has more than doubled since the 1960s, totaling nearly 7 million metric tons in 2000. The greater use of fertilizers and pesticides, as well as the increased mechanization, that have produced these higher yields are environmentally damaging. The problem does not end with growing tobacco leaves cause massive deforestation. There are millions of tobacco farmers worldwide. There are millions of tobacco industry exploits them by contributing to their debt burden, while using their economic plight to argue against efforts to control tobacco. In the USA, the bond between the tobacco industry and the tobacco farmer finally is beginning to break down, and partnerships are developing between the farmers and the public health community.

Production climbed markedly when a cigarette-making machine was developed in the 1880s by James Albert Bonsack which vastly increased the productivity of cigarette companies, who went from making approximately 40,000 hand-rolled cigarettes daily to around 4 million. In the English-speaking world, the use of tobacco in cigarette form became increasingly widespread during and after the Crimean War, when British soldiers began emulating their Ottoman Turkish comrades and Russian enemies, who had begun rolling and smoking tobacco in strips of old newspaper for lack of proper cigar-rolling leaf. This was helped by the development of tobaccos suitable for cigarette use, and by the development of the Egyptian cigarette export industry.

The use of tobacco for smoking has been practiced for centuries. The tobacco plant has been grown in America since the 17th century and tobacco has been used in various forms since. The form of smoking tobacco by rolling the leaves in fine paper was frequently done by hand for those who practiced it, which limited the habit of smoking. In 1865, a man named Washington Duke from North Carolina began to roll cigarettes and sell them to others for profit.

In 1883, James Bonsack invented a machine that could roll cigarettes and produce thousands per day. Bonsack began a business called the American Tobacco Company, which was the first company to produce cigarettes on a large scale. The mechanized production of cigarettes widely increased the popularity of smoking, and made cigarettes much more accessible to those who wanted to smoke. Premade cigarettes were available for those who did not wish to roll their own tobacco and cigarettes became available in quantities by the pack.

In the late 19th century, cigarettes were being sold in packs and marketed throughout the United States. Cigarettes were packaged into containers of 10 that were marked with the name of the company that manufactured them and various logos or designs. The packs of 10 cigarettes sold for 5 cents each. Cigarette packages were made of paper with a small card inserted to reinforce the package. These cards were designed with attractive prints that served as a form of advertisement for the cigarette, and people began to collect and trade these cigarette cards, a practice called cartophily. The manufacturers of cigarette packs began to design cards specifically with the purpose of trading in mind, which in turn boosted their sales.

Cigarette brands varied in their blends of tobacco and the advertising on their cards. Fragrant Rose cigarettes, sold in the 1880s, issued cards with romantic and flowery images on them to correspond with their name. Creole cigarettes, created by SF Hess and Company were known for issuing baseball cards for the Newsboys League in 1888. Other popular brands of the late 19th century were Sweet Caporal, Lone Jack and Three Kings. It was not until the early 20th century that companies such as Philip Morris Tobacco, the founder of Marlboro cigarettes, began.

The evolution of the cigarette industry continued into the first half of the 20th century. Cigarette usage initially began as a habit for soldiers; but with the mechanization of cigarette production, followed by the popularity of cards due to advertising, many more people began to smoke cigarettes as a fun and even healthy activity. In the 1920s, the cost of a pack of cigarettes ranged from 15 cents to a quarter each, depending on quality.

The major cigarette companies that are still in production today have evolved into giants of the industry. Two of the largest producers, RJ Reynolds Tobacco Company and Philip Morris have bought out many of the smaller industries throughout the last century, becoming international corporations with holdings around the world. The use of cigarettes and the tobacco industry has changed several times since its early beginnings. Many people have their own opinions about smoking tobacco, but its history is a fascinating story of the evolution of a widespread habit.

Cigarettes may have been initially used in a manner similar to pipes and cigars and not inhaled; for evidence, see the Lucky Strike ad campaign asking consumers "Do You Inhale?" from the 30s. As cigarette tobacco became milder and more acidic inhaling may have become perceived as more agreeable. On the other hand, Moltke noticed in the 1830s (cf. *Unter dem Halbmond*) that Ottomans (and he himself) inhaled the Turkish tobacco and Latakia from their pipes (which are both initially sun-cured, acidic leaf varieties).

As early as 1888, cigarettes were described colloquially as "coffin nails". The widespread smoking of cigarettes in the Western world is largely a 20th-century phenomenon—at the start of the 20th century the per capita annual consumption in the USA was 54 cigarettes (with less than 0.5% of the population smoking more than 100 cigarettes per year), and consumption there peaked at 4,259 per capita in 1965. At that time about 50% of men and 33% of women smoked (defined as smoking more than 100 cigarettes per year). By 2000, consumption had fallen to 2,092 per capita, corresponding to about 30% of men and 22% of women smoking more than 100 cigarettes per year, and by 2006 per capita consumption had declined to 1,691; implying that about 21% of the population smoked 100 cigarettes or more per year.

German doctors were the first to identify the link between smoking and lung cancer which led to the first anti-tobacco movement in Nazi Germany. During World War I and World War II, cigarettes were rationed to soldiers. During the Vietnam War, cigarettes were included with C-ration meals. In 1975, the US government stopped putting cigarettes in military rations. During the second half of the 20th century, the adverse health effects of tobacco smoking started to become widely known and text-only health warnings became commonplace on cigarette packets. Warnings became prevalent but unpopular, mainly due to the political influences held by tobacco growers. The United States has not yet implemented graphical cigarette warning labels, which are considered a more effective method to communicate to the public the dangers of cigarette smoking. Canada, Mexico, Belgium, Sweden, Thailand, Malaysia, India, Pakistan, Australia, Brazil, Chile, Greece, the Netherlands, New Zealand, Norway, Hungary, United Kingdom, France, Romania, Singapore and Turkey however, have both textual warnings and graphic visual images displaying, among other things, the damaging effects tobacco use has on the human body.

The cigarette has evolved much since its conception; for example, the thin bands that travel transverse to the "axis of smoking" (thus forming circles along the length of the cigarette) are alternate sections of thin and thick paper to facilitate effective burning when being drawn, and retard burning when at rest. Synthetic particulate filters may remove some of the tar before it reaches the smoker.

Tobacco smoking first reached Australian shores when it was introduced to Northern-dwelling indigenous communities by visiting Indonesian fishermen in the early 18th century. British patterns of tobacco use were transported to Australia along with the new settlers in 1788; and in the years following colonization, British smoking behavior was rapidly adopted by indigenous people as well. By the early 19th century, tobacco was an essential commodity routinely issued to servants, prisoners and ticket-of-leave men (conditionally released convicts) as an inducement to work, or conversely, withheld as a means of punishment. Following the American Civil War, the tobacco industry struggled as it attempted to adapt. Not only did the labor force change from slavery to sharecropping, but a change in demand also occurred. As in Europe, there was a desire for not only snuff, pipes and cigars, but cigarettes appeared as well. With a change in demand and a change in labor force, James Bonsack, an avid craftsman, in 1881 created a machine that revolutionized cigarette production. The machine chopped the tobacco, then dropped a certain amount of the tobacco into a long tube of paper, which the machine would then roll and push out the end where it would be sliced by the machine into individual cigarettes. This machine operated at thirteen times the speed of a human cigarette roller.

Smoking Restrictions

Many governments impose restrictions on smoking tobacco especially in public areas. The primary justification has been the negative health effects of second-hand smoke. Laws vary by country and locality. Bhutan is currently the only country in the world to completely outlaw the cultivation, harvesting, production and sale of tobacco and tobacco products under the "Tobacco Control Act of Bhutan, 2010". However, small allowances for personal possession are permitted as long as the possessor can prove that they have paid import duties. The Pitcairn Islands had previously banned the sale of cigarette, however, it now permits sales from a government run store. The pacific island of Niue hopes to become the next country to prohibit the sale of tobacco. Iceland is also proposing banning tobacco sales from shops, making it prescription only and therefore dispensable only in pharmacies on doctor's orders. New Zealand hopes to achieve being tobacco free by 2025 and Finland by 2040. Singapore and the Australian State of Tasmania have proposed a "tobacco free millennium generation initiative" by banning the sale of all tobacco products to anyone born in and after the year 2000. In March 2012, Brazil became the world's first country to ban all flavored tobacco including menthols. It also banned the majority of the estimated 600 additives used, permitting only 8. This regulation applies to domestic and internationally imported cigarettes. Tobacco manufacturers have 18 months to remove the noncompliant cigarettes, 24 months to remove the other forms of noncompliant tobacco.

ITC and Cigarette

ITC is the market leader in cigarettes in India. With its wide range of invaluable brands, ITC has a leadership position in every segment of the market. ITC's highly popular portfolio of brands includes **Insignia, India Kings, Lucky Strike, Classic, Gold Flake, Navy Cut, Players, Scissors, Capstan, Berkeley, Bristol, Flake, Silk Cut, Duke and Royal.** The Company has been able to consolidate its leadership position with single minded focus on continuous value creation for consumers through significant investments in creating and bringing to market innovative product designs, maintaining consistent and superior quality, state-of-the-art manufacturing technology, and superior marketing and distribution. With consumers and consumer insights driving strategy, ITC has been able to fortify market standing in the long-term, by developing and delivering contemporary offers relevant to the changing attitudes and aspirations of the constantly evolving consumer.

ITCs pursuit of international competitiveness is reflected in its initiatives in overseas markets. In the extremely competitive US market, ITC offers high-quality, value-priced cigarettes and Roll-your-own solutions. In West Asia, ITC has become a key player in the Gulf Cooperation Council (GCC) markets through its export operations. ITCs cigarettes are manufactured in state-of-the-art factories at Bengaluru, Munger, Saharanpur, Kolkata and Pune, with cutting-edge technology and excellent work practices benchmarked to the best globally. An efficient supply-chain and distribution network reaches India's popular brands across the length and breadth of the country.

"Best Manufacturer of Cigarettes" for the year 2008 and 2007 and Best Exporter of Cigarettes for 2008 by the Tobacco Board based on previous 3 years' performance.

ITC launched its hand-rolled cigar, Armenteros, in the Indian market in March 2010. Armenteros cigars have been developed to suit the discerning taste of the Indian cigar connoisseur. The perfect balance of flavor, aroma and taste, Armenteros hand-rolled cigars are the perfect option for the cigar connoisseur. Armenteros cigars are being sourced from the Dominican Republic, the largest producer of hand-rolled cigars in the world. The cigars are being manufactured at La Aurora, which is one of the oldest cigar companies in the world and is run by the reputed Leon Jimenes family. The products and the packaging are custom-made to ITC specifications and stringent quality parameters. Armenteros is a trademark owned by ITC Limited.

Armenteros Handrolled Cigars have a unique blend comprising tobacco from the best growing regions of the world. The exquisite wrapper leaf comes from Cuban seed tobaccos grown in the mountains of Ecuador. This full bodied and aromatic wrapper leaf has a smoothness of texture considered among best in the world. The Sumatra seed, grown in Brazil, is used as the binder. These tobaccos take a great deal of care to mature, but once the leaf reaches its peak maturity, it offers a rich wisp of spicy and sweet flavor to the cigar. The exceptional filler is a masterful blend of tobaccos. The strength and earthiness of the Nicaraguan and Brazilian tobaccos are balanced with the mild yet rich taste of tobaccos from the Dominican Republic and Peru. Expert cigar rollers and robust quality control measures ensure that Armenteros is a truly world class cigar.

Armenteros Hand-rolled Cigars are packed with utmost care. They are placed inside a specially designed wooden box, created with a unique hand crafted inverted curves design and polished till it radiates perfection. The box also carries a Certificate of Authenticity signed by the Master Blender and the Production Director as a pledge to deliver the best products. The Cedar inlayer inside the box compliments the woody and earthy aromas of the cigars. The entire packaging design and graphics portray the rich and exclusive Armenteros lineage.

Available in the most popular cigar sizes (Churchill, Torpedo, Corona, Petit Corona and Robusto), the Armenteros portfolio consists of 8 pack sizes comprising 3, 5 and 10 cigars. Armenteros cigars are available exclusively at tobacco selling outlets in select hotels, fine dining restaurants and exclusive clubs.

Production of Imports/Exports

Production of cigarettes pieces in India increased from 20.7 billion in 1950–1951 to 101 billion in 1998–1999. India started exporting cigarettes from 1990–1991 which increased from in 1988–1999. The country has also been importing cigaretts starting from 1992–1993, 51 million in 1992–1993 and reached a peak of 252 million in 1997–1998, but came down to 35 million next year in 1998–1999.

Some E-cigarettes may Pose Cancer Risk

Electronic cigarettes appear to be safer than ordinary cigarettes for one simple—and simply obvious —reason: people don't light up and smoke them. With e-cigarettes, there is no burning tobacco to produce myriad new chemicals including some 60 carcinogens.

But new research suggests that, even without a match, some popular e-cigarettes get so hot that they, too, can produce a handful of the carcinogens found in cigarettes and at similar levels. A study to be published this month in the journal Nicotine and Tobacco Research found that the high-power e-cigarettes known as tank systems produce formaldehyde, a known carcinogen, along with the nicotine-laced vapor that their users inhale.

The toxin is formed when liquid nicotine and other e-cigarette ingredients are subjected to high temperatures, according to the study. A second study that is currently being prepared for submission to the same journal also points to similar findings. The long-term effects of inhaling nicotine vapor are unclear, but there is no evidence to date that it causes cancer or heart disease as cigarette smoking does. Indeed, many researchers agree that e-cigarettes will turn out to be much safer than conventional cigarettes, an idea that e-cigarette companies have made much of in their advertising.

For instance, the website for Janty, a company that manufactures popular tank systems, says the benefits of e-cigarettes include having "no toxins associated with tobacco smoking". Nonetheless, the new research suggests how potential health risks are emerging as the multibillion-dollar e-cigarette business rapidly evolves, and how regulators are already struggling to keep pace. While the US's FDA last month proposed sweeping new rules that for the first time would extend its authority to e-cigarettes, the FDA has focused largely on what goes into these products—currently, an unregulated brew of chemicals and flavorings—rather than on what comes out of them, as wispy plumes of flavored vapor.

The proposed rules give the FDA the power to regulate ingredients, not emissions, although the agency said it could consider such regulations in the future. Even so, some experts contend that the current approach is akin to examining the health risks associated with tobacco leaves rather than with cigarette smoke. "Looking at e-cigarette ingredients is one thing, and very important", said Maciej L Goniewicz, who led the first study, which is scheduled to be published on May 15. "But to have a comprehensive picture, you have to look at the vapor".

Moving from E-cigarettes

Quitting cigarettes is agony. But Anil Budhiraja, a Delhi-based management professional who had been smoking for 30 years, found a way to quell his cravings.

The 50-year-old went to a clinic where a pen-like device was held to his ears. An hour later, Budhiraja, who used to go through at least 10 cigarettes a day, says he walked out with no desire to light up ever again.

Budhiraja has not smoked for the last nine months. "I have regained my taste buds, become energetic and more confident". Budhiraja had opted for IQS (I Quit Smoking), the latest smoking-cessation treatment on the block. Developed by Irish organization Quit Smoking International in 2001, IQS involves the use of electro-auriculotherapy, basically ear acupuncture with electric currents instead of needles, to beat the smoking habit.

The therapy triggers the release of beta-endorphins or "happy hormones"—usually released during a workout—which mask the urge to smoke, say promoters.

IQS promises to eliminate cigarette cravings altogether and in this era of lunchtime surgeries, the promise of a quick solution—advertisements claim it helps you quit smoking in "just 1 hour"—has made IQS much sought after in Europe, South Africa and the Middle East, even though no large scale research has been conducted to test its efficacy.

The therapy made its Indian debut last March with the first clinic opening at a plush mall in Delhi's Vasant Kunj area. At least 25–30 smokers—most of them are 30–50 year-old males in senior corporate positions—enroll every month, says Kunal Sekhri, managing director of the IQS India franchise.

Considering India is home to a 110 million smokers, Sekhri foresees a surge in demand over the coming years. "We will open centers in Mumbai, Chandigarh and Vadodara soon".

IQS finds its roots in the traditional practice of auriculotherapy, which is based on the belief that the ear is a micro system reflecting the brain and that its points are linked to our organs. The US FDA has approved auriculotherapy for smoking cessation. While IQS is not FDA-approved, promoters say the device used to deliver electric charges has been sanctioned for use as a "nonmedical wellness product" by the US and UK health departments.

During treatment, a doctor stimulates precise nerve endings on the patient's ear lobes with a patented RISE (Reflection Instrument Scanning Electro-pulse) device. "We activate 19 points on the left ear lobe and 18 on the right for 30–50 seconds each over a 45-minute session", says Dr Shiwani Braskon, who works at the Delhi IQS clinic. The power and frequency of the electric charge varies according to the level of addiction. The client just feels a "mild prick-like sensation".

"When one has been smoking for a long time, certain brain cells are converted into nicotine receptors. The endorphins mask these receptors and reduce the urge to introduce more nicotine into the body. They also eliminate the usual withdrawal symptoms such as irritability or headaches," explains Braskon".

Normally, when one quits, it takes 3–4 weeks for the receptors to deactivate. Braskon says IQS makes the process "easier and faster". Although IQS involves the use of electric charges, the franchise says their intensity is too low to have any adverse effects. Clients are warned of only minor side effects including drowsiness, a sensation in the ears, migraines and a slight sense of emptiness in the stomach in the first few weeks.

Independent medical experts, however, are sceptical as there has been no "randomized control trial" to gauge the efficacy of electro-auriculotherapy and its possible side effects. "Even though the current used is very small, it is given quite close to the head and we are not aware of the potential harms it can cause. The physiology and neurology of the process need to be studied", says Dr Surendra Shastri, who heads the de-addiction clinic at Mumbai's Tata memor.

As Cigarette Sales Drop, Cancer Relief Fund Dwindles

The Punjab Government's ambitious plan to hike value-added tax (VAT) on the sale of cigarettes and contribute 33% of the collections toward the cancer relief fund has hit a roadblock. The sale of cigarettes has declined.

The taxation department is now contemplating a proposal to lower the VAT on cigarettes to propel a rise in sales and thus ensure greater funds for cancer relief.

Till date, the department has collected Rs 25 crore through the VAT on cigarettes. Sources said the government had expected an additional revenue of Rs 100 crore. "However, the increase in VAT from 22% to 59% saw cigarette sales declining", they said.

Two major companies, ITC and Godfrey, have both seen a dip in their sales. While the ITC had earned Rs 33.58 crore in the first two quarters of fiscal 2012–2013, it has earned only Rs 39.46 crore till date, a marginal rise. Godfrey, which made Rs 27.90 crore in the fiscal year 2012–2013, has collected Rs 24.90 crore till date.

"The low sale is attributed to a high tax structure. The companies have approached us to decrease the tax to 40% so that they can be more sales. This would ensure a greater more flow of funds for cancer relief", said Jaspal Garg, Deputy Excise and Taxation Commissioner (VAT).

Sources said that VAT evasion on cigarettes could not be ruled out as the market was flooded with packets smuggled from other States where the taxes were low.

Cancer Relief Fund

- The cancer relief fund has been setup to give assistance to cancer patients for treatment at empanelled hospitals.
- The government has directed all departments, semi-government institutions and local bodies to contribute 2% of the income generated from the sale of their properties toward the fund.
- It has made it mandatory that 1% of the tender amount of all infrastructural projects, costing over Rs 50 crore will be contributed toward the fund.

State Emerging as North India's Smoking Capital: Survey

Jammu and Kashmir is fast emerging as the smoking capital of North India. The monthly spending on tobacco products far outstrips the national average. National statistics say smokers aged 15 years and above spend Rs 399.2 a month on cigarettes and Rs 93.4 on bidis while smokers in the state spend Rs 513.6 and Rs 134.2, respectively. This has been revealed in a survey by an NGO Voluntary Health Association of India (VHAI).

As per the GATS India 2009-10, released by the Ministry of Health and Family Welfare, 26.6% of the population in the state is using tobacco products in one or other form.

"The state has 12% cigarette smokers, 3.8% bidi smokers and 8% smokeless tobacco users. State's cigarette use prevalence (12%) is almost double the nationwide prevalence of 5.7%. It has also come to light that the highest proportion of adults

(67.9%) who are exposed to tobacco smoke in offices are in the state and the lowest (15.4%) are in Chandigarh", Dar.

To protect the health of people, the Center had enacted the Cigarettes and other Tobacco Products (Prohibition of Advertisement and Regulation of Trade and Commerce, Production, Supply and Distribution) Act, commonly known as COTPA-2003.

"Section 4 of the Cigarette and Other Tobacco Products Act 2003 protects people from second hand smoke. Creating smoke- free jurisdiction and declaring cities smoke-free are some of the conscious efforts of the health and other responsible authorities that take collaborative steps toward increased compliance".

In Jammu district a monitoring committee on the enforcement of the Act (COTPA-2003) is working to make all public places smoke-free. Efforts were also being made by the VHAI and the civil society network to generate awareness and build the capacity of the managers of public places, enforcement officials, sensitize the media and generate awareness among the common man on tobacco control issues.

Scientists Warn WHO not to Stub Out E-cigarettes

A leaked Document shows UN Body's plans to classify it as a Regular Tobacco Product.

In London, a confidential document of the WHO has been leaked which shoes the UN body's plans to classify e-cigarettes with regular cigarettes. The leaked document is from the organization's FCTC preparatory meeting. This comes just ahead of the WHO sponsored FCTC in Moscow in October.

The document confirmed that WHO considers e-cigarettes a threat public health use as an accessible alternative to regular tobacco and cigarettes. The move has made over 50 of the world's top researchers and specialists from 15 countries submit a signed letter saying e-cigarettes had the potential to save millions of lives. If asked WHO to reconsider warning that they risk missing an opportunity to drastically reduce smoking with illness and death associated with it. If the WHO gets its way and extinguishes e-cigarettes it will not only have passed up what is clearly one of the biggest public health innovations of the last three decades that could potentially save millions of lives but it will have abrogated its own responsibility under it won charter to empower consumers to take control of their own health, something which they are already doing themselves in their millions. Gerry Stimson, Emeritus professor at the Imperial College in London. He is a signatory to the letter and organizer of the upcoming inaugural Global Forum on Nicotine. Globally, 1.3 billion people smoke and the WHO estimates that up to 1 billion tobacco-related premature deaths are possible in the 21st century—all preventable.

For the WHO to suggest that e-cigarettes are as risky as other tobacco products would send an erroneous and bleak message to the millions of current e-cigarette users who have used them to quit smoking. West also signatory to the letter and Professor of Health Psychology and Director of Tobacco Studies at University College in London. It would discourage smokers from trying them and we would miss out on a major opportunity to reduce smoke-related deaths globally.

Scientists have known for some years that people smoke for the nicotine but die from the smoke. The death and disease from smoking arises from inhalation of tar particles and toxic gases drawn into the lungs.

The signatories to the letter believe that tobacco harm reduction tools such as e-cigarettes and other less harmful products such as snus could be the solution. People who currently smoke will do much less harm to their health if they consume nicotine in low-risk, noncombustible form.

E-cigarettes use has been a consumer led revolution and grown as a bottom up public health initiative that could save millions of lives, said John Britton, professor of Epidmiology at the Universtiy of Nottingham, United Kingdom.

Ads Term Gutkha Ban Unfair

The photographed ad on this page is one of the many ads that has been appearing in leading print and electronic media of the country since September. Issued by the gutkha industry, the ads term the ban on the chewing tobacco unfair and question why the government has not banned cigarette.

Since the introduction of the Food Safety and Standards Authority (FSSA) Act rules in August 2011, as many as 14 states have banned gutkha, known to be responsible for 80% of oral cancer cases in the country.

The ads prompted nonprofits campaigning against gutkha to call an urgent press meet on October 18. The meet was also participated by representatives from the health Ministry. Justifying the ban, Amal Pusp, Director with the Ministry, said, the Government chose to ban gutkha as a higher number of people consume it. Of the 274.9 million adult tobacco users in India, 75% consume smokeless tobacco, Pusp said. Vulnerable groups like women and teenagers consume more gutkha than cigarette. About 18% women consume smokeless tobacco, while only 3% smoke tobacco including bidi, he said, citing figures from GATS of 2010.

Pusp, however, showed helplessness when fielded questions related to weak regulations on cigarette. "I agree that cigarette is equally harmful but till now there is no legislation under which it can be banned", he said. Both cigarette and gutkha are covered under the COTPA of 2003, which only regulates tobacco products. Gutkha could be banned only after FSSA came into being. The Act considers gutkha as a food product and allows banning any food item containing injurious substance like nicotine. Unfortunately, cigarette is not a food item, Pusp added.

A representative of Smokeless Tobacco Association, who does not wish to be named, alleges that the Ministry is siding with the cigarette lobby using the policy loopholes. While supporting the ban, Jagdeep Chhokar of the Association of Democratic Reforms, says, "ITC Ltd, which controls 80% of the Indian cigarette market, has been one of the major donors for political parties, including the Congress." The Delhi nonprofit recently studied the source of funds to political parties.

Claims Busted

One of the many facts cited in the advertisement reads like this: "1 pouch of gutkha contains 0.2 gram of tobacco verses 0.63 gram in cigarette". Bhavna Mukhopadhyay, executive director of nonprofit VHAI, terms this misleading. "The size of gutkha pouch varies from 1 gram to 3.5 gram, which changes the percentage of tobacco in the mix. Moreover, there is no authentic estimate of contents for gutkha", she says. Another fact claims that a cigarette contains 4,000 chemicals while gutkha has only 3,000. Monika Arora, Director, Health Promotion and Tobacco Control of Nonprofit

PHFI, says, smokeless tobacco may have fewer chemicals but as many as 28 of them are carcinogenic. "Even a single cancer-causing chemical is enough to cause disease, disability and death", she adds.

The ad also claims that over 40 million people have lost their livelihood because of the ban. "Government estimates show that the total employment in the formal sector by the tobacco industry was seven million in 2004–2005. It can't come close to 40 million even if one adds employment by the informal sector", Arora says.

She also refutes the claim that farmers are growing tobacco in around 700,000 hectare in the country. As per the Directorate of Tobacco Development, the area under cultivation for smokeless tobacco is just 40,000 hectare. "The industry is trying to hide behind the livelihood issue when it is only concerned with its profits that are badly affected due to the ban", says Mukhopadhyay. The CTRI in Andhra Pradesh has identified that crops like sugarcane, maize, paddy and cotton can be grown on the same soil, offering the farmers an alternative livelihood option. Besides, according to a 2010 Planning Commission report, the annual revenue generated by the gutkha industry is US $1.62 billion. But, the expenditure on treatment of major diseases caused by it is six times more.

"Constitutionally, all states should have implemented the ban", Pusp said at the press meet. "We have written to all states but they are taking their time". However, the main contention of the ad that cigarette should be banned remains and the government has no plan for it.

Bidi History

Bidi is a leaf-rolled cigarette made of coarse, uncured tobacco, tied with a string at one end. Bidis (beedis or biris) dominate the smoking market of India—for every cigarette ten bidis are smoked. The word bidi is derived from beeda (a word in Marwari—a dialect of Hindi Predominantly spoken by the trader caste from Marwar of Gujarat and Rajasthan, which is a betel leaf-wrapped offering of betel nuts, herbs and condiments. The beeda is a symbol of esteem, and display of respect and reverence across the Indian subcontinent, and the bidi gradually started being equated with it. The Indian medicinal system, especially Ayurveda, also prescribe inhalation of the fumes of medicinal herbs, rolled in leaves. The myth of tobacco's medicinal properties along with parallels in Ayurveda, led to easy acceptance of the bidi in subcultures.

Birth of Bidi and the Industry

There is no historical record of the exact period during which the practice of smoking tobacco rolled in leaves started in India. The cultivation of tobacco started in Southern Gujarat in the late 17th century. Hookah smoking was popular among local people. Men of the same caste or subcaste gathered around in the evenings to share a common hookah. Because the hookah was tedious to carry around, a cheaper and portable form of the hookah was developed called the chillum. Bidis were developed soon after, possibly around the Kheda and Panchamahal districts of Gujarat, where cultivation of tobacco was high laborers would roll leftover tobacco in leaves of the astra tree (Bauhinia variegate) and smoke at lesifure. Communities across India experimented using leaves of mango (*Mangifera* spp). jackfruit (*Artocarpus* spp.), banana sal (*Shorea robusta*), pandanus (*Pandanus odoratissimus*, kewda) and palash (*Butea monosperma*) initially, communities in Gujarat made bidis for their own consumption, but their increasing popularity inspired to make it into a home-grown business. Soon bidis made locally became more popular than hookahs, largely because bidis overcame the obstacle of sharing the hookah, as individuals could smoke without hurting caste and religious sentiments and also because they were portable and did not require assembling and extensive preparation to light up. The early business model of the bidi industry in Gujarat involved businessmen and their workers rolling their own bidis, putting them in a thali (tray) and selling them along with tobacco and matches in local haats. Gujarat families that had settled down in Bombay saw the potential of the bidi business and soon started manufacturing bidis business and soon started manufacturing bidis on a larger scale. Bidis penetrated into other parts of the country outside of Bombay, but until 1900 bidi manufacturing was largely restricted to Bombay and Southern Gujarat.

It was during the severe drought of 1899 in Gujarat, which completed many families to migrate in search of a livelihood that the bidi become a small scale industry. The father of the modern bidi and the industry is possibly Mohanlal Patel of Gomtipur District. Ahmedabad, who migrated from Gujarat to Jobalpur. Patel worked as an agent of small contracts in Bineki and Bargi town on the Bengal-Nagpur Railway (BNR). Soon his cousin Hargovindas joined him. Mohanlal and Hargovindas would visit Jabalpur to get contracts and also traded in petty goods. During these visits to Jabalpur, they noticed that bidis were only available in the general—purpose shop of Bhatia Morarji (another Marwari expatriate who had escaped the famine). Morarji obtained bidis from Bombay and sold them at a premium to the gentry in Jabalpur. The Patel brothers saw an opportunity of making bidis in Jabalpur. Raw materials: tobacco and astra leaves were initially obtained from Ahmdabad, and soon bidis made by the brothers gained acceptance.

The secret of their phenomenal success however, came when Mohanlal and Hargovindas made the significant discovery that leaves of the tendu tree are best for making bidis. Tendu was found abundantly around the degraded forests of Jabalpur, and was far better than astra leaves. The tendu tree (Diospyros melanoxylon, family *Ebanaceae*, or the black or East Indian ebony) grows in the degraded deciduous forests of peninsular India, Tendu flourished, once the forests which had been stripped of sal trees (used to make railway sleepers) and other precious tropical timber trees. More importantly, tendu leaves were widely available soon after the tobacco crop was ready and cured, when most other trees had shed their leaves. The tendu leaves have all the characteristics of an excellent wrapper material-they are large and pliable, and to not crack on rolling when dry; their leathery texture was more acceptable than the veins and rough textures of other leaves, and they matched well with the taste of tobacco, without interfering with the tobacco flavor. Bidis rolled in tendu leaf soon found wide consumer acceptance.

The rapid expansion of the railways in Central India in 1899 opened new tobacco markets to this region, which made it cheaper for Mohanlal and Hargovindas to source tobacco and sell bidis more efficiently. Bidis had no brands before this. The first trademark was registered by Haribhai Desai of Bombay (using astra leaves) in 1901, while Mohanlal and Hargovindas obtained their brand trademark in 1902. In 1903, the BNR opened its link westwards towards the Nagpur sector, which led to the creation of another important bidi-manufacturing cluster in Govinda. Between

1912 and 1918, the rapid expansion of the railways established more such clusters in Vidharbha, Telangana, Hyderabad, Mangalore and Madras. The bidi cult rapidly spread to all parts of the country, gaining a strong foothold in the informal urban and rural economics. The habit of smoking trickled down from cities and towns to remote villages with the development of the railways.

The "Swedeshi andolan" a civil disobedience movement to boycott imperial good) which was started by Mahatma Gandhi in 1920 as an anti-British movements, uplifted the prestige of the Indian cottage industries. The bidi received a further impetus when the educated class started smoking it instead of cigarettes, to show solidarity to the swadeshi movements. Several Muslim leaders like Hassan Imam openly supported the bidi and said. Foreign cigarettes are haraam (illiet), used bidis instead of cigarettes.

Around World War II, the industry became an important and widespread cottage industry in urban shanties and rural areas. It was a part of the rations of the Indian jawan when he went to fight in foreign soils. The outbreak of World War II saw an increase in the production of bidis, which also accompanies the Indian soldiers. The demand for bidis increased at such a fast rate that the opening of new productions centers became an everyday activity for bidi manufacturers. Bidi gained widespread social acceptance in a short period and the industry became a role model for small Indian businesses.

Apart from human skill, there is little or no processing technique required in making the bidi. In the early 1940s, the engine of growth for the bidi industry was the urban shanties in the textile cities of Western India. Migrants and their families came to Bombay, Surat, Bhawandi and Sholapur, and would roll bidis through the day, to supplement the income of the waves and loom operators. By the 1960s, with the coming of the powerloom, many weavers were left without jobs and were forced to migrate back from these textile centers. Many of them found employment in the bidi industry in the Telangana region, Andhra Pradesh. More than 60% of the bidi workers in this region hail from the displaced weaver community (the Padmashalis), while the others are Dalits and Muslims.

By the 1950s and 1960s, there were so many brands that strong competition emerged among bidi manufacturers. Companies focused on building and consolidating their brands to establish brand loyalty, just as cigarette companies did in the West. They extolled the medicinal properties of tobacco (jeevan chhap): aroused patriotism Hindmata, named brands after gods and deities (ganesh); lured youth using modern names (with brand names like telephone, train, telegram) and endorsement of film actors, sportsmen and even wrestlers. Bidis became so popular that the more powerful cigarette industry became wary of them.

Quality became an important factor for bidis and products were defined by their provenance and quality of their inputs. For example, tendu leaves of Orissa are better than those in many other States. Similarly, tobacco based on origin, coarseness and curing techniques had its own followers. The industry also got boosts from creation of tobacco cultivation institutes (one specifically for bidi tobacco in Anand, Gujarat), and national and state policies to exploit tendu.

Bidi tobacco growing is concentrated in Kaira in Karnataka while most manufacturing clusters are in Mangalore, Mysore and Nipani (Karnataka); Pune and Nashik (Maharashtra); Jabalpur, Damoh and Sagar (Madhya Pradesh; MP Raipur Chhattisgarh), Tirunelveli and Chennai (Tamil Nadu); Cannoore (Kerala), and Nizamabad, Karim Nagar, and Warangal (Andhra Pradesh). By the mid, 1970s, production of bidis had reached nearly the same level as of today, between 800 billion and 1.2 trillion bidis. While new clusters were being created rapidly, several old clusters like Vidharba dissipated. Even strongholds like Madhya Pradesh, which accounted for more than half the bidis produced till the 1980s, have lost out to new epicenters of bidi rolling like West Bengal, Bihar an Orissa, where labor is cheaper. The bidi industry has been affected by forces of sustained competition and new legislations (like restrictions in child labor), but has been more or less stable since the mid-1980s. The industry wields an immense locals and national political clout and resists any modernization efforts like mechanization, contributing revenues through taxes and adopting better labor standards.

Conclusion

There is nothing traditional or historical about the use of tobacco and its forms of consumption like the bidi. The invention and the phenomenal commercial success of the bid has been spurred by a series of fortuitous events. Coupled with these, the creation of institution, favorable government policies and little regulation have helped the bidi (industry) to endure. In about 140 years since its invention and less than a century since its mass production, the bidi has become a leading agent of death among adults in the Indian subcontinent. The true success of the bidi, however, has to be the consummate case with which it has been accepted by local communities and how it has permeated into folklore, cultures and tradition in a short-span of time.

Bidi rolling is an entirely manual process. Laborers must painstakingly place tobacco inside a small tendu leaf, tightly roll the leaf and secure the product with a thread. This process is largely home-based and is dominated by women and children. An average roller can achieve a daily output of about 1,000 bidis per day. An already vulnerable sector of society, women and children engaged in bidi rolling face abuse, financial enslavement, and a number of health problems.

Women, Families, and the Bidi Industry

- Women make the largest proportion of labor in the bidi industry. Published literature estimate women makeup 76% of total bidi employment. The All India Bidi, Cigar, and Tobacco Workers Federation estimates women comprise 90–95% of total employment in bidi manufacture.
- Women are primarily bidi rollers. Workers typically operate from their homes. Other members of the family actively assist in the bidi rolling, especially children. In many cases, several women from the same household will all engage in bidi rolling to fulfill quotas.
- The industry is male dominated, and often contributes to the economic exploitation of women.
- Middlemen are known to supply female laborers with low quality tendu leaves. They also reject bidis deemed poor quality, but eventually take them without paying.

A Dangerous Occupation

- Entire households relying heavily on bidi production for survival are often forced to go into debt to bidi contractors when raw materials to complete the production process are scarce. Contractors then gain financial control over them.

- Minimum wages are fixed by the state governments and revised from time to time. However, International Labor Organization findings indicate that such provisions had scarcely any impact on home-based workers. Fixed wages for rolling 1,000 bidis varies from Rs 29.0 in Tripura to Rs 64.8 in Gujarat.

Exploiting Our Children

- Government estimates find 15–25% of children are employed by the industry. NGO estimates indicate that this is a gross underestimation of the size of the child workforce.
- Under the Child Labor Protection Act, 1986, permitting children under 14 to work in hazardous industries is illegal.
- Section three of the Child Labor Protection Act, 1986, allows for the employment of children under age 14 in home-based work. Bidi production units regularly exploit the loophole by giving work to families and enabling them to employ children. Children as young as 3–5 years are known to assist in the family's work.
- It is estimated that roughly 10% of all female bidi workers and 5% of all male bidi workers are children.
- Children are made to workup to a 14-hour day, 7 days per week, with very short breaks.
- Children working in factories are commonly subjected to punishment for working late, making a mistake, working slowly, or even talking to another child. They are reprimanded by being hit with a stick on the open hand or even beatings.
- For women and children engaged in rolling bidis a myriad of occupational hazards exist.
- The process releases large amounts of coarse particles and dust into the work environment (typically the home).
- Rollers do no wear protective clothing, gloves or masks, and are exposed to tobacco dust through their skin and by inhaling the harmful particles.
- The Factory Advisory Services and Labor Institute in Bombay, a unit of the Labor Ministry of India, found the incidence of bronchial asthma and tuberculosis to higher among bidi workers than any other group in the general population.
- Further health effects include pain and cramping in the shoulders, neck, back, lower abdomen, anemia and eye problems.

AIIMS to have Tobacco Cessation Clinic

The All India Institute of Medical Sciences (AIIMS) is putting in place a new tobacco cessation clinic as part of the Health Ministry's drive to check smoking or use of tobacco. More government hospitals including Safdarjung Hospital and Lady Hardinge Hospital will also be following suit. The move comes after TCCs, as tobacco cessation clinics are called, have proved to help addicts quit the habit.

Expected to start in July this year, the center manned with trained health workers would offer counseling services to all potential quitters. It is believed that, the TCCs, based on the cessation algorithm having a combination of behavioral and pharmacotherapy, would help arrest the ever-rising graph of tobacco consumers, with as much as 57% of men and 11% of young women addicted to some form of tobacco use.

As popular hospitals like AIIMS draw a large number of patients, a majority of whom coming from modest social and economic backgrounds, TCCs in these hospitals would be of big help, officials said.

Official sources said there are only 19 TCCs across the country, run by the government and the WHO together, apart from some private centers. "People are not much aware of the fact that tobacco can be controlled with counseling and other help, and this is going to be the thrust of the TCCs", Dr Jagdish Kaur, Chief Medical Officer with the Health Ministry told The Tribune.

"The government has been working towards introducing a multisectoral approach for improving the condition and a process of mapping various stakeholders' participation including smokers' profile in controlling tobacco spread has been initiated".

Officials said the marginal show of tobacco control program is due to the perception among people that tobacco consumption is not addictive in nature and it also enjoys society's acceptance. With more hospitals going to have TCCs, this perception is likely to change.

Going by the dismal success rate of quitting tobacco in India, the government is also likely to go in for a national toll-free line for upscaling the cessation exercise under the National Tobacco Control Program.

Anti-tobacco Curricula in Schools Soon

India is planning to introduce a comprehensive anti-tobacco curriculum and teachers' guide at school level across the country to reduce the growing dependence of students on nicotine. The move is part of the National Tobacco Control Program which is set for a major expansion through the coverage of school students whose addiction to tobacco as well as exposure to second-hand smoke through contact with smoker parents is increasing.

The teachers' manual, complete with worksheets for children on the A to Z of tobacco—its extent, how it impacts the physical and psychological health of users, how it kills, what are the laws governing tobacco use in India; the motive behind pictorial warnings on tobacco packs; the adverse effects of smokeless tobacco like gutka, and the best ways quitting tobacco - is ready for circulation to all the CBSE, ICSE and State Board Schools.

Guide ready

- Non-smoking teachers will help students quit smoking
- Chapters for parents who tend to affect their children's health by smoking

What is disturbing?

- Percentage of students who initiated smoking before the age of 10 increasing15% of India's students are nicotine dependent
- Boys aged 15–24 smoking 5 cigarettes a day while girls of that age smoking 9 sticks a day.

The manual, developed by the Ministry of Health, also carries chapters for parents who tend to affect their children's health by smoking in their presence. The chapter is named, "Effects of second-hand smoke and what the parents need to do" and comprises joint tasks with children. Interestingly, the Ministry has said in the manual that those instructing students in the anti-tobacco curricula should themselves be non-smokers and non-tobacco users. Asked how they would ensure this requirement, a Health Ministry Official said, "we expect the schools to respect the contents of the manual considering we and the school authorities have a shared objective—that of reversing the alarming trend of increasing tobacco use among our students". The manual would be included in the school system under the ongoing School Health Program, currently underway in 27 States.

It is inspired by the growing evidence of more and more students becoming regular tobacco users. The latest Global Tobacco Youth Survey for India reveals a rise in the number of tobacco-addicted students from 13.7% in 2006 to 14.7% now. The addiction has been reported for both smoking (cigarettes and bidis) and smokeless (gutka, areca nut, khaini, zarda) forms of tobacco, with the prevalence of smoking among boys being three times higher than that among girls, who are more addicted to smokeless tobacco forms.

Moreover, the percentage of students who initiated smoking before the age of 10 years has been increasing, much to the discomfort of policy planners. It was 26 in 2006 and is 45.4% now. The percentage of boys exposed to second-hand smoke is 29.3% while that of girls is 22.4.

The findings of the Youth Survey were most recently corroborated by those from the Global Adult Tobacco Survey which showed that boys aged 15–24 years were smoking 5 cigarettes a day while girls of that age were smoking 9 sticks a day. That means girl students in India are more nicotine dependent than boys though the average tobacco use continues to be higher for the boys.

Government Calls National Meet to Regulate Smokeless Tobacco

Alarmed by the mounting cancer burden attributable to the use of smokeless tobacco in India, the government today decided to hold a national consultation to devise strategies for the regulation of this most dangerous form of tobacco. India has no regulatory standards on smokeless tobacco as of now. The decision comes within weeks of The Tribune reporting the Center for Tobacco Research in India's findings regarding high nicotine and pH levels in several sampled smokeless tobacco products—including pan masalas, khaini, zarda and gutkha—being sold in the markets.

The most striking discovery was high nicotine even in pan masalas being marketed as tobacco-free. Rajnigandha was found to have 2.26 gram of nicotine per 100 gram of pan masala. High nicotine was found in all six tested samples of smokeless tobacco. Their pH levels were such as were aiding quick absorption of nicotine in the blood, thus adding to the product's addiction value. Evidence in hand, the Health Ministry has on April 4 called stakeholders to debate the critical need to ban or regulate smokeless tobacco, considering the GATS India Report findings that 26% Indian adults were consuming these products.

Globally, the highest smokeless tobacco prevalence rate of 53.1% among male consumers has been observed in Yemen. In Bangladesh, the prevalence of use of smokeless tobacco among females (27.9%) exceeds that of males (26.4%).

The Government has finally been constrained to call a consultation on the issue in view of the fact that smokeless tobacco, as per latest evidence, is known to contain over 3,000 chemical compounds; 29 of these are proven carcinogens. The Indian Council for Medical Research, which is partnering with the Health Ministry and WHO for the consultation, says 50% cancers among men and 25% among women in India are related to tobacco use; 90% oral cancers are related to the use of chewing tobacco.

Importantly, though some State Governments had tried banning smokeless tobacco, the industry moved the Supreme Court which asked the Center to take a call on the regulation of smokeless forms considering COTPA, 2003, a Central Act, is in place to regulate smoking tobacco use.

School-Going Children at Risk

Recent studies have also shown increasing addiction among youth to smokeless forms of tobacco. As many as 12.5% youngsters (16.2% boys and 7.2% girls) used tobacco products other than cigarettes in India. The Youth Tobacco Survey Indian Report confirms that school-going children aged 13–15 years are more likely to use non-cigarette tobacco than smoking cigarettes.

The Gutkha Menace

- 25% Indians addicted to gutkha, khaini, cancer burden rising.
- In India, khaini followed by gutkha is the most common smokeless tobacco product in use, with Bihar, Chattisgarh and Jharkhand topping in its usage along with Northeast.
- The lowest use is Himachal, Goa, Chandigarh, Punjab and Haryana.

Exports

India is exporting both unmanufactured and manufactured products. Total quantity exported constituted 75 million kg (20.6% in 1974–1975) which increased to 176 million kg (1%) in 2010–2011 (Table 1.4) of total production. The share of manufactured products in the total exports went up from 4.2% in 1960–9661 to 19% in 1998–1999 (Table 1.4A) and came down to 15.7% in 2010–2011. From among the manufactured products, nearly 2.5% is the share of Hooka tobacco paste. Chewing tobacco and cigarettes constitute other major component (Table 1.4B). India is exporting both manufactured and unmanufactured tobacco. Exports of unmanufactured tobacco increased from 32.2 thousand tons in 1940–9441 to 82 thousand tons in 1940–1941 to 82 thousand tons in 1998–9999. During 1940–1991, Indian exports were 10% of the total world, occupying 3rd position. (Tables 1.4C and 1.4D). From among the variety wise exports FCV is at the top with 66.7% share in 1990–1991 increasing to 85% in 1997–1998. (Table 1.4E). Europe is the main importer of Indian tobacco, accounting for 51% of India's total-exports in 2011–0112. The other major importing regions were South and South-East Asia (19% of exports). Africa (14%), North and South Americas (9%) and West Asia (7%) (Tables 1.4F) and Table 1.4G is shown in Annexure at the end of chapter.

Table 1.4: Production and exports of tobacco and production of cigarettes

Year	*Tobacco production (mn kg)*	*Tobacco yield (kg/ha)*	*Tobacco export (mn kg)*	*(Rs cr)*	*(Rs/kg)*	*Cigarette production (mn pieces)*
1974-75	363	954	75	80	11	62,400
1980-81	481	1,065	79	125	16	79,500
1981-82	520	1,172	115	203	18	86,800
1982-83	582	1,157	100	214	21	94,000
1983-84	497	1,120	90	181	20	80,447
1984-85	450	1,113	75	158	21	85,028
1985-86	442	1,097	64	139	22	80,080
1986-87	462	1,186	67	145	22	84,360
1987-88	367	1,155	72	108	15	75,420
1988-89	491	1,309	52	101	18	80,400
1989-90	552	1,335	71	143	20	82,800
1990-91	558	1,361	87	263	30	85,200
1991-92	587	1,304	84	312	37	87,600
1992-93	599	1,185	88	474	54	61,300
1993-94	565	1,361	105	461	44	72,000
1994-95	590	1,349	54	255	47	71,038
1995-96	535	1,355	87	447	51	69,588
1996-97	599	1,387	117	757	65	73,842
1997-98	650	1,430	145	1,061	74	83,162
1998-99	700	1,430	89	762	86	79,314
1999-00	524	1,210	138	993	72	82,859
2000-01	488	1,318	108	871	56	75,094
2001-02	530	1,565	99	580	58	60,577
2002-03	500	1,506	120	730	61	54,991
2003-04	550	1,486	150	721	48	50,009
2004-05	600	1,498	136	1,255	92	54,747
2005-06	700	1,481	167	1,413	85	75,711
2006-07	700	1,407	181	1,723	95	85,747
2007-08	700	1,750	173	1,932	111	85,991
2008-09	725	1,813	225	3,388	151	87,047
2009-10	725	1,813	260	4,402	169	90,199
2010-11	725	1,813	224	3,821	170	96,124
2011-12	735	–	176	4,006	227	94,086
2012-13(P)	735		128	2,297	179	57,345

P- provisional.

Table 1.4A: Exports of tobacco, tobacco products and total since 1974-75

Year	*Tobacco*		*Tobacco products*		*Total*		
	Qty. (Tons)	*Value (Rs.Crs.)*	*Qty. (Tons)*	*Value (Rs.Crs.)*	*Qty. (Tons)*	*Value (Rs.Crs.)*	*MUS$.*
1974-75	74982	80.36	2973	1.86	77955	82.22	98.20
1975-76	74276	93.10	4181	5.27	78457	98.37	109.80
1976-77	80134	96.62	5372	5.40	85506	102.02	116.70
1977-78	89427	113.21	3814	4.03	93241	117.24	143.10
1978-79	78557	110.71	5734	5.59	84291	116.30	143.00
1979-80	64810	99.53	5627	5.30	70437	104.83	133.10
1980-81	78501	124.85	12337	16.27	90838	141.12	162.30
1981-82	114562	202.86	17759	30.53	132321	233.39	269.50
1982-83	100430	214.26	21784	33.44	122214	247.70	245.30
1983-84	89985	181.05	16172	22.46	106157	203.51	179.10
1984-85	74745	157.87	21738	27.79	96483	185.66	149.70
1985-86	64433	139.98	19663	32.62	84096	172.60	139.60
1986-87	66824	144.87	21489	39.72	88813	184.59	144.44
1987-88	48111	96.98	13307	19.32	61418	116.30	89.67
1988-89	39917	108.72	10379	16.14	50296	116.86	80.70
1989-90	58183	152.24	15512	19.79	73695	172.03	103.32
1990-91	70375	209.16	13299	54.53	83674	263.69	147.00
1991-92	71792	342.69	14662	47.71	86454	390.40	164.49
1992-93	81294	434.41	13424	73.33	94718	507.74	175.32
1993-94	91998	406.00	9221	79.72	101219	485.72	154.87
1994-95	44600	207.83	10822	59.95	55422	267.78	85.29
1995-96	72052	361.36	11883	59.68	83935	421.04	126.06
1996-97	117466	733.66	13115	92.86	130581	826.52	234.32
1997-98	136739	972.83	7795	88.36	144534	1061.19	272.52
1998-99	82366	634.48	18957	171.71	101323	806.19	199.10
1999-2k	122590	864.77	13631	185.45	136221	1050.22	245.55
2000-01	100537	677.04	15393	226.34	115930	903.38	203.55
2001-02	86010	602.89	16076	285.63	102086	888.52	189.04
2002-03	107715	770.62	19842	325.33	127557	1095.95	224.95
2003-04	128186	825.48	22776	350.15	150962	1175.63	251.04
2004-05	138159	968.90	24774	393.28	162933	1362.18	305.77
2005-06	142007	1027.52	24862	385.95	166869	1413.47	322.49
2006-07	152618	1241.05	28370	482.37	180988	1723.42	381.54
2007-08	174690	1478.51	30657	544.27	205347	2022.78	502.67
2008-09	197127	2713.28	27740	675.15	224867	3388.43	738.06
2009-10	229632	3655.49	29934	746.80	259566	4402.29	928.37
2010-11	212573	3192.39	39725	1018.02	252298	4210.41	923.94
2011-12	203294	3090.21	37101	1010.09	240395	4100.30	854.94
2012-13	228023	3831.84	35552	1147.21	263575	4979.05	914.43
2013-14*	93635	1832.74	11478	415.27	105113	2248.01	386.19

* April - August, 2013.

Table 1.4B: Exports of tobacco from India (product wise) from 1991-92 to 1996-97 and 2005-06 to 2007-08

(Quantity : Tons; Value : Rs Crores)

Product		*1991-92*	*1992-93*	*1993-94*	*1994-95*	*1995-96*	*1996-97*	*2005-06*	*2006-07*	*2007-08*	*Percent of increase in 2007-08 over 2006-07*
Beedis	Q	400	668	569	633	676	662	694	1,079	1,003	13.15
	V	692.13	1122.91	1227.91	1537.91	1152.28	1596.43	32.92	39.08	44.22	
Cigarettes	Q	1753	2644	3226	1028	884	714	5,885	6,424	5,833	4.31
	V	1610.68	3971.56	4898.98	1574.98	1392.79	1414.43	119.24	148.39	145.14	
Cigar & Cheroot	Q	–	–	–	a	–	–	–	–	–	–
	V	–	–	–	0.11	–	–	–	–	–	
Chewing Tobacco	Q	77	54	111	811	424	643	5,739	5,953	8,338	27.44
	V	152.22	351.82	215.05	661.27	607.00	2606.33	171.27	198.48	252.95	
Hookah Tobacco Paste	Q	12129	9578	5285	8145	9376	10759	9,930	10,594	10,656	7.83
	V	2179.64	1514.37	1566.19	2150.39	2612.26	3408.98	37.37	42.38	45.70	
Snuff	Q	69	3	2	4	6	20	108	87	147	3.59
	V	10.13	2.24	3.70	8.24	8.16	27.84	1.26	1.39	1.44	
—Zarda Scented Tobacco	Q	21	3	2	4	–	–	–	–	–	–
	V	36.96	29.83	26.20	34.12	–	–	–	–	–	
Cut Tobacco	Q	–	440	20	70	512	317	2,506	4,229	4,680	4.31
	V	–	319.15	15.79	15.60	177.60	232.10	23.89	52.55	54.82	
Other Products	Q	213	34	6	127	5	–	–	–	–	–
	V	89.05	20.80	18.85	12.15	17.94	–	–	–	–	
Total	Q	14662	13424	9221	10822	11883	13115	24,862	28,370	30,657	12.83%
	V	4770.81	7332.68	7971.95	5994.77	5968.03	9286.11	385.95	482.37	544.27	

Q: Quantity
V: Value
Source: Tobacco Board, Guntur, Ministry of Commerce, Government of India.

Table 1.4C: Exports of unmanufactured tobacco from India

(Qty : Tons; Value Rs: Crores)

Year	*Unmanufactured tobacco (Qty)*	*Value (Rs)*	*India's total export of all items (Rs.)*	*World percentage*	*Emports Indian rank*
1940-41	32187	1.77	380*	10	3rd
1947-48	22694	5.03	450*	5	4th
1950-51	42198	13.05	606	8.6	3rd
1960-61	20762	14.61	642	2.5	5th
1970-71	47524	31.40	1535	5.8	5th
1980-81	78501	124.85	6711	5	5th
1990-91	70375	209.16	32553	4	8th
1996-97	117466	733.66	117525	6.6	6th

* Approximate
Source: Tobacco Board, Guntur.

Table 1.4D: India's tobacco exports in selected years

	Unmanufactured		*Manufactured*		*Total*	
Year	*Quantity ('000 tons)*	*Value (Rs million)*	*Quantity ('000 tons)*	*Value (Rs million)*	*Quantity ('000 tons)*	*Value (Rs million)*
1960/61	*46*	*146*	*2*	*11*	*48*	*157*
Share (%)	*95.8*	*93.0*	*4.2*	*7.0*	*100*	*100*
1970/71	48	314	2	12	50	326
1980/81	79	1 248	12	163	91	1 411
1990/91	70	2 062	17	699	87	2.761
1991/92	72	3 427	15	477	87	3 904
1992/93	81	4 344	13	733	94	5 077
1993/94	92	4 060	9	797	101	4 857
1994/95	45	2 078	12	598	57	2 678
1995/96	72	3 614	12	597	84	4 211
1996/97	117	7 336	13	920	130	8 256
1997/98	137	9 722	8	890	145	10 612
1998/99	82	6 345	19	1 717	101	8 062
Share (%)	*81.2*	*78.7*	*18.8*	*21.3*	*100*	*100*

Sources: Tobacco Development Board (various issues) *Handbook of Tobacco Statistics*. Directorate of Tobacco Development. *Status Paper on FCV Tobacco*. Ministry of Finance, Government of India. *Budget Documents*.

Table 1.4E: Exports of tobacco from india (variety-wise) from 1990-91 to 1997-98

Quantity: Tons Value: Rs. Crores

Year		*FCV*	*S(N)*	*SCV*	*Burley*	*Lalcho-padia.*	*Judi*	*Rustica*	*Others*	*Total*
1990-91	Q	47017	4551	–	4402	6578	6297	1390	140	70375
	V	165.66	7.75	–	13.48	11.25	8.83	1.90	0.27	209.16
1991-92	Q	49622	5426	670	7528	4010	2619	949	968	717792
	V	268.36	17.00	1.76	43.68	5.56	2.79	1.60	1.90	342.69
1992-93	Q	56468	5799	1654	7193	3760	2249	3030	1141	81294
	V	366.96	15.72	4.15	29.64	6.41	2.41	6.57	2.55	434.41
1994-95	Q	27209	2210	550	5800	4405	2497	722	1851	45244
	V	159.38	6.21	2.47	20.18	10.08	4.59	1.71	5.1	209.72
1995-96	Q	54573	2489	556	5405	4042	2410	252	2324	72052
	V	298.11	8.55	1.30	23.66	10.28	5.94	0.65	12.78	361.36
1996-97	Q	95985	3224	1958	2911	8112	1536	8	3732	117466
	V	658.08	14.08	7.45	17.46	20.05	3.69	0.02	12.50	733.65
1997-98	Q	102381	5960	7854	5249	5926	1093	–	8276	136737
	V	825.64	21.94	35.84	35.04	19.73	2.90	–	31.73	972.63

Q = Quantity
V = Value
Source: Tobacco Board, Guntur.

Table 1.4F: Production, exports and imports of cigarettes in India

Year	*Production*	*Imports*	*Exports*
	Million pieces		
1950/51	20 700		
1960/61	35 000		
1970/71	63 100		
1980/81	78 600		
1981/82	90 600		
1982/83	89 100		
1983/84	87 300		
1984/85	96 100		
1985/86	82 400		
1986/87	81 100		
1987/88	77 800		
1988/89	80 300		
1989/90	83 500		
1990/91	86 100		800
1991/92	85 700		6428
1992/93	80 800	51	2410
1993/94	78 800	25	3456
1994/95	84 000	86	3463
1995/96	95 600	134	1461
1996/97	102 300	157	1206
1997/98	104 600	252	1446
1998/99	101 000	35	2543

Source: Union Budget, and foreign trade data from Directorate General of Commercial Intelligence.

TOBACCO BOARD

Tobacco is an important commercial crop grown in India. It occupies the third position in the world with an annual production of about 725 million kg. Of the different types grown, flue-cured tobacco, country tobacco, burley, bidi, rustica and chewing tobacco are considered important. India, as an exporter of tobacco, ranks 6th in the world next to Brazil, China, USA, Malawi and Italy.

Tobacco and tobacco products earn a whopping annual sum of about Rs 15,502.38 crore. to the national exchequer by way of excise revenue, and Rs 4210.41 crore (2010–2011) by way of foreign exchange. Furthermore, tobacco is a source of gainful employment. Several lakhs of people thrive on this weed crop.

Flue-cured growth, with an annual production of about 300 million kg, is the singular type, which contributes huge amount of forex and excise earnings. More or less, 50% of the FCV tobacco produced is consumed domestically while the rest is exported to more than 100 countries across the globe. Other tobacco types viz. Burley, Country tobacco, Chewing tobaccos (Lal chopadia, Judi and Rustica) are also exported whereas bidi tobacco—a poor man's smoke—is consumed only within the country.

Flue-cured Virginia tobacco is the principal type grown in the States of Andhra Pradesh and Karnataka under varied agroclimatic conditions. It is grown in the light soils of Karnataka as rain-fed crop and in the heavy soils of Andhra Pradesh under conserved moisture in the aftermath of Southwest monsoon rains. The crop is grown under irrigated conditions in the of Andhra Pradesh and Eastern Light Soils (ELS) of Orissa and as a semi-monsoon crop in Southern Light Soils (SLS) of Andhra Pradesh. Thus, India is endowed with a vast potential to produce different types of tobacco so as to cater to the interests of the discerning customers.

The Government of India established the Tobacco Board under an Act of Parliament in the year 1975 (brought to effect from 1.1.1976) and opened its head quarters at Guntur, Andhra Pradesh with a view to bring about an all-round development to the tobacco industry.

The Tobacco Board is interested in entry of MNCs into tobacco cultivation, assuming a better deal for the tobacco farmers. But, the industry feels otherwise. It says that foreign cigarette multinationals have no real interest in the Indian tobacco industry as they use Indian tobacco only as filler tobacco; they do not consider Indian tobacco worthy of use as semi-flavored or flavorful variety.

According to section 8(1)(a) of the Tobacco Board Act, one of the important functions of the Tobacco Board is to regulate the production and curing of Virginia tobacco having regard to the demand for tobacco in India and abroad, marketability of different types of FCV tobacco and other factors. This objective is sought to be achieved through crop planning and fixing crop size of FCV Tobacco for Andhra Pradesh and Karnataka separately every year and by registering commercial nurserymen, tobacco growers and barn operators.

The majority of European Union (EU) Health Ministers, meeting at Brussels on December 4, 2002, agreed to outlaw tobacco advertising by July 2005. The new rules will also prohibit advertisements promoting events, and on radio and the Internet. Of course, there was opposition to the new rules from the UK and Germany.

ISO 9001:2008 Certification to Indian Tobacco Board

The Indian Tobacco Board, in furtherance of its objectives strive to provide superior service to its customers namely, growers and traders in a systematic manner. M/s Det Norkse Veritas (DNV), Netherlands bestowed the honor of ISO 9001:2008 certificate to the Indian Tobacco Board for establishing quality management systems. The Tobacco Board has implemented systems aimed at achieving product integrity and traceability, model project area and quality circles concept to improve the quality of tobacco leaf so as to meet the specifications of importers. The Board, committed to meeting the needs of customers, advises all the Indian exporters to obtain ISO certification with a view to meet the expectations of the global market.

Board Activities

Mission

"To strive for the overall development of tobacco growers and the Indian Tobacco Industry".

Vision

"Tobacco Board is committed to accomplishing its role—the expressed will of parliament—for the smooth functioning of a vibrant farming system, fair and remunerative prices to tobacco growers and export promotion".

Activities

The Tobacco Board Act aims at planned development of tobacco industry in the country. The various activities of the Board outlined in the Act for the promotion of the industry are: regulating the production and curing of Virginia Tobacco with regard to the demand in India and abroad. Constant monitoring of the Virginia tobacco market, both in India and abroad and ensuring fair and remunerative price to the growers and reducing wide fluctuations in the prices of the commodity.

The Tobacco Board undertakes the following export promotion activities:

1. Inviting official and business delegations from abroad.
2. Organizing visits of Indian official and trade delegations abroad.
3. Participation in international trade fairs, and exclusive world tobacco exhibitions and symposiums.
4. Publicity through an extensive advertisement campaign in the international media to promote Indian tobacco.
5. Dissemination of information and various enquiries received from overseas customers to the exporters.
6. Problem solving with government agencies and organizations: RBI, customs; import/export procedures; problems with importers through Indian missions abroad, etc.

Activities of the Board

Soil and Water Testing

1. The Board had established two soil testing laboratories – one at Ongole in AP and another at Periyapatna in Karnataka State. The Board also avails the services of soil testing laboratories of the Governments in AP and Karnataka, whenever required.

2. The Board organizes the collection and analysis of soil and water samples of growers, free of cost.
3. It advises concerned growers about the correct dose of fertilizers and requirements for irrigation.

Insurance facilities: The Tobacco Board facilitates group personal accident policies and barn insurance policies for the registered tobacco growers of Andhra Pradesh, Karnataka, Maharashtra and Orissa at competitive rates.

Financing Tobacco Growers

The Board helps get crop loans from banks and helps banks in recovery by routing sale proceeds through the concerned banks. It arranges additional loans at about 7% interest rate from nationalized banks for procuring inputs like coal, fertilizer, etc.

It has organized the setting up of four ATMS in different places of West Godavari district by ICICI bank, which is extending crop loans and input loans at 7% interest to growers, through these ATMs.

Trade participation in crop development: The Tobacco Board had successfully roped in some international tobacco merchants and domestic manufactures to take-up low productivity areas for agronomical development with a view to improving quality and thus promoting exports.

Awards to growers: The Tobacco Board honors the best growers for achieving higher yields every year as a step toward inculcating a spirit of competition among them.

You have no chance, put that in you pipe and smoke it.

Is it fair that governments understandingly increase the tax on cigarettes with almost every budget they pass? No doubt this happens all over the world. In Britain, in fact, cigarettes can't even be displayed on open shelves. They are stocked out of sight. But, the fact practically every Finance Minister does it doesn't detract from my question. You could actually say it makes it more pertinent.

Certainly Mummy, who is 97 agrees with me. Cigarettes are a pleasure she refuses to forego. Even though she hasn't been given one for 2 years or more, her memory, which can now play delightful tricks, has convinced her she's only just put one out. So far as she is concerned, she is remained a smoker and enjoys every puff she can get.

What's he done to fags. Mummy asked of Mr Jaittley's efforts on budget day, I could tell she dearly wanted to know. Increased the tax-six-fold, I said knowing that would rile her. It most certainly did. Hmm, she snorted or perhaps it was an expletive I dialed to hear. Well, tell him that won't put me off I'm going to carry on smoking till I snuff it.

Actually, it is sort defiance and determination that Finance Ministers bank upon when they sharply increase the tax on cigarettes. They may claim they are doing it because smoking is unhealthy. That is for our own good. But, if that were the case the logical thing to do would be to ban cigarettes altogether. Simply making a health hazard more expensive is inadequate protection. You could even say it is an irresponsible response.

It is when you look at the revenue expectation figures Finance Ministers assume in their budgets that you can clearly see they do not expect anyone to give up.

Mr Jaitley, for instance, hopes to garner an additional Rs 4,000 crore by kicking up excise duty from 11% to 72%. As Bill Clinton might have said it is the revenue stupid.

In fact, the blunt truth goes one critical, if obvious, step further Finance ministers know smokers won't give up and, therefore, when they increase taxes they are making money out of this addiction. I call that exploitation. But, when I put this point to Mr Jaitley in an interview it left him completely stumped. Of course, he did not agree. But, I have a further point to make consider this: the Jaitley budget has increased the excise on cigarettes six-fold but left that on bidis untouched. Yet, eight times more people smoke bidis than cigarettes. Now, what do you make of that.

There can be only two answers. Either Mr Jaitely cares more for the health of cigarette smokers, who are better off, than bidi smokers, who tend to be poor, or bidi smokers constitute a lobby that is so powerful Mr Jaitely dare not increase the excise. He knows he can not handle their wrath.

In fact, it is the second answer and Mr Jaitley was honest enough to say so. My predecessor tried it on bidis and had to retract in Parliament. I have his experience before me, he admitted. You do not come out with proposals that are bound to meet a road block at some stage.

Unfortunately, this does not work for Mummy, when I suggest she switch to bidis she dismissed the idea with a imperious wave of her hand. What about a hookah? I asked. No thank you, she shot back. Till stick to cigarettes and hereafter you can bloody well pay for them.

WORLD TOBACCO

About 100 countries produce tobacco, but the major producers are China, India, Brazil, United States, Turkey, Zimbabwe and Malawi, which together produce over 80% of the worlds' tobacco. China alone accounts for over 35% of world production, and thus variability of production in China directly affects variability of production figures at world level.

World area under tobacco was 3398 thousand hectares in 1961. It crossed 4 million hectares. By 1981 and 5.0 million by 1992. Started declining and came to 3,675 thousand hectares by 2007 (Table 1.5). Production on the other had increased from 3.57 million tons in 1961 to 6.2 million tons in 2007. Thereafter, hovered around this figure and touched 6.4 million tons (Table 1.5A). There are a number of tobacco varieties produced in the world-flue cured out of them occupies around. 68.70%. Burley for behind next covers hardly 12–13%. Details about the production of various types are as in (Table 1.5B). Major producer of FCV variety is China-nearly 56% Brazil comes next with 14% followed by India (7.4%). There are quite member of other countries in North/South America, Europe, Africa and Asia/Oceana which contribute their smaller shares (Table 1.5C).

During 2012, world FCV production is projected to increase marginally. Production in South America and Africa has declined due to various factors such as weather conditions and global demand-supply equations. Important FCV producing countries such as Brazil, Tanzania have produced lower crop. In all the remaining countries also the crop size is expected to decline except in USA and China. In India, the crop has declined because of incessant rains which caused production of more low grade leaf in Andhra Pradesh Except in NLS region where quality is reported to be good which is ripe to over ripe with medium to firm body

Table 1.5: Tobacco production (unmanufactured)

Countries	*Unit*	*2002*	*2003*	*2004*	*2005*	*2006*	*2007*
Albania	Tons	2600	1416	2100	1900	2000	900
Algeria	Tons	5847	5674	7600	6500	6889	6043
Argentina	Tons	132437	115837	157294	161064	144345	127740
Armenia	Tons	2714	1204	1100	500	171	268
Australia	Tons	9000	6461	3782	3605	4000	3346
Austria	Tons	300	332	234	247	304	400
Azerbaijan	Tons	3273	4685	6518	7135	4845	2914
Belarus	Tons						
Belgium	Tons	1200	1300	1221	777	209	158
Bosnia and Herzegovina	Tons	5173	3279	4246	4421	3916	3265
Brazil	Tons	670309	656200	921281	889426	900381	908679
Bulgaria	Tons	62250	61539	69569	58336	41956	41100
Canada	Tons	54550	46338	42430	43000	48525	44000
Chile	Tons	6976	7713	9321	9850	8349	8341
China	Tons	2454108	2262663	2411490	2685743	2746193	2397152
Colombia	Tons	26475	34458	32486	34940	20557	18109
Croatia	Tons	10905	9680	10293	9579	10851	12639
European Union	Tons	452321	450794	454062	428467	291076	282692
France	Tons	24329	25467	25568	22947	18880	15805
Georgia	Tons	2065	1384	1461	1094	300	100
Germany	Tons	11490	11625	10101	10888	8500	7700
Ghana	Tons	1350	1350	1350	2500	2500	2700
Greece	Tons	133000	136000	133937	124351	37405	29370
Hungary	Tons	11288	11437	11413	11385	9145	6300
India	Tons	550000	490000	549900	549100	552200	520000
Indonesia	Tons	192083	200875	165108	153470	146265	164851
Iran	Tons	27000	22195	12521	22180	15479	11600
Italy	Tons	122231	124985	117882	115983	96600	110000
Japan	Tons	58200	50662	52659	46800	37700	37800
Kazakhstan	Tons	15830	15898	14314	16000	14060	11030

Table 1.5: Tobacco production (unmanufactured) *(Contd.)*

Countries	*Unit*	*2002*	*2003*	*2004*	*2005*	*2006*	*2007*
Kenya	Tons	20000	17084	22000	25000	17605	11153
Kyrgyzstan	Tons	6154	8690	12988	13396	13361	14429
Macedonia	Tons	22044	21592	21140	27691	25036	22056
Malaysia	Tons	12404	13526	13850	11400	8900	6453
Mexico	Tons	21936	22437	21763	16122	19381	13008
Moldova	Tons	11806	6692	7900	6690	4850	3632
Morocco	Tons	6500	4035	2467	1888	2000	1890
Nigeria	Tons	17000	16000	15000	15000	14000	9000
Pakistan	Tons	94500	88200	86200	100500	112592	103240
Peru	Tons	9832	2466	1770	2230	2300	2350
Philippines	Tons	50174	52903	48308	45093	38368	34289
Poland	Tons	20728	22000	29065	33483	40512	39482
Portugal	Tons	5603	5735	5357	4749	2298	1311
Romania	Tons	16000	7900	7471	3682	1686	1128
Russia	Tons	260	80	140	80	10	10
Serbia	Tons					10808	11136
Slovakia	Tons	2020	1932	1298	1038	668	390
South Africa	Tons	33000	37400	22200	20000	17500	13000
South Korea	Tons	47549	35666	36380	35000	34000	32000
Spain	Tons	41525	40192	40596	40251	32563	29248
Switzerland	Tons	1462	1584	1320	1527	1176	870
Tajikistan	Tons	4081	744	2675	1609	1301	516
Thailand	Tons	77693	75290	68249	71953	65835	58562
Turkey	Tons	152856	112158	133913	135247	98137	74584
Turkmenistan	Tons	3000	3000	3000	3135	3500	3100
Ukraine	Tons	1600	1450	1100	490	340	160
USA	Tons	395134	364035	400012	292574	330169	357273
Uzbekistan	Tons	19000	19000	19000	20000	17602	19400
Venezuela	Tons	6504	7239	3677	3714	5035	5082
Vietnam	Tons	33200	31800	23400	25900	41900	31900
World	Tons	6517129	6028965	6590379	6757713	6598315	6186893

Table 1.5A: Area and production of tobacco in India and world

[Area (hect.) production in tons]

	India		World	
Year	*Area*	*Production*	*Area*	*Production*
2007	370,000	520,000	3,675,420 A	6,202,127 A
2006	372,800	552,200	3,850,735 A	6,642,977 A
2005	366,500	549,100	3,961,779 A	6,738,602 A
2004	369,700	549,900	3,880,473 A	6,534,041 A
2003	330,000	490,000	3,799,305 A	6,027,052 A
2002	350,000	550,000	3,924,206 A	6,515,821 A
2001	260,000	340,000	3,849,588 A	6,153,931 A
2000	433,400	520,000	4,169,891 A	6,691,906 A
1999	508,100	736,200	4,326,222 A	6,988,557 A
1998	464,000	646,000	4,447,697 A	6,937,122 A
1997	428,000	618,000	5,380,654 A	8,980,184 A
1996	394,000	535,200	4,649,761 A	7,407,222 A
1995	381,000	566,700	4,146,431 A	6,286,406 A
1994	384,800	562,900	4,242,745 A	6,477,594 A
1993	418,500	596,500	5,293,667 A	8,343,170 A
1992	427,000	584,400	5,319,972 A	8,330,385 A
1991	410,800	555,900	4,868,647 A	7,563,143 A
1990	413,100	551,600	4,648,967 A	7,137,437 A
1989	377,000	492,800	4,796,417 A	7,065,400 A
1988	318,000	367,400	4,527,657 A	6,839,755 A
1987	389,200	461,800	4,256,949 A	6,177,950 A
1986	397,000	441,200	4,273,688 A	6,007,986 A
1985	436,600	485,900	4,694,860 A	7,049,189 A
1984	439,700	492,500	4,204,665 A	6,554,452 A
1983	502,700	581,600	4,248,027 A	5,987,789 A
1982	443,800	520,100	4,541,214 A	6,948,556 A
1981	451,500	480,800	4,119,048 A	5,981,468 A
1980	425,400	438,500	3,897,572 A	5,258,295 A
1979	409,300	453,800	4,095,796 A	5,434,067 A
1978	504,400	493,600	4,565,925 A	5,987,668 A
1977	432,400	418,800	4,439,484 A	5,582,693 A
1976	368,200	349,800	4,383,883 A	5,732,973 A
1975	380,600	363,100	4,131,474 A	5,418,558 A
1974	461,500	462,100	3,933,032 A	5,299,463 A
1973	444,900	372,200	3,912,073 A	4,949,319 A
1972	458,300	418,900	3,922,702 A	4,934,530 A
1971	446,900	361,900	3,716,936 A	4,567,459 A

Table 1.5A: Area and production of tobacco in India and world *(Contd.)*

Area (hect.) production in tons

	India		*World*	
Year	*Area*	*Production*	*Area*	*Production*
1970	437,900	337,100	3,770,286 A	4,663,176 A
1969	439,800	361,000	3,850,104 A	4,675,245 A
1968	423,500	368,700	3,772,567 A	4,766,053 A
1967	423,500	353,400	3,868,635 A	4,891,506 A
1966	377,000	293,000	3,824,275 A	4,591,428 A
1965	394,000	346,000	3,793,646 A	4,355,632 A
1964	441,000	360,000	3,881,609 A	4,660,809 A
1963	405,000	341,000	3,898,915 A	4,265,315 A
1962	418,000	339,000	3,558,852 A	3,935,808 A
1961	401,000	307,000	3,398,158 A	3,573,815 A

A , May include official, semi-official or estimated data.

and has distinct chemistry blocks. In India, 2011 Karnataka auctions were concluded on 10th April 2012 with a marketed quantity of 104.29 million kg. Where as in AP, 2012 crops is estimated to be about 160 million kg with good quality leaf except in first two harvests. Country-wise graph details are as below:

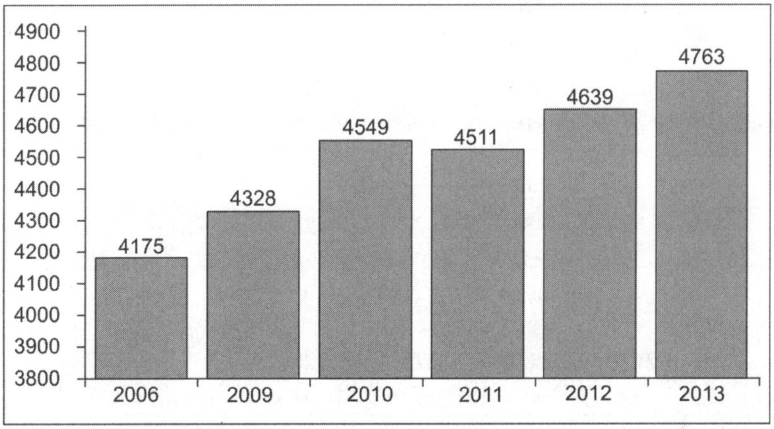

World FCV tobacco production in million kg

Brazil: In 2012, Brazilian FCV crop is expected to be around 587 million kg down by 20% as against 708 million kg during 2011 due to lack of rain and high temperatures which have affected the quality in a big way and yield to some extent. Harvesting is complete and the marketing slow in tune with higher expectations by farmers. Most of the buyers have agreed to pay 4% more in average over the prices paid last year. As per the latest updates, the average pices are higher by 26%. Increase in prices is partly cushioned (12%) by declining Brazilian Real against US Dollar. Orders for 2012 Brazilian FCV remain low on quality concerns.

Table 1.5B: World flue cured production by crop year and country-wise

Million kg (green)

Region/country	*2006*	*2007*	*2008*	*2009*	*2010*	*2011(E)*	*2012(P)*	*+/–*
North and Central America and Caribbean								
USA	210	220	219	236	222	170	227	57
Canada	25	16	10	11	22	22	23	1
Others	6	6	6	4	5	4	5	1
Subtotal	241	242	235	251	249	196	255	59
South America								
Brazil	632	643	608	608	567	708	587	–133
Argentina	81	85	82	81	95	87	80	–7
Others	21	21	23	22	20	27	20	–7
Subtotal	734	749	713	711	682	817	687	–135
Europe and CIS								
EU	121	125	130	140	135	129	116	–13
CIS	27	16	20	18	20	20	18	–2
Subtotal	148	141	150	158	155	149	134	–15
Africa and Middle East								
Zimbabwe	55	73	49	60	120	132	13450	3
Tanzania	48	49	51	57	89	122	90	–32
Malawi	30	23	24	21	24	24	12	–12
Zambia	23	19	14	17	21	27	25	–2
South Africa	13	10	7	8	8	10	10	0
Uganda	10	11	16	18	18	20	20	0
Kenya	N.A	11	14	16	23	22	24	2
Others	50	36	27	21	22	18	32	14
Subtotal	229	232	203	218	325	375	348	–27
Asia and Oceania								
India	242	260	275	320	335	278	260	–18
Bangladesh	49	57	53	63	100	87	90	3
Indonesia	37	41	42	41	46	48	50	2
Philippines	22	25	23	33	42	50	50	0
Thailand	15	15	15	15	18	18	18	0
China	2050	1950	2300	2350	2461	2341	2569	228
Others	181	163	168	168	136	136	135	–1
Subtotal	2596	2511	2876	2990	3138	2958	3172	214
World total	**3949**	**3875**	**4175**	**4328**	**4549**	**4500**	**4596**	**–96**

E: Estimate; P: Provisional.
Source: Universal Crop Reports dated February 2, 2012, Tobacco Magazines, Alliance One Crop Reports, Internet Data.

Table 1.7.5C: Production of tobacco

(Tons)

Countries	*1994-1996*	*1999-2001*	*2003-2005*	*2006*	*2007*	*2008*	*2009*
Argentina	86,390	108,673	133,102	165,000	170,000	170,000	
Bangladesh	38,917	33,667	38,000	38,000	39,180	40,248	
Brazil	482,755	592,160	822,302	900,381	908,679	851,058	862,355
Canada	71,503	60,610	43,923	43,000	44,000	44,000	
China	2,609,480	2,466,997	2,453,297	2,746,193	2,397,152	2,836,725	3,001,725
Greece	141,313	139,461	131,429	37,252	29,370	28,000	28,000
India	554,933	532,067	529,667	552,200	520,000	520,000	
Indonesia	140,443	162,000	173,151	177,895	164,851	169,668	
Italy	125,220	128,925	119,617	110,000	110,000	110,000	
Japan	69,441	62,043	50,040	38,000	37,800	38,500	36,600
Korea, Democratic People's Republic of	61,667	62,667	64,467	65,000	63,000	63,000	
Korea, Republic of	81,189	63,076	35,682	34,000	35,500	35,500	
Malawi	123,454	88,591	98,032	115,000	118,000	160,238	
Pakistan	87,018	100,533	91,633	112,600	103,240	107,765	
Philippines	61,820	49,733	48,767	38,368	34,289	32,466	36,383
South Africa	20,530	31,267	26,533	17,500	20,000	20,000	
Thailand	53,133	72,500	68,000	70,000	70,000	70,000	
Turkey	205,537	196,178	127,106	98,137	74,584	93,403	85,000
United States of America	660,947	504,584	352,207	329,918	357,273	363,103	373,440
Zambia	4,580	9,916	38,519	4,800	48,000	48,000	
World	**6,724,434**	**6,612,629**	**6,432,650**	**6,615,424**	**6,264,243**	**6,724,338**	**6,911,396**

Zimbabwe: In 2011/12, crop was harvested totally and sales were conducted between 15th February and 7th August 2012 for sale of the said tobacco. Even though the target is 150 million kg, the crop size is 141.67 million kg only, mainly due to long dry spells prevailed in Northern part. However, this is 9 million kg more than previous year.

Bangladesh: The production in Bangladesh has increased marginally to 90 million kg this year. Marketing of 201 crops is completed and the processing of the same is underway. The average grower prices-realized is US$ 1.76 per kg.

USA: During 2012, the crops is expected to increase to 227 million kg from that of 170 million kg during 2011. Most of the flue-cured buyers have contracted volumes for the 2012 crops and the seedbeds sowing are in progress. Prevailing below average soil moisture conditions are a cause for worry but the same are expected to normalize before the scheduled planting commences.

China: During 2012, FCV tobacco crops is projected to be at the level of 2569 million kg, i.e. about 228 million kg more as compared to 2011. Coupled with 115 million kg of Burley, this is going to be one of the biggest tobacco crop sizes for China in the last 5 years. Leaf development is good due to wide spread rainfall received in all tobacco growing zones. However, higher than normal rainfall has resulted in higher incidence of pests and disease. The average farm price is expected to increase by 20% compared to last year.

Argentina: During 2012, crop size is estimated to be 80 million kg 10% which is lower when compared to 2011 due to extreme difficulties in reaching price agreements by growers and dealers. This led to a cautious approach by farmer associations and they could succeed in getting a 9% hike in average price for this crop over last year which almost all the buyers have honored. The sowings for 2013 crop are in progress and were completed to the extent of 80%. The amount of seedbeds will be similar to last year, nevertheless farmers are waiting for the outcome of negotiations with national government on the special tobacco fund to decide on the area they will plant.

Malawi: During 2012, crop in Malawi is projected to be 19 million kg against 24 million kg during 2011. Revised estimate suggest that the crop will be in the range of 12 million kg. Overall crop quality is better than last year though yields are marginally lower in some of the regions due to prolonged dry spells. Estimated cost of production for FCV tobacco is about US$2.73 per kg. Sales commenced on the 26th of March 2012 amidst uproar over low prices. Marketing is almost completing by the end of July 2012 and the farmer has realized an average price of US$ 3.23 per kg as against a season ending average of US$ 2.12 per kg realized during 2011. This is partly due to lower crop produced during the current year in neighboring Zimbabwe.

Tanzania: During 2012, crop in Tanzania expected to be around 90 million kg down by 32 million kg as against 122 million kg during 2011. Most of the regions have experienced shortage rainfall with prolonged hot dry spells from late January to middle of February. Crop is graded and made ready by all farmers. Marketing for the 2012 crops is complete to the extent of 20% with an average price of US$ 1.81 per kg as against season ending average of US$ 1.61 during last year.

Canada: FCV production has more or less remained at the same level as that of last year with 23 Mkg of production during this year.

Indonesia: The production of FCV Tobacco during 2012 is projected to be 50 million kg which is more by 2 million kg when compared to 48 million kg produced during last year. Production of Burley is set to increase to 3.5 million kg this year up from 1.35 million kg of last year. Harvesting is in progress and most favorable weather conditions prevailed cross the country may positively impact the quality as well as output of 2012 crop.

Kenya: FCV production during this year stood at 24 million kg which is slightly higher when compared to 22 million kg produced in 2011. The crop quality has significantly improved besides being NTRM free. The weather has been extremely hot and dry which has a slowed and in some cases stopped the markets. Marketing of 2012 crop has concluded.

WHO Agreement

In keeping with the WHO agreement, while there is short decline in the world while area under tobacco, the pattern, however, varies widely from country to country. Major producer USA has reduced production from 0.66 million to 0.35 million tons.

There are, however, countries like Thailand, Tanzania, Pakistan, Nicaragna and Indonesia where there is a substantial increase in the production. Production in India a major producer has remained more or less constant as shown below:

Table-I
Leading tobacco producing countries-2002

Country	Production (metric tons)
China	2,161,697
India	599,400
Brazil	493,100
USA	408,200
Zimbawe	208,988
Turkey	178,742

Table-II
Leading tobacco exporting countries-2002

Country	Production (metric tons)
Brazil	350,000
Zimbabwe	195,977
USA	182,000
India	123,185
China	113,594
Malawi	101,250
Turkey	100,900

Most countries have agreed to WHOs recommendations on cohtrolling tobacco consumption. However, authoritative estimates of tobacco consumption indicate that Europe and the US, which now account for approximately 39% and 18% of tobacco consumption, respectively, are already showing deceleration unconsumption while Asia is registering a rise.

> According to WHO estimates, there are 1.1 billion smokers in the world, and this number is expected to rise to 1.64 billion by 2025. About 4 million people die each year from tobacco use, and if current trends continue, this number will escalate to 10 million by the early 2030s, with 70% of those deaths occurring in developing countries. Exports say tobacco will soon become the major cause of deaths worldwide, causing more deaths than HIV, material mortality, automobile accident, homicides, and suicides combined.

Future Course

According to the FAO, by 2010, tobacco consumption may experience some changes:

1. Tobacco consumption in rich countries may decline by about 0.2% annually. On the other hand, consumption in the developing countries may go up 3.1% annually. Tobacco consumption in the developing countries may increase at an annual growth rate of 1.7% between 1988 and 2010.
2. The increase in world tobacco demand in the developing countries may be mainly due to increase in population and income growth.
3. World tobacco demand is expected to increase to 7,100 million kg by 2010 (an increase by 29% in developed countries and 71% in developing countries. In recent times, the research efforts of Central Tobacco Research Institute (CTRI) have significantly contributed to the improvements in productivity, quality and overall production of FCV tobacco in different States.

The Tobacco Institute of India (TII) has urged the government to formulate a pragmatic and equitable taxation policy to reduce the disparity in the rates between cigarettes and other tobacco products. The present taxation policy is highly discriminatory, with 85% of the tax burden falling on the cigarettes sector, which accounts for only 15% of domestic consumption. The shift to lightly taxed and cheaper products has led to an increase in overall tobacco consumption, thereby defeating the social objectives of tobacco control.

World Flue-cured Exports and Prices

Brazil, USA and China, the world's leading exporters of FCV tobaccos had increased their exports significantly in 2011. In the case of India, the exports of FCV tobacco during 2011 have declined by 10% in quantity terms. Exports of USA have started looking up with its Asian customers picking up most of its leaf. Fifty percentage of its entire production is being exported. Even though the export volumes by leading exporter countries could be compiled, no authentic or at least reliable industry data on average export prices is available (Tables 1.6 and 1.6A).

Table 1.6: Estimated flue-cured exports (by calendar year)

(In million kg)

Country	*2003*	*2004*	*2005*	*2006*	*2007*	*2008*	*2009*	*2010*	*2011*
Brazil	381	478	501	466	535	516	521	413	455
India	86	103	112	128	138	145	165	159	144
China	135	130	105	101	108	105	100	91	100
USA	84	75	68	96	87	101	107	109	129

Table 1.6A: Global FCV export prices

(In US$/kg)

Country	*2003*	*2004*	*2005*	*2006*	*2007*	*2008*	*2009*	*2010*	*2011*
USA	7.36	7.31	6.35	6.47	6.66	7.25	7.94	7.23	7.05
Brazil	2.28	2.92	2.71	3.01	3.19	3.98	4.70	5.64	4.76
Argentina	2.46	2.74	2.84	–	4.11	4.64	–	–	–
China	1.37	–	1.64	1.95	2.12	2.19	4.14	4.84	5.00
India	1.54	1.73	1.76	1.90	2.20	2.90	3.61	3.65	3.78
Zimbabwe	3.21	3.25	3.21	3.06	3.18	3.22	4.80	4.68	4.76

Source: Various tobacco magazines and Tobacco Board.

World Flue-cured Stocks

Latest information on world flue-cured stocks is not readily available, as Universal Corporation has not released its demand and supply report since 2008. As per the industry sources, the global uncommitted FCV tobacco stocks at the end of 2011 are in the order of 125 million kg which have come down to about 65 million kg by the end of June 2012 whereas the same are projected to decrease to 35 million kg by the end of 2012.

Global Farm Prices of FCV Tobacco

During 2011, global farm prices for FCV tobaccos have declined except in USA and Canada, as seen from the reports of the markets where ever the sales were concluded. The prices which were exorbitant during the previous 3 years have started downtrends owning to the price correction by International merchants/manufacturers, excess production in Brazil and African countries and also the reported understanding between the major merchant groups. But, the same are on increasing trend during 2012 in almost all the ongoing/concluded markets which is attributed to balancing out of demand-supply scenario and reduction in uncommitted stocks (Tables 1.7 and 1.8).

Table 1.7: Global FCV tobacco grower prices

(In US$ per kg)

Country	*2002*	*2003*	*2004*	*2005*	*2006*	*2007*	*2008*	*2009*	*2010*	*2011*	*2012(P)*
USA	4.02	4.08	4.07	3.30	3.42	3.48	3.92	3.86	3.75	3.98	NA
Zimbabwe	2.27	2.25	2.00	1.61	2.01	2.34	3.24	3.01	2.89	2.73	3.67
Malawi	1.86	1.60	1.60	1.71	1.56	1.93	2.81	2.91	2.60	2.12	3.23
Brazil	1.18	1.19	1.43	1.76	1.92	2.13	3.24	2.79	3.69	3.30	4.16
Canada	2.54	2.96	3.25	3.10	3.07	3.53	3.48	NA	4.55	4.62	NA
Argentina	1.92^ (0.83*)	1.85^ (1.16*)	1.90^ (1.37*)	1.74^ (1.25*)	2.05^ (1.45*)	2.25^ (1.63*)	2.26^ (1.89*)	2.53^ (2.44*)	2.54 NA	2.41 NA	2.63 NA
Tanzania	0.58	0.72	0.82	0.83	0.88	1.01	1.20	2.14	2.40	1.61	1.81
India	0.74	0.76	0.84	0.92	1.03	1.30	2.11	2.20	1.85	1.83	1.75

^ Includes and *Excludes Govt. subsidy of about US$ 1.20 to 0.57/kg. P- Provisional; NA-Not Available.

Table 1.8: Soil region-wise-grower prices of FCV tobacco in India

(In US$ per kg)

Region	*2002*	*2003*	*2004*	*2005*	*2006*	*2007*	*2008*	*2009*	*2010*	*2011*	*2012(P)*
KLS	0.90	0.82	1.05	1.08	1.26	1.50	2.46	2.34	2.01	1.88	*
NLS	0.82	0.87	0.91	0.98	1.26	1.35	2.20	2.75	2.31	2.15	1.87
SLS	0.65	0.72	0.75	0.82	0.93	1.12	1.73	2.05	1.53	1.68	1.58
BCS	0.64	0.67	0.70	0.77	0.94	1.12	1.81	2.02	1.33	1.32	1.50

* Marketing for KLS 2012 crop not yet commenced. P- Provisional.

In India during 2012, AP marketing season, the average prices realized by growers (as on 08.08.2012) were lesser in all soil regions except in NLS and SLS when compared to the final prices during last year. Even the gains in SLS and NLS regions were cushioned by declining rupee against dollar.

In Zimbabwe during 2012, tobacco selling season concluded on 07.08.2012 and a total quantity of about 141.67 million kg as against 132.4 million kg marketed during previous year. The average unit realization by the farmers was US$3.53 per kg in auctions and US$3.75 per kg under contract making the total average realization

US$3.67 per kg. This is as against the average prices of US$2.42, US$2.97 and US$2.73 per kg respectively realized during 2011. The uncommitted stocks out of 2012 Zimbabwe crop are projected to be almost zero.

In Brazil, most of the buyers have agreed to pay 4% more in average for 2012 crop over the prices paid last year. As per the latest updates, the average prices are higher by 26%. Increase in prices is partly cushioned (12%) by declining Brazilian Real against US Dollar. Orders for 2012 Brazilian FCV remain low on quality concerns.

In Canada, all FCV tobaccos are currently grown under contract as compared to traditional auction system that has been in place for the last 50 years.

In USA, the average grower prices for FCV tobacco in 2011 are estimated to be higher at US$ 3.98 per kg when compared to US$ 3.75 per kg realized during 2010 and the same is partly attributed to lower global output of flavor tobacco during 2011.

Prices for all other types of tobaccos in India, except bidi tobacco have marginally increased during 2011/12 due to the reduction in crop sizes world over (Tables 1.8A to C).

Table 1.8A: Exports of tobacco and tobacco product

Item	*April-August, 2013*			*April-August, 2012*		
	Qty. tons	*Value*		*Qty. M. tons*	*Value*	
		Rs. Cr.	*M.US$*		*Rs. Cr.*	*M.US$*
Unmanufactured tobacco	93635	1832.74	314.85	93583	1493.08	272.63
Tobacco products	11478	415.27	71.34	13702	435.42	79.50
Total	105113	2248.01	386.19	107290	1928.60	352.13
Change (%)	–2	17	10	13	27	4
FCV	67587	1478.90	254.06	70411	1228.37	224.28
Change (%)	–4	20	13	22	35	10

Table 1.8B: Exports of tobacco products

Products	*August, 2013*		*August, 2012*		*April-August, 2013*		*April-August, 2012*	
	Qty.	*Value*	*Qty.*	*Value*	*Qty.*	*Value*	*Qty.*	*Value*
Cigarettes	802	4221.65	580	1996.05	3806	17194.04	3512	13529.55
Beedies	24	258.23	54	400.85	144	1185.16	118	845.85
Hookkah tobacco paste	524	502.39	1303	979.40	3315	2753.99	4814	3666.82
Chewing tobacco/zarada	699	4749.11	792	4870.75	3238	18338.88	4325	23498.25
Cut tobacco	148	348.12	296	618.29	955	19988.05	893	1871.80
Snuff and others	0	1.15	3	9.01	20	66.74	40	129.63
Total	**2197**	**10080.65**	**3028**	**8874.35**	**11478**	**41526.86**	**13702**	**43541.90**

Table 1.8C: Region wise exports of unmanufactured tobacco

(Qty: Tons; Value: Rs Crores)

Region	*April-August, 2013*				*2011-12*				*2010-11*			*Change (%)*		
	Qty	%	*Val.*	%	*Qty*	%	*Val.*	%	*Qty*	%	*Val.*	%	*Qty*	*Val.*
West Europe	25882	27.64	58762.27	32.06	75332	37	1282.11	41	74651	35	1222.93	38	1	5
East Europe	14375	15.35	29532.48	16.11	27916	14	448.36	15	28125	13	427.45	13	–1	5
Middle East	11805	12.61	17396.19	7.49	13531	7	133.66	4	13514	6	131.24	4	0	2
South and South East Asia	20911	22.33	44460.84	24.26	39247	19	622.72	20	43716	21	673.9	21	–10	–8
Africa	12226	13.06	21414.28	11.68	27521	14	386.53	13	36338	17	519.36	16	–24	–26
North and South Americas	8146	8.70	11024.06	6.02	17660	9	174.57	6	13456	7	167.52	5	31	4
Australia	290	0.31	684.16	0.37	2087	1	42.26	1	2773	1	49.99	2	–25	–15
Total	**93635**	**100**	**183274.28**	**100**	**203294**	**100**	**3090.21**	**100**	**212573**	**100**	**3192.39**	**100**	**–4**	**–3**

PROJECTIONS OF PRODUCTION OF TOBACCO LEAF

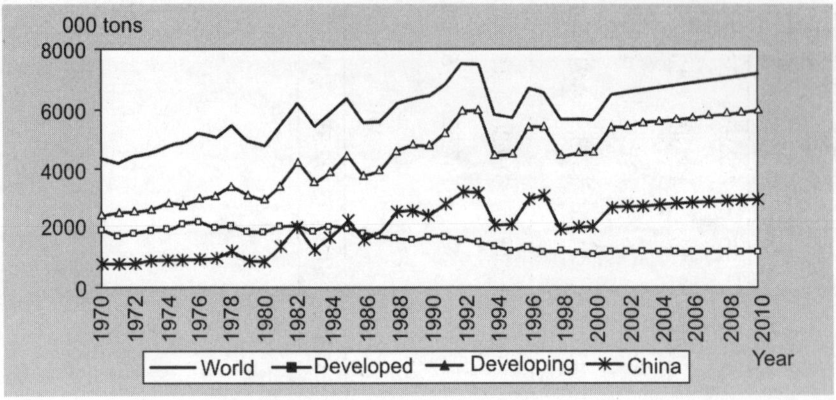

Tobacco leaf - production trends, 1970-2010 (baseline scenario) (dry weight)

The volatility in world production is mainly due to China, which exhibits substantial volatility in the area used for tobacco cultivation. China is expected to account for over 40% of world production in 2010.

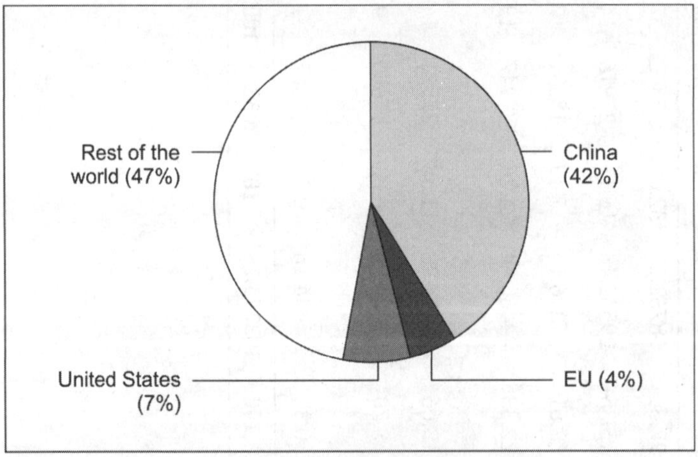

Tobacco leaf - production share, 2010 (baseline scenario)

After reaching a maximum level of over 1.8 million tons in the early 1980s, production of tobacco leaf in the developed countries declined to 1.6 million tons in the early 1990s and further to 1.3 million tons in 1998. This contraction is expected to continue to about 1.1 million tons in 2010 (Table 1.9) in the baseline scenario.

In developing countries, however, tobacco leaf production continues to increase, thus expanding their share in world production from about 76 % in 1991 to 87% million tons in 2010. China is projected to remain the world's largest producer with 2.6 to 2.9 million tons in 2010, well above India with 0.68 million tons and Brazil with 0.58 million tons. Malawi and Zimbabwe, although major exporters, have much lower production levels and are projected to produce about 0.13 and 0.21 million tones, respectively.

Table 1.9: Tobacco leaf production-actual and projected (scenarios-baseline and policy) (dry weight)

(000 tons)

	Actual			
	1970-72	*1980-82*	*1990-92*	*1997-99*
World	**4 269.4**	**5 455.3**	**6 936.2**	**5 938.3**
Developed	**1 797.6**	**1 959.5**	**1 659.0**	**1 178.6**
North America	*815.9*	*882.7*	*745.0*	*593.8*
United States	729.7	795.5	682.7	536.6
Europe	*544.6*	*648.3*	*602.5*	*418.8*
EU	248.9	320.3	397.7	278.9
Other Europe	*295.7*	*328.0*	*204.8*	*139.9*
Area of the former USSR	*249.0*	*258.6*	*55.2*	*85.3*
Oceania	*19.4*	*15.0*	*11.7*	*6.3*
Other developed	168.7	155.0	94.4	74.4
Developing	**2 471.8**	**3 495.8**	**5 282.3**	**4 759.6**
Africa	*157.7*	*218.8*	*362.0*	*391.3*
Malawi	23.8	49.1	109.3	102.5
Zimbabwe	56.0	88.7	156.1	174.7
Latin America	*489.7*	*652.8*	*679.3*	*714.4*
Brazil	225.4	357.3	430.6	450.6
Near East	*203.7*	*237.8*	*312.8*	*268.3*
Turkey	151.1	181.2	261.4	210.5
Far East	*1 620.7*	*2 386.2*	*3 927.9*	*3 385.6*
China	755.2	1 413.6	2 780.4	2 345.6
India	335.4	431.8	507.6	514.1
Indonesia	62.6	92.1	122.5	108.4

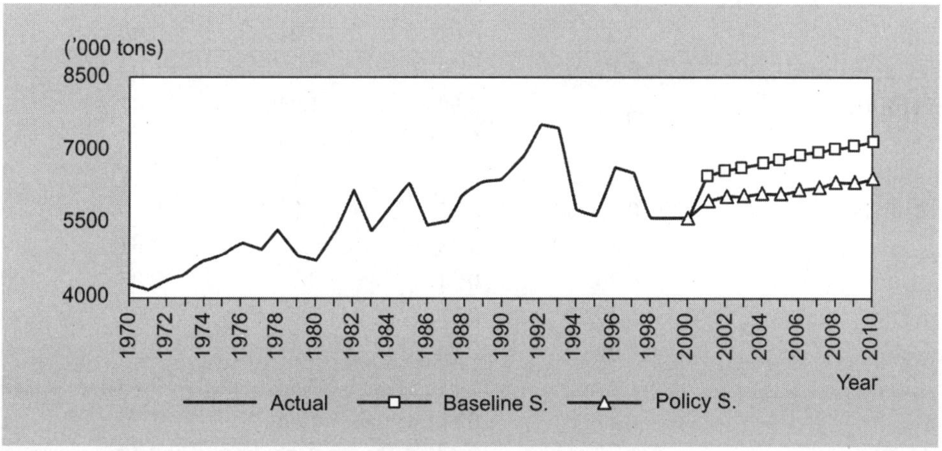

Tobacco leaf production, world, 1970–2010 (scenarios-baseline and policy) (dry weight)

In the policy scenario, world production of tobacco leaf is projected to be significantly lower, reaching 6.1 million tons in 2005 and 6.4 million tons in 2010, or about 7.5% lower than in the baseline scenario. These projections imply that production in 2010 will remain below the high levels of the 1990s.

Yields and Area Under Tobacco Production

Tobacco yields (production per hectare) are determined mostly by technological factors and have increased slightly over time with the exception of cases, such as China, where the expansion of production into new, less fertile, areas has reduced average yields. Price effects on yields are much smaller and for all practical purposes can be ignored in an exercise of this kind. Therefore, yields are assumed to increase modestly in the period to 2010 at a rate determined from past trends. Yields are projected to increase in developed countries from 2.2 tons/hectare in 1998 to 2.3 tons/hectare in 2010 and in the developing countries from 1.6 tons/hectare in 1998 to 1.7 tons/hectare in 2010.

The total area used for tobacco production is projected to change little. A small decline is expected in developed countries and a small increase in developing

Table 1.9A: Tobacco leaf area harvested-actual and projected (scenarios-baseline and policy)

(Million hectares)

	Area actual				
	1970-72	*1980-82*	*1990-92*	*1997-99*	*2000*
World	**3.80**	**4.18**	**4.99**	**4.77**	**4.17**
Developed	**1.16**	**1.19**	**0.91**	**0.70**	**0.60**
North America	*0.39*	*0.42*	*0.34*	*0.32*	*0.22*
United States	0.35	0.38	0.31	0.30	0.19
Europe	*0.47*	*0.49*	*0.41*	*0.27*	*0.27*
EU	0.18	0.20	0.21	0.15	0.14
Other Europe	*0.29*	*0.29*	*0.20*	*0.12*	*0.12*
Area of the former USSR	*0.18*	*0.18*	*0.10*	*0.06*	*0.07*
Oceania	*0.01*	*0.01*	*0.01*	*0.00*	*0.00*
Other developed	0.11	0.09	0.05	0.04	0.04
Developing	**2.64**	**2.99**	**4.08**	**4.07**	**3.58**
Africa	*0.23*	*0.25*	*0.33*	*0.38*	*0.36*
Malawi	0.05	0.07	0.12	0.12	0.11
Zimbabwe	0.05	0.05	0.07	0.10	0.09
Latin America	*0.51*	*0.58*	*0.51*	*0.61*	*0.53*
Brazil	0.25	0.31	0.30	0.35	0.32
Near East	*0.40*	*0.27*	*0.36*	*0.35*	*0.35*
Turkey	0.34	0.20	0.31	0.29	0.29
Far East	*1.49*	*1.89*	*2.88*	2.73	2.33
China	0.41	0.81	1.84	1.70	1.30
India	0.45	0.44	0.42	0.45	0.46

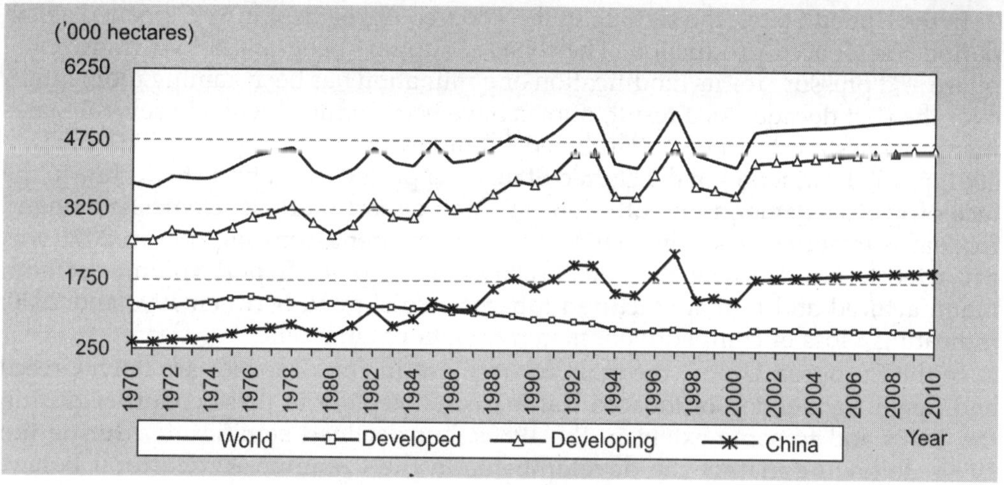

Area under tobacco, 1970-2010 (baseline scenario)

countries. As shown in Table 1.9A, the area under tobacco production in the developed countries is expected to decline slightly from 0.7 million hectares in 1998 to 0.68 million hectares in 2010. On the other hand, in developing countries, the area under tobacco is projected to increase slightly from 4.07 million hectares in 1998 to 4.57 million hectares in 2010 in the baseline scenario and remain at 4.08 million hectares in 2010 in the policy scenario.

Prospects for Tobacco Production in Developed Countries

The major developed country producers are the United States, the EU, some other countries of Europe (such as Bulgaria) and some countries of the area of the former USSR. Trends in tobacco supply in developed countries in the baseline and the policy scenario are shown in the below Figure.

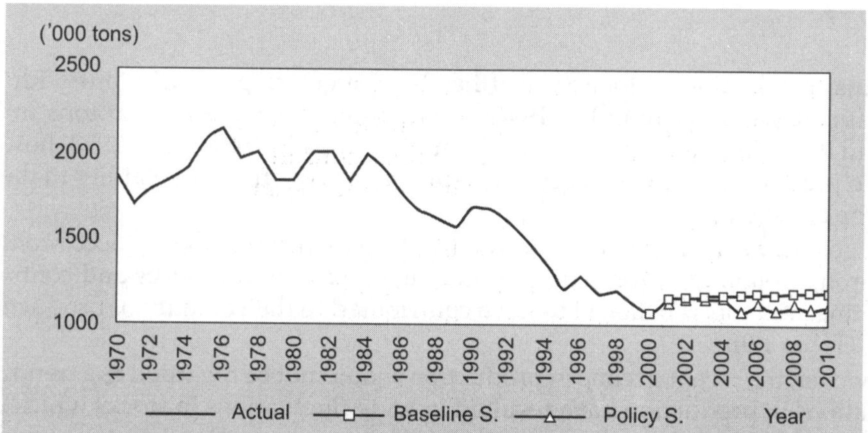

Tobacco leaf production, developed countries, 1970-2010 (scenarios-baseline and policy) (dry weight)

In the United States, the signing of the Tobacco Agreement in 1997 opened a new period for tobacco production. The tobacco support program is in a transitional phase and pressure for its modification or elimination has been gaining momentum over the past decade. As a result, quotas have been reduced while in several States the quota system has been abandoned following referenda held in 2001 (USDA, 2001, p. 16). Production in the United States is expected to continue to decline in the face of weaker demand on both domestic and export markets. Domestic demand for leaf is expected to decline since domestic cigarette consumption in 2001 was projected to be 2% lower than 2000 (USDA, 2001, p. 4). Export volumes of both manufactured and unmanufactured tobacco also slipped between 1990 and 2000, indicating a loss of competitiveness in international markets.

In the European Union, the main tobacco producing countries are Italy, Greece and Spain. Production of tobacco leaf increased rapidly in these countries during the 1970s and to some extent in the 1980s, but declined significantly during the 1990s, following mainly the developments in the Common Agricultural Policy. Under the policies in place at present, tobacco production in the EU is expected to continue to decline while further changes in tobacco support policies may be expected to reduce tobacco production even more.

Production in other European countries and the area of the former USSR is recovering to pre-reform levels. Some of these countries, such as Bulgaria and Bosnia, have been major tobacco producers and exporters in the past but their production contracted severely during the transition period in the 1990s. With the normalization of market conditions, production may be expected to continue to recover in these countries.

Production of tobacco leaf in other developed countries, such as Japan and Australia, is expected to follow the negative trends of the 1990s.

Prospects for Tobacco Production in Developing Countries

The developing countries account for 80% of world production of tobacco leaf and are projected to increase their share to 87% in 2010. China remains by far the major producer in the world.

China

In China, production of tobacco leaf has been increasing rapidly, but with wide fluctuations, particularly in the 1990s. Production reached 3 million tons in 1991, up from 0.8 million tons in 1971 and 1.5 million tons in 1981. Since 1993, however, tobacco production has been highly volatile mainly because of volatility in the area used for production.

The government has effective control over tobacco through the Tobacco Monopoly and through planning production, contracting areas, setting prices and controlling marketing, and this is believed to have contributed to the volatility of production in China (Table 1.9B).

However, the recent decline in production should not be regarded as a trend, since fluctuations in production have resulted in wide fluctuations in stocks which at the beginning of 1999 were standing more than 50% above normal levels but have declined significantly since then. Thus, although production in next few years may remain low, it will most probably return to normal trends in the medium term.

Table 1.9B: Area and production on tobacco in China

Year	*Area*	*Production*
	Million hectares	*Million tons farm weight*
1993	2.09	3.45
1994	1.49	2.24
1995	1.47	2.31
1996	1.85	2.23
1997	2.35	4.25
1998	1.36	2.36
1999	1.60	2.60

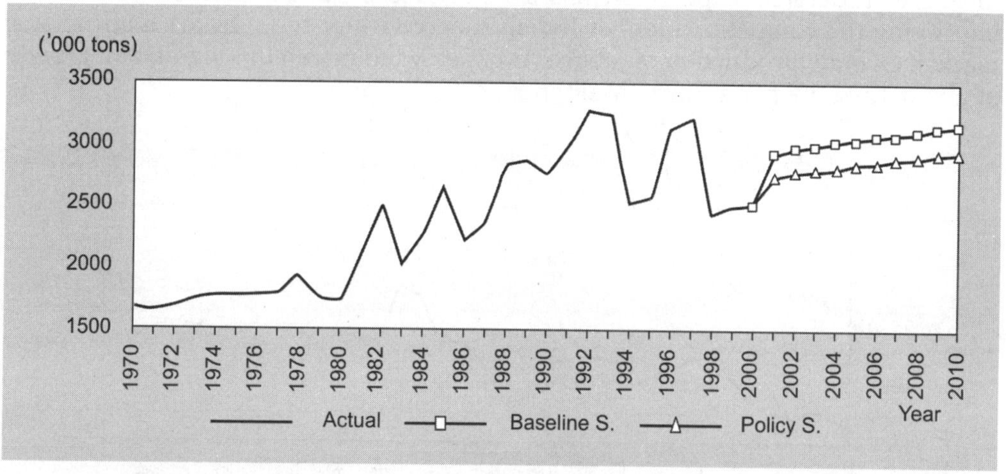

Tobacco leaf production, China, 1970-2010 (scenarios-baseline and policy) (dry weight)

Demand for tobacco leaf by cigarette manufacturers in China is declining (by as much as 30%) due to the introduction of new processing technologies and new manufacturing equipment in cigarette production. Thus, the pattern of production during the 1990s indicates that in the period to 2010 the growth rates in tobacco leaf production would be substantial, but would remain modest compared to historical rates.

Other Developing Countries

Among the rest of the developing countries, India is the most significant, producing over half a million tons of tobacco leaf in dry weight annually during the 1990s. Brazil, Turkey, Zimbabwe, Malawi are also important producers. Trends in supply from developing countries are presented in below.

In 1998, India grew 0.46 million hectares of tobacco, around 0.25% of the total cropped area, and produced about 0.64 million tons. Non-cigarette tobacco varieties, such as those used for bidi, account for 75% of total production. Production of tobacco has been encouraged by State Governments by providing subsidized inputs, price and market support and export promotion. Farmers, also, favor tobacco cultivation as it generally yields higher returns than other crops, although costs are also higher. However, marketing of non-Virginia tobacco has been a problem for farmers, while the introduction of the auction system by the Tobacco Board for Virginia types has fetched better prices for farmers and has led to excess supply of Virginia type tobacco. As a result of the above it seems easier for farmers to reduce production of non-cigarette types (such as bidi) than Virginia types by shifting to other alternative cash crops. Thus, the potential for shifting from tobacco to alternative cash crops appears limited and would be likely to disturb the economic conditions of tobacco-cultivating households.

On the basis of the above observations, under the present policy regime, the area under tobacco is likely to grow only modestly although the area under Virginia and burley tobacco may continue to increase. Yields are expected to accelerate because there is considerable scope for increases in productivity and for cost reduction, thus improving the competitiveness of Indian tobacco (filter type) in the international market. Overall, production of tobacco is expected to maintain a significant growth of about 1.5–2.0% per annum (Malhotra, 2000).

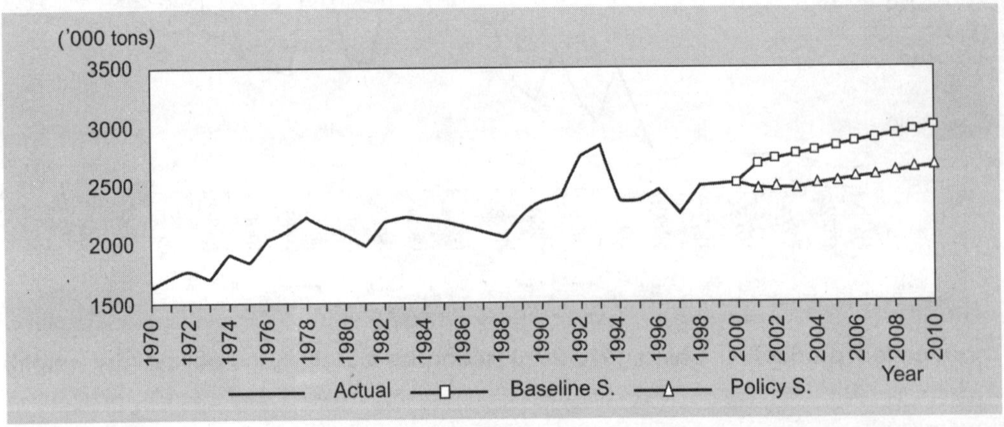

Tobacco leaf production, developing countries, 1970-2010 (scenarios-baseline and policy) (dry weight)

In Latin America, the main producers are Brazil and Argentina. In Brazil, strong growth in production in the 1970s (4.7% per annum) was followed by lower growth rates (1.9 and 2.7% per annum in the 1980s and 1990s, respectively). Given that demand in its main trading partners (the United States and Europe) may decline substantially, growth rates in the medium term are expected to moderate. However, there are few alternative crops available to farmers, and also, as the tobacco industry has invested heavily in tobacco production, there is little prospect for tobacco land to be switched to other crops. Overall, a growth rate a little lower than in the past is expected.

Argentina's tobacco production is much smaller then Brazil's but after some decline in the 1980s. It now exhibits strong growth. In fact, output growth in the 1990s exceeded expectations, due to the introduction of burley and Virginia types in areas where previously dark tobacco was grown and to the strengthening demand for exports. Given that the country has limited cash crop alternatives, low production costs and several multinational tobacco companies, tobacco production is expected to continue to grow.

Africa's major tobacco producers are Zimbabwe and Malawi. In both countries production expanded rapidly in the 1970s and the 1980s, due mainly to the expansion of the area under tobacco cultivation. The growth rate was higher in Malawi, which started, however, from a lower base. The tobacco industry is well organized in both countries, and is well equipped with technology following recent substantial investments. Although demand by the major trade partners, such as the United States and the EU, is expected to be weaker in the longer term, production is expected to decline in developed countries giving an opportunity for expanding production from Africa. Overall, growth of exports during the period to 2010 is expected to be stronger than that in the base period.

In the Near East, the major producer is Turkey, producing almost entirely Oriental tobacco. Turkey ranks fifth in the world in tobacco production after China, India, the United States and Brazil and produces about 4% of the world's tobacco. Oriental tobacco which constitutes 97% of total Turkish production amounts to less than 10% of global tobacco production and it is used for blended cigarettes. Turkey produces about 65% of the world's oriental tobacco, the rest being produced by Greece, Bulgaria, Bosnia and countries of the area of the former USSR. Export demand for oriental tobacco is declining while production of burley and Virginia types is increasing to accommodate the shift in demand. Under the present price support policies, the upward trend in production observed in the 1970s and 1980s was reversed in the 1990s but production is expected to stabilize with growth rates maintained at around present levels.

Future Outlook for FCV Tobacco Production

There is reduction in crop sizes in major producing countries like Brazil, India, Malawi and Tanzania during current crop season due to adverse weather conditions and fall in prices during the year before. At global level, a level of equilibrium is expected to creep back into Global Tobacco Leaf markets going forward by October/ November 2012. The short crop sizes in Brazil, India, Malawi and Tanzania should help drawdown and absorb uncommitted accumulated inventories and thereby strengthen overall pricing.

However, the factors such as climatic changes increasing the production risks have become a major factor affecting the security of supply of leaf.

As per the industry sources, about 15 million kgof uncommitted stocks remain with the trade at the end of June 2012. Crop size during 2011–2012 in AP is estimated to be about 160 million kg.

Productivity levels of Indian tobacco need to be improved at reduced cost of production in order to sustain and to remain competitive in the world market. Product integrity measures have to be taken up effectively by the Government agencies and the stakeholders together by addressing the problems of pesticide residues and more particularly the NTRMs menace in order to sustain the exports.

Keeping all the above factors in view, the valued opinion of the industry analysts/ experts is that there appears to be a reasonable demand for the Indian FCV tobacco in 2012–2013 crop season in AP as also in Karnataka. A total crop size in the range of 260–270 million kg (AP + Karnataka) during 2012–2013 will augur well for the welfare of the entire tobacco industry in general and growing community in particular.

Cigarette Production

World cigarette production during the recent years is around 600 million. China has been increasing its share in the total production: 36–46% during the last 4 years. Next comes Russia with 6.5% India is not among the top producer of cigarette its share being just 1.7% (Table 1.10). Percent of people smoking daily in a member of developed countries is declining. Britain where 40% of people smoking daily is 1980, has come down to 20%. In USA, it is from 30% to 15% is shown at the next page chart. Surveys show smoking is falling among adults and kids in the developed world. Alcohol consumption is also on the decline. Among British teens, the number of young people who abstain totally from alcohol is rising, but those who do drink are guzzing more. Something similar is happening with the consumption of drugs.

Table 1.10: World cigarette production trends

Country	*2008*			*2009*			*2010*			*2011*		
	Qty.	*% of world*	*Rank*	*Qty.*	*% of world*	*Rank*	*Qty.*	*% of world*	*Rank*	*Qty.*	*% of worl d*	*Rank*
China	2205900	36.35	1	2290150	38.14	1	2354150	39.40	1	2424500	40.29	1
Russia	400900	6.61	2	398960	6.64	2	389250	6.51	2	387000	6.43	2
USA	396552	6.53	3	334159	5.56	3	321640	5.38	3	318892	5.30	3
Indonesia	240060	3.96	4	244480	4.07	4	244000	4.08	4	294000	4.89	4
Germany	221200	3.64	5	217200	3.62	5	204100	3.42	5	204000	3.39	5
Japan	204200	3.36	6	177400	2.95	6	169900	2.84	6	131800	2.19	6
Ukraine	129813	2.14	7	114391	1.90	7	101861	1.70	1	95529	1.59	
South	119162	1.96	8	113273	1.89	8	111464	1.87	7	126800	2.11	8
Poland	117550	1.94	9	109320	1.82	1	105080	1.76	9	129703	2.16	7
Turkey	112237	1.85	1	106995	1.78		97600	1.63		103200	1.72	1
Netherland	110800	1.83		110500	1.84	9	108550	1.82	8	85300	1.42	
India	102000	1.68		101000	1.68		101700	1.70		109721	1.82	9
Others	1716476	28.28		1693072	28.19		1665705	27.88		1606887	26.70	
Total	**606900**	**100**		**600500**	**100**		**597500**	**100**		**601733**	**100**	

Source: TMA.

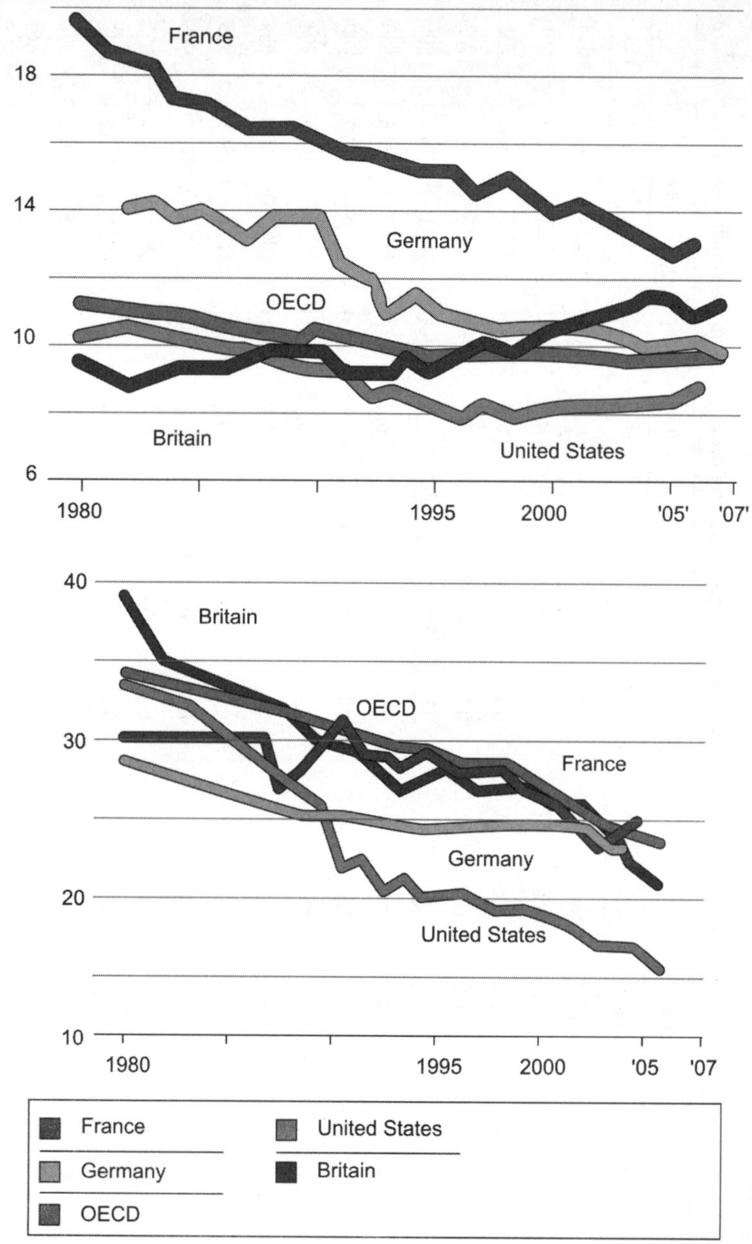

Source: OECD Health at a Glance, 2009.

Annexures

Table 1.2: Area production and average yield for hectare-statewise-tobacco

(Area: in thousand hectares; Production: in million nuts; Yield: number of nuts per hectare)

Year	Haryana			Himachal Pradesh			Jammu & Kashmir			Punjab			Andhra Pradesh		
	Area	Produ.	Yield	Area	Produ.	Yield	Area	Produ.	Yield	Area	Produ.	Yield	Area	Produ.	Yield
1970-71	0.5	0.7	1400	0.7	0.3	429	0.3	0.5	1667	0.1	0.2	2000	222.1	144.0	648
1971-72	0.5	0.3	600	0.7	0.2	286	0.2	0.3	1500	0.1	0.2	2000	238.1	205.0	861
1972-73	0.9	0.6	667	0.7	0.2	286	0.3	0.4	1333	0.2	0.3	1500	222.7	163.2	733
1973-74	0.4	0.6	1500	0.5	0.3	600	0.2	0.1	500	0.1	0.1	1000	236.5	237.1	1003
1974-75	0.6	0.5	833	0.4	0.2	500	0.4	0.2	500	0.1	0.1	1000	177.1	159.4	900
1975-76	0.6	0.6	1000	0.6	0.2	333	0.2	0.1	500	0.1	0.2	2000	156.2	129.6	830
1976-77	0.5	0.4	800	0.4	0.2	500	0.2	0.1	500	0.1	0.2	2000	188.4	133.2	707
1977-78	0.3	0.3	1000	0.6	0.2	333	0.4	0.2	500	0.1	0.1	1000	290.7	262.8	904
1978-79	0.4	0.4	1000	0.4	0.1	250	0.4	0.2	500	0.1	0.1	1000	198.7	190.6	959
1979-80	0.2	0.2	1000	0.4	0.2	500	0.2	0.1	500	0.1	0.1	1000	171.6	154.9	903
1980-81	0.2	0.1	500	0.4	0.1	250	0.1	0.1	1000	0.1	0.1	1000	169.4	164.0	968
1981-82	0.2	0.1	500	0.3	0.1	333	0.1	0.1	1000	Neg.	0.1	–	183.9	193.4	1052
1982-83	0.1	0.2	2000	0.3	0.1	333	0.1	Neg.	0	–	–	–	253.2	270.2	1067
1983-84	0.1	0.1	1000	0.2	0.1	500	0.1	0.1	1000	–	–	–	186.8	185.6	994
1984-85	0.2	0.2	1000	0.2	0.1	500	0.1	0.1	1000	–	–	–	177.9	170.6	959
1985-86	0.1	0.1	1000	0.2	0.1	500	0.1	Neg.	0	–	–	–	149.3	145.5	975
1986-87	0.1	0.1	1000	0.2	0.1	500	0.1	0.1	1000	–	–	–	146.5	152.0	1038
1987-88	0.1	0.1	1000	0.1	Neg.	–	0.1	0.1	1000	–	–	–	107.4	104.9	977

Table 1.2: Area production and average yield for hectare-statewise-tobacco *(Contd.)*

(Area: in thousand hectares; Production: in million nuts; Yield: number of nuts per hectare)

Year	Haryana			Himachal Pradesh			Jammu & Kashmir			Punjab			Andhra Pradesh		
	Area	Produ.	Yield	Area	Produ.	Yield	Area	Produ.	Yield	Area	Produ.	Yield	Area	Produ.	Yield
1988-89	Neg.	Neg.	–	0.1	Neg.	–	Neg.	Neg.	–	–	–	–	150.5	185.6	1233
1989-90	0.1	0.1	1000	0.1	0.1	1000	0.1	Neg.	–	–	–	–	163.5	203.1	1242
1990-91	0.2	0.2	1000	0.1	0.1	1000	Neg.	Neg.	–	–	–	–	166.8	187.0	1121
1991-92	Neg.	Neg.	–	0.1	Neg.	1000	Neg.	Neg.	–	–	–	–	205.5	256.8	1250
1992-93	Neg.	Neg.	–	0.1	Neg.	0	Neg.	Neg.	–	–	–	–	173.5	236.4	1363
1993-94	Neg.	Neg.	–	0.1	Neg.	0	0.2	0.1	500	–	–	–	149.1	188.2	1262
1994-95	0.0	0.0	0	0.4	0.1	250	0.0	0.0	0	–	–	–	130.5	164.5	1261
1995-96	0.0	0.0	0	0.1	0.1	1000	0.0	0.0	0	–	–	–	136.2	170.3	1250
1996-97	0.0	0.0	0	Neg.	0.1	0	0.0	0.0	0	–	–	–	163.0	184.2	1130
1997-98	Neg.	Neg.	–	Neg.	0.1	–	Neg.	Neg.	–	–	–	–	201.9	201.5	998
1998-99	Neg.	Neg.	–	Neg.	Neg.	–	0.1	Neg.	0	–	–	–	193.0	246.0	1275
1999-2000	Neg.	Neg.	–	Neg.	Neg.	–	0.1	Neg.	0	–	–	–	171.4	193.5	1129
2000-01	Neg.	Neg.	–	Neg.	Neg.	–	0.1	Neg.	0	–	–	–	52.0	88.0	1692
2001-02	–	–	–	–	–	–	–	–	–	–	–	–	127.3	168.6	1324
2002-03	–	–	–	–	–	–	–	–	–	–	–	–	116.8	167.7	1436
2003-04	–	–	–	–	–	–	–	–	–	–	–	–	132.5	195.5	1475
2004-05	–	–	–	–	–	–	–	–	–	–	–	–	132.5	195.5	1475
2005-06	–	–	–	–	–	–	–	–	–	–	–	–	134.0	198.0	1478
2006-07	–	–	–	–	–	–	–	–	–	–	–	–	127.0	182.0	1433
2007-08	–	–	–	–	–	–	–	–	–	–	–	–	120.0	175.0	1458

(Contd.)

Table 1.2: Area production and average yield for hectare-statewise-tobacco

(Area: in thousand hectares; Production: in million nuts; Yield: number of nuts per hectare)

Year	Karnataka			Kerala			Tamil Nadu			Madhya Pradesh			Uttar Pradesh			Gujarat		
	Area	Produ.	Yield	Area	Produ.	Yield	Area	Produ.	Yield	Area	Produ.	Yield	Area	Produ.	Yield	Area	Produ.	Yield
1970-71	42.8	20.9	488	0.8	1.6	2000	14.6	23.9	1637	2.3	1.2	522	10.9	9.7	890	86.9	113.0	1300
1971-72	39.6	16.6	419	0.8	1.7	2125	10.8	16.1	1491	2.4	1.3	542	11.2	9.8	875	85.6	116.4	1360
1972-73	37.0	20.3	549	0.7	1.5	2143	13.9	20.7	1489	2.4	1.1	458	11.1	10.8	973	87.2	110.1	1263
1973-74	38.3	17.9	467	0.7	1.4	2000	12.6	18.6	1476	2.4	1.2	500	10.0	8.9	890	90.6	131.0	1446
1974-75	35.5	19.2	541	0.8	1.3	1625	6.1	5.8	951	1.9	0.9	474	7.7	5.8	496	88.5	127.4	1440
1975-76	38.0	22.9	603	0.8	1.5	1875	13.4	18.9	1410	2.7	1.5	556	11.7	9.4	870	78.6	116.6	1483
1976-77	36.2	27.2	751	0.5	1.0	2000	19.0	27.1	1426	3.1	1.7	548	10.8	10.7	1202	99.2	164.6	1659
1977-78	42.1	30.5	724	0.4	0.8	2000	11.3	16.7	1478	2.5	1.3	520	8.9	10.2	1097	81.5	125.3	1537
1978-79	43.5	29.6	680	0.4	0.8	2000	12.7	19.0	1496	1.7	0.9	529	9.3	10.4	990	74.6	153.6	2059
1979-80	44.5	26.6	598	0.4	0.8	2000	12.9	19.1	1481	1.2	0.5	417	10.5	13.8	896	114.7	174.9	1525
1980-81	51.6	33.9	657	0.4	0.8	2000	14.5	22.4	1545	2.0	1.0	500	15.4	20.2	1656	121.5	185.2	1524
1981-82	50.0	29.0	580	0.5	1.0	2000	14.8	22.9	1547	1.3	0.7	538	12.2	15.4	1375	113.0	209.5	1854
1982-83	49.7	38.4	773	0.5	1.0	2000	8.1	9.2	1136	1.1	0.5	455	11.2	15.3	1195	110.6	197.1	1782
1983-84	49.5	29.3	592	0.6	1.0	1667	12.3	16.7	1358	1.3	0.7	538	12.8	17.7	912	108.3	186.9	1726
1984-85	48.9	31.2	638	0.5	1.0	2000	12.3	25.7	2089	1.3	0.6	462	19.4	28.1	1951	108.4	173.5	1601
1985-86	47.2	31.9	792	0.5	0.9	1800	13.2	18.3	1386	1.0	0.5	500	14.4	21.5	1581	106.2	167.8	1580
1986-87	46.7	37.4	715	0.4	0.8	2000	9.2	11.4	1239	0.9	0.4	444	13.6	20.4	1594	110.4	182.8	1656
1987-88	43.8	33.4	941	0.4	0.7	1750	9.0	12.5	1389	0.8	0.4	500	12.8	38.3	2736	81.5	121.8	1494
1988-89	51.2	41.2	674	0.4	0.6	1500	5.8	7.3	1259	1.0	0.5	500	14.0	48.0	3429	90.1	151.0	1676

Table 1.2: Area production and average yield for hectare-statewise-tobacco *(Contd.)*

(Area: in thousand hectares; Production: in million nuts; Yield: number of nuts per hectare)

Year	Karnataka			Kerala			Tamil Nadu			Madhya Pradesh			Uttar Pradesh			Gujarat		
	Area	Produ.	Yield	Area	Produ.	Yield	Area	Produ.	Yield	Area	Produ.	Yield	Area	Produ.	Yield	Area	Produ.	Yield
1989-90	50.5	34.5	683	0.4	0.7	1750	7.3	9.2	1260	1.2	0.7	583	15.8	64.2	4063	112.6	182.9	1624
1990-91	46.5	31.4	675	0.3	0.6	2000	10.4	16.0	1538	1.1	0.6	545	15.0	75.1	5007	109.6	192.9	1760
1991-92	52.9	44.7	845	0.3	0.6	2000	7.3	11.1	1521	0.7	0.4	571	14.7	70.3	4782	85.3	154.3	1809
1992-93	58.4	52.9	906	0.2	0.3	1500	8.4	12.2	1452	0.5	0.3	600	14.5	76.7	5290	105.5	172.1	1631
1993-94	61.2	46.0	752	0.1	0.3	3000	9.2	13.5	1467	0.7	0.4	571	16.6	94.1	5669	96.7	179.2	1853
1994-95	59.4	45.2	761	0.2	0.3	1500	7.2	10.7	1486	0.6	0.3	500	16.7	90.7	5431	113.4	213.2	1880
1995-96	59.6	48.8	819	0.2	0.5	2500	8.6	13.0	1512	0.5	0.3	600	13.1	61.1	4664	121.8	196.0	1609
1996-97	70.3	57.0	811	0.1	0.1	1000	11.8	17.6	1492	0.4	0.3	750	17.1	105.5	6170	112.6	211.5	1878
1997-98	70.8	62.2	879	0.1	0.8	8000	7.9	11.9	1506	0.4	0.2	500	19.8	136.2	6879	111.0	183.9	1657
1998-99	83.7	59.0	705	0.1	0.5	5000	7.5	11.5	1533	0.3	0.2	667	22.1	151.7	6864	110.6	103.7	938
1999-2000	75.4	44.5	590	Neg.	0.2	0	7.7	11.9	1545	0.3	0.2	667	18.1	126.5	6989	110.6	103.7	938
2000-01	70.5	52.1	739	0.2	1.2	6000	8.3	12.6	1518	0.3	0.1	333	1.1	4.6	4182	87.8	148.6	1692
2001-02	72.4	58.6	809	0.1	0.4	4000	6.0	9.0	1500	0.3	0.1	333	18.8	129.3	6878	85.5	145.3	1699
2002-03	82.4	59.2	718	0.1	0.5	5000	5.2	8.1	1558	0.2	0.1	500	19.6	113.7	5801	66.4	114.7	1727
2003-04	98.1	55.1	562	0.1	0.4	4000	6.0	9.0	1500	0.3	0.2	667	22.9	125.8	5493	68.2	124.9	1831
2004-05	91.0	62.0	681	0.1	0.4	4000	4.6	6.9	1500	0.3	0.1	333	22.0	119.0	5409	71.3	113.9	1597
2005-06	101.0	62.0	614	neg.	0.1	0	5.1	7.8	1529	0.2	0.1	500	20.2	121.5	6015	71.3	113.9	1597
2006-07	103.0	46.0	447	neg.	0.1	0	5.0	7.7	1540	0.2	0.1	500	23.0	125.0	5435	71.3	113.9	1597
2007-08	113.0	46.0	407	0.0	0.0	0.0	5.9	9.1	1542	0.2	0.1	500	25.5	140.8	5522	46.0	79.0	1717

(Contd.)

Table 1.2: Area production and average yield for hectare-statewise-tobacco

(Area: in thousand hectares; Production: in million nuts; Yield: number of nuts per hectare)

Year	Maharashtra			Rajasthan			Bihar			Orissa			West Bengal			Arunachal Pradesh		
	Area	Produ.	Yield	Area	Produ.	Yield	Area	Produ.	Yield	Area	Produ.	Yield	Area	Produ.	Yield	Area	Produ.	Yield
1970-71	13.2	6.1	462	3.6	2.7	750	13.5	12.0	889	14.2	12.3	866	10.1	7.7	762	–	–	–
1971-72	13.3	6.6	496	5.5	3.8	691	12.5	12.4	992	14.0	11.8	843	12.1	8.6	711	–	–	–
1972-73	10.6	4.4	415	5.5	3.3	600	13.3	5.4	406	15.3	13.2	863	13.1	10.0	763	–	–	–
1973-74	12.7	5.9	465	4.2	3.2	762	13.2	6.0	455	15.4	12.4	805	14.1	10.5	745	–	–	–
1974-75	12.7	5.8	457	3.6	2.9	806	9.1	7.4	813	15.4	11.1	721	11.9	8.8	739	–	–	–
1975-76	11.2	5.2	464	5.9	3.9	661	11.0	11.7	1064	16.7	11.0	659	11.7	10.5	897	–	–	–
1976-77	10.4	6.1	587	9.4	5.4	574	15.7	13.0	828	14.8	6.9	466	14.9	15.0	1007	–	–	–
1977-78	10.8	5.6	519	3.7	3.0	811	11.8	9.8	831	16.6	7.1	428	14.9	14.5	973	–	–	–
1978-79	12.8	7.4	578	2.7	2.8	1037	10.9	10.6	972	19.6	9.6	490	13.2	12.7	962	–	–	–
1979-80	14.3	7.9	552	3.1	2.7	871	12.7	11.7	921	18.1	8.6	475	12.7	11.5	906	–	–	–
1980-81	11.9	6.8	571	3.4	2.5	735	12.5	9.7	776	21.2	11.3	533	18.9	17.4	921	0.2	0.2	1000
1981-82	12.0	7.3	608	3.0	2.4	800	13.9	12.3	885	16.6	7.8	470	14.1	13.3	943	0.2	0.1	500
1982-83	12.2	7.1	582	2.4	2.2	917	13.7	12.9	942	15.9	7.2	453	16.1	15.8	981	0.3	0.1	333
1983-84	10.1	7.9	782	2.5	2.6	1040	13.4	13.4	1000	18.6	10.2	548	15.2	15.4	1013	0.3	0.1	333
1984-85	7.1	4.9	690	3.2	3.1	969	15.9	16.1	1013	17.8	9.4	528	15.7	16.5	1051	0.3	0.1	333
1985-86	9.9	7.7	778	2.8	2.8	1000	12.7	15.3	1205	18.2	9.6	527	14.5	14.9	1028	0.1	0.1	1000
1986-87	8.4	7.9	940	2.4	2.6	1083	14.1	16.9	1199	16.2	9.7	599	14.1	15.2	1078	0.1	0.1	1000
1987-88	11.2	10.3	920	1.8	2.3	1278	14.9	18.9	1268	14.4	5.0	347	14.1	15.2	1078	0.1	0.1	1000
1988-89	9.9	8.5	859	2.4	3.4	1417	14.5	17.3	1193	14.0	6.3	450	17.9	19.9	1112	0.1	0.1	1000

Table 1.2: Area production and average yield for hectare-statewise-tobacco *(Contd.)*

A(Area: in thousand hectares; Production: in million nuts; Yield: number of nuts per hectare)

Year	Maharashtra			Rajasthan			Bihar			Orissa			West Bengal			Arunachal Pradesh		
	Area	Produ.	Yield	Area	Produ.	Yield	Area	Produ.	Yield	Area	Produ.	Yield	Area	Produ.	Yield	Area	Produ.	Yield
1989-90	9.2	9.9	1076	3.6	4.4	1222	15.5	15.8	1019	15.2	9.1	599	12.8	13.8	1078	–	–	–
1990-91	10.1	10.4	1030	2.9	3.7	1276	15.3	12.7	830	15.0	9.5	633	12.7	12.8	1008	–	–	–
1991-92	9.7	8.0	825	1.9	2.2	1158	15.2	8.6	566	14.9	10.8	725	14.0	13.7	979	–	–	–
1992-93	10.2	11.8	1157	1.8	2.4	1333	16.4	9.3	567	12.9	9.9	767	11.7	9.3	795	–	–	–
1993-94	9.5	13.0	1368	1.4	2.4	1714	13.9	7.4	532	10.0	6.1	610	12.0	9.5	792	–	–	–
1994-95	9.8	12.8	1306	1.7	2.7	1588	14.9	7.7	517	10.3	6.0	583	12.6	10.0	794	–	–	–
1995-96	9.4	13.5	1436	1.3	2.1	1615	18.2	10.4	571	9.1	6.7	736	13.3	10.4	782	–	–	–
1996-97	9.5	10.8	1137	1.7	2.4	1412	17.2	11.7	680	9.3	5.5	591	11.8	9.1	771	–	–	–
1997-98	9.0	12.0	1333	1.2	1.9	1583	20.6	14.9	723	8.6	4.4	512	10.7	6.1	570	–	–	–
1998-99	9.1	7.7	846	1.0	1.7	1700	19.5	13.4	687	8.6	4.4	512	11.8	6.7	568	–	–	–
1999-2000	9.2	11.0	1196	1.1	1.6	1455	17.4	17.6	1011	7.4	4.6	622	11.5	6.7	583	–	–	–
2000-01	8.1	9.3	1148	0.6	1.2	2000	15.4	17.9	1162	4.0	2.0	500	10.5	5.7	543	–	–	–
2001-02	6.0	7.0	1167	0.8	1.4	1750	13.7	15.1	1102	5.7	3.6	632	9.7	5.3	546	–	–	–
2002-03	6.7	9.4	1403	0.8	1.3	1625	15.0	16.8	1120	4.1	2.6	634	7.7	4.2	545	–	–	–
2003-04	6.0	7.0	1167	0.5	0.9	1800	14.4	16.0	1111	5.3	3.5	660	13.0	9.6	738	–	–	–
2004-05	6.0	7.0	1167	0.7	0.9	1286	16.1	18.7	1161	4.8	3.2	667	15.0	20.1	1340	–	–	–
2005-06	6.0	7.0	1167	0.4	0.5	1250	14.9	17.3	1161	3.7	2.7	730	13.9	19.9	1432	–	–	–
2006-07	6.0	7.0	1167	0.4	0.6	1500	14.1	16.1	1142	4.1	3.0	732	12.0	16.6	1383	–	–	–
2007-08	6.0	7.0	1167	0.5	0.6	1200	13.5	15.5	1148	3.8	2.8	737	11.7	16.5	1410	–	–	–

(Contd.)

Table 1.2: Area production and average yield for hectare-statewise-tobacco

(Area: in thousand hectares; Production: in million nuts; Yield: number of nuts per hectare)

Year	Assam			Meghalaya			Mizoram			Tirpura			All-India		
	Area	Produ.	Yield	Area	Produ.	Yield	Area	Produ.	Yield	Area	Produ.	Yield	Area	Produ.	Yield
1970-71	8.4	6.3	750	0.3	0.2	667	0.2	0.1	500	1.4	0.5	357	446.9	361.9	810
1971-72	8.7	6.6	759	0.3	0.2	667	0.4	0.3	750	1.4	0.5	357	458.3	418.9	914
1972-73	8.0	6.0	750	0.4	0.3	750	0.4	–	0	1.2	0.3	250	444.9	372.2	837
1973-74	7.1	5.5	775	0.4	0.3	750	0.9	0.6	667	1.2	0.4	333	461.5	462.1	1001
1974-75	6.9	5.1	739	0.4	0.3	750	0.4	0.4	1000	1.1	0.4	364	380.6	363.1	954
1975-76	6.6	4.9	742	0.4	0.3	750	0.8	0.4	500	1.0	0.3	300	368.2	349.8	950
1976-77	6.7	4.9	731	0.4	0.3	750	0.7	0.4	571	1.0	0.3	300	432.4	418.8	969
1977-78	6.0	4.3	717	0.4	0.3	750	0.5	0.3	600	0.9	0.3	333	504.4	493.6	979
1978-79	5.3	3.9	736	0.5	0.3	600	1.2	0.5	417	0.9	0.3	333	409.3	453.8	1109
1979-80	5.1	3.7	725	0.6	0.4	667	1.2	0.5	417	0.9	0.3	333	425.4	438.5	1031
1980-81	5.7	4.0	702	0.5	0.4	800	0.7	0.3	429	0.9	0.3	333	451.5	480.8	1065
1981-82	5.5	3.7	673	0.6	0.4	667	0.7	0.3	429	0.9	0.2	222	443.8	520.1	1172
1982-83	5.0	3.3	660	0.6	0.4	667	0.7	0.3	429	0.8	0.3	375	502.6	581.6	1157
1983-84	5.3	3.6	679	0.8	0.5	625	0.7	0.3	429	0.8	0.3	375	439.7	492.5	1120
1984-85	5.4	3.5	648	0.8	0.6	750	0.4	0.3	750	0.8	0.3	375	436.6	485.9	1113
1985-86	4.5	2.9	644	0.7	0.5	714	0.6	0.5	833	0.8	0.3	375	397.0	441.2	1111
1986-87	3.9	2.4	615	0.7	0.5	714	0.5	0.8	1600	0.7	0.2	286	389.2	461.8	1187
1987-88	3.4	2.1	618	0.7	0.5	714	0.7	0.6	857	0.7	0.2	286	318.0	367.4	1155
1988-89	3.0	1.7	567	0.7	0.5	714	0.8	0.7	875	0.6	0.2	333	377.0	492.8	1307

Table 1.2: Area production and average yield for hectare-statewise-tobacco *(Contd.)*

(Area: in thousand hectares; Production: in million nuts; Yield: number of nuts per hectare)

Year	Assam			Meghalaya			Mizoram			Tirpura			All-India		
	Area	Produ.	Yield	Area	Produ.	Yield	Area	Produ.	Yield	Area	Produ.	Yield	Area	Produ.	Yield
1989-90	2.9	1.6	552	0.7	0.5	714	0.9	0.7	778	0.7	0.3	429	413.1	551.6	1335
1990-91	2.6	1.4	538	0.7	0.5	714	0.8	0.7	875	0.7	0.3	429	410.8	555.9	1353
1991-92	2.2	1.3	591	0.8	0.5	625	1.0	0.8	800	0.5	0.3	600	427.0	584.4	1369
1992-93	2.1	1.2	571	0.8	0.5	625	1.0	0.9	900	0.5	0.3	600	418.5	596.5	1425
1993-94	1.8	0.9	500	0.8	0.5	625	1.0	1.0	1000	0.5	0.3	600	384.8	562.9	1463
1994-95	1.7	0.9	529	0.8	0.5	625	1.0	0.9	900	0.5	0.2	400	381.7	566.7	1485
1995-96	1.6	0.8	500	0.7	0.5	714	0.5	0.5	1000	0.4	0.2	500	394.6	535.2	1356
1996-97	1.6	0.8	500	0.7	0.5	714	0.5	0.6	1200	0.4	0.2	500	428.0	617.9	1444
1997-98	1.6	0.8	500	0.7	0.5	714	0.4	0.4	1000	0.3	0.2	667	465.0	637.9	1372
1998-99	1.5	0.7	467	0.7	0.5	714	0.3	0.4	1333	0.3	0.1	333	470.2	608.2	1293
1999-2000	1.0	1.0	1000	0.7	0.5	714	0.4	0.4	1000	0.3	0.1	333	432.6	524.0	1211
2000-01	1.3	0.6	462	0.7	0.5	714	0.4	0.2	500	0.3	0.1	333	261.5	344.7	1318
2001-02	1.0	1.0	1000	0.7	0.5	714	0.3	0.2	667	0.2	0.1	500	348.5	545.5	1565
2002-03	1.0	1.0	1000	0.7	0.5	714	0.3	0.3	1000	0.2	0.1	500	327.2	500.2	1529
2003-04	1.0	1.0	1000	0.7	0.5	714	0.5	0.4	800	0.2	0.1	500	369.7	549.9	1487
2004-05	0.7	0.4	571	0.7	0.5	714	0.5	0.4	800	0.2	0.1	500	366.5	549.1	1498
2005-06	0.7	0.4	571	0.7	0.5	714	0.5	0.4	800	0.2	0.1	500	372.8	552.2	1481
2006-07	1.0	0.3	300	0.7	0.5	714	0.5	0.4	800	0.2	0.1	500	368.5	519.4	1409
2007-08	1.0	0.3	300	0.7	0.4	571	0.1	0.0	0	0.2	0.1	500	348.1	493.3	1417

Source: Area and Production of Principal Crops in India (Various Issues), Directorate of Economics & Statistics, Department of Agriculture & Co-operation, Ministry of Agriculture.

Table 1.4G: India's tobacco exports by commodities-countries/destination, 1995-1996

(Qty: Kg; Value: Rs)

Articles	*Countries/ destination*	*Quantity*	*Value*
1	2	3	4
Unmanufactured tobacco, tobacco refuse, stemmed/stripped FCV tobacco not stemmed.	Australia	131400	9940306
	Bangladesh	1108400	78887567
	Belgium	971302	43027318
	Canada	5000	115079
	Chile	1600	121294
	Cyprus	22000	1169498
	Egypt ARP	53000	1140471
	Estonia	127000	5030643
	France	135400	4539351
	German F. Rep.	512343	32457992
	Guinea	2000	1199067
	Indonesia	69600	2380762
	Ireland	39600	2415165
	Israel	13000	740484
	Malaysia	39600	2985479
	Maldives	750	69240
	Nepal	103712	3471869
	Netherland	763100	39777453
	Newzealand	9600	908773
	Oman	27400	1123936
	Papua N. GNA	30000	2147918
	Poland	103200	4060457
	Russia	4587236	155897124
	Saudi Arabia	219100	5180215
	Slovak Rep.	205425	7692877
	Singapore	139821	12268892
	South Africa	209630	13691944
	Sri Lanka	190656	9575755
	Sweden	159840	1604366
	Switzerland	80000	3811406
	Trinidad	28000	1504749
	Tunisia	147	1470
	UAE	126600	4811288
	UK	1876464	115074984
	USA	1340800	24570950
	Vietnam Soc Rep.	320000	11835828
	Yemen Rep.	301000	7718392
	Total	14071726	612950362

Table 1.4G: India's tobacco exports by commodities-countries / destination, 1995-1996 *(Contd.)*

(Qty: Kg; Value: Rs)

Articles	*Countries/ destination*	*Quantity*	*Value*
1	*2*	*3*	*4*
Suncured country (natu) tobacco Not stemmed	Bangladesh	12000	75048
	Belgium	10000	631625
	Dijibouti	51000	1194847
	Ethiopia	35000	723845
	Indonesia	20000	824777
	Nepal	36788	1213254
	Saudi Arabia	35656	790506
	Sri Lanka	39448	395422
	UK	57000	991322
	USA	33160	1113240
	Yeman Rep.	313000	5603682
	Total	643052	13557568
Suncured Virignia tobacco not stemmed	China P. Rep	79200	5678263
	Egypt A. Rep	495600	34189305
	France	11400	589757
	Hong Kong	19200	285221
	Indonesia	20000	686986
	Russia	1095200	34022500
	Signapore	39600	2396542
	Srilanka	57600	4335456
	UAE	19000	1019560
	Total	1836800	83203590
Burley tobacco not stemmed	Belgium	17820	1004279
	German F. Rep.	68352	4353142
	Italy	53460	1839128
	Russia	51000	1614003
	South Africa	105952	2491977
	UK	53460	1839128
	Total	350044	13141657
Tobacco for MNFRD of bidis not stemmed	Bangladesh	26000	387125
	Digibouti	220400	5437125
	Nepal	43065	1046168
	Reunion	150	6124
	Russia	382000	15587895
	Sri Lanka	179065	1904578
	UAE	2500	176094
	UK	59400	3877628
	USA	16800	561609
	Yeman Rep.	145000	3448030
	Total	1074380	32432376

(Contd.)

Table 1.4G: India's tobacco exports by commodities-countries/destination, 1995-1996

(Qty: Kg; Value: Rs)

Articles	*Countries/ destination*	*Quantity*	*Value*
1	2	3	4
Tobacco MNFR of chewing tobacco not stemmed	Behrain IS	3230	272829
	Bangladesh	3000	73350
	Canada	3700	233316
	Dijibouti	293000	6481496
	France	7500	159477
	Israel	60690	3757398
	Jordon	47000	3087445
	Kuwait	40600	1653011
	Nepal	1440	35925
	Oman	12750	862248
	Saudi Arabia	2400	1493783
	Trinidad	70000	1575391
	UAE	129250	7491291
	Yemen Rep.	4832250	109334129
		5528410	136511089
Tobacco for MNFR of cigar, cheroots not stemmed	Belgium	368640	28252947
	Egypt A. Rep.	60000	2086094
	German F. Rep.	957333	58647337
	Indonesia	20000	620328
	Netherland	172870	6105627
	Papua N. GNA	20000	1199067
	Poland	20000	713674
	Russia	1443200	53200945
	Sri Lanka	153600	9823811
	Trinidad	11600	895757
	UK	631142	45145151
	Zaire Rep.	35640	1216320
	Total	3894025	207907058
Tobacco for MNFR of hooka tobacco not stemmed	Bangladesh	11000	67794
	Hong Kong	800	21246
	Nepal	7950	212450
	Saudi Arabi	760309	14371921
	South Africa	9000	176600
	UAE	52600	1876900
	USA	59280	925099
Other tobacco not stemmed/stripped	Afghanistan	3170	95577
	Australia	75600	5681625
	Austria	25488	1008638

Table 1.4G: India's tobacco exports by commodities-countries / destination, 1995-1996 *(Contd.)*

(Qty: Kg; Value: Rs)

Articles	*Countries/ destination*	*Quantity*	*Value*
1	2	3	4
	Bangladesh	1030100	72552329
	Belgium	801716	52930895
	Belarus	540000	12433758
	Chinese Taipet	198000	11148811
	Chena P. Rep.	413400	42638581
	Denmark	70260	6100270
	Dijibouti	11000	177062
	Egypt A. Rep.	1329440	79530462
	Estonia	254295	10026815
	France	702676	42338827
	German F. Rep.	1404147	135791379
	Greece	974300	63109119
	Guinea	30000	1408824
	Hong Kong	236400	13179466
	Indonesia	50000	1884157
	Israel	4000	162604
	Italy	852970	58422499
	Kazakhastan	400000	21324677
	Laivia	453619	13962932
	Libya	222500	14240768
	Malaysia	98280	7775018
	Maldives	172500	6631903
	Nepal	4571627	179124912
	Netherland	946420	45766970
	New Zealand	49200	52840097
	Norway	18000	1598587
	Oman	648	55960
	Papua N. GNA	60200	3846423
	Poland	214176	8964534
	Portugal	372487	24339124
	Russia	10483340	379426867
	Saudi Arabia	103296	1362100
	Singapore	363416	27591231
	Solomon IS	35000	497825
	South Africa	60000	3915619
	Sri Lanka	895811	43940871
	Sudan	248640	3716605
	Surinam	197140	12624439

(Contd.)

Table 1.4G: India's tobacco exports by commodities-countries/destination, 1995-1996

(Qty: Kg; Value: Rs)

Articles	*Countries/ destination*	*Quantity*	*Value*
1	2	3	4
	Sweeden	195520	5198802
	Trinidad	9600	548528
	UAE	200415	9952442
	UK	3386080	225028260
	Ukraine	1122500	27368739
	USA	501692	13848699
	Uzbekistan	264000	8254669
	Vietnam Soc. Rep.	1044800	40394716
	Yemen Rep.	344000	8137764
	Subtotal	36041869	1755345779
	Total	64341245	2872701489
Tobacco partly or wholly stemmed/stripped flue-cured Virginia tobacco stemmed	Argentina	304000	19546401
	Baharains	2500	184493
	Bangladesh	1522800	109094713
	Belgium	873000	10448822
	Cameroon	103000	10945880
	Estonia	100000	4028875
	German F. Rep.	119200	8534490
	Italy	160000	15018711
	Korea DP Rep.	39775	2758579
	Netherland	32000	2145258
	New Zealand	100000	10317698
	Poland	130000	4096370
	Russia	2450800	82012018
	Saudi Arabia	13750	1141335
	Singapore	50225	3891551
	Spain	286000	30811935
	Sri Lanka	6000	376894
	UAE	99625	6683158
	UK	4735000	385847624
	USA	1900	144215
	Vietnam Soc. Rep.	120000	6157688
	Total	11249575	805886708
Sun cured country (NATU) tobacco, stemmed	Malaysia	36000	6387092
	Russia	100000	342138
	Singapore	4000	176488
	Total	140000	6905718

Table 1.4G: India's tobacco exports by commodities-countries / destination, 1995-1996 *(Contd.)*

(Qty: Kg; Value: Rs)

Articles	*Countries/ destination*	*Quantity*	*Value*
1	2	3	4
Sun-cured Virginia tobacco, stemmed	Bangladesh	281000	24618694
	Egypt A. Rep.	60000	1336029
	Estonia	20000	625845
	German F. Rep.	10000	516867
	Greece	59400	2610631
	Myanmar	4000	172823
	Russia	20000	381114
	Sri Lanka	19800	1350154
	Total	474200	31612157
Burley tobacco stemmed	Belgium	69000	5943802
	Total	69000	5943802
Tobacco for MNFR of bidis	Canada	650	32000
	Sri Lanka	63890	695630
	Total	64540	727630
Tobacco for MNFR of chewing tobacco atemmed	Canada	277	10695
	Jordan	6000	664016
	Kuwait	1650	128207
	Nepal	9000	431340
	Oman	2000	223906
	UAE	7705	597243
	Total	26632	2055407
Tobacco for MNFR of hookah tobacco stemmed	France	216000	1210686
	UAE	40000	788004
	Total	256000	1998690
Other tobacco partly or wholly stemmed / stripped	Afghanistan	10000	942325
	Bangladesh	50000	4405740
	Belgium	30000	1454055
	Egypt A. Rep.	120000	2487823
	German F. Rep.	18000	1245000
	Israel	2000	100064
	Italy	51840	3900292
	Jordan	11109	38082
	Kuwait	7750	561297
	Malaysia	9000	1596773
	Maldives	4100	187952
	Mozambique	300	22356
	Nepal	187337	14793297
	Netherland	10000	497267

(Contd.)

Table 1.4G: India's tobacco exports by commodities-countries/destination, 1995-1996

(Qty: Kg; Value: Rs)

Articles	*Countries/ destination*	*Quantity*	*Value*
1	2	3	4
	Oman	388	34620
	Saudi Arabia	38790	3314941
	South Africa	40000	1055442
	UAE	321700	18355680
	USA	117130	3417816
	Yemen Rep.	37312	686784
		1056766	59097606
		13336713	914227718
	Total	-	3786929207
Cigar cheroots cigarillo and cigarettes of tobacco or of tobacco substitute cigar cheroot and of cigarillos CNTNG tobacco bidis	Afghanistan	61892	914208
	Australia	8305	1307659
	Baharain IS	13111	3293548
	Belgium	100	19544
	Canada	609	116723
	Chinese Taipet	842	154781
	Hong Kong	873	206264
	Jamaica	150	51942
	Japan	1153	260198
	Kuwait	18672	5161902
	Malaysia	18438	5002783
	Mexico	1824	385347
	Netherland	1478	319459
	Oman	38251	8742907
	Phillippines	40	8631
	Saudi Arabia	154970	37962859
	Singapore	28085	6209808
	South Africa	444	101750
	Spain	92	18602
	Sri Lanka	46320	2593684
	Switzerland	8424	2073820
	Trinidad	395	80827
	UAE	289711	69806908
	USA	39606	8099815
	Total	733785	161103969
Cigar & cheroots	Afghanistan	25280	4057260
	China P. Rep.	45	6332
	UAE	23040	4042940
	USA	4113	348853
	Total	52478	8455385

Table 1.4G: India's tobacco exports by commodities-countries / destination, 1995-1996 *(Contd.)*

(Qty: Kg; Value: Rs)

Articles	*Countries/ destination*	*Quantity*	*Value*
1	2	3	4
Other cigarillos & cigarettes cigarettes containing tobacco	Nepal	8500	1016000
	Afghanistan	55849	8666131
	Austria	520	51657
	Baharain IS	1000	187933
	Bangladesh	579	77644
	Chinese Taipet	34	134110
	China P. Rep.	80	33846
	German F. Rep.	24120	2836920
	Guinea	6517	515642
	Hong Kong	36	3409
	Iran	63308	8436918
	Ireland	13260	1155554
	Jordan	6034	689786
	Kenya	5750	774996
	Korea Rep.	35360	5469030
	Kuwait	15700	2150733
	Liberia	6573	585959
	Malaysia	20000	16716766
	Nepal	560	145851
	Nigeria	7000	614328
	Oman	44313	6513412
	Pakistan	32079	4554739
	Russia	185545	27409700
	Saudi Arabia	45729	4747279
	Senegal	12555	1405338
	Sierra Leone	6517	515642
	Slovak Rep.	6500	783221
	Singapore	40	5656
	Sri Lanka	30	7000
	Surinam	53440	5716601
	Switzerland	9868	1226584
	UAE	312288	38895350
	UK	35305	4416809
	Ukraine	44116	2051210
	USA	155731	19840765
	Total	1206336	167215519
Cigar cheroots & cigarettes of tobacco substitute	Maldives	1000	143080
	Netherland	30	9624

(Contd.)

Table 1.4G: India's tobacco exports by commodities-countries/destination, 1995-1996

(Qty: Kg; Value: Rs)

Articles	*Countries/ destination*	*Quantity*	*Value*
1	*2*	*3*	*4*
	New Zealand	20	1564
	Russia	12555	1819527
	Subtotal	13605	1973795
	Total	-	339764668
Other MNFRD tobacco & MNFRD tobacco substitutes homogenized or reconstituted tobacco, tobacco extracts & essences. Smoking tobacco W/N CONTNG tobacco substitutes hookah/goouku tobacco	Australia	335	8859
	Beharains	5940	60146
	France	114000	589757
	German F. Rep.	80900	512164
	Kuwait	62000	1072800
	Nepal	4560	110600
	Russia	54975	237719
	Saudi Arabia	5429124	161732051
	South Africa	240094	7400773
	UAE	346000	7141095
	UK	30000	498365
	Ukraine	33075	1589082
	USA	34432	1327287
	Total	6435435	182280698
Other smoking tobacco excluding hookah tobacco	Saudi Arabia	155906	3102547
	UAE	39600	2138913
		195506	5241460
	Total	6630941	187522158
Other MNFRD tobacco extract & essences NES chewing tobacco	Australia	40	32527
	Beharain IS	4470	1538314
	Bangladesh	158	32396
	Canada	5421	634405
	German F. Rep.	19800	3873682
	Israel	2000	152461
	Jordan	6000	511265
	Kenya	2122	518952
	Nepal	29600	2007566
	Oman	12789	3381725
	Phillipines	49	9381
	Saudi Arabia	22049	7313152
	Singapore	750	37890
	South Africa	100	12488
	Spain	700	282560
	Tanzania Rep.	510	100033

Table 1.4G: India's tobacco exports by commodities-countries / destination, 1995-1996 *(Contd.)*

(Qty: Kg; Value: Rs)

Articles	*Countries/ destination*	*Quantity*	*Value*
1	2	3	4
	UAE	71310	20855394
	UK	4531	1334886
	USA	5496	2602346
	Total	187895	45231423
Jarda-scented tobacco	Beharain IS	7159	5748969
	Bangladesh	3716	675934
	Canada	150	78261
	Japan	66	87708
	Kenya	550	295798
	Malagasy Rep.	110	121170
	Myanmar	4100	1171461
	Nepal	740	395880
	Phillipines	30	17644
	Saudi Arabia	31180	19128698
	South Africa	297	192095
	Switzerland	2	2400
	Tanzania Rep.	774	306965
	UAE	35975	23716252
	UK	3016	558846
	USA	9441	8126375
	Zambia	55	55035
	Total	97361	60679491
Snuff	Baharain Is	300	47019
	Kenya	1775	227393
	Kuwat	6280	826526
	Nepal	94635	2280105
	Oman	2228	197282
	South Africa	1052	145702
	Tanzania Rep.	320	45580
	UAE	7561	828924
	UK	3017	553481
	USA	1956	560561
	Total	119124	57125713
Tobacco extracts essences (CRD solenesol)	Japan	60060	1825411
	USA	510	123420
	Total	60570	18377531
Tobacco manufactured NES	Australia	1026	55327
	Beharain IS	600	42374

(Contd.)

Table 1.4G: India's tobacco exports by commodities-countries/destination, 1995-1996

(Qty: Kg; Value: Rs)

Articles	*Countries/ destination*	*Quantity*	*Value*
1	2	3	4
	Canada	27	26063
	German F. Rep.	230	19603
	Japan	16000	1457911
	Malaysia	18000	3102480
	Nepal	24200	3403239
	Netherlands	1650	181000
	Oman	3668	521811
	Phillipines	60	32197
	Saudi Arabia	1200	324563
	Tanzania Rep.	413	49006
	UAE	193867	12304423
	UK	52311	2260507
	USA	1063	211890
		314315	23992394
		779265	153993412
	Total		341515570

Source: Monthly Statistics of the Foreign Trade (1995-96) Directorate General of Commercial Intelligence and Statistics, Ministry of Commerce, Government of India, Kolkata.

Annexure 1: Expensive cigar

One box of Gurkha's, his majesty's reserve cigars costs around $25,000. That price is expected to increase to about $30,000 by next year. Each cigar costs nearly $1,000 and feature aged tobacco fermented in Louis XIII Cognac, Gurkha, the manufacture, produces about 20,000 boxes per year, and has a 3-year waiting list of the cigars.

Delhi Government to Ban All Raw Chewable Tobacco Products

Delhi government will ban production, storage, sale and purchase of all kinds of raw chewable tobacco products (like khaini and zarda) in the Capital soon. The sale and production of gutkha, a mixture of raw tobacco and supari (betel nut), was banned in Delhi in September 2012.

Rooting out the menace:·

- 90% of oral cancer cases are related to chewing tobacco products.
- 90% of lung cancer cases are due to tobacco consumption.
- 40% of all cancers are due to tobacco consumption.
- 11 lakh cancer cases reported in India each year.

"Even though gutkha was banned in 2012, the retailers started selling the components of gutkha (betel nut and raw tobacco) in separate pouches. People would buy them separately, mix them, and turn it into gutkha. So, our purpose of banning gutkha was not served. Then, we realized that we need to ban raw chewable tobacco products completely", said Dr SK Arora, Additional Director Health, Tobacco Control Program, Delhi Government.

We have already prepared a file to ban raw chewable tobacco products in Delhi and submitted it to the higher authorities for approval.

Even after the ban, there was an unstinted supply of gutkha to the Capital from neighboring States of Uttar Pradesh and Haryana. Once we set a precedent of banning them, they must also follow suit.

Even after the ban, there was an unstinted supply of gutkha to the capital from up and Haryana. Once we set a precedent of banning them. They must also follow suit.

According to sources in the Delhi Health Ministry, the proposal was approved by the Chief Secretary, Delhi Government in May 2014 and was sent to the Lieutenant Governor for final approval. Delhi Government had already declared last day of every month as dry day for tobacco.

According to doctors, 90% of oral cancer is directly related to chewing tobacco products. It is a welcome decision because chewable tobacco products play a predominant role in causing oral cancer. About 90% of lung cancer is related to tobacco and 40% of all cancers can be directly attributed to tobacco Dr Durgatosh Pandey, Assistance Professor Surgical Oncology of Dr BRA Institute Rotary Cancer

Hospital (IRCH), All India Institute of Medical Sciences (AIIMS) "This initiative will have an impact gradually and it will reduce tobacco consumption by more than 50%. I will benefit people who have never been exposed to the effect of tobacco consumption and do not run the risk of developing cancer".

Cigarette Packets to Now Carry Health Warnings Covering 85% of Space

The government has made it mandatory for tobacco companies to carry health warnings covering at least 85% of the surface of cigarette packets, making India the world leader in implementing plain packaging of tobacco products as advocated by the World Health Organization.

The Health Ministry on Wednesday amended the rules under the Cigarettes and Other Tobacco Products Act (COTPA) through a gazette notification, fixing April 1, 2015, as the deadline and leaving cigarette makers with less than 6 months for compliance. The development has come in the wake of an international report by the Canadian Cancer Society, which ranked India at 136 out of 198 countries with regard to the size of health warnings on cigarette packets. Thailand (85%), Australia (82.5%) and Uruguay (80%) were the top three countries as per the report.

As per earlier rules, pictorial warnings covered 40% of just the front surface of the cigarette packs in India. With the drastic revision in rules, India will share the top spot with Thailand. Tobacco Institute of India (TII) which represents the interest of cigarette makers including ITCBSE 1.48% and Godfrey Phillips said the proposed warnings are unreasonable, drastic and impractical to implement and enforce. "The existing graphic health warnings at 40% are adequate to inform and caution a person. The proposal to further increase the size of the warnings is completely unwarranted and unnecessary. Even countries like USA, Japan and China have textual warnings which are not disproportionately large", said Syed M Ahmad, Director at TII.

Tobacco Institute of India said the proposed warnings are unreasonable, drastic and implement and enforce.

Ahmad said even global consultancy firms like Deloitte and London Economics have established through their studies on graphic health warnings that there is no correlation between implementation of such warnings and reduction in consumption. According to the notification, 60% of each cigarette packet will have "pictorial representation" while another 25% will be covered by text warning against the ill-effects of tobacco on a smoker's health. Each side of the packet will have a different picture provided by the government and text will not be in more than two languages.

According to Health Minister Harsh Vardhan, the decision to increase size of health warnings is the first of many such changes to come. "I am a practicing ENT surgeon and I have personally seen people dying because of cancer caused by smoking and consumption of tobacco. We have made a number of suggestions to the Cabinet on curbing tobacco consumption and this decision is just one step in that direction", the Minister said at a function organized by the WHO to observe Global Handwashing Day.

ET was the first to report on September 10 that the Narendra Modi-led NDA Government was mulling a number of changes to COTPA including increasing size of health warnings on cigarette packets, raising age limit of tobacco consumption from 18 years to 25 years, banning sale of loose cigarettes and increasing fine for smoking in public, among other measures.

Tobacco, TB and Female Mortality

With over 12.1 million women smokers, India is home to second highest number of women smokers globally. Illiteracy, poor healthcare and malnutrition add to an alarming rate of growth in cancer, cardiovascular and respiratory disorders among women due to smoking and tobacco chewing.

Tobacco consumption among Indian women doubled during the period 1995–96 to 2009–10 from 10% to 20%. Much of this increase was due to the use of smokeless tobacco among women, which rose from 8.6% in 1995–96 to 18% in 2009–10. In fact, one in every five female tobacco users in the country consumes the smokeless form, as against one in 10 who smoke.

Studies have found the initiation for smokeless tobacco is higher among the poor and those with no formal education. Poor awareness of the insidious impact of tobacco and the social acceptability of chewing tobacco are the primary reasons for this worrying trend, say experts. Tobacco consumption is the cause of more than half of cancer deaths and a majority of the cardiovascular and lung disorders.

Worrying Trends

A direct consequence of the increase in smokeless tobacco is increased burden of disease and mortality in the country. Women's share in the economic burden of diseases related to tobacco was highest for cancer, at 38% *vis a vis* respiratory diseases, tuberculosis (TB) and cardiovascular diseases according to a recent 2014 study by the WHO in India and the Delhi-based Public Health Foundation of India (PHFI). It also found women contributed 29% of the total burden for smokeless tobacco including gutkha, pan masala and khaini.

The sale, manufacture and distribution of gutkha, khaini and pan masala containing tobacco has been banned by 23 States, including Himachal Pradesh, Haryana and Punjab after the 2011 regulation issued by the Food Safety and Standards Authority of India, a statutory body under the Health Ministry.

However, gutkha, a popular concoction of tobacco, areca nut, slaked lime, catechu, and flavoring is among the 22 different types of smokeless tobacco products that are readily available. Its consumption along with other chewable forms like khaini and zarda is not a taboo; hence it is high among women.

Reproductive Health

Ironically, talking about women's sexual and reproductive health remains a taboo which means that little or nothing is discussed about the impact of smokeless tobacco on the reproductive health of women including infertility and delays in conception. In particular, poor women in rural areas with little or no education who consume smokeless tobacco are rarely counseled about the adverse effect of continuing with smokeless tobacco during pregnancy. They are not told they risk complicated pregnancies and adverse outcomes including sudden death, preeclampsia, and preterm delivery. Neither are they informed why their babies are low weight or stunted.

According to the latest National Family and Health Survey (NFHS-3), the proportion of births with a low-birth weight is greater among children born to women who use tobacco. In the Northern region, Haryana has the highest percentage of low-birth weight babies followed by Punjab. It is estimated that in Punjab, 91% of female tobacco users use smokeless products; betel quid with tobacco, followed by gutkha and khaini, according to Voice of Tobacco Victims, a nongovernmental organization working to raise awareness on the impact of tobacco use.

Mother and Child Care

Nicotine reaches the brain within 10 seconds after the smoke is inhaled and can be found in all parts of the body including breast milk. It would help to incorporate easy to understand information related to tobacco use in maternal and child health programs and provide related services. Antenatal clinics should include appropriate screening and ensure pregnant women are counseled about the negative effects of tobacco use and exposure to passive smoking.

The link between smoking and TB is well established. Over 1,000 Indians die of TB each day and 2 million develop it each year, making the country among the top 10 countries with the highest burdens of tuberculosis and tobacco use. With over 12.1 million women smokers, India is home to the second highest number of women smokers globally. Also, an average woman in India is starting to smoke at 17.5 years compared to 18.8 years among men according to a Lancet study. However, there are no recent figures on how many female smokers died of TB. Women fall through the cracks as they tend to stay at home and have a lower awareness of TB symptoms. More than 300,000 children leave school each year on account of parental TB.

Stigma and TB

Lack of proper data also stems from the stigma associated with TB that prevents women from coming forward to seek treatment. They are often reluctant to reveal they might have TB due to potential rejection from their families. Women also delay seeking care because they are hesitant to use family resources, often meagre. They wait until they are severely ill and more likely to die. Many times, even when they do access the health services, women tend to discontinue treatment early in the absence of a strong healthcare support system to ensure follow-up.

An innovative use of technology has shown that this problem can be overcome. Operation ASHA, a NGO based in Delhi, has developed a biometric system that has taken TB treatment to the doorsteps with local community health workers, also known as Directly Observed Therapy (DOTS) providers and making sure they take their medicine as part of DOTS model for tuberculosis treatment introduced by the WHO. A cadre of trained, well-compensated, full-time counselors ensures compliance. If a patient misses a dose, a counselor goes to the patient's home to bring him or her back into the system. The counselors receive a cash incentive for tracking missed doses and administering them to the patient. They are also responsible for linking patients with hospitals, taking them for sputum testing, and getting boxes of medicine allotted, which is more helpful to women.

Innovative Approach

At the time of swallowing the medicine under DOTS guidelines, the provider identifies the patient with the fingerprints saved in the system. The data is then sent by SMS several times per day to a server located in Delhi, and if patients miss doses, text messages are sent at the end of the day to the appropriate counselors and health workers when noncompliance is detected. Those who do not show up to take their medication are sent reminders and tracked down.

The e-compliance system is highly interactive and easy to use even for semi-illiterate health workers and illiterate microentrepreneurs. The system is linked to an electronic medical system at the back-end, which improves transparency and reliability. So far, 175,000 visits have been logged in at the 58 centers with e-compliance terminals located in various States, including Punjab and Haryana. About 1,600 patients are tracked by the system bringing down the default rate considerably.

The Nepal Experiment

Its success also lies in its working in close coordination with the government and following its Revised National Tobacco Control Program (RNTCP) guidelines. The RNCTP is the largest TB control program in the world. However, merely having DOTS services in a district does not necessarily translate into ensuring that all those who have symptoms of the diseases are being diagnosed and treated by DOTS services.

If the e-compliance technology can be scaled up to reach out to marginalized populations living in remote areas, it would give women a chance to seek treatment and save their lives.

Another good initiative that needs to be adapted is the integration of tobacco control into a TB control program as shown in Nepal by the WHO Tobacco Free Initiative (TFI) and the WHO Stop TB program, in collaboration with the International Union against TB and Lung Diseases. This integration showed improved detection and management of TB cases.

Every 40 seconds a person adds to the numbing statistic on death from tobacco in India. The number of people dying of tobacco-related diseases annually is higher than the combined toll from AIDS, accidents, alcohol and other addictions according to the WHO.

Only a Smoke Screen: Electronic Cigarettes are not Entirely Harmless and need to be Regulated

In recent years, the electronic cigarette industry has been rapidly expanding, evolving from just one manufacturer in 2005 to a $3 billion global business with 466 brands. Electronic nicotine delivery systems (ENDS), of which e-cigarettes are the most common prototype, are battery-powered devices that use electricity to aerosolize a nicotine containing fluid for inhalation.

We know that nicotine is addictive and harmful. But as ENDS are not made from tobacco leaves, they have largely escaped any regulation. Rapid global growth of ENDS represents an evolving frontier filled with both promise and threat for tobacco control. There is an urgent need to regulate the use of ENDS to maximize their potential and minimize health threats.

ENDS are frequently marketed by the industry as an aid to quit smoking or a healthier alternative to tobacco. The argument for ENDS is that they don't contain the toxic by-products found in cigarettes, such as tar, and don't produce smoke. But, the fact is that there is very little research on ENDS and no convincing evidence that they are effective as a "quit smoking device". In fact, with almost 8,000 different flavors added, including fruit and candy-like flavors, there is legitimate concern that instead of reducing the number of smokers, they will actually serve as a gateway to nicotine addiction, and ultimately smoking, particularly for young people. Evidence supports this—experimentation with e-cigarettes is increasing rapidly among adolescents, doubling from 2008 to 2012.

Existing evidence shows ENDS aerosol is not merely "water vapor". It contains cancer-causing agents such as formaldehyde, which in some brands reach concentrations close to those of some conventional cigarettes. They deliver nicotine, which we know is a potent vasoconstrictor that may contribute to cardiovascular disease.

There is sufficient evidence to show that nicotine itself, and not just the smoke from cigarettes, can affect brain development in fetuses and adolescents just from passive inhalation. ENDS contain varying levels of nicotine. Frequently these levels are similar to those in cigarettes, and without regulation there is no way to control this amount.

There is also evidence that ENDS use indoors increases second-hand exposure of nonsmokers and bystanders, to nicotine and a number of toxicants. While some evidence does show that ENDS are likely to be less toxic than conventional cigarettes, it is not known how much less toxic they are.

Until we have sufficient evidence to determine the extent of their health impacts, the industry must be regulated. If we wait to implement regulations until the research is available, it may be too late.

While some steps have been taken to regulate ENDS, there are huge variations in country policies. Singapore and Brazil have completely banned e-cigarettes. In the WHO South-East Asia Region, many countries are considering implementing regulations. In India, a governmental round-table discussion in July decided to consider banning ENDS. While these are steps in the right direction, several countries in the developing world have no regulations or measures to regulate e-cigarettes.

It is for this reason that WHO recently released a report on the regulation of ENDS, which will be the primary topic of discussion at the sixth session of the Conference of the Parties to FCTC, to be held on October 13–18 in Moscow.

In this report, WHO calls for regulations to prohibit addition of flavors which may make ENDS more attractive to youth, ban the use of ENDS indoors and in public and workplaces, and restrict its advertising, promotion, and sponsorship to ensure that adolescents and nonsmokers are not targeted.

Such regulations should impede ENDS promotion to nonsmokers and young people, minimize potential health risks to both users and nonusers, prohibit the dissemination of unproven health claims, and protect existing tobacco control efforts.

WHO is urging countries to choose the best regulatory framework available to implement the suggested regulatory objectives. In some cases, this might be the existing tobacco control legislation, or the existing medicines and medical devices regulations while in other cases it may be in other government sectors.

Regardless, these regulations must be implemented in a timely manner to protect the public from any potential harm while more tests regarding the health impacts of ENDS are carried out. These regulations should be adaptable to be able to respond to new data as it is gathered on the health impacts of ENDS.

We have made remarkable progress in terms of tobacco control, but the increasing popularity of e-cigarettes threatens to undermine years of hard work. There is urgent need therefore to act now, to protect public health.

Anti-tobacco Drive: Government Issues Challans of Over Rs 40,000

The Delhi Government on Sunday issued challans to several authorities including New Delhi Railway station of over Rs 40,000 for selling banned tobacco products.

On the occasion of "Dry Day for Tobacco Drive" today the Health Department of Delhi Government sensitized 500 people including general public and staff of various departments on tobacco-related issues and filed a total of Rs 43,350 challans. Dr SK Arora, Additional Director of Health Department said "few illegal advertisement boards were removed from tobacco vendor shops and a strict warning was also issued to them".

Apart from this few challans were also issued for violation of law on the point of sale, he said. "People should stop consuming tobacco because it kills and not because of the fear of being getting challaned". Challans of Rs 25,200 were issued in the name of ISBT authorities for multiple violations and challans of Rs 3,850 were made for violations by the public. At New Delhi Railway Station, inspection was done only at two platforms, 1 and 14, and here also large number of violations were seen among the staff of the railway station. An amount of Rs 14,000 of challan was issued in the name of New Delhi Railway Station Authority for multiple violations".

"No smoking" signages were not found in adequate number and as per guidelines and people were also sensitized regarding it. The crackdown was a part of the drive being carried out by Delhi Government on the last day of every month. The official also said that the drive was conducted with the support of police and representatives of concerned departments and the activities were focused mainly at ISBT, Kashmiri Gate and New Delhi Railway Station in Central Delhi. The drive was focused on ban on direct or indirect advertisement of tobacco products, ban on smoking in public places and warning regarding ban on sale of tobacco products to minors. The observations made by the team included that the entire premises of ISBT was not having even a single "no smoking" signage.

Directory to Warn Public of Tobacco Ills

The Delhi Government has launched an innovative drive which proposes to create a "Tobacco Aware Citizens' Directory" to spread the word about its harmful effects. Sharing the details of the campaign, Dr SK Arora, Additional Director (Health) of the Tobacco Control Program under the Directorate of Health Services, said that one of the most interesting aspects of the campaign is that it is being conducted at zero cost to the exchequer. "The aim is to sensitize people to the harmful effects of tobacco use by creating a large network". Arora said.

Those who actively participate in the drive will be given a merit certificate and be termed a bonafide "Tobacco Aware Citizen of Delhi". Their names will be included in the Tobacco Aware Citizens of Delhi Directory, he added.

Beedis a Bigger Killer, Tax them Like Cigarettes

There is a glaring omission in your crusade. Why don't you and other politicians crusade against beedis too, which are infinitely bigger killers than cigarettes? In 2009, Swaminomics explained that Indians consume 1 trillion lightly taxed beedis per year; against 106 billion highly taxed cigarettes (both figures will be higher today). Why focus only on the 10% smoking cigarettes? Why not equalize taxes on beedis and cigarettes? At the time, I calculated that equalizing the tax on beedis to the rate for nonfilter microcigarettes would yield an additional Rs 15,000 crore per year. And if the beedi tax was equated with the standard filter cigarette rate, it would yield an additional Rs 80,000 crore a year. This would provide huge revenues to slash the fiscal deficit and finance important health-related measures like the Swachh Bharat Scheme.

The big reason is, of course, that the beedi is the poor man's smoke, and the beedi industry employs millions. So what? These are horrifying reasons for justifying huge tax breaks for proven killers. The poor want low prices, but is a cheap killer like the beedi the solution? Are you worried only about the health of richer folk who smoke cigarettes?

Dr Prabhat Jha of Toronto University estimates that 930,000 Indians die annually of tobacco-related diseases. His research reveals that smoking even a few beedis per day is harmful. Global experience shows that people give up smoking when high cost and social inconvenience provide proper incentives. Around 30% of all smokers in the US and Europe have given up the habit. But in India, only 2% of beedi smokers ever give it up, because the costs and social pressures are so low.

Politicians say the beedi industry employs millions, and tendu leaves used by the industry provide employment to lakhs of tribals gathering such leaves in forests. But, Dr Harsh Vardhan, can you justify encouraging an industry that kills millions just to provide employment? Surely you can create other, less harmful jobs?

A research study of 2010, "The Economics of Tobacco and Tobacco Taxation in India", concluded that "raising beedi taxes to Rs 98 per 1,000 sticks would add Rs 36.9 billion to tax revenues and prevent 15.5 million current and future smokers dying prematurely. Increasing cigarette taxes to Rs 3,691 per 1,000 sticks would further add Rs 146.3 billion to tax revenues and prevent 3.4 million premature deaths".

Another study in 2008, by Emily Sunley estimated that beedis account for 77% of all tobacco consumption but only 5% of excise taxes. She highlighted the fact that the tax per thousand was Rs 14 for handmade beedis and Rs 26 for machine-made ones. The tax break for handmade beedis was supposed to encourage employment, but actually encouraged corruption and misdeclaration of factory-made beedis as handmade ones.

However, even the low duty on handmade beedis was largely evaded by cottage industries producing unbranded beedis. Only 360 billion out of the trillion beedis produced annually paid any taxes at all. Sunley suggested banning unbranded beedis. This could be facilitated by obliging tobacco curers, blenders and processors to file electronic reports on whom they sold tobacco to. If the tax on handmade and machine-made beedis was equalized, this would facilitate a shift in production to machine-made production in factories, where tax collection was easier and evasion more difficult.

Sunley noted that against the tax of Rs 14–26 per thousand on beedis, the tax on cigarettes was Rs 168 for micro nonfilter cigarettes, Rs 819 for standard 70 mm filter cigarettes, and a whopping Rs 2,163 for filter cigarettes longer than 85 mm. On health grounds, how can anybody justify this wide spread? Clearly, the taxation of cigarettes and beedis is more politics than healthcare.

THE SMOKING GUN

India with 12.7 million women smokers was second only to the US, beating China to this dubious position. While the number of women smokers in China went down over the last three decades, in India, it more than doubled, even as the prevalence remained almost unchanged since 1980. Most developed countries, barring a few like France and Russia, have successfully brought down both smoking prevalence among women and the number of women smokers. Smoking is the third top risk

Source: "Smoking prevalence and cigarette consumption in 187 countries 1980-2012" by the Institute for Health Metrics and Evaluation (IHME) at the University of Washington.

for health loss in India, leading to nearly 1 million deaths each year in the country, according to a global study.

Another Reason to Quit Tobacco

Risk of HPV16 Infection Higher Among People Who Consume Tobacco

New Research has indicated a possible link between tobacco use and infection with oral human papillomavirus (HPV) type 16. This is a sexually transmitted virus that causes cancers of mouth and throat. The study examined 6,887 people in the United States and looked for HPV16 infection among those who tested positive for tobacco-related chemicals in their blood and urine samples. The virus was detected from a 30-second oral rinse and gargle that collected mouth and throat cells. It was found that people who had higher levels of tobacco compounds in their body were more likely to be infected with HPV16. Although the exact reason is not known, researchers suspect that the virus may not be cleared easily from the body of those who use tobacco.

SMOKING THEM OUT

The Union Health Minister told Parliament that the Government has accepted a proposal to ban sale of loose cigarettes. A 2013 WHO report suggests that curbing smoking needs simultaneous implementation of several measures, collectively known as MPOWER-monitoring tobacco use, banning smoking at public places and offices, putting large warning labels on cigarette packs, mass media anti-smoking campaigns, advertisement bans and higher taxation. By implementing all six MPOWER measures, Turkey, for instance, was successful in reducing smoking prevalence among adults from 31.2% in 2008 to 27.1% in 2012. Data shows that

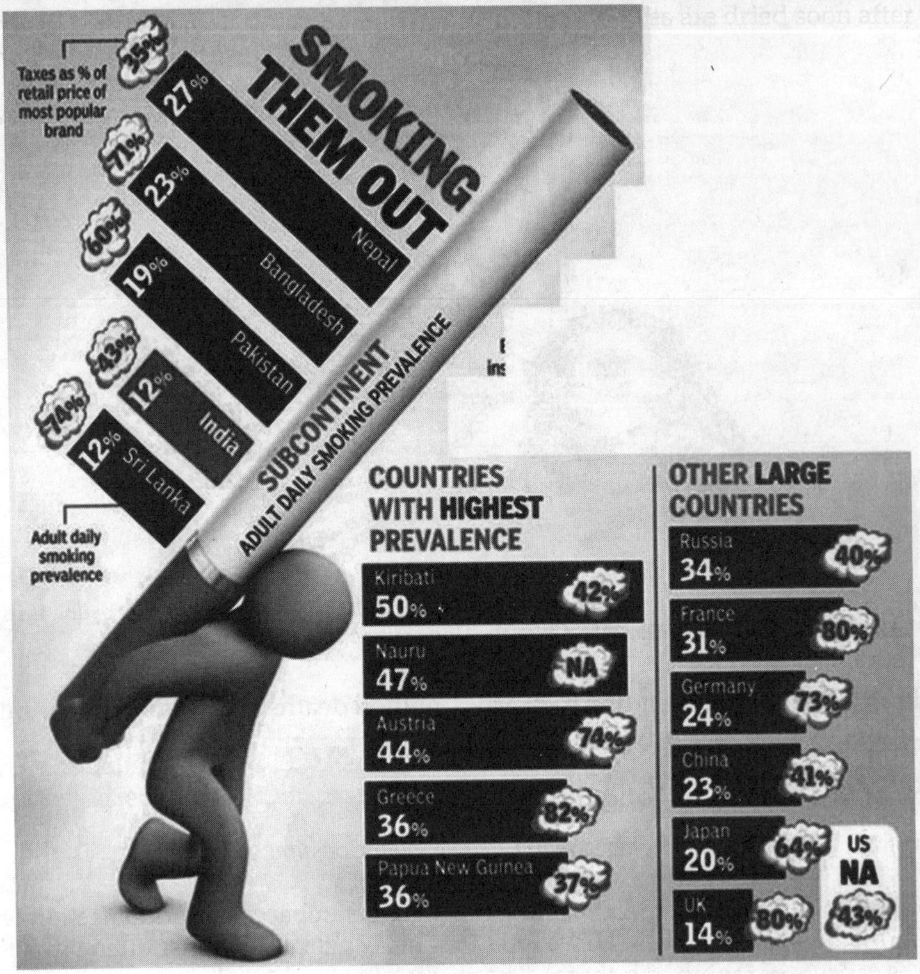

Source: WHO Report on the Global Tobacco Epidemic, 2013

when compared to advanced economies or even its own neighbors, India has among the lowest taxes on cigarettes.

Government may ban sale of loose cigarettes, allow only those over 25 to buy tobacco. There may soon be a ban on sale of loose cigarettes in India. The Union Government has accepted a new tougher framework for tobacco sale as part of recommendations of an expert panel which prompted it to also consider raising the minimum age of those who can be sold tobacco products, to 25 years from the current 18 years. Another proposal under government's consideration is increasing the fine for smoking in public and violation of other provisions of COTPA, 2003. Loose cigarettes account for over 75% of all cigarette sales, according to some industry estimates. In his reply in the Rajya Sabha, Health Minister JP Nadda said the ministry has accepted the suggestions made by the expert committee on "prohibition on sale of loose or a single stick of cigarette, increasing the minimum legal age for sale of tobacco products, increasing the fine or penalty amounts for violation of certain provisions of the Act as well as making such offences cognizable".

The ministry has circulated a draft note on the new norms, seeking comments from other ministries. As a result, shares of tobacco giants ITC and Godfrey Phillips India tanked 5% and 9% on Tuesday. The panel was formed by the Health Ministry to review COPTAs (Prohibition of Advertisement and Regulation of Trade and Commerce, Production, Supply and Distribution), 2003. The WHO-FCTC States that countries "shall endeavor" to prohibit sale of loose cigarettes because it makes them more affordable for minors to consume them. India is a signatory to the WHO's FCTC convention. It entered the convention on 2003 and started implementing the norms in 2005.

Soon after assuming office, the Narendra Modi Government had raised the excise on cigarettes and called for a countrywide ban on sale of tobacco products. The government is now also considering a ban on branding on cigarette packets. The expert panel had also recommended increased penalties for smoking in public. Six years ago, India had banned smoking in public places. However, implementation of the law has been weak, experts say. Once the inter-ministerial consultation is over, the draft proposal by the Health Ministry is likely to be taken up by the Cabinet.

Tobacco Stocks Tank on Plan to Ban Loose Sticks

Led by cigarette major ITC, stocks of tobacco companies witnessed major selling in Tuesday's market after JP Nadda, the Health Minister in Narendra Modi's Government, told Rajya Sabha that it has accepted the recommendations of a panel that had proposed a ban on sale of single cigarette sticks. The main reason behind such a ban is a WHO report that says single sticks promote smoking among minors since they are more affordable. On their part, tobacco companies say they do not promote selling single sticks of cigarettes and warned, given the number of shops selling cigarettes, enforcement will be tough. In Tuesday's session on the BSE, after Nadda informed Rajya Sabha members that his ministry was in favor of such a ban, stocks of tobacco companies came in for heavy selling with sensex major ITC closing 5% lower at Rs 356.

Along with ITC (makers of Classic, Gold Flake, etc), stocks of Godfrey Phillips (makers of Marlboro) tanked 8.9% to Rs 2,966, while Golden Tobacco (makers of Panama) closed 7.6% lower at Rs 37 and VST Industries (makers of Charms and Charminar) closed 2% lower at Rs 1,833.

UP in Smoke

Stock	Closing price (Rs)	Change (%)
Godfrey Philips	2,966	–8.9
Godfrey Tobacco	37	–7.6
ITC	356	–5.0
VST Inds	1,883	–2.0

Annexure 2: Big Tobacco's future: Big pot

You may like technology (who doesn't these days) or the energy sector (where would we be without it)—but if you are making a long-term bet as an investor, there is a lot going for Big Tobacco. It is not just that tobacco boasts the best historical performance of all US industries. The industry's future seems especially bright. As marijuana gradually becomes a legal drug, Big Tobacco is poised to dominate the market.

According to the 2015 edition of Credit Suisse's Global Investment ReturnsYearbook (I thank my Bloomberg View colleague Justin Fox for bringing it to my attention), a dollar invested in tobacco in 1900 would have turned into $6.3 million by the end of 2014, by far the best performance of all the industries that existed at the start of the 20th century.

That, of course, reflects the decline of some old industries, like coal, railroads and shipbuilding, and fails to account for the emergence of new ones. (A small investment in "some kind of fruit company," called Apple, is how Forrest Gumpearned his fortune.) So, perhaps the last 10 years are a better indicator of tobacco's resilience. Since the beginning of 2005, the MSCI Global Tobacco Index has risen 196.4%, providing an 11% annual return. It far outperformed the catch-all MSCI World Index, which went up 50.6% in the same period.

It even did better than the MSCI World Information Technology Index, which rose 94.4% in the past decade. Despite governments' efforts to get people to quit smoking, a lot of them still do, and they represent a stable core market for Big Tobacco. In the US, for example, 20.9% of adults smoked in 2004 and 19% still had the habit in 2011.

Markets for addictive products are less susceptible to economic crises than any others, and – in part because they are so politically toxic – they are less bubbly. So, investors tend to get a steady return.

Right now, the industry is undergoing a vaping revolution. A Bloomberg Intelligence analytical report from last December predicted sales of vapour products in the US could climb 44% to $2.6 billion this year. So far, much of that market has been in vaping liquids and the e-cigarettes that use them, but that technology is growing obsolete. The new cutting edge is in "heat not burn" devices, which, according to the Bloomberg Intelligence report, "may be highly disruptive to the existing tobacco industry" because they use real tobacco.

A "heat not burn" vapouriser heats ground tobacco leaves and delivers a nicotine hit to the user without producing much smoke or ashes. This still amounts to using an addictive substance in a slightly different way, but it's not hard to imagine why smokers might find it appealing to inhale less smoke, none of which contains burned paper. Such "heat not burn" devices are already available from a host of smaller companies, but the bigger tobacco companies, such as Philip Morris and Reynolds, have made it clear they are intent on catching up.

It may seem that Big Tobacco is merely cannibalizing its existing sales by putting out such products. Yet, it may be something of a bet on the future, too. "Heat not burn" vapourizers can just as easily be used to smoke marijuana as tobacco. And they are already gaining popularity among cannabis users.

Tobacco companies have never said publicly that they had like to get in on the marijuana business. That's understandable. Selling marijuana is still largely illegal in Europe and in the US, and it would be politically suicidal for companies that face as many regulatory barriers as tobacco companies do to suggest that they want to go into soft drug dealing. But, they have long watched marijuana as a potential market.

In a 2014 paper entitled "Waiting for the Opportune Moment: The Tobacco Industry and Marijuana Legalization", the political scientist Rachel Ann Barry and her colleagues quoted internal documents from Philip Morris expressing an interest in marijuana as a tobacco competitor. These letters and memos date back to 1969. In 1970, an adviser to the board of British American Tobacco, Sir Charles Ellis, penned a proposal for a marijuana product to the company, claiming that "smoking such a cigarette is a natural expansion of current smoking habits which, if a more tolerant attitude were ever taken to cannabis, would be a change in habit comparable to moving over to cigars". The discussions and research paused in the 1980s as marijuana legalization prospects became more remote, but resumed in the 1990s.

More than 19 million Americans aged 12 and older reported using marijuana in 2012. If recreational marijuana is ever legalized beyond the four states where it is currently permitted, the tobacco companies will be perfectly positioned to capture this vast market. They already have distribution systems (licensed tobacco sellers already dispense medical marijuana in a number of states), marketing machines, industrial facilities to make marijuana cigarettes and package cannabis for use in vaporizers, patented designs for the vaporizers themselves, research laboratories (and possibly even a head start on commercial product development) and, last but not least, cash resources.

"Marijuana legalization advocates", Barry and her colleagues wrote, "have not considered the potential effects of the multinational tobacco companies entering the market (or other corporations such as the food and beverage industries), with their substantial marketing power and capacity to engineer marijuana cigarettes to maximize efficacy as drug delivery systems, in the way that modern cigarettes are designed, whose primary objective is maximizing profits through higher sales". I am not sure that is true: the legalization advocates probably would not mind Big Tobacco's participation in developing the market.

After all, these corporations can do it better than the tiny companies that have attracted the early marijuana investment into their penny stocks. Companies listed on Marijuanastocks.com may survive on the fringes of the post-legalization industry, but many of them will be put out of business or acquired by the big league players who have survived all the upheavals of the last 115 years while producing top returns for their investors. For those not overly worried about the moral strings attached to investing in companies that pander to addictions, a greener future for Big Tobacco may be one of the biggest opportunities of a lifetime.

Annexure 3: Govt issues fresh notification to ban raw tobacco products

The Delhi health department has reissued last year's notification to ban the production, storage, sale and purchase of all kinds of raw chewable tobacco products such as khaini, zarda, tobacco and nicotine mixed pan masala in the Capital.

A fresh notification was issued because the earlier one had lapsed. HT had reported in October last year that the previous proposal of banning raw chewable tobacco products was pending with the Lieutenant Governor (L-G) for final approval for 6 months.

"The updated proposal of notification is going to bring about clarity in the ambiguity of the use of all forms of chewable tobacco products. The sale of raw chewable tobacco products in Delhi henceforth will be considered illegal in keeping with the Cigarette and Other Tobacco Products Act (COPTA) and the Supreme Court directions of banning tobacco products", said a Delhi government official.

"This notification has been finalised on the directions of health minister Satyendar Jain", said the official. The sale and production of gutkha, a mixture of raw tobacco and supari (betel nut) was banned in Delhi in September 2012.

"Even though gutkha was banned in 2012, retailers used to sell the components of gutkha (betel nut and raw tobacco) in separate pouches. People buy them separately, mix them, and turn it into gutkha. Therefore, the purpose of banning gutkha was not served. Then we realised we need to ban all forms of raw chewable tobacco products completely. The earlier proposal was pending because there was no government in Delhi for at least 1 year", said Dr SK Arora, additional director health, Tobacco Control Programme, Delhi government.

Banned in Delhi

Notification proposes to ban raw tobacco items.
90% of oral cancer is related to chewing tobacco products.
90% of lung cancer is due to tobacco consumption.
40% of all cancers are due to consumption of tobacco.
11 lakh cancer cases area reported in India every year.

2

Cadbury

Cadbury was founded almost 200 years ago. 1824 John Cadbury opened Bull Street shop in 1824, John Cadbury opened a grocer's shop at 93 Bull Street, Birmingham. Among other things, he sold cocoa and drinking chocolate, which he prepared himself using a pestle and mortar. John's wares weren't just inspired by his tastes, they were driven by his beliefs. Tea, coffee, cocoa and drinking chocolate were seen as healthy, delicious alternatives to alcohol, which Quakers deemed bad for society.

1831 John cadbury opens factory in crooked lane: The Cadbury manufacturing business was born in 1831, when John Cadbury decided to start producing on a commercial scale and bought a four-storey warehouse in nearby Crooked Lane.

1842 the range expands: By 1842 John Cadbury was selling no less than 16 varieties of drinking chocolate and 11 different cocoas! The earliest preserved price list shows that you could buy drinking chocolate in the form of both pressed cakes and powder.

The chocolate varieties boasted titles like "Churchman's Chocolate", "Spanish Chocolate", and "Fine Brown Chocolate". Cocoa was sold as flakes, in powder and in nibs, and went by names including, "Granulated Cocoa", "Iceland Moss", "Pearl" and "Homeopathic". It is intriguing to imagine what the ingredients might have been!

1847 the business moves to bridge street: In 1847, the Cadbury brothers' booming business moved into a new, larger factory in Bridge Street in the center of Birmingham. The new site had its own private canal spur, which linked the factory to the Birmingham Navigation Canal and from there to all the major ports in Britain.

1847 Fry's produce the first chocolate bar: In 18th century, France produced pastilles (tablets) and bars. But, it wasn't until Bristol company Fry and Son made a "chocolate delicieux a manger" in 1847 that the first bar of chocolate appeared as we know it today. The first ever chocolate bar was made from a mixture of cocoa powder and sugar with a little of the melted cocoa butter that had been extracted from the beans. The result was a bar that could be molded. It might have been coarse and bitter by today's standards, but it was still a revolution. Shaped into blocks and bars, and poured over fruit-flavored centers, this plain chocolate was a real breakthrough. But, there were many more treats in store.

Cadbury chocolate is renowned worldwide, but the Cadbury legacy is more than just a chocolate factory: The Cadbury family, with their Quaker beliefs that—all human beings should be treated equally and should live in peace, believed in social responsibility and social reform. They improved working and social conditions for their employees and the community.

This was made possible by the success of their business. The Cadbury story began in 1824 when John Cadbury, a young Quaker, opened a shop in Birmingham. He sold coffee, tea, drinking chocolate and cocoa amongst other things. John believed alcohol was a main cause of poverty and hoped his products would serve as an alternative. He started manufacturing on a commercial scale in 1831 and his brother Benjamin joined the company in the 1840s to form Cadbury Brothers.

Cadbury

- 1824 John Cadbury opened a shop
- 1854 Royal warrant issued
- 1861 George and Richard took over the business
- 1879 Bournville factory opened
- 1918 Cadbury opened first overseas factory in Tasmania
- 1919 Cadbury merged with JS Fry and Sons Limited
- 1969 Cadbury merged with Schweppes
- 2008 Cadbury Schweppes split.

Royal Approval

The brothers opened an office in London and received a Royal Warrant as manufacturers of chocolate and cocoa to Queen Victoria in 1854. John's sons George and Richard took over the business in 1861 and set about expanding it. Richard looked after sales and marketing and George took care of production and buying. In the late 1870s the growing business needed a larger site, so they purchased land 4 miles out of Birmingham. This was in the countryside at the time.

George Cadbury's Vision

A new factory, planned by George, was built on the site, and the area became known as Bournville after the small stream that runs through the site. George was driven by a passion for social reform and wanted to provide good quality low cost homes for his workers in a HEALTHY environment—giving an alternative to grimy city life. So, he set about building a village where his workers could live.

George said of his plans: "If each man could have his own house, a large garden to cultivate and healthy surroundings—then, I thought, there will be for them a better opportunity of a happy family life". His aim was that one-tenth of the Bournville estate should be "laid out and used as parks, recreation grounds and open space". The brothers set new standards for working and living conditions in Victorian Britain and the Cadbury plant in Bournville became known as "the factory in a garden".

1861 Richard and George Cadbury Take Charge

John's health rapidly declined and he finally retired in 1861, handing over complete control of the business to his sons Richard and George. The brothers were just 25 and 21 when they took charge of the business. Although they'd both worked for the company for a number of years, taking control must still have been a daunting prospect for Richard and George. Other cocoa manufacturers were going bust, and they must have been worried that Cadbury Bros would soon be joining them. Luckily, they had a financial lifeline: each invested £4,000 in the business, money that had been left to them by their mother. It was the equivalent of about £600,000 today, but it didn't solve all their problems. The first few years were tough. To keep the business alive, the brothers worked long hours and lived frugally. George looked after production and buying. Richard looked after sales and marketing, which wasn't in good shape—he commented that if the business ever made a profit of a thousand pounds a year he would retire a happy man!

1866 an Innovative Processing Technique is Introduced

The turning point for the Cadbury business was the introduction of a new processing technique, resulting in the 1866 launch of "Cadbury Cocoa Essence", the UKs first unadulterated cocoa.

Before Cocoa Essence, the cocoa Cadbury produced, like that of many other manufacturers, contained high levels of cocoa butter. They had to add starches to mask its taste and texture. But, George Cadbury had heard about an innovative cocoa press being used by a Dutch manufacturer called Coenraad Johannes van Houten. The press squeezed out much of the cocoa butter from the beans, so it wasn't necessary to add starches. Could this be the way forward? Buying the press was a massive gamble. It was expensive and the brothers had little money. It had to be used for mass production and no one knew if there'd be enough demand for the product. But, the Cadbury brothers decided to go for it—the first British manufacturer to go down this route. It was a momentous step, one that changed the British cocoa business and led to the future prosperity of Cadbury. The press was installed in their factory in Bridge Street, Cadbury Brothers' new product appeared. Cocoa Essence was extensively advertised as "Absolutely Pure". Therefore, "Best", alongside medical testimonials. The marketing of Cocoa Essence helped to increase sales dramatically and transformed a small business into the worldwide company that Cadbury is today.

1875 First Milk Chocolate Bar

In 1875, a Swiss manufacturer called Daniel Peter added milk to his recipe to make the first milk chocolate bar. This wasn't a completely new idea; Cadbury produced their milk chocolate drink based on Sir Hans Sloane's recipe between 1849 and 1875. And Cadbury added their own milk chocolate bars in 1897. But, Daniel Peter was still way ahead of them—using condensed milk rather than powdered milk to produce a chocolate with a superior taste and texture. Another Swiss manufacturer invented the conching machine in 1879. This refined chocolate, giving it the smooth texture we know today. Swiss milk chocolate dominated the British market—a situation the Cadbury family set out to challenge in the 20th Century.

1875 Cadbury Makes their First Easter Egg

The first Cadbury Easter egg was made in 1875. The earliest eggs were made with dark chocolate and had a smooth, plain surface. They were filled with sugar-coated chocolate drops known as "dragees". Later, Easter eggs were decorated and had their plain shells enhanced with chocolate piping and marzipan flowers.

1878 the Cadbury Brothers are Inspired by their Vision

When the Bridge Street factory became too small, George Cadbury had a new vision of the future. "Why should an industrial area be squalid and depressing?" he asked.

His vision was shared by his brother Richard, and they began searching for a very special site for their new factory.

In 1878, the brothers found their new home. They chose a 14½ acre greenfield site between the villages of Stirchley, King's Norton and Selly Oak, about four miles South of Central Birmingham. The site comprised a meadow with a cottage and a trout stream – the Bourn. The cottage isn't there anymore, but the pear tree from its garden still stands outside the main Cadbury reception at the Bournville factory. The factory was initially going to be called, Bournbrook, after the cottage and Bournbrook Hall which stood nearby. But instead, "Bournville" was chosen—combining the name of the stream with "ville", the French word for town. At Bournville, workers lived in far better conditions than they'd experienced in the crowded slums of the city. The new site had canal, train and road links and a good water supply. There was lots of room to expand, which was lucky, because George's plans for the future were ambitious. He wanted to build a place full of green spaces, where industrial workers could thrive away from city pollution. "No man ought to be condemned to live in a place where a rose cannot grow", George Cadbury.

1879 Bournville "the Factory in a Garden" is Born

Birmingham architect, George H Gadd worked closely with George Cadbury to draw up plans for the factory. The first bricks were laid in January 1879 and 16 houses for foremen and senior employees were built on the site. These mostly semi-detached houses were well-built and spaced out with ample gardens. Production began at the Cadbury Brothers' "Bournville factory in a garden" in September 1879. When the workers arrived they found facilities that were simply unknown in Victorian times. There was a field next to the factory where men were encouraged to play cricket and football; a garden and playground for the girls; a kitchen where workers could heat up their meals, and properly heated dressing rooms where they could get changed.

As George said, "if the country is a good place to live in, why not to work in?" Keen sportsmen, Richard and George encouraged sports and recreations, often playing cricket themselves. Sports facilities grew to include football, hockey and cricket pitches, tennis and squash racquet courts and a bowling green. Gradually women's and men's swimming pools were built and every young boy and girl joining the company was encouraged to become a good swimmer. Work outings to the country were organized together with summer camps for the young boys. Morning prayers and daily bible readings, first started in 1866, helped to preserve the family atmosphere and continued for another 50 years, until the workforce grew too large for such an assembly. For workers who still needed to travel to the new factory from their homes in Birmingham, the Cadbury brothers negotiated special workmen's train fares to Bournville's Stirchley Station with the local railway company. Cadbury duly became famous not just for its prosperity, but also for the advances in conditions and social benefits for its workforce.

1893 George Cadbury Adds another 120 Acres to Bournville

George Cadbury had already created some houses for key workers when the Bournville factory was built. Then, in 1893, he bought another 120 acres near the works and started to build houses in line with the ideals of the embryonic Garden City movement.

George's wife, Dame Elizabeth Cadbury, planned Bournville Village alongside her husband, and her memoirs tell us how these plans became reality. "When I first came to Birmingham and we were living at Woodbrooke, morning after morning I would walk across the fields and farmland between our home and the works planning how a village could be developed, where the roads should run and the type of cottages and buildings". Gradually, she realized this dream. Many of the first tenants were men in Mr Cadbury's Adult School Class, who had previously lived in the centre of Birmingham without gardens. Now, they enjoyed healthy surroundings and cultivated their gardens, many with their own apple trees.

1895 George Cadbury Builds a Further 143 Cottages in Bournville

George Cadbury decided not to go for tunnel-backs because it limited the amount of light in the houses. Instead he chose rectangular cottages, each one with a large garden. In 1895, 143 cottages were built on the land he had bought privately, a total of 140 acres. When building started at Bournville, the basic house type built in the Midlands was the "tunnel-back". It was cheap, large-scale housing complying with the Public Health Acts that had condemned "back-to-back" housing. They were built in long rows with entrances to the back through common passages, built over on upper floors. Though they were an improvement on the previous houses, they didn't look that attractive—lots of tunnel-backs meant endless rows of dreary monotonous housing. George Cadbury decided not to go for tunnel-backs because it limited the amount of light in the houses. Instead he chose rectangular cottages, each one with a large garden. In 1895, 143 cottages were built on the land he had bought privately, a total of 140 acres. The first houses were built in straight rows with no more than four houses in a terrace, but this soon gave way to more interesting layouts.

Bournville was developed to be a "garden village" and these were the guiding principles—cottages grouped in pairs, threes or sometimes fours. Groups were set back from tree-lined roads, each house with its own front garden and vegetable garden with fruit trees at the back. All cottages were well built with light airy rooms and good sanitation. A typical cottage had a parlour, living room and kitchen downstairs and three bedrooms upstairs. Some early houses didn't have bathrooms, but it was easy to add them later on. Houses should cost at least £150 to build: they were to house honest, sober, thrifty workmen, rather than the destitute or very poor. Building was restricted on each plot to prevent gardens being overshadowed and keep the rural feel. The first houses were sold on leases of 999 years to keep the rural appearance of the district: mortgages were available for would-be purchasers. Bournville's green environment reflected the aim of George Cadbury that 1 of 10 of the Estate should be "laid out and used as parks, recreation grounds and open space". It attracted great interest from housing reformers including the Garden City Association. In fact, George Cadbury was instrumental in developing the Garden City Movement along with other reformers including Sir Ebenezer Howard, who founded the Association in 1900 and was the father of modern town planning. He once said that Bournville gave him the drive to carry out his ideas. The first Garden City, Letchworth, was begun in 1902. Bournville became included within the boundary of the city of Birmingham in 1911, so it is now a "garden suburb", like Hampstead Garden Suburb in London.

1897 Cadbury Milk Chocolate is Launched

When Cadbury started making Cocoa Essence they had lots of cocoa butter left over, so they used it to make bars of chocolate! Cadbury milk chocolate hit the shelves in 1897, but it probably wouldn't be much to our taste now. Made of milk powder paste, cocoa mass, cocoa butter and sugar, the first Cadbury milk chocolate bar was coarse and dry and not sweet or milky enough to be a big hit.

Building a Legacy

Richard died unexpectedly in March 1899 of diphtheria whilst in Jerusalem. George continued to provided better working conditions for employees, setting up workers committees and providing facilities. Over the years George invested a lot of his money in businesses which placed a high priority on the welfare of the workers and despite running a large company he also dedicated a lot of time to helping those less privileged in his local community.

George gave the Bournville estate to the Bournville Village Trust in 1901. The trust was founded, to administer and develop the village and its surroundings. One of George Cadbury's former homes, Woodbrooke, a Georgian style mansion built by Josiah Mason, has retained a Quaker connection and is Europe's only Quaker Study Center. Since 1903, it has provided education for people from around the world. George's second wife Elizabeth, was also heavily involved in philanthropy. Together they opened Woodlands Hospital in Northfield and built The Beeches, where children from the city slums could holiday. George also donated the Lickey Hills Country Park to the people of Birmingham.

1900 Early Outdoor and Press Advertising

Cadbury produced some of the finest examples of posters and press advertisements during this period. A popular local artist, Cecil Aldin, was commissioned to illustrate for Cadbury. His evocative images featured in early magazine campaigns and graced poster sites all over the country.

1905 Cadbury Dairy Milk is Launched

Swiss manufacturers were leading the field in milk chocolate, with much better products than their rivals. In 1904, George Cadbury Junior was given the challenge to develop a milk chocolate bar with more milk than anything else on the market. All sorts of names were suggested, "Highland Milk", "Jersey" and "Dairy Maid". But, when a customer's daughter suggested "Dairy Milk", the name stuck. Dairy Milk was launched in June 1905. It was sold in unwrapped blocks that could be broken down into penny bars. Gradually it became more and more successful until it was Cadbury's biggest seller by the beginning of the First World War. By the early 1920s, it had taken over the UK market. And of course, it is still with us today. Cadbury Dairy Milk has become what's known as a "megabrand", hugely popular and available in many different varieties, all over the world.

1905 First Cadbury Logo Commissioned

In 1905, William Cadbury commissioned the first Cadbury logo. He was in Paris at the time and chose Georges Auriol to create the design—Auriol also designed the signs for the Paris Metro. The logo was an image of a stylized cocoa tree interwoven with the

Cadbury name. Registered in 1911, it was used on presentation boxes, catalogues, tableware and promotional items, and imprinted onto the aluminum foil that was used to wrap molded chocolate bars. Although we might not recognize it today, it was used consistently from 1911–1939 and again after the Second World War.

1906 Bournville Cocoa is Launched

At first, Cadbury resisted creating an alkalized cocoa (a product made less bitter by adding harmless carbonate of potash) having emphasized the purity of their own cocoa. But, eventually, the company realized that alkalized cocoa was the future and created Bournville Cocoa.

1908 Bournville Chocolate is Launched

Bournville chocolate was launched in 1908. It was named after the Bournville factory where it was made, and was originally launched just as a plain chocolate bar. Many variants have been added to the range over time including Bournville Nut, Bournville Fruit, Bournville Roasted Almond and Bournville Fruit and Nut.

1914 Fry's Turkish Delight is Launched

JS Fry and Sons merged with Cadbury in 1919 but the name of the bar remains. Fry's Turkish Delight—rose-flavored Turkish delight draped in milk chocolate—is a long-standing favorite. This luxurious treat was flavored with genuine Otto of Roses, and molded without starch for a smoother finish. The slogan "Full of Eastern Promise" has been used since the end of the 1950s. It was particularly well known in the 1970s and 1980s through popular TV advertising, which tended to involve mysterious ladies in exotic desert settings.

1915 Milk Tray is Launched

Boxes of chocolates had been produced at Cadbury since the 1860s. But they were expensive, sold in small quantities and would only have been bought for very special occasions. Milk Tray was different: a chocolate assortment, affordable enough to be an everyday treat. To start with, the chocolates were sold in 5½ lb boxes, which would be put out in trays to sell to customers, which is where the name originated from. One was Milk Tray and one was Plain Tray. Then, in 1916, Cadbury produced a half-pound box of chocolates, followed by a 1Ib box in 1924. By the mid 1930s it was outselling all its competitors. Later in 1961, it was made more sophisticated, while in 1971 a William Morris-style pack was introduced. In 1978, it changed again, to an elegant pack with a white orchid on the purple background. Milk Tray of course became hugely famous for its "Milk Tray Man" TV commercials, featuring a daring, dark and handsome action hero who dives off cliffs, pilots helicopters through storms and speed boats over waterfalls, "All because the lady loves Milk Tray". Today, over 8 million boxes are sold every year.

1919 Cadbury Purchases Fry's

Cadbury bought Fry's in 1919 and the company grew, producing delicious chocolate on a grand scale, so it could be enjoyed by everyone. Cadbury already had close links with JS Fry and Sons Limited, and in 1919 they signed an agreement, creating a new holding company, the British Cocoa and Chocolate Company, to take over the assets of both businesses. A new site was found for Fry's outside Bristol, at Keynsham, and this was named Somerdale. The Fry's business had many good things going for it including Countlines. Countlines were popular in America and Canada; they were chocolate bars with different centers and got their name because they were sold by bar, not by weight. Crunchie, Fudge and Picnic are all tasty examples.

1920-1960

1920 Cadbury Dairy Milk Goes Purple

Cadbury dairy milk started out in pale mauve with red script, in a continental style "parcel wrap" at its launch in 1905. The full dairy milk range became purple and gold in 1920.

1920 Flake is Launched

The "crumbliest flakiest chocolate" was first developed in 1920. A canny Cadbury employee noticed that, when the excess from chocolate moulds was drained off, it fell in a stream and created flaky, folded chocolate.

From that simple observation, came a mouth-watering new chocolate bar! It started off as a Cadbury Dairy Milk product with a see-through wrapper. The yellow wrapper appeared in 1959, without the "Dairy Milk" label. Sales of Flake quadrupled in the 1970s with the popularity of the sensual TV commercials, showing beautiful, bohemian Flake Girls enjoying luxurious "Flake" experiences.

1921 Cadbury Script Logo First Appears

The Cadbury script logo, based on the signature of William Cadbury, appeared first on the transport fleet in 1921. It was quite fussy to start with and has been simplified over the years. It wasn't until 1952 that it was used across major brands.

1928 the "Glass and a Half" Symbol is Introduced

It was originally used in 1928 on press and posters, but since then it hass been in TV ads and on wrapper designs, where you can still see it to this day. First of all it was just on Cadbury Dairy Milk, but it is become the face of the company in recent years.

1928 Investment Begins in Cadbury Dairy Milk Ads

A huge success from day one, Cadbury Dairy Milk first hit the shelves in 1905. But surprisingly, little money was put into advertising it until 1928. No one knew quite what to say about it—some ads talked about its "rich nutty flavor" others said "rich in cream". It didn't matter though—by 1928 it was the biggest selling chocolate product in Britain. At this point, Cadbury ploughed investment into advertising, stressing its high milk content. From 1928 a series of poster campaigns using the iconic "glass and a half" measure of milk established Cadbury Dairy Milk as one of the first truly recognizable brands on the high street. The "glass and a half" simple message of food value combined with enjoyable eating has found its way on to TV ads and wrappers. And it is still there today—becoming synonymous with Cadbury Dairy Milk worldwide.

1929 Crunchie is Launched

A Fry's product, Crunchie was launched to rival an Australian bar called the Violet Crumble, which first appeared in 1913. It is a bar with literary credentials—well, sort of. It was mentioned in Enid Bagnold's book "National Velvet" in 1935, as the Brown sisters' candy of choice for the year. It used to be smaller than it is now—the size was increased in 1982. Over a million bars are produced a day.

1938 Cadbury Roses are Launched

Cadbury Roses were introduced to compete in the twist wrapped assortment market. Early designs incorporated a sampler or embroidery rose design which was later replaced by a simpler rose. Bournville—where the chocolates were conceived and produced—was renowned as 'a factory in a garden. Roses were one of the most popular flowers at the time—hence the name for this popular assortment. The early 1 lb drum was described as a "wonderful lot" of chocolates for two shillings (10 p).

1939 King George VI and Queen Elizabeth Visit Bournville

Bournville welcomes King George VI and Queen Elizabeth on a tour that formed part of the program of their visit to Birmingham on March 1st 1939. 10,000 employees lined the route to welcome the King and Queen.

1939 Second World War Begins

During the War, rationing was enforced and raw materials were in short supply so it was a question of making do and concentrating on those products they were still able to produce. Cadbury Dairy Milk came off the shelves in 1941 when the government banned manufacturers from using fresh milk. Instead there was Ration Chocolate, made with dried-skimmed milk powder.

1945 Post War Expansion

Once the war ended, the company worked hard to restore business as usual. In due course of time, its efforts were rewarded and sales climbed. Cadbury expanded its biscuit range, launched a lot of promotional work and fended off competitors by keeping a direct distribution system.

1947 Milk Tray Bar is Launched

Eight Milk Tray Chocolates in a bar, imagine a box of Milk Tray Chocolates. Now, imagine picking eight of the most popular chocolates—keeping their distinctive shapes—and putting them in a bar! The Milk Tray Bar had a cult following back in the 1970s and people still reminisce about it to this day. It was originally launched in 1947 and was a favorite through to 1981.

1948 Fudge is Launched

Launched in 1948, Fudge is most famous for its 1980s and early 1990s advertising jingle "a finger of Fudge is just enough to give your kids a treat". The words were new, but the tune was borrowed and based on a traditional English folk song, "The Lincolnshire Poacher".

1955 First Cadbury TV Advert

Cadbury's ad for drinking chocolate was one of 24 that were shown on TVs launch night. The advert was based on the popular panel game "Twenty Questions".

1957 the Making of a 50s Cadbury TV Advert

Ever wondered how an early TV ad was made? We found this footage in the Cadbury archive showing the making of an early Roses TV ad.

1958 Lucky Numbers are Launched

In 1958, Cadbury launched a new assortment of chewy sweets, some covered in chocolate and some not. These lucky numbers each had an individual number on the wrapper, hence the name. The brand was retired in 1968.

1960 Skippy is Launched

The milk chocolate bar with a caramel and wafer center launched in 1960 with the slogan "It is got a crunch in the biscuit and a munch in the middle". A classic 1960s TV ad for Skippy shows a swinging London couple getting off their scooter and going into a trendy coffee bar to pickup their Skippys.

1961-1970

1967 Aztec Bar is Launched

Made of milk chocolate, nougatine and caramel, the Aztec made a big impact on its launch in 1967.

1967 Toffee Buttons are Launched

A button-shaped chocolate sweet with toffee inside launched in 1967 and withdrawn in 1971. The packs featured brightly colored cowboys and Indians.

1969 Cadbury Merges with Schweppes

The merger happened after the new Cadbury Chairman, Adrian Cadbury, was approached by his opposite number, Lord Watkinson. Cadbury commented "We had great opportunity, which was that of broadening the market for Cadbury brands geographically. That required the concentration of effort behind major brands, the ability to give better value to the customer and more in the way of financial resources than the Firm then possessed".

1970-1999

1970-A Decade of Sales Growth

Many Cadbury brands: Flake, Cadbury Dairy Milk, Whole Nut and Fruit and Nut—saw vast increases in sales in the 1970s, partially due to hugely successful and memorable TV advertising campaigns.

1970 Curly Wurly is Launched

Curly Wurly, made of chewy caramel covered in milk chocolate, first appeared in 1970. It is evolved over the years—the recipe was changed so that the middle was softer, making the milk chocolate less likely to drop off. It is still popular and seems to remind grown-ups of when they were young.

1970 Old Jamaica is Launched

Old Jamaica was a special blend of milk and plain chocolate with rum flavored raisins. This Cadbury Classic Selection bar is no longer made for the UK market, but you can still stock up on Old Jamaica if you look around on the Internet.

1971 Creme Egg is Launched

Cream-filled eggs first appeared back in 1923. But the Cadbury Creme Egg, we know and love today didn't hit the shelves until 1971. Sales really took off in 1975, when Cadbury Creme Egg became a cult through the power of TV advertising. The eggs are delivered to the trade for sale between January and Easter every year. About 1.5 million Cadbury Creme Egg eggs can be made every day at the Bournville factory. They're made in two halves, both filled with white and one additionally filled with yellow fondant. The two halves are closed together quickly and there it is a Cadbury Creme Egg. With its milk chocolate shell, creme fondant and yellow "yolk" Cadbury Creme Egg is absolutely unique in the market, and over 200 million of them are sold in the UK every year.

1981 Wispa is Launched

Launched nationally in 1983 after a trial run in the North East of England, Wispa was available throughout the 1980s and 1990s and was re-born in 2007. Early TV campaigns used the power of celebrities to create impact featuring comedians and comic actors including Mel Smith, Paul Eddington, Nigel Hawthorne, Victoria Wood, Julie Walters, Peter Cook, John Le Mesurier and Arthur Lowe who talked about it in a series of ads. A teaser campaign in the press asked "Have you heard the Wispa?" But didn't divulge that they were ads for a new chocolate bar. Wispa was discontinued in 2003 but relaunched, first temporarily in 2007 and then permanently in 2008 following pressure through social media channels to bring it back!

1985 Boost Coconut is Launched

Milk chocolate covered bar with a toasted coconut and caramel center. A variant of the mighty Boost, this coconut flavor was discontinued in 1994.

1987 Twirl is Launched

Twirl was launched in the UK in 1987. The brand was developed by the Cadbury Ireland business using Flake technology. It was originally launched in Ireland in 1985 as a single finger product and became a two-finger product on its UK launch.

1989 Inspirations are Launched

Textured fruit flavored centers covered in milk, white and dark chocolate. Inspirations launched in 1989, in a carton with sliding drawers. Initially highly successful, it was retired in 1998.

1990 Cadbury World Opens

Factory tours had always been popular but it was impossible to run a factory smoothly if it had thousands of visitors. In 1988, Cadbury began planning a visitor attraction to take the place of the factory tours—Cadbury World.

It cost £6 million to build, but was worth the expense. In 1990 Cadbury World opened in Bournville on a site next to the Cadbury factory and headquarters, attracting 350,000 visitors in its first year—100,000 more than were expected.

1996 Cadbury Fuse is Launched

Fuse exploded into the UK marketplace on "Fuesday" 24th September 1996. It was a chocolate bar with a difference—instead of having a milk chocolate coating on the outside, the yummy ingredients were suspended right the way through it. 40 million bars were sold in the first week, and within 8 weeks it was the UK's favorite confectionery. Alas, 10 years later and Fuse fizzled off the shelves, but it is fondly remembered to this day.

2000 Today

2003 Cadbury Schweppes Buys Adams and Becomes the World's Leading Confectionery Company

Cadbury bought the world's number 2 gum manufacturer, Adams, in 2003 and achieved its aim of leading the market. Cadbury Schweppes had the ambition to become the world's leading confectionery company but it was going to be hard to achieve through chocolate or sugar. Large chocolate companies tended to be family-owned and not for sale, and in sugar confectioners, a field in which there were few major brands. However chewing gum had big brands, growth and margins. Cadbury bought the world's number 2 gum manufacturer, Adams, in 2003 and achieved its aim of leading the market.

2007 the Gorilla Advert Premiers

"Gorilla" showed the eponymous primate enthusiastically playing the drums on the Phil Collins record "In the Air Tonight". It proved hugely popular and cleaned up at advertising awards ceremonies, winning many prizes including the prestigious Grand Prix Lion at Cannes in 2008.

2008 Cadbury and Schweppes Demerge

The two companies demerged to allow each to concentrate on its area of expertise.

2008 Cadbury Cocoa Partnership Launched

In January 2008, Cadbury launched the Cadbury Cocoa Partnership. £45 million was put aside to put into cocoa farms in Ghana, India, Indonesia and the Caribbean over a decade.

Today's cocoa farmers face big problems—average production has dropped and it can be hard to make a living. The Cadbury Cocoa Partnership has been setup to help them. It is a groundbreaking initiative, now funded by Mondelçz International, which is carried out in partnership with the United Nations Development Program and others, and marking 100 years since the Cadbury brothers first began trading in Ghana. Seventy percent of the Partnership funds will be invested into small farms and farming villages in Ghana, which provide the cocoa beans for Cadbury's UK chocolate, giving it its unique and much loved taste. So what will the Partnership do? Help farmers increase their yields and produce top quality beans; help start new rural businesses; improve life in cocoa communities by supporting education, the environment and building wells for clean and safe water; develop a pioneering way for cocoa farmers to work together with governments, NGOs, local organizations and international agencies. All in all, around a million people—cocoa farmers and the communities they live in—will benefit.

2009 Cadbury Dairy Milk Becomes Fairtrade

The move to Fairtrade has the impact of tripling the sales for cocoa farmers in Ghana under Fairtrade terms, both increasing Fairtrade cocoa sales for existing certified farming groups, as well as opening up new opportunities for thousands more farmers to benefit from the Fairtrade system. This move, which also includes Cadbury's hot chocolate beverage, marked the first anniversary of the Cadbury Cocoa Partnership.

2010 Cadbury Becomes Part of Mondelçz International

Cadbury became part of Mondelçz International family on the 2nd of February 2010.

2012 Chocolate Center of Excellence Opens in Bournville

A new global research and development center opens in Bournville as part of a £17 million investment in R&D in the UK. The "Center of Excellence" includes brand new innovation laboratories, a test plant facility and a collaboration kitchen to put new ideas to the test.

Over View

This case study explains the history and product development of Cadbury World; aspects of its operational and marketing functions, as well as providing some key numerical data. It is intended to provide students and other interested parties with a snapshot view of and insight into one of the UK's leading leisure attractions. It is strongly recommended that the case study is used in association with a visit to the attraction.

Cadbury World in Context

Seen as a new venture into the leisure industry when it opened in 1990, Cadbury World began its life principally as a public relations tool, but quickly became a popular half-day venue for people of all ages looking for quality leisure time. The original attraction was very educational and historical-based with mainly static displays. Over time, Cadbury World has grown to be a family attraction of much bigger dimensions. It has maintained visitor numbers comfortably in excess of half a million annually, and returns a healthy paper profit back into Cadbury UK as well as bringing value to the company in terms of public interface and direct communication to the consumer.

The original vision for Cadbury World was to provide a tourist attraction experience and provide an alternative to the demands from the general public denied access to the Bournville factory tour, which ceased due to health and safety practicalities around the time of the merger between Cadbury and Schweppes in 1969.

In setting up Cadbury World, in the face of strict health and safety and hygiene legislation, the vision was to underpin the central message of "Cadbury means chocolate means fun" with the interpretation of cocoa and Cadbury's chocolate both past and present. Responding to these principles, Cadbury World was conceived as a continuation of the message *"Cadbury means chocolate, means fun"*, through the interpretation of cocoa and Cadbury chocolate both past and present.

The original vision for Cadbury World developed as follows:

To significantly enhance consumers' perceptions of Cadbury and develop long-term brand loyalty by:

- Giving the visitor a memorable enjoyable, and unique Cadbury chocolate experience
- Offering high quality and good value for money
- Delivering Cadbury values of fun and quality, whilst achieving a break-even cost target for Cadbury Limited (at the time the UK chocolate operation of Cadbury Schweppes plc).

The Early Years

Opened on 14 August 1990, Cadbury World's first weeks proved to be successful beyond initial projections and led to a number of operation concerns and issues.

Huge queues built up at the start of each day and most visitors came with the expectation of taking part in the resumption of the Bournville factory tour (although it was thought by Cadbury World management that this perception had been overcome in its launch publicity and literature.

Free samples were not deemed to be as freely available as the public expected, and prices in the retail shop were more "gift shop" than "factory shop". The team's response to these initial problems were quick and comprehensive: including the immediate introduction of a timed-ticketing system (later a formal pre-booking system), and a greater access gained to a small part of the factory.

Free samples gradually became more plentiful and – as today – are distributed to visitors at intervals throughout the tour. The prices in Cadbury World took longer to resolve as the Cadbury World "gift shop" strategy needed to be aligned to serious and real business concerns relating to the threat to some serious and well-established commercial relationships. The belief from retailers in the Birmingham area was that unlike the Cadbury staff shop, the Cadbury World offering was open to the general public and would prove so successful that it would represent serious competition to those local traders if prices and offers were misaligned with those available from other retailers.

A policy was developed whereby there would be no more than a token reduction in the prices the Cadbury World gift shop charged, compared with prices in normal retail outlets. In reality, where the major retail organizations exerted substantial buying power, they were able to charge well below Cadbury World rates. Eventually, a "bargain corner" (now called the factory area) was established, the "gift shop". The retail offer developed and Cadbury World now has two retail outlets: "The World's Largest Cadbury Shop" and the "Essence Emporium" offering themed gifts and merchandise, standard retail offerings from the Cadbury brand portfolio and exclusive chocolate novelties hand-crafted in Cadbury World's "Demonstration Area".

In its early years, due to both visitor comfort and also health and safety provisions, Cadbury World's limited capacity required a robust control on the numbers of visitors allowed inside at any one time, as well as their flow and passage through the exhibition. Initially, a system of timed ticket entry was introduced—based on a first come first served approach—and enabled visitors to have a known time when they would go into the main exhibition.

As popularity for the attraction grew, even this measure proved to be inadequate to the increasing visitor numbers, and queues began to trail outside the main building once more. In March 1993, a reservations system was introduced, whereby visitors could prebook the date and time of their entry into Cadbury World, and eliminated much of the need to queue.

From 1993 onward, all publicity material for Cadbury World emphasized the reservations service and still strongly recommends that the visitor pre-book via the booking office telephone number or via the internet in order to avoid disappointment.

Whilst the reservations system had an immediate benefit, around 30% of admissions on a busy day would consist of visitors "rolling-up" (as awareness of the need to pre-book increased, the number of "roll-ups" has fallen to a more manageable of no more than 20% during peak periods). Indeed, during school holidays and bank holidays, it is not unknown for a visitor arriving at 10 AM without reservation to sometimes have to wait four hours before being admitted into the main exhibition.

During these peak times, this allows the visitor to "reverse their visit" and visit the Essence and Bournville Experience zones (accessed separately from the main building), enjoy any complimentary entertainments, utilize the outdoor play area for those visitors with children, or pick up a map from reception and take a walking tour of places of interest in the Bournville area.

Within the main exhibition itself, the "smoothing" of the visitor flow has been a key consideration in the development of Cadbury World's features and shows with the introduction of new or updated sets in a process of continuous improvement to meet demands. Visitors are admitted to the exhibition at a maximum rate of 80 individuals at intervals of every 10 minutes. Thus, certain presentations such as *The Cadbury Story* and the following set: *Making Chocolate*, will accommodate up to 80 people seated, and last no longer than 10 minutes including the audience's entry to, and exit from, each set.

The *Cadabra* ride is also carefully timed, to allow for an average of three passengers in each of the 12 cars (plus wheelchair-adapted car), and a circuit taking in the region of 5.5 minutes. All of this is careful orchestrated to ensure a steady and constant flow through the exhibition. On busy days, the delay from the slightest technical hitch on *Cadabra* is very difficult to recover, and this, with the queue of ticket holders in reception, is the main source of queuing nowadays in Cadbury World.

Ongoing Development and Continuous Improvement

Early improvements to Cadbury World were more reactive, addressing the issues raised by a new product from a company whose traditional expertise was not in the leisure industry. As time progressed, and as would be expected from a business unit whose parent company is a leading consumer brand, improvements became more proactive as the needs of the visitor changed and were driven more by a desire to offer the same service any visitor or leisure attraction would adopt.

The first significant development occurred in 1993 when parts of the exhibition were moved up onto the ground floor of the East Cocoa Block, and renamed the Cadbury Collection. Finally, some Cadbury-sponsored outdoor play equipment was recovered from the now defunct National Garden Festival of Wales in Ebbw Vale and used to expand the play facility.

Early feedback indicated that Cadbury World was surprisingly adult in appeal, and, during 1993, plans were laid to create the first exhibition feature aimed specifically at younger children, up to age 10. "The Fantasy Factory" was opened in March 1994, to provide a child's eye view of the production of liquid chocolate, from bean to bar, using interactive techniques, and, with the mirror room, to provide a grand finale.

In 1995, the child appeal was further increased by the installation of the Astros Set from the TV commercial that launched the brand in the UK, and then in 1997 with the opening of Cadabra, a Magical Cadbury Journey on specially constructed beanmobiles through various lands and scenes populated by the Cadbury World mascot—the Chucklebean

With the launch of Cadbury Land in July 2000, in a separate building to the rear of the site, and the complete replacement of the play area with a state-of-the-art themed play area, Cadbury World had achieved a shift in appeal to encompass the entire age range "from 090 and beyond".

Feedback from visitors in 2001 indicated that the attraction had shifted from a very adult profile, to a strong child profile. The improvements made to the attraction since 2001 have been of more adult interest in order to re-address this balance, whilst more recent additions and improvements have attempted to be cross-generational.

Attraction Structure – Spring, 2009

Cadbury World is now divided into 14 distinct and separate zones each dealing with a unique aspect of the history of cocoa and chocolate, the origins of the Cadbury business and the vision of its founding fathers, the production of chocolate and popular Cadbury brands, or just fully immersing the visitor in a truly "chocolatey" experience. Each zone broadly follows on from the previous one to give a logical and consistent story for the visitor's self-guided journey.

On entry to the main exhibition, the story of cocoa begins, in the jungles of Central America, in the area now known as Mexico. The Aztec Jungle zone was "re-laid" in January 2005, to incorporate water features and a more detailed explanation of the culture and beliefs of the various peoples who lived there up to the time of the Spanish conquest.

Moving on, the visitor goes into the Journey to Europe zone describing the way that the taste for cocoa and chocolate eventually made its way to high society in England in Cromwellian times. This zone leads into the last remaining set from 1990, now known as Bull Street Zone, covering regency London and the earliest days of John Cadbury's business in Birmingham in the 1820s in a re-creation of Victorian Birmingham.

Since 2001, the *Cadbury Story* Zone and *Making Chocolate* Zone, have controlled the visitor flow within the exhibition with automatic doors. Updated to include subtitles, these visually compelling zones tell the story of the origins of the Cadbury business, the Factory in a Garden and the Quaker principles important to the development of the company, and the manufacturing processes involved in producing Cadbury chocolate. The *Making Chocolate* Zone is multisensory experience and was one of the first of its kind in the UK leisure industry.

Exiting *Making Chocolate*, the visitor moves into the *Manufacturing* Zone (originally created in 2000) where they can select from a series of consoles' various stories relating to the manufacturing of seven popular brands within the Cadbury product portfolio.

Walking up stairs (or accessing via the lift provided), the visitor stops off for their first souvenir photograph opportunity next to an over-sized version of the Cadbury World Chucklebean mascot before moving through a time tunnel (constructed 2005) to commemorate the 100 years of Cadbury Dairy Milk.

Moving onto the Packaging Plant Zone, subject to scheduling, the visitor gets to see a snapshot of the real Bournville factory in operation as various Cadbury Dairy Milk products move their way along the conveyor belt on their journey to the outside world. The visitor then makes their way to the Cadbara Zone (updated in 2008) – consistently voted as being one of the most popular Zones—and a second souvenir photograph opportunity.

Downstairs, the visitor has the chance to purchase their first two photographs before seeing a replica of a water well and learning more about Cadbury's Ghana Well program. Visitors often toss spare change into the replica well and to date, have helped Cadbury World to construct 15 wells to help improve the lives of the Ghanaian cocoa farming community (for more details on the Cadbury Cocoa Partnership, Cadbury Corporate Social Responsibility, Fair-trade and a case study on the Ghana Wells.

Since mid-2004, the *Demonstration Area* Zone has allowed visitors to see how chocolate was made before mass-manufacturing methods were introduced. Here, the visitor can write their name in liquid chocolate and watch as skilled Cadbury World Chocolatiers hand-craft novelties which can be purchased later in the tour.

As part of the program of continuous improvement, in the summer of 2009, the next three sets comprising of the Happiness Room (2005), Coronation Street (built in 1996 and showcasing Cadbury's 10-year sponsorship of ITV's flagship drama), and the Advertising Room (constructed in 2001) will be replaced by the *Advertising Avenue* Zone. *Advertising Avenue* will give the visitor the opportunity to walk through a chronologically-themed life-sized street of chocolate houses, lampposts and trees as they enjoy the history of Cadbury's advertising past from posters through to interactively-selected television commercials.

In 2006, the *Purple Planet* Zone gave visitors the opportunity to participate in a uniquely interactive chocolate environment. *Purple Planet* allows the opportunity to play in chocolate rain, grow and care for a cocoa bean tree, and chase a Cadbury Creme Egg. Recent 2009 updates to *Purple Planet* see the inclusion of "Magic Planet"—a touch-screen information terminal with content projected through an illuminated globe which provides an overview of Cadbury operations around the world and "Mould Me", a capture of the visitor's image digitally transformed to give the appearance of the visitor sculptured in chocolate. This provides the visitor with their third souvenir photograph opportunity which can be purchased at a later stage.

Exiting the main exhibition into the *World's Biggest Cadbury Shop* Zone, the visitor is presented with various retail offerings, merchandise and exclusive Cadbury World merchandise. In Spring 2009, various aspects of the shop were updated with specialized display units relating to Cadbury UK's "Power Brands" including

Cadbury Dairy Milk, Cadbury Dairy Milk Caramel, Cadbury Milk Tray, and Bassett's Liquorice Allsorts and Jelly Babies.

Upon leaving the *World's Biggest Cadbury Shop*, the visitor has the choice of either purchasing refreshments from Café Cadbury (a 240-seat visitor restaurant offering a selection of both hot and cold meals and snacks) or walking outside of the main building and following the yellow painted footsteps to the final two zones.

The *Essence* Zone (constructed in 2005 and replacing *Cadburyland*) tells the story of the magical creation of Cadbury Dairy Milk before allowing the visitor to create their own confectionery concoction in a tub of liquid chocolate. Opened in 2007, *The Bournville Experience* Zone replaced the Cadbury Collection Museum and presents the unique creation of Bournville village through a series of models, multi-media view ports and videos as well as memorabilia from Cadbury's past including John Cadbury's original pestle and mortar used in his shop to create cocoa based concoctions in the early 19th century.

With ample free parking space, an outdoor catering kiosk, the children's play area, the Cadbury No. 14 train and a picnic area—the grounds of Cadbury World offer the visitor plenty to see and do (with easy access to Bournville village) whilst they wait for their entry into the main exhibition or enjoy any complimentary entertainments.

Opening Schedule

Cadbury World is generally open between 315 and 325 days each year—which tends to be every day from early February through to early November, and four or five days a week outside that time. It is necessary for there to be complete closure to the visitor from New Year's Eve through to the third week in January, in which time major installations, refurbishment and renovations take place.

Originally, Cadbury World opened every day except Christmas Day, for the same length of time each day. However, experience of the natural patterns of business, and the waste of opening on a day when variable costs are likely to outweigh the marginal revenue from visitor attendance, has led to a distinctive schedule of opening times. At the quietest (offpeak) times, Cadbury World opens at 10 AM and ceases admissions at 3 PM or often 4 PM, allowing the final visitors the opportunity to view the exhibition at their leisure, and browse the shop. Generally, closing time will be about 2 hours after the last admission. Average dwell time on site at Cadbury World is 3.5 hours currently.

On busier days, particularly during the school holidays, opening hours are extended up to a maximum admission span of 9 AM to 5 PM. The visitors are admitted at the maximum rate of 80 every 10 minutes, which allows in excess of 3,000 visitors.

Cadbury World and Education

Cadbury World is a company committed to education. Tracing back to 1879 and the move to Bournville, George Cadbury introduced the first employee and community education program. Cadbury World has maintained this same enthusiasm and commitment to education to the present day.

Whilst touring Cadbury World you will discover the history and heritage of the company and learn how it developed from a small Birmingham based business into a global company. Cadbury World feels that it is important to teach the young people of today about business and the way in which we operate. With the information we provide through visuals and exhibitions, we hope that it will give them a good understanding, which will then prepare them for the readily awaiting world of work.

One of the first attractions to be awarded the Learning Outside the Classroom Quality Badge from the Council of Learning, Cadbury World's Education offers have gone from strength to strength. Cadbury World is committed to the education of young people and has tailor-made packages to support the education needs from Key Stage 1 through to Key Stage 5 and beyond. Educators can bring their students for a standard visit around the exhibition—complimenting this with downloadable workbooks, or can attend one of a series of talks from Aztecs to Victorians aimed at a Primary-level audience through to talks supporting various GCSE subject's national curriculum. Indeed, education talks have proved so successful over recent years that a second purpose-built education room was opening in January 2009 to accommodate growing demand.

Awards

Over the years, Cadbury World has won a number of industry-recognized awards from its offers, its services, through to its marketing and advertising campaigns. Recent awards and nominations include:

- 2008 (Finalist & Highly Commended) Access for All Category, Excellence in Tourism Awards
- 2008 (Bronze Winner) "Gordon" Radio Campaign, created by BIG, Cream Awards
- 2008 (Winner) "You Can't Eat the Exhibits in a Zoo" print campaign, created by Big, Roses Award
- 2008 (Runner Up) Recognition of Disability Facilities, Group Travel Awards
- 2007 (Finalist) Group Leisure Awards.

Marketing Cadbury World

"In the early 1960s, Professor Neil Borden at Harvard Business School identified a number of company performance actions that can influence the consumer decision to purchase goods or services. Borden suggested that all those actions of the company represented a 'Marketing Mix'. Professor E Jerome McCarthy, also at the Harvard Business School in the early 1960s, suggested that the Marketing Mix contained four elements: product, price, place and promotion", (Wikipedia).

The "4 p's" are good place to start when looking at any marketing strategy and its effectiveness. Overtime, the main concept of the "4 p's" has developed to become the "7 p's" (with the inclusion of "Process", 'Physical Evidence", and "People"). As techniques and technology develops, even these "7 p's" have been deemed too restrictive in terms of marketing analysis and now some commentators have even point to a recently devised "Web 4.2 (the new 4 p's)" including "Personalization", "Participation", "Peer-to-Peer", and "Predictive Modeling".

Whilst not giving a comprehensive overview into Cadbury World's marketing strategy, broadly in-line with the relevant 'P's' of the marketing mix, the below gives an insight into the way Cadbury World goes about talking to visitors, potential visitors and generating awareness for its products and services.

Product

As a leading tourist attraction, Cadbury World operates in a service industry and is almost unique in being owned by a major manufacturer. The product that Cadbury World delivers is "a memorable, exciting and great day out"; whereas for the main Cadbury business, the product delivered is chocolate, candy, gum brands and drinking chocolate products.

The actual *product* Cadbury World delivers has been built up over nearly 20 years. As discussed in previous sections, it has changed, developed and evolved overtime. Whilst being intrinsically-linked to the main Cadbury business; Cadbury World as a profit-making business unit would not survive if it wasn't for the desire to offer a quality day out.

Visitor Numbers

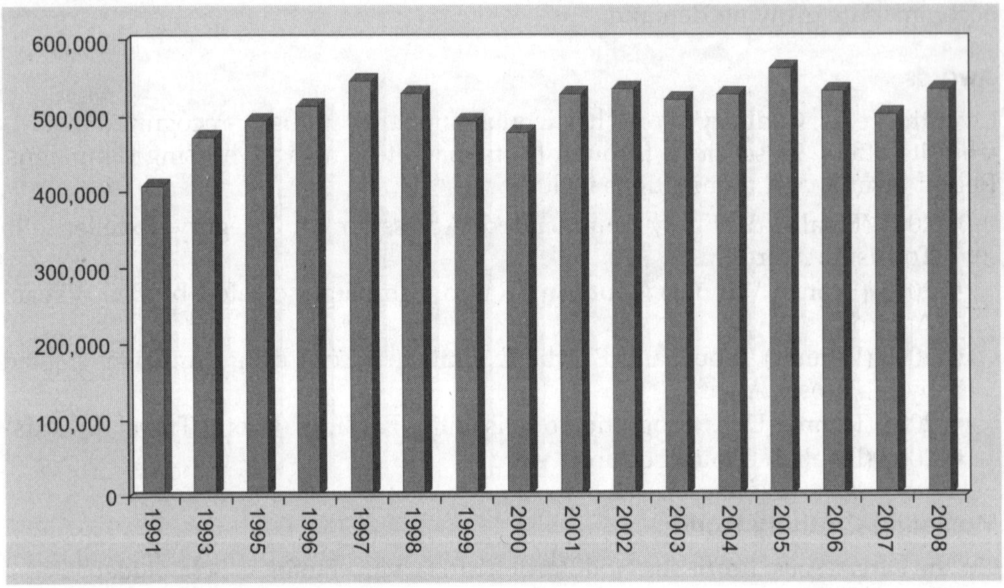

Primary Demographics and Targeted Visitor

- Adults 55% / Children 45% / UK (domestic) 90+%
- ABC1 50% vs. 38% population
- Key catchment area 75–150 miles radius to the south of Birmingham.

Pricing

In the confectionery market, the price of the products, and the amount of planning prior to purchase are both relatively small. In the leisure industry generally, and specifically for a visit to Cadbury World, the commitment, e.g. admission price, travel costs and time to plan the visit are significant.

Cadbury World offers various pricing structures to meet the expectations of different visitors and changing economic situations. For instance, in the third quarter of 2008, the pricing structure for 2009 had already been agreed and printed on marketing literature for use during the following year.

Current 2009, Cadbury World pricing is split into peak (classed as school holidays) for Group parties (special Group packages are offered including a Memory Lane Tour, Choc and Cruise, Choc and Steam, and meal deals—designed to meet the different needs of different Groups) and off-peak prices. A special rate for educational visits (nontalk) and educational visits (with talk/study day).

The standard adult ticket costs £13.45, child ticket is £10.10, with a concessionary rate offered to seniors and students at £10.30. Both family tickets and annual passports are also available.

In a need to respond to the reduction in VAT at the start of December 2008, not only did all the prices offered in the retail outlets change but the proposed admission prices for 2009 were reduced even though on the marketing literature they're higher. Consequently, a potential visitor looking at a 2009 Cadbury World leaflet will see a slightly different price than the one they will ultimately pay upon their arrival.

One element of Cadbury World's pricing strategy growing in importance and requiring constant review and monitoring is that of its discount strategy. Cadbury World works with a number of third party promoters and businesses in order to offer a discount on the entry price. This strategy helps to increase visitor footfall, whilst using the third party's databases and own marketing budget to promote Cadbury World and its products.

Other considerations in determining the pricing strategy would be the participation costs for competing leisure activities (other attractions, cinemas, etc) as well as the price Recommended Selling Price (RSP) for merchandise and confectionery.

Promotion

Promotion of Cadbury World to various target audiences to build visitor numbers is proving to be a vital part of the management function and encompasses every method for generating awareness of the Cadbury World offer.

In the past, and as alluded to in previous sections, Cadbury World has been seen as having a bias towards a certain age demographic. Indeed, it was concluded through research, that the potential visitor may not be fully aware of what Cadbury World is or what its position is in the leisure market. Some members of the public thought it was a theme park, whilst others thought it was a museum, and others still being confused about what age group it appealed to.

In 2008, working with Big Communications, it was deemed that in order to execute a successful campaign, Cadbury World should start by talking to the consumer at a very basic level in terms of what Cadbury World is and what there is to offer. Launched in 2008, all Cadbury World marketing material now leads with the visually compelling and emotionally charged "Where Chocolate Comes to Life", with an additional tag line to tell the visitor that there is quite a lot on offer: "Fourteen Amazing Zones, One Fantastic Day Out".

To support and reinforce this message further, each Zone has had its own instantly identifiable Icon designed which is used to signpost the separate areas within the exhibition on promotional communications.

3

Guar and Guar Gum

India is native of guar or cluster bean where it is used as a vegetable. From hundreds of years, guar has been used as vegetable in India. It is also used as a cattle food, and as a green manure crop in agriculture. Guar gum comes from the endosperm of the seed of the legume plant *Cyamopsis tetragonoloba*; an annual plant, grown in dry regions of India as a food crop for animals. There are various grades of guar gums pure or derivative. Guar gum is a white to creamy colored, free flowing powder and free from extraneous matter. Its ability to suspend solids, bind water by hydrogen bonding, control the viscosity of aqueous solutions, form strong tough films have accounted for its rapid growth and use in various industries. For example guar gum is used in paper, textile, oil drilling, mining, explosives, ore flotation and other various industrial applications. The growing season of guar is 14–16 weeks and requires reasonably warm weather and moderate flashing rainfall with plenty of sunshine. Too much rain can cause the plant to become more "leafy" resulting thereby reducing the number of pods or the number of seeds per pod which affects the size and yield of seeds. The crop is generally sown after the monsoon rainfall in the second half of July to early August and is harvested in late October early November. The guar is a naturally rain fed crop. Depending on the monsoon rainfall the total size of guar crop varies from year to year. After harvesting, when the pods become dry through sunlight, they are beaten off and during this process, the seeds come out of the pods.

What is Guar Gum

The guar plant *"Cyamopsis Tetragonalobus"* is an annual plant. The legume is an important source of nutrition to animals and humans. It also regenerates soil nitrogen and the endosperm of guar seed is an important hydrocolloid widely used across a broad spectrum of industries. The "Guar" legume plant is fodder as well as soil restorative crop extremely drought resistant fodder as well as soil restorative crop and thrives in semiarid regions where most plants perish. It grows best in sandy soils and areas of West, Northwest India and parts of Pakistan are the ideal areas for it is farming. Jodhpur City in the North Western State of Rajasthan in India is the most ideal and important processing center of guar gum and contributes approximately 40% of the worlds' guar gum supply.

Guar requires reasonably warm weather and a growing season of 14–16 weeks. It needs moderate intermittent rainfall with plenty of sunshine. It cannot withstand excessive moisture water logging. Too much precipitation can cause the plant to become more "leafy", thereby reducing the number of pods and/or the number of seeds per pod which affects the size and yield of seeds. The crop is generally sown after the monsoon rainfall in the second half of July to early August and is harvested in late October to early November. The guar is a naturally rain fed crop and the total size of guar crop varies from year to year depending on the monsoon rainfall.

As a forage crop, it is often sown mixed half and half with fodder jower to provide a highly balanced cattle feed. The seed pods grow in clusters giving guar the common name cluster-bean. A gum extracted from the guar beans forms a gel in water, commonly referred to as guar gum. Guar gum is also known as guarkernmehl, guaran, goma guar, gomme guar and galactomannan. Guar seed is also highly nutritive and is often fed as a contentrative to all livestock except horses.

After harvesting, when the pods become dry through sunlight, they are beaten off and during this process, the seeds come out of the pods.

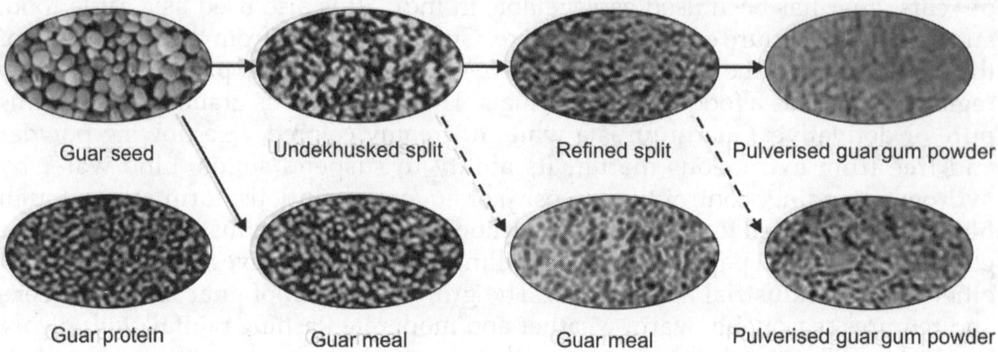

The molecular structure reveals that GEMPOLYM is a straight chain galactomannan with galactose on every other mannose unit. Beta 1–4 glycosidic linkages couple the mannose units and the galactose side chains are linked through alpha 1–6. The mannose to galactose ratio has been estimated at 1.8: 1 to 2: 1.

The molecular weight of guar has reported as 1–2 × 106. Further studies indicate that GEMPOLYM is a rigid rod like polymer because of the beta-linkage between the monomer units. The guar hydroxyls are in the CIS positions. The CIS position is important since adjacent hydroxyl groups reinforce each other in hydrogen bonding reactions.

GEMPOLYM has excellent cold water solubility because of the high galactose: mannose ratio. The special properties of GEMPOLYM make it most suitable for various industrial applications.

Guar is a native to the Indian subcontinent and is grown mainly in India, Pakistan, United States and also in some part of Africa and Australia. In old times, guar was only used as rich protein to feed cattle. It is also used as green vegetable in India. After Second World War, there was major shortage of locust bean gum which adversely affected the textile and paper industries. At that time, guar gum was found as the most suitable substitute for scarce locust bean gum.

Guar gum, also called guaran, is a galactomannan. It is primarily the ground endosperm of guar beans. The guar seeds are dehusked, milled and screened to obtain the guar gum. It is typically produced as a free-flowing, off-white powder.

Guar gum powder is extracted from the guar seed after a multistage industrial process. The most important property of guar gum is its ability to hydrate rapidly in cold water to attain uniform and very high viscosity at relatively low concentrations. Its colloidal nature gives excellent thickening to the solution. Guar gum, either modified or unmodified is a very versatile and efficient natural polymer covering a number of applications in various industries like food, beverages, pharmaceuticals, cosmetics, paper, textile, construction, oil and gas well drilling, mining, etc due to its cost-effective emulsifying and thickening properties.

Guar gum can best be described as a natural food thickener, similar to locust bean gum, comstarch or tapioca flour. It is said to have significantly more thickening ability than cornstarch, at a fraction of the cost. This has made it a popular additive in products such as puddings and ice creams. Until recently, it was also an ingredient in non-prescription diet pills designed to create a sense of fullness. The guar plant, also known as a cluster plant, grows primarily in Pakistan and the northern regions of India. It thrives on the drought / monsoon cycles present in those areas. The plants are harvested after the monsoon season and the seeds are allowed to dry in the sun. The seeds are then manually or mechanically separated and processed into a flour or sold as split seeds. Guar gum is an important cash crop for the Indian and Pakistani economies.

While consumers may balk at such "exotic" ingredients as locust bean gum, carageenan and guar gum, the truth is many icecreams, puddings, and canned sauces would be fairly inedible without them. Guar gum is not just a thickening agent, but a binder and plasticizer as well. When untreated icecream melts and refreezes, grainy ice crystals often form. This substance has the natural ability to bind with water molecules, preventing them from forming the unwanted crystals. Processed foods with creamy textures are primarily held together with binders such as this. Without a binder, the individual ingredients might separate into a watery mess.

Guar Gum is an important ingredient in producing food emulsifier, food additive, food thickener and other guar gum products. India is the largest producer of guar gum products. Its guar gum exporters, guar gum manufacturers, guar gum products suppliers, food emulsifier exporter have reached to many countries and today there is a lot of demand for Indian guar gum products, food additives, food thickener and other allied guar gum products. Guar gum is extracted from the seed of *Cyamopsis tetragonoloba*, an annual leguminous plant originating from India and Pakistan, also cultivated in the United States. Guar gum grows best in sandy soils, in areas of West, Northwest India and parts of Pakistan, which are ideal for its farming. Jodhpur City in the North Western State of Rajasthan in India is the most important processing center of guar gum and contributes approximately 40% of the world's guar gum supply. Indian guar gum products are exported and supplied all over the world by different guar gum exporters, guar gum manufacturers, guar gum suppliers and guar gum exporter. Many food emulsifier exporter also exports superior quality food additive, food thickener and food emulsifier.

Guar gum is an emulsifier, thickener, and stabilizer approved for use in a wide range of foods, cosmetics, and pharmaceuticals. Gum technology stabilizers are carefully controlled blends of various food ingredients. They are mostly natural vegetable gums which come from sources such as seeds, plant exudate and marine plants. These may be blended with other hydro-colloids or food ingredients such as fats or emulsifiers. India is famous for guar gum products and food additives. It is sold as a white to yellowish odorless powder, which is available in different viscosities depending on the desired one. One advantageous property of guar gum is that it thickens without the application of heat. Guar gum has the following properties, which make it useful in variety of applications:

- Easy solubility in cold and hot water
- Film forming property
- Resistance to oils, greases and solvents
- Better thickening agent
- Water binding capacity
- High viscosity
- Functioning at low temperatures.

Industrial application of guar gum includes the textile industry where guar gum's excellent thickening properties are used for textile sizing, finishing and printing. In the paper industry, guar is used as an additive where it gives denser surface to the paper used in printing. And in the explosive industry guar is mixed in ammonium nitrate, nitroglycerine and oil explosives, where it helps to maintain the explosive properties of the product even in wet conditions.

In the food, pharmaceutical and cosmetics industry, guar gum is used as an effective binder, stabilizer, disintegrator and thickener. In bakeries, diaries and in production of meat and dressings and sauces, guar is an important natural food supplement with high nutritional value for weight gain and cholesterol reduction. In cosmetics, especially shampoos and toothpastes, guar gum is used primarily as a thickening and suspending agent. In beverages, it is used as stabilizer for preparing chocolate drinks and juices. Guar is also widely used in tobacco, leather, insecticides and pesticides, crayons, adhesives, etc. Guar gum comes in different forms—from seeds to powder. Main types of guar gum include guar seed, undehusked split, refined split, pulverized guar gum powder, guar protein and guar meal.

Varieties

a. Hydroxy alkylated guar gum
b. Carboxy methylated guar gum
c. Oxidised guar gum
d. Acetates of guar gum
e. Cationic derivatives of guar gum
f. Sulphated guar gum
g. Guar gum formate
h. Guar gum acryl amide
i. Borate cross-linked guar gum
j. Reticulated guar gum.

Manufacturing Process

Depending upon the requirement of end product, various processing techniques are used. The commercial production of guar gum normally uses roasting, differential attrition, sieving, and polishing. Food-grade guar gum is manufactured in stages. Guar split selection is important in this process. The split is screened to clean it and then soaked to prehydrate it in a double-cone mixer. The prehydrating stage is very important because it determines the rate of hydration of the final product.

The soaked splits, which have reasonably high moisture content, are passed through a flaker. The flaked guar split is ground and then dried. The powder is screened through rotary screens to deliver the required particle size. Oversize particles are either recycled to main ultra fine or reground in a separate regrind plant, according to the viscosity requirement. This stage helps to reduce the load at the grinder. The soaked splits are difficult to grind. Direct grinding of those generates more heat in the grinder, which is not desired in the process, as it reduces the hydration of the product. Through the heating, grinding, and polishing process, the husk is separated from the endosperm halves and the refined guar split is obtained. Through the further grinding process, the refined guar split is then treated and converted into powder.

The split manufacturing process yields husk and germ called "guar meal", widely sold in the international market as cattle feed. It is high in protein and contains oil and albuminoids, about 50% in germ and about 25% in husks. The quality of the food-grade guar gum powder is defined from its particle size, rate of hydration, and microbial content. E412 guar gum is an important natural food supplement with high nutritional value.

Manufacturers define different grades and qualities of guar gum by the particle size, the viscosity generated with a given concentration, and the rate at which that viscosity develops. Coarse-mesh guar gums will typically, but not always, develop viscosity more slowly. They may achieve a reasonably high viscosity, but will take longer to achieve. On the other hand, they will disperse better than fine-mesh, all conditions being equal. A finer mesh, such as a 200 mesh, requires more effort to dissolve. Modified forms of guar gum are available commercially, including enzyme-modified, cationic and hydropropyl guar.

PRODUCTION AND TRADE

Production of Guar in India

Area production and yield statewise shows that production increased from 651 thousand bales 100 kg in 1970-71 to 1,169.3 thousand bales in 2006-07. India produces 600,000 lakh tons of guar annually, i.e. the maximum level of production in the world. It contributes to around 80% share in the world's total production. The major producing regions of this crop in India are: Rajasthan, Gujarat, Haryana, Punjab, Uttar Pradesh, Madhya Pradesh, Tamil Nadu, Maharashtra, Karnataka and Andhra Pradesh.

Area under Guar Seed Increases 10 Times in Punjab

In Punjab, farmers normally sow guar seed in 3,000-4,000 acres. However following meteoric rise in prices during the previous season, farmers have sown guar seed in nearly 50,000 acres during this season. According to experts, the crop not only produces highly nutritive green manure, it also makes soil fertile by fixing the nitrogen and increasing organic content. 2013 was a strong year for guar sowing and production in India. The total sowing area rose by 21% in 2013 to reach 10.6 million acres. Rajasthan, Haryana, and Gujarat—the three key guar-producing states—exceeded the sowing area target set by their respective agriculture departments. Nontraditional guar cultivators in other Indian States also showed keen interest in the crop in 2013.

Guar and the Shift to Consumer-Driven Agriculture

How responsive is agriculture to consumer demand? More than any other industry in the world, agriculture only appears to be slow, traditional and caught in a time warp. In reality, it is more agile and nimble than manufacturing.

When consumers rush to buy any product, and prices rise, they clearly signal a business opportunity. A company usually needs a couple of years to put up a factory of any significant size for this new demand. Farmers take 6 months. The moment they realize a crop has profit potential, wham goes more area under it.

A classic Indian example is guar. In 2011, when American drilling companies discovered money in shale gas, Indian farmers immediately understood guar's golden moment had come. As demand trebled, guar gum became India's most valuable commodity export, beating jewelery. American companies spent $2.5 billion that year on this small neglected bean with an outsized role in shale gas extraction.

By 2012, guar production had doubled. Acreage jumped 25%. Traditionally, guar was grown on malnourished, arid farms with little or no investment by the farmer. Today, this virtually orphan crop is planted in irrigated areas, displacing grains and cotton.

Almost overnight, guar made geography history. News of the windfall gains in Rajasthan and Gujarat spread like wild fire and farmers in Andhra Pradesh, Karnataka, Haryana, Punjab and Chhattisgarh jumped onto the bandwagon.

What makes the guar story truly remarkable is the complete absence of any government policy, subsidy or even a minimum support price to encourage farmers. Farmers just kept their ears to the ground and in 14 weeks reaped what they sowed.

Agri-business was equally quick to seize the opportunity. Capacity to manufacture guar gum and powder was rapidly scaled up. More than 100 companies sprang up around Jodhpur and grabbed 40% of the $3 billion export market. No one waited for an SEZ, an export sop or an Apeda scheme. Entrepreneurs were pumping in capital because the profits in 2012 were 10 times more than those in 2011. Price signals created an automatic inflow of investment. In Pakistan, guar and guar products export was just $29 million in 2006-07. It shot up to a record $152 million in 2011-12.

Agriculture doesn't have high entry barriers like industry. So, abnormal profits are short-lived. Guar is no longer enjoying triple-digit price increases because supply has caught up with demand. The consumer too is becoming wiser. Halliburton, an oil company, is reportedly spending $800,000 annually in Texas on guar research. Food ingredient companies, worsted by drilling companies in the scramble for supply, are searching for chemical substitutes. Companies like the US-based Guar Global Ltd are using technology to help Rajasthan farmers increase yields and make the supply chain more efficient. These are all welcome signs of a maturing market and sustainable prosperity.

But, those crazy profits are not the real story anyway. Guar shows how intelligently Indian farmers were tracking consumer demand. Not just demand here but thousands of miles away in Texas. Easier access to real-time information—mobile phones, internet, futures trading—allowed them to pick up the earliest signs of a boom. Business decisions—what to plant and when to sell—were made looking through the front windshield, not the rear view mirror.

Guar also shows the future of Indian agriculture. More and more farms will shift to demand-driven agriculture. They will grow more of the crops that people value highly—be it guar, onions, cotton, fruits, or maize. Unlike in the past, farmers won't grow a crop and then go seeking a buyer. They will analyze what people want to buy and then decide what to grow.

The success of demand-driven agriculture rides on one crucial factor—the price signal from buyer to seller. If the price signal is clear and correct, farmers will decide well. If signals are distorted by market aberrations, politics or industry cartels, farmers will remain victims of circumstance.

But, if we can get the price signals right for all crops, demand-driven agriculture can change the lives of 600 million Indians. Their finances will strengthen. Consumers want variety, convenience, affordability. Farmers will invest in technology that creates this extra value. Since the stakes are higher, farmers will use their computer, social networking and communications skills to find multiple marketing channels for capturing higher margins and mitigating risk. Both consumers and farmers will demand more transparency. Eventually, both will come out ahead.

It is a myth that agriculture is a slow-moving behemoth that requires government support and large subsidies to move with the times. All that farmers today need is a phone signal and a price signal.

Green Gold

Guar itself is termed as "green gold" by its cultivators and traders in Rajasthan and the neighboring Haryana and Punjab. Jokes like "what now the thieves look for is guar, and not ornaments", abounded during the dizzy days when the berry price went up to Rs 30,000 per quintal in the international market in 2012. Overnight hundreds of farmers in Sriganganagar-Hanumangarh area and in neighboring Haryana's Abhor-Sirsa belt seemed to be reaping a fortune.

India and Pakistan are the main growers of guar. Guar is grown in Punjab, Haryana and Gujarat as well but Rajasthan accounts for 70% of the crop. Cluster beans have replaced traditional crops of cotton, bajra, soybean and mustard in Rajasthan's canal belt, stretching up to Bikaner, Jodhpur and Barmer.

The area under guar report doubled in Rajasthan in the past one decade. In the wake of heightened demand for the product, 3.5 million hectares were brought under guar cultivation in 2013 in the state. Guar is considered a valuable plant for the farmers as it increases soil fertility, growing in symbiosis with nitrogen-fixing bacteria in soil and is drought tolerant as well.

Traditionally used for human and animal consumption and in pharmaceuticals, paper manufacturing and the textile industry, guar (*Cyamopsis tetragonoloba*) in powder form of late is put to use in oil drilling and as an adhesive in shale gas. Guar gum is exported to some 30 countries and multinational companies including Nestle, Mars, Heinz and Unilever are among its users.

Taking the initiative, instead of waiting for the State Government to act on its plans for agricultural diversification, has paid rich dividends for farmers in the Malwa belt of Punjab. Last summer for the first time in more than 10 years, farmers in this region decided to grow the cluster bean guar in what has traditionally been a cotton belt. The crop was sown in more than 40,000 hectares under contract farming in Bathinda, Faridkot, Muktsar and Fazilka districts and the farmers earned Rs 40,000 per acre when they harvested in November–December, double the earnings from cotton.

The idea was mooted by Vikas WSP, a private company in Ganganagar, which also promised the farmers an assured price of Rs 40,000 per acre. With the switch having paid off handsomely last year, a large number of farmers are waiting for a similar promise from Vikas as they want to move away from cotton, which is highly labor-intensive and involves spraying pesticides several times. "Farmers opted for guar, but it was their personal agreement with the private company and they got good prices", said Dr Rajinder Singh Brar, Bathinda's chief agriculture officer.

"Guar is a desert crop and it was grown in areas where farmers otherwise were not able to do much. The area under cotton in our district reduced from 1.5 lakh hectares to 1.45 lakh hectares only. In fact, the barren land was used by farmers for this crop because it is a rain-fed crop which requires not more than one or two rainfalls in a season", Brar added.

While small farmers are known to have sold all their produce, landlords have kept some stocks hoping for higher prices as it is linked to the commodity market. The so-called "neglected crop" is priced at around Rs 11,500 per quintal at present and some farmers are waiting for it to rise to Rs 20,000. An acre of land produces 3–6 quintals of guar.

Last season, cotton did not earn more than Rs 3,500 per quintal, said Kuldeep Singh, a Maur Mandi farmer who has kept his land vacant for guar this year too. Vikas had even paid a harvesting charge of Rs 700 per acre, said Harbhajan Singh, another farmer in the same area.

The Guar Story

- Guar is in demand for its derivatives; a special gum is made from its seeds and used as coolant for drilling and also in thermal power stations.
- Guar gives back to the land on which it is grown instead of draining groundwater. Studies show it helps nitrogen growth in the soil.
- Nearly, 80% of the world's guar is grown in India and Pakistan.
- The crop is best grown in semiarid zones and Rajasthan is the main producer, with Jodhpur being the main center.
- Poor prices had forced Punjab farmers to stop growing guar until last year.

Guar Gums Market Influencing Factors

- Changes in production due to rainfall fluctuation
- Demand and supply mismatch
- Hoarding and black marketing
- Government policies.

Supply varies largely between years while the demand is almost constant over the years. There are involvement of speculators and stockiest in the physical market. The commodity is subjected to a long storage period based on demand and market prices. There are no Government rules and regulations governing the production, distribution, marketing, exports or imports of the commodity and the market forces determine the prices.

Industrial Applications

- Textile industry: Sizing, finishing and printing
- Paper industry: Improved sheet formation, folding and denser surface for printing

- Explosives industry: As waterproofing agent mixed with ammonium nitrate, nitroglycerin, etc.
- Pharmaceutical industry: As binder or as disintegrator in tablets; main ingredient in some bulk-forming laxatives.
- Cosmetics and toiletries industries: Thickener in toothpastes, conditioner in shampoos (usually in a chemically modified version)
- Hydraulic fracturing shale oil and gas extraction industries consume about 90% of guar gum produced from India and Pakistan.
- Mining
- Hydroseeding: Formation of seed-bearing "guar tack"
- Medical institutions, especially nursing homes: Used to thicken liquids and foods for patients with dysphagia
- Fire retardant industry: As a thickener in Phos-chek
- Nanoparticles industry: To produce silver or gold nanoparticles, or develop innovative medicine delivery mechanisms for drugs in pharmaceutical industry.

Uses

Guar gum being a natural polymer is used everywhere and in almost everything.

1. Frozen Foods

- Used in: Icecreams, soft serves, frozen cakes, etc.
- Functions: Guar gum works as crystal growth controller, moisture loss controller, freezer burn reducer, syneresis controller, freezing point and thaw separation controller.

2. Confectionery

- Used in: Breads, cakes, pastries, biscuits, chocolate, jellies, etc.
- Functions: As moisture retaining agent, dough controller, binding agent, film forming agent, jelling agent, bloom controller, agar and gelatin replacer, glazing agent, etc.

3. Beverages

- Used in: Cocoa drinks, fruit juices, sugarless and alcoholic beverages.
- Functions: Guar gum acts as a suspending agent in fruit beverages, maintains viscosity, improves mouth feel.

4. Dairy Products

- Used in: Yogurt, desserts, mousse, cheese, etc.
- Functions: It prevents syneresis in cheese formation, improves texture and tenderness, maintains color and viscosity uniformly. It adds mouth feel to the dairy products.

5. Ketchup and Pickles

- Used in: Sausage, pickles, barbecue, salad dressing, etc.
- Functions: It improves free flowing properties of sauce and reduces separation between water and oil phases. It is unique cold water dispersible, acid resistant, free water binder in salad dressings, sauce, pickles and relishes.

6. Pet Food

- Used in: Veterinary preparations, calf milk replacer, etc.
- Functions: It is a good thickener, stabilizing and suspending agent for veterinary preparations, it forms gels and retains moisture.

7. Oil and Gas Well Drilling

Functions: It is widely used in oil and gas well drilling due to its multifunction such as fluid and water loss control, lubrication and cooling of drill bits, shale inhibitor and solids carrier. It has excellent solution rheology, stability, solubility and compatibility with other auxiliaries used in oil well drilling.

8. Mining and Construction

- Used in: Concentration of ore, filtration, etc.
- Functions: Floating agent, flocculating or setting agent, foam stabilizer, back water generator.

9. Pharmaceuticals

- Used in: Laxatives, sustained release drug, vitamins, syrups.
- Functions: Used as a binder and disintegrating agent in tablet perpetration. Used in laxatives to increase intestinal transit time and to increase stool. Suitable suspending agent in anti-inflammatory drugs, etc.

10. Paper Industry

- Used in: Wrapping papers, crafts, photographic paper, filter, etc.
- Functions: Guar's cost-effectiveness and properties make it a useful polymer for paper industry. It increases fold, tensile, strength, pick and pulp hydration. Simultaneously, it decreases the porosity and improves finish.

11. Textile Industry

- Used in: Cotton, rayon, silk, wool sizing, carpet printing, etc.
- Functions: In sizing, it increases the strength of the wrap thereby reduces its breakages and also reduces the dusting of sizing machine. It is used as a dispersant and thickening agent for dyes in textile printing.

12. Tobacco Industry

- Used in: Cigar, cigarette, kreteks, gutka, etc.
- Functions: Guar gum is used as a binder for fragmented tobacco fins of reconstituted tobacco. It is used as a binding and strengthening agent.

13. Toothpaste

- Used in: Toothpaste, ointments, conditioners, etc.
- Functions: Its high viscosity and lubrication property, imparts slip for extruding the paste from the tube without any excessive function. It is used as detergent compatible thickener, lubricator, suspender and film forming agent, etc.

14. Cream and Cosmetics

- Used in: Lipstick, shaving cream, hair shampoos, etc.
- Functions: Used as thickening agent, lubricating agent, suspending agent, detergent compatible thickener, protective colloids, film forming agent.

15. Miscellaneous

Used in: Water based paints, explosives, photography, water treatment, fire fighting, incense sticks, mosquito coils and mats, soups, snacks, puddings, noodles, gem, ceramics, synthetic resin, wallpapers, polishes, battery electrolytes, printing inks, etc.

The largest market for guar gum is in the food industry. In the US, differing percentages are set for its allowable concentration in various food applications. In Europe, guar gum has EU food additivehttp://en.wikipedia.org/wiki/EU_food_additive_code code E412. Xanthan gum and guar gum are the most frequently used gums in gluten-free recipes and gluten-free products.

Applications include:

- In backed goods, it increases dough yield, gives greater resiliency, and improves texture and shelf life; in pastry fillings, it prevents "weeping" (syneresis) of the water in the filling, keeping the pastry crust crisp. It is primarily used in hypoallergenic recipes that use different types of whole-grain flours. Because the consistency of these flours allows the escape of gas released by leavening, guar gum is needed to improve the thickness of these flours, allowing them to rise as a normal flour would.
- In dairy products, it thickens milk, yogurt, kefir, and liquid cheese products, and helps maintain homogeneity and texture of ice creams and sherbets. It is used for similar purposes in plant milks.
- For meat, it functions as a binder.
- In condiments, it improves the stability and appearance of salad dressings, barbecue sauces, relishes, ketchups and others.
- In canned soup, it is used as a thickener and stabilizer.
- It is also used in dry soups, instant oatmeal, sweet desserts, canned fish in sauce, frozen food items and animal feed.

Nutritional and Medicinal Effects

Guar gum, as a water-soluble fiber, acts as a bulk-forming laxative, so is claimed to be effective in promoting regular bowel movements and relieving constipation and chronic related functional bowel ailments, such as diverticulosis, Crohn's disease, colitis and irritable bowel syndrome. Several studies have found significant decreases in human serum cholesterol levels following guar gum ingestion. These decreases are thought to be a function of its high soluble fiber content. Guar gum has been considered of interest in regard to both weight loss and diabetic diets. It is a thermogenics substance. Moreover, its low digestibility lends its use in recipes as a filler, which can help to provide satiety, or slow the digestion of a meal, thus lowering the glycemic of that meal. In the late 1980s, guar gum was used and heavily promoted in several weight-loss products. The US Food and Drug Administration eventually recalled these due to reports of esophageal blockage from insufficient fluid intake, after one brand alone caused at least 10 users to be hospitalized, and a death (http://en.wikipedia.org/wiki/Guar_gum - cite_note-15). For this reason, guar gum is no longer approved for use in over-the-counter weight loss aids in the United States. Moreover, a meta-analysis combining the results of 11 randomized, controlled trials found guar gum supplements were not effective in reducing body weight.

Two Japanese studies using rats showed guar gum supports increased absorption of calcium occurring in the colon instead of in the small intestine. This means lesser amounts of calcium may be consumed to obtain its recommended minimum daily intake. This has obvious implications for reduced calorie diets, since some calcium-rich dairy products tend to be high in calories. Guar gum, though, is also capable of reducing the absorbability of dietary minerals (other than calcium), when foods or nutritional supplements containing them are consumed concomitantly with it, but this is less of a concern with guar gum than with various insoluble dietary fibers.

Some studies have found guar gum to improve dietary glucose tolerance. Research has revealed the water-soluble fiber in it may help people with diabetes by slowing the absorption of sugars by the small intestine. Although the rate of absorption is reduced, the amount of sugar absorbed is the same overall. This may help diabetic patients by moderating glucose "spikes".

Guar Gum Food

- Guar gum can best be described as a natural food thickener, similar to locust bean gum, cornstarch or tapioca flour.
- Lack of air will make a food item dense and tough instead of light or flaky. Guar gum can result in a thinner, more stringy mixture.

Gum Guar

- Although xanthan tends to be more successful at creating a product reminiscent of gluten, it is often avoided in favor of guar gum by people who have corn allergies or diets that limit corn. Guar gum is also more affordable than xanthan gum, which can be up to triple the price.
- While consumers may balk at such "exotic" ingredients as locust bean gum, carageenan and guar gum, the truth is many ice creams, puddings, and canned sauces would be fairly inedible without them.

Guar Gum Products

- While consumers may balk at such "exotic" ingredients as locust bean **gum**, carageenan and **guar gum**, the truth is many ice creams, puddings, and canned sauces would be fairly inedible without them.
- While both xanthan or **guar gums** can be substituted for gluten **products** in recipes, xanthan tends to produce a texture that is more similar to gluten.

Guar Bean Gum

- While consumers may balk at such "exotic" ingredients as locust bean gum, carageenan and guar gum, the truth is many ice creams, puddings, and canned sauces would be fairly inedible without them.
- Some people with food allergies may be sensitive to the product, however, and it can cause headaches, stomach pain, and diarrhea. Other "gums", such as guar gum, carageenan, and locust bean gum, can be substituted if needed.

Guar Gum Icecream

- While consumers may balk at such "exotic" ingredients as locust bean gum, carageenan and guar gum, the truth is many icecreams, puddings, and canned sauces would be fairly inedible without them.
- This is just one example; for as many types of icecream there can be a protein ice cream. Another recipe, at the Healthy Foodie Web site, utilizes cottage cheese in the mix as well as other ingredients to make raspberry almond chocolate protein icecream.

Guar Gum Supplement

- Recent additions to fiber supplements are those containing guar gum or acacia. These are natural thickening agents one often sees added to other products.
- Some dieters claim success against hunger pangs by consuming certain herbs or other natural supplements. Powdered guar gum can be purchased at many health food stores and used as a natural appetite suppressant.

Guar Gum Thickener

- While consumers may balk at such "exotic" ingredients as locust bean gum, carageenan and guar gum, the truth is many ice creams, puddings, and canned sauces would be fairly inedible without them. Guar gum is not just a thickening agent, but a binder and plasticizer as well.
- Although xanthan tends to be more successful at creating a product reminiscent of gluten, it is often avoided in favor of guar gum by people who have corn allergies or diets that limit corn. Guar gum is also more affordable than xanthan gum, which can be up to triple the price.

Allergies

Some studies have found an allergic sensitivity to guar gum developed in a few individuals working in an industrial environment where airborne concentrations of the substance were present. In those affected by the inhalation of the airborne particles, common adverse reactions were occupational rhinitis and asthma. Soy protein occurs as an impurity in manufactured guar gum, and can make up as much as 10%. The guar gum can therefore adversely affect those with sensitivity to soy.

Dioxin Contamination

In July 2007, the European Commission issued a health warning to its member states after high levels of dioxins were detected in a food additive - guar gum - used as thickener in small quantities in meat, dairy, dessert or delicatessen products. The source was traced to guar gum from India that was contaminated with pentachlorophenol, a pesticide no longer in use. PCP contains dioxins as contamination. Dioxins damage the human immune system.

Guar Gum: Stagewise Process

Guar Seed

- First, the pods are dried in sunlight, manually separated from the seeds.
- The seeds are supplied to the industry for processing.
- Guar by-products, churi and korma are used for Cattle feed.

Undehusked Guar Splits

- The gum is commercially extracted from the seeds essentially by a mechanical process of roasting, differential attrition, sieving and polishing.
- The seeds are broken and the germ is separated from the endosperm.
- Two halves of the endosperm are obtained from each seed and are known as Undehusked Guar Splits.

Refined Guar Splits

Refined Guar Splits are obtained when the fine layer of fibrous material, which forms the husk, is removed and separated from the endosperm halves by polishing.

Guar Powder

The refined guar splits are then treated and finished into powders by a variety of routes and processing techniques depending upon the end product desired.

Guar Gum: Method of Marking

- The grade designation mark shall be securely affixed or stenciled on each container in a manner approved by the Agricultural Marketing Adviser and shall also indicate the number of the certificate of authorization issued to the packer by the Agricultural Marketing Adviser.
- The authorized packer may, after obtaining the prior approval of the Agricultural Marketing Adviser, mark his private trade mark on a container in a manner approved by the said officer, provided the private trade mark does not represent quality or grade of the guar gum different from that indicate by the grade designation mark affixed on the container in accordance with these rules.
- In addition to the grade designation mark every container shall be clearly marked with the following particulars, namely:
  - o Date of packing
  - o Lot number
  - o Name and address of the packer
  - o Net weight
  - o Any other particulars as may be specified by the Agricultural Marketing Adviser.

The Food Ministry will Decide on Relaunching Guar Complex Futures

According to Forward Markets Commission, guar complex futures will be launched soon. All the members of the advisory committee have agreed upon starting of guar futures. FMC will submit the report to the Food Ministry and decision will be taken accordingly. Around 37,000 tons of guar gum (splits and powder) exported to various countries in August month 2013 as reported. It is notable that India has exported 45,000 tons of guar gum (splits and powder) in July month 2013. Despite of sharp fall in Rupee, free flow buying has not been seen from foreign countries of guar gum which depicts that demand is very less in foreign countries of guar gum at present.

Exports

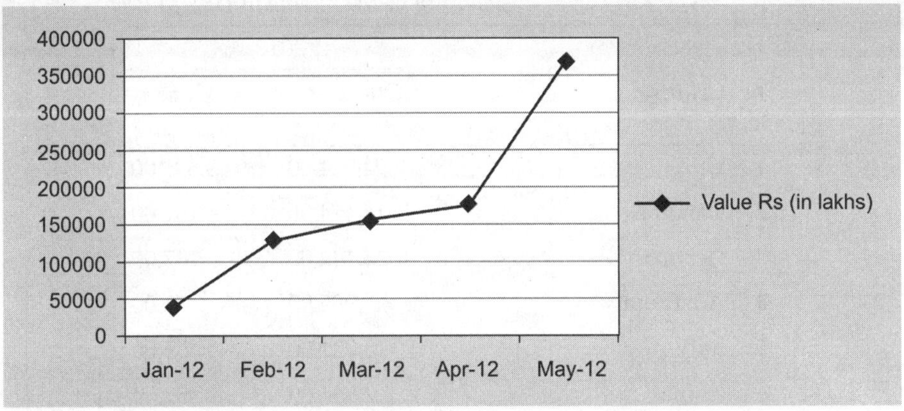

Trend of total export of guar gum to USA from India based on value

India's farmers were responding by planting new areas with guar with suitable weather conditions. Weather conditions is the main reason why efforts to grow Guar gum commercially in other countries, such as the US, have been unsuccessful. Pakistan is the only other significant producer of guar.

In March, the US purchased a record 33,800 tons of guar gum from India, up from an average 22,000 tons a month last year. In April 2012 more than 50 US companies procured guar gum from 60 different exporters of India. Most US companies procure guar gum from multiple Indian suppliers.

The major importing countries of Indian guar gum and its derivatives are:

- United States of America
- Germany
- France
- United Kingdom
- South Africa
- Netherlands
- Italy
- Japan.

Major Exporter of Guar Gum

India is also the world leader in the exports of guar and its derivatives followed by Pakistan. The major countries exports guar gums are India, Pakistan, USA, Italy, Morocco, Spain, France, Greece and Germany. Data are shown on page 536 at top.

Analysis of Guar Gum Export to United States from India

India is the world's biggest guar gum producer, with an average annual output of a million tons. This year, the American oil industry is expected to import 300,000 tons of guar gum – 75% of the India's export total. Till May 2012 India has already exported guar gum worth Rs 873967 lakh to US.

Major importing countries of guar gum

(Quantity in MT Value in US$ Mill.)

Sr No.	*Country*	*2012*	
		Qty	*Value*
1	USA	2,94,224.00	3,535.00
2	Canada	16,474.00	152.00
3	Germany	25,142.00	147.00
4	Australia	7,985.00	73.00
5	Italy	15,721.00	59.00
6	China	7,534.00	59.00
7	Japan	5,436.00	55.00
8	Russian Federation	6,932.00	47.00
9	Denmark	4,593.00	42.00
10	Netherlands	4,965.00	41.00
		3,89,006.00	**4,210.00**

The dramatic rise of guar powder, which has climbed from $US4/$US5 per kilo to $US30 within 18 months, and a limited supply of beans are creating a headache for the oil industry. Several American oil companies have been forced to halt drilling because of guar shortages. It said that guar gum now represented as much as 30% of the cost of fracking, or hydraulic fracturing. About nine tons of the material is needed per well.

With shale gas drilling now taking off in Argentina, Australia, China and Eastern Europe, the demand is expected to grow further. China, which is completely dependent on India for guar gum, levies an import duty of 15% on guar gum powder and seven per cent gum splits. The Directorate General of Foreign Trade (DGFT) is

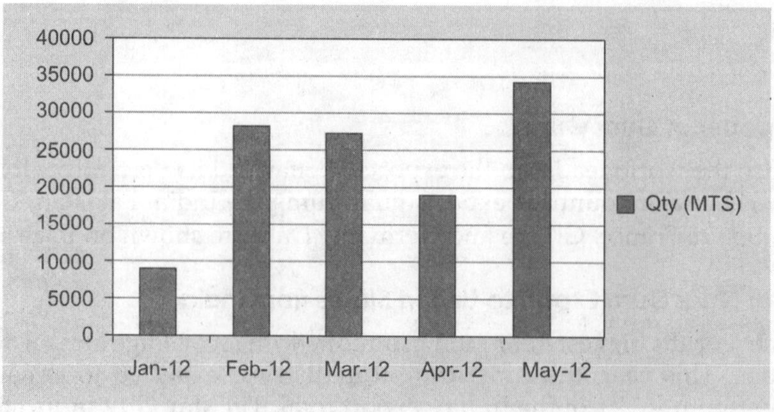

Month-wise guar gum from India to USA

considering levy of 20% export duty on guar gum, a derivative of guar seed, with application in oil drilling, paper, textiles, mining, explosives, ore floatation and many other industries.

Guar Gum: Method of Packing for Export

- The guar gum shall be packed only in sound clean, dry and un-used containers made of B-twill just or in polythene bags placed in gunny bags or multiply craft paper sacks or any other material as may be approved by the Agricultural Marketing Adviser.
- The container shall be free from any insect infestation or fungus contamination.
- The container shall be free from any undesirable smell.
- The container shall be securely closed and sealed in the manner approved by the Agricultural Marketing Adviser.
- Each package shall contain Guar Gum of one trade description and one grade designation only.

During last decade, guar has immerged as an important industrial raw material and produced by man for thousands of years. India has been the single largest producer and exporter of guar gum accounting for more than 80% of the global output and trade.

GUAR GUM MANUFACTURER AND EXPORTER IN INDIA

Guar Gum Manufacturing Process

Depending upon the requirement of end product various processing techniques are used. In India, the commercial production of guar gum is normally undertaken by using process of roasting, differential attrition, sieving and polishing. The stage wise process of manufacturing food grade guar gum is as under. It is very important to select guar split in this process. The split will be screened to clean and then it will be soaked to prehydrate in a double cone mixer. Prehydrating stage is very important in the process as it derives the rate of hydration of the final product. The soaked splits, which has reasonably high moisture content, will be passed through flacker to take them. The flaked guar split will be ground to desired particle size followed by drying of the material. The power will be screened through rotary screens to deliver required particle size. The oversize will be either recycle to main ultrafine or regrind in separate regrind plant, as per viscosity requirement.

This stage helps to reduce the load at the grinder. The soaked splits are difficult to grind. Direct grinding of those generates more heat in the grinder which is not desired in the process as it results in insoluble or reduced hydration of the product. Through heating, grinding and polishing process the husk is separated from the endosperm halves and the refined guar gum split are obtained. Through grinding process the refined Guar split are then treated and converted into powder.

During the split manufacturing process, husk and germ are obtained which are used as a cattle feed as they are rich in protein. It is widely sold in the international market as "Guar Meal" and has contents of "Oil and Albuminoids". These contents are about 50% in germ whereas it is about 25% in husks. Quality of the food grad guar gum powder is defined from its particle size, rate of hydration and the microbial in it. E412 guar gum is an important natural food supplement with high nutritional value.

Guar Gum Export Increases 75%

Uttar Pradesh and Rajasthan farmers are raising a cheer each time a global oil major announces exploration plans. Guar gum, grown in north India and used as an important lubricant in the drilling of oil wells across the world, has seen a 75% jump in export as the largest producer, India, is currently the only supplier to the world market. This rise in global demand, coupled with tighter supplies this year, has led to bumper profits for local producers.

A closer look at the movement of guar gum price shows that it has appreciated by a whopping 72% in March this year *vis-a-vis* same period previous year. Currently, the guar gum price is hovering around Rs 85,000 per ton compared to Rs 49,500 per ton in the corresponding period of 2010.

Exports of guar gum from India in FY11 are likely to be in the range of 260,000 ton to 270,000 tonne as against 220,000 ton in FY10. US, China and Europe are the major importers of guar gum. Rajasthan, Gujarat and Haryana are the biggest manufacturers in the country. The projected export earnings in FY11 is likley to be Rs 1,405.93 crore. Talking to ET, PK Hissaria, MD of Sunita Hydrocolloids, said: "There is a good demand for guar gum in the oil drilling sector, which has pushed up the prices.

China Imposes Duty on Guar Exports

Guar splits and guar powder attract a duty of 7% and 15%, respectively. China accounts for 25-30% of total exports of guar gum splits.

Guar gum exporters from India are at a distinct disadvantage. China has imposed customs duty of 7–15% on guar exports from India, the world's largest exporter. But import from Pakistan is duty free. This preferential treatment is costing India in global market share. The guar splits and guar powder attract a duty of 7–15%, respectively. China accounts for 25–30% of the total exports of guar gum splits. Due to the higher duty on guar powder, India's exports to China are decreasing while exports of refined guar gum splits is increasing.

Guar gum refined split is refined endosperm derived from guar seed or cluster bean. Guar gum refined split is mechanically separated from guar seed which yields 28–30% of refined split. PK Hissaria, managing director of Sunita Hydrocolloids, said: "Many manufacturing units have come up in China over the last several years to manufacture the value-added finished guar gum powder from refined guar gum splits. Due to this duty disparity, China has been able to compete Indian guar gum powder manufacturers in the world market. This has put Indian guar gum powder manufacturers at a disadvantage and also reduced the exports of value-added products like guar gum powder".

Guar gum industry feels that Indian guar gum is qualitatively superior to guar gum in Pakistan. "Pakistan exports guar gum products to China at a nil duty. Parity in import duty levied by China for guar gum exported by India and Pakistan will enhance export of about Rs 300 crore of Indian guar gum", said Debjani Roy, executive director of Shefexil. There is also a disparity in the export duty structure of sesame seeds.

Indian Guar Market

- India has been a major player in the context of guar and guar gum in the global market.

- India's production contributes to 80% of the world's total production figuring up to 6 lakh tons.
- Rajasthan wholly retains the credit for India's position producing 70% of the production itself.
- Guar is largely consumed as a vegetable in the Indian subcontinent. It is also used in making pickles.
- 25,000 tons of the total production in the country constitutes to the domestic market.
- Guar gum has a vast range of industrial applications and the major share of demand comes from various industrial sectors only.
- India is the leading net exporter of guar seeds and guar gum. The country exports over 117,000 tons of guar and its derivatives, which is comprised by 33,000 tons of refined split guar gum, and 84,000 tons of treated and pulverized guar gum.
- The net worth of the Indian exports is estimated over Rs 500 crores.
- The production list of guar is dominated by India as a leading producer of this crop. The consumption pattern of guar seeds is largely influenced by the demands from the petroleum industry of United States of America and the oil fields in the Middle East as the derivative products of these seeds are quite useful in the petroleum drilling industries.
- United States alone constitute to around 40 thousand tons of guar and its derivatives demand.
- Also, in rest of the world, the trend of consumption has increased with time that has lead to the introduction of this crop in many countries.

WORLD

The United States has produced 4,600–14,000 tons of guar over the last 5 years. As many as 50,000 acres of guar have been grown in West Texas over the last 50 years. The world production for guar gum and its derivatives is about 1.0 million tons. Industrial guar gum accounts for about 70% of the total demand. Mainly it is used as a proppant transport/proppant suspending agent in Hydraulic Fracturing Process. In 2012, guar prices increased by 900–1,000%. The main reason for this large scale price rise was the inventory build up by companies like Halliburton and Schlumberger, amidst the fear of shortage of guar gum for drilling due to ongoing drought in Rajasthan.

4

Hops

Hop History

The hop is a perennial climbing plant of the hemp family (*Cannabinaceae*). The wild hop (*Humulus mas*) is very different from its cultivated cousin (Humulus lupulus) which not only gives beer its aroma and bitter flavor but also preserves it. The high-quality brewer's hop is the result of a process of cultivations spanning several centuries. As hops are used almost exclusively in brewing, this development is closely linked with the history and geographical distribution of beer.

Hops are the female flower clusters (commonly called seed cones or strobiles), of a hop species, Humulus lupulus. They are used primarily as a flavoring and stability agent in beer, to which they impart a bitter, tangy flavor although hops are also used for various purposes in other beverages and herbal medicine. Hops were cultivated continuously around the 8th or 9th century AD in Bohemian gardens in the Hallertau district of Bavaria and other parts of Europe However, the first documented use of hops in beer as a bittering agent is from the 11th century. Prior to this period, brewers used a wide variety of bitter herbs and flowers. Dandelion, burdock, marigold, horehound (the German word for horehound means "mountain hops"), ground ivy and heather were often used prior to the discovery of hops. Hops are used extensively in brewing today for their many purported benefits, including balancing the sweetness of the malt with bitterness, contributing a variety of desirable flavors and aromas, and having an antibiotic effect that favors the activity of brewer's yeast over less desirable microorganisms. Historically, it is believed that traditional herb combinations for ales were abandoned when it was noticed that ales made with hops were less prone to spoilage.

A Brief History of Hops in Beer Hops is a relatively new addition to the brewmaster's toolkit. Prior to the widespread adoption of hops, beer was bittered and flavored with spice and herb mixtures sometimes called gruit. Any number of herbs and spices went into fruit including henbane, wild rosemary, heather, ginger, spruce, juniper, and bog myrtle, just to name a few. In parts of Europe the blending of gruit was the closely held province of Gruit Guilds that had exclusive rights and kept the specific ingredients secret. The first documented link between hops and brewing is from 822 AD when a Benedictine abbot wrote a series of statutes covering the running of the monastery that included gathering sufficient hops for making beer. Evidence suggests that commercial hop cultivation began in northern Germany during the 12th or 13th century and that the Germans were exporting hopped beer from the 13th century onward. The first evidence of hopped beer being brewed in England is from 1412 and for a time English brewers produced both un-hopped "ale" and hopped "beer". On April 23, 1516 the Bavarian Reinheitsgebot was put into effect declaring hops one of the three allowable beer ingredients (Yeast hadn't yet been discovered). In 1710, the English parliament banned the use of non-hop bittering agents, at least in part to prevent brewers from evading the new penny-per-pound hop tax. Thus, hops became the dominant bittering agent in beer.

History and Production

Known by the Romans as a culinary delicacy, and by medieval monks for their herbal properties, hops began to be grown extensively in northern Europe in the 13th and 14th centuries as a preservative and flavoring for beer. In England, a thriving hop industry developed, initially in Kent where the plentiful supply of coppiced chestnut provided poles for the hop gardens and fuel for drying, and then in Herefordshire and Worcestershire which also had ideal conditions and proximity to the Midlands with its thirsty industrial workforce. Even small farms in these areas had their own hop gardens with their distinctive oast-houses.

Hops, Humulus lupulus, are in the same *Cannabinaceae* family as hemp and nettle—and have similar tough, fibrous stems and a rough hairiness to the stalks and leaves. Vigorous perennial plants, they thrive in rich, moist soils, establishing deep rooting systems that enable them to survive summer droughts and winter frosts. The young shoots emerge in March and twine clockwise up and around any suitable support, following the sun.

In commercial production, the strongest shoots are selected (and the rest removed) and twined up rough coir string. They grow as much as 10 cm a day during May and June, reaching about 5 m in height. Lateral shoots develop in July and the flowers form in August. The large hop flowers or "cones" used for brewing and decoration are the fruiting bodies borne on the female plants and are composed of collections of green bracts or "petals" protecting the seeds. At the base of these bracts is a yellow pollen-like substance—the plant's essential oil (lupulin) glands that provide the bittering and preservative element used in beer-making.

Hops are "dioecious"—the males and females flower on separate plants—but, it is only the female plant that produces the big, soft, flowering cone that is used for beer and decoration. Male plants are sometimes planted in hop gardens to produce seeded hops. The full length of the growing hop climbing on its string is known in Kent as a bine (or as a vine elsewhere).

Sensitivity to day length influences their viability as a horticultural crop, so even though the universal popularity of beer has made hops a world-wide commodity, the main commercial production is in areas of specific latitude: Europe, China and North-West America in the northern hemisphere, and Tasmania, parts of New Zealand, Southern Australia, and the tip of South Africa in the southern hemisphere.

Needless to say, as a garden plant or for home-brewing, hops will grow happily throughout many parts of the UK if given good soil and protection from strong winds. In the wild it will reproduce readily from seed but commercially is always grown from setts or root cuttings established in the winter or early spring in frost-free ground.

In the UK, hops are harvested in the first few weeks of September. Once needing gangs of hand-pickers (a traditional working "holiday" for London's East-enders), the job is now done by machines, picking the hop flowers off the "bines" to be quickly air-dried and compressed into sacks for transport to the brewers. The plants, being perennials, are then cut back to ground level and lie dormant until the spring.

Hops at Castle Farm

Hops add the crucial bittering and aromatic elements that help distinguish one brew of beer from another, but they have herbal, culinary and decorative uses too, as well as being attractive climbing plants for the garden. Old maps from 1720 show hop gardens at Castle Farm in the same area where they remain now—the best soil on the farm. Being a traditional Kentish crop, hops were always a specialty here and each September gangs of pickers would descend from London to camp in our hopper huts and enjoy a working family holiday. In those days the hops were grown purely for brewing but, for the past 25 years, The Hop Shop has been developing diverse uses for hops—exploring their versatility to the full!

Hops Overview

Hops is a plant. The dried, flowering part of the plant is used to make medicine. Hops is used for anxiety, inability to sleep (insomnia) and other sleep disorders, restlessness, tension, excitability, attention deficit-hyperactivity disorder (ADHD), nervousness, and irritability. It is also used to improve appetite, increase urine flow, start the flow of breast milk, as a bitter tonic, and for indigestion. Other uses include prostate cancer, breast cancer, ovarian cancer, high cholesterol, tuberculosis, bladder infections, intestinal cramps, an intestinal disorder called mucous colitis, nerve pain, and prolonged painful erection of the penis (priapism).

Hops is sometimes applied to the skin for leg ulcers and as an antibacterial agent. In foods and beverages, the extracts and oil are used as flavor components. Hops are also used in brewing beer. In manufacturing, the extract is used in skin creams and lotions.

HOPS: THE BITTER HERB

Hops were first used in beer in Asia 10,000 years ago. It appears that hops were used in Babylon before 200 AD. Hops Latin name appears in records of Jews' captivity in Babylon. They mention *sicera* (strong drink) *ex luplis confectam* (made from hops). Hops spread into Europe from Asia through Eastern Europe. The most consistent fact about the spread of hops is that in almost every country, the use of hops was resisted. Hops are a distant relative of stinging nettle and cannabis. This is a major reason for the relaxing effect of hops. They have been used for insomnia since their earliest mention in literature. Pliny (61–113 AD) discusses hops in his study of natural history. To the Romans, it was *Lupus Salictartius*, from the way they originally grew. As the ancients said, hops grew "wild among willows, like a wolf among sheep", hence the name *Humulus Lupulus*.

The hop has its place in folklore. Along with the animals who are supposed to receive the gift of speech late on Christmas Eve, the hop is supposed to turn green in the same night. The first mention of hops is in reference to a hop garden in the Hallertau district in 736 AD.

The first EUROPEAN mention of hops being added to beer was in 1079 by Abbess Hildegarde of St. Ruprechtsberg. "If one intends to make beer from oats, it is prepared with hops. Brewing was traditionally a monastic task, and much mention is made of hops gardens in monasteries.

In Germany which was the center from which hops conquered all Europe, it was not until the 13th century that the traditional flavoring of gruit was seriously threatened. In some places, like Cologne, monopolistic rights were associated with gruit, generally the Church's. The Archbishop of Cologne possessed the "Grutrecht" (gruit rights) and tried to suppress the use of hops, which of course the brewers saw as a commercial as well as technical advance. While the composition of gruit was subject to local variations, it commonly contained bog myrtle, rosemary, yarrow, alecost, and many others. The herbs were not chosen only for their flavor, but for their reputed medicinal properties as well. The hopped beer of the middle ages was extremely heavily hopped 7 lb to the hogshead, or 5 lb to the barrel were not uncommon.

Records reflect the use of hops in beer in France in 1268 during the reign of Louis IX. the law stated that beer should only contain good malt and hops. In Holland, by the 14th century, the Netherlanders had already developed a taste for Hamburg beer, which was hopped beer, in contrast to the normal Dutch beer, which was still based on gruit. The Dutch nobility tried to exclude foreign beers by prohibition and high import duties, but the reputation of Hamburg beer as so great, that it all came to naught. In 1376 there were no less than 126 "braxatores de Almsetlredamme" (Amsterdam breweries). The Dutch were apt pupils and by 1517, Antonio de Beatis stated the *"the beer in these regions is better than in Germany and brewed in larger quantity"*. The English developed a taste for hopped Dutch beer while soldiering in the Low Countries. Hopped beer, or beer (as opposed to ale) was imported into Winchelsea as early as 1400, with the first hops being planted in England in 1428.

In 1524, hops were condemned as an adulteration by Henry VIII, and an injunction against their use was issued. However, in 1536, Edward VI (Henry's successor) commended hopped beer as *"notable, healthy, and temperate"*. The Brewer's Company, formed in 1437 and made up of ale brewers, concerned about the spread of beer petitioned the Lord Mayor of London in 1484 that *"no hops, herbs, or other like thing be put into any ale or liquore wherof ale shall be made—but only liquor, malt, and yeast."* This was intended to keep clear the demarcation between ale and beer. In 1493, the beer brewers themselves became a definite craft (guild) and ale and beer were to remain quite distance for over 100 years.

Although unhopped ale had ceased to be brewed in England by the 16th century, it could still be found in Scotland. We read of Jerome Cardan, a French physician, who traveled to Scotland in 1552. He frequently mentions food and approves of Scotch ale and says that it *"it differs from beer in the omission of hops"*.

Botany of the Hop

The hop is a dioecious plant; this means that a single plant bears only male or only female flowers. Only the female plant forms cones. The hop is propagated by means of cuttings. The part of the plant above ground is cut off at harvest time; only the rootstock remains, from which new shoots grow the following spring. The rootstock stores the reserves which will enable the plant to grow to a height of 30 inches in the spring with virtually no other nourishment. In spring, the rootstock puts out shoots. These are covered with hooked hairs to give the bines a better grip as they climb. In the Yakima Valley, bines can grow by up to 14 inches in a single day, but the average is about 4 inches. The leaves of the hop plant grow from the nodes of the bine. The underside of the leaves sis smooth, the top surface is very hairy. When the hops have climbed halfway up their trellises, the laterals start to grown. The total length of a plant's laterals can reach up to 360 feet. As the hop cones grow almost exclusively on the laterals, their development is very important for the yield.

After a flowering period of 3–4 weeks the cones form, mature and are ready for harvest. The cone itself contains the substances which make the hop so valuable to the brewer. Experts can recognize the different varieties of hop, not only by the shape and aroma but also the colors of the different parts of the plant.

What are Hops?

Hops (*Humulus lupulus*) are a perennial plant of the *Cannabaceae* family that also includes the genus Cannabis. In beer, hops provide bitterness to balance the sweetness of malt sugars, as well as flavors, aromas, resins that increase head retention, and antiseptics to retard spoilage. Often referred to as a "vine", hops are actually a "bine", using a strong stem and stiff hairs to climb rather than tendrils and suckers to attach. It is the flower of the hop plant that is used in brewing. Hop flowers or cones resemble pine cones but are composed of thin, green, papery, leaf-like bracts. At the base of these bracts are waxy, yellow lupulin glands that contain alpha acids responsible for bitterness and essential oils that give beer flavor and aroma. The plant has separate male and female bines, but only the female bines develop cones. If male plants are allowed to pollinate them, the flowers will produce seeds, rendering them useless for brewing. Aside from their use in beer, hops also have medicinal application as a sleep aid. Hop filled pillows were once a common remedy for insomnia. Hops also aid in clarification as well as head retention.

Cultivation

The hop plant flourishes in certain climates and soils in temperate zones. The plant flourishes in areas with direct sunlight with access to plenty of moisture in the spring and warm sun in the summers. It requires approximately 4 months of frost free conditions. Ideally for cultivation, the soils should be moist, rich and well drained with pH levels of 6 to 7.5. The hops grow well on sandy and loamy soils. Fertilizers containing potassium, phosphate, and nitrogen can be used for optimum production. Given the right conditions, the vines can grow to heights of upto 30 feet. The soils should be tilled to create a weed free zone and are to be planted during the early spring when no frost is present. The hop plant requires regular but light supply of water.

When the hops plants reach a size of around 1 foot, a few are to be selected for further growth and the rest are to be removed. In the month of July, the lowest parts of the hops are carefully removed to enable greater air circulation and stop the developments of diseases. When the season is over, the healthy vines can be buried in the soil for producing new plants in preparation for next spring. The flowering of the hops plants occurs in the month of July and the ripening of the fruits occurs during the months of September and October.

Uses

Hops function as flavoring agents and stabilizers in the making of beer. It is a cheaper substitute for making beers. It is used to make beautiful garlands and also for decorative purposes. In the medieval age, the poorer sections of society ate the young hop shoots during the spring time. It substituted vegetables like the asparagus. Hop shoots can be eaten raw with vinegar, boiled or fried form. In Italian cuisine, it is eaten with risotto or frittata. Hops are used to make the Julmust, a popular beverage from Sweden. Farmers feed their livestock with wild hops. The hop is associated with good luck. The flexible and fiber rich stem of hops can be used to fabricate cloth and paper. Ongoing research is being done to understand fully the medicinal value of the plant. Hop contains ingredients like humulene and lupulin. With a high presence of antibacterial qualities, it increases in the production of gastric juices. Hops are also antiviral in nature and contain high amounts of flavonoids.

Hops Cultivation Becoming Popular with Himachal Farmers

Farmers in Keylong region of Himachal Pradesh are getting good returns by cultivating hops. Hops are female flower clusters, commonly known as cones or strobiles, of the hop plant, which are primarily used as a flavoring and stability agent in beer. Hops have emerged as one of the main cash crops of the region and are being cultivated in around 63 hectares of the land area. More and more farmers are taking to cultivating hops because of its lucrative value as one kilogram of hops fetches the farmers anywhere from between rupees 60–70. "It is very easy to grow. We do not have to sow it again and again. We have to only change the its rope or thread, to support the plant. People are benefiting a lot from it", said Shamsher Singh, a farmer. he various varieties of hops cultivated in the region are the hybrid and late cluster. The hybrid cluster is rich in alpha acid content and is much in demand in the beer industry. "The hops grown here is the hybrid two variety which has a high content of alpha acid and last year we found that it has approximately 13.1 alpha content in it, and it has got a boost because of its use in the beer industry", said SK Gupta, Deputy Director, Horticulture, Lahaul and Spiti. The cultivation of hops began since 1979. Last year, there was 41.80 metric tons production of hops in the region.

Hop Plants for the Garden

Hop plants are used in gardens to cover unsightly structures, to provide contrasting foliage - and to provide a resource for home-brewing! They have a fast and vigorous growth rate and thrive in rich, moist soils, establishing a deep rooting system that enables them to survive summer droughts and winter frosts. The young shoots emerge in March and need a rough support through which they can climb and twine. They grow happily in many parts of the UK if given good soil and protection from strong winds. The flowers develop in August and mature in early September. Being perennials, the stems need to be cut back to ground level in the Autumn and the plant will lie dormant until the Spring.

The most popular commercial varieties for decorative use in gardens or for home-brewing are Fuggles (a well-known brewing variety with a large showy hop flower) and Wye Challenger (good for lager-type beers, with a mass of smaller compact flowers). Fuggles is excellent for sleep pillows, Wye Challenger is perfect for decorative use. Both these varieties will grow to about 5 m (15–16 feet) in height in a season, once established. For smaller gardens or for growing along fences, we recommend Prima Donna—a dwarf variety growing to about 2.5 m (8 ft) and with brewing characteristics similar to Wye Challenger. For mail order, the rootstocks (or rhizomes) of hop plants are available for immediate planting (if ground conditions are suitable) from December until April (the earlier the better!). They are supplied with full growing instructions. Potted hop plants, complete with a screw peg, string and growing instructions, can be purchased direct from the farm shop from December until May.

All our plants are certified disease-free: An important consideration when buying hops which can be susceptible to soil-borne viruses.

Hops to Eat and Drink

Known as "Poor Man's Asparagus", young hop shoots, cut in April when they are less than 15 cm long, can be gently fried in butter and garlic for salads or as a garnish for fish. In baking, a tiny pinch of hop flowers (ground in a coffee grinder) can add a distinctive zing to savory biscuits, but don't overdo it—hops are very bitter! Small quantities of hops can be used as an ingredient in herbal teas to aid relaxation. Our special Sleepy Tea with hops, chamomile, lavender and rose petals is available by Mail Order. Of course, we sell hop flowers for the home-brewer too. Our hop flowers are of the aromatic Fuggles variety. They are dried as soon as they have been harvested and are stored in the dark in dehumidified stores to retain the best color and quality. Unlike hops supplied for commercial brewing, which need to be tightly packed for storage, our hops are unpressed therefore minimizing loss of the aromatic oils.

Types of Hops for Brewing

- Hops are available to brewers in whole-leaf, pellet, or extract form. American craft brewers have also started using fresh, unprocessed hops to brew "harvest" or "fresh-hop" ales. Each of these forms has advantages and disadvantages.
- Whole-leaf Hops: Whole-leaf hops are simply the dried hop cones that have been compressed into bales. They are believed to have greater aromatic qualities than the other forms and are easier to strain from wort. However, because they retain more of the vegetative matter greater volumes must be used. They soak up more wort than other forms resulting in greater loss to the brewer. Their bulk also makes them more difficult to store and more susceptible to spoilage.
- Pellets: To make pellet hops the dried cones are shredded, compressed, and extruded into pellets that resemble rabbit food. The shredding process exposes the lupulin glands and removes a percentage of the vegetative matter, meaning smaller volumes can be used in the brewery. Their lighter weight and compressed state also makes them easier to store and less susceptible to spoilage. On the down side, they tend to lose some of their aromatic quality in processing and they create sludge at the bottom of the brew kettle that can be difficult to remove from the wort. The majority of hops used in the craft brewing industry are pellet hops.
- Extract: For hop extracts, the alpha acids and essential oils are pulled from the cones using heat and various solvents. These concentrated liquid extracts can be used in the brewing process just like hops. There are separate extracts for bittering, flavor, and aroma. They are mostly used by large breweries, although they are sometimes used by smaller breweries to reduce wort in highly hopped beers. Hop extracts are easy to store and can be kept for long periods

of time without spoilage. Their concentrated state and lack of vegetative matter reduces the amount that must be used and eliminates wort loss. Their concentration can make them difficult to use properly in small batches however, and some claim undesirable flavors from their use.

- Fresh or Wet Hops: Fresh hops are green, unprocessed cones, often added to the beer within hours of harvest. Wet hops give beers an intense, bright hop flavor and aroma. However, because they lack the concentration that comes with drying, a much larger volume is needed to achieve the same result as from dried hops. The additional vegetative matter can lend beer a grassy character and results in greater wort loss for the brewer.

Hop Varieties

Hops can be generally divided into two broad categories, bittering and aroma. Those hop varieties that contain high levels of alpha acids are called bittering hops because a lower volume is needed to achieve high levels of bitterness. Those with lower alpha acid content but higher levels of essential oils are called aroma hops. Beyond this broad division, general characterizations can be made based on the traditional area of origin.

- Continental or Noble Hops: The noble hops originate in central Europe and are among the most prized of the aroma hops. There are four noble hops, Hallertau, Tettnang, Spalt, and Czech Saaz. These hops impart a smooth bitterness and spicy/floral aromas. The noble hops are often used in lagers. Common descriptors for these hops include spicy, black pepper, licorice, perfume, floral, and herbal. English Hops: The most traditional English hop varieties fall into the low alpha acid aroma hop category. The most common are East Kent Goldings and Fuggle. Other higher alpha English hop varieties include Challenger, Target, and Progress. Common descriptors for the English hops include herbal, grassy, earthy, floral and fruity.
- American Hops: Bright, fruity, and resinous, these are the signature hops of American pale ale and IPA. The United States grows a number of hop varieties that can be considered duel use hops, with high alpha acid content and pleasant aromatic qualities. Commonly used American hop varieties are Cascade, Centennial, Chinook, Willamette, and Amarillo. Common descriptors for the American hop varieties are citrus, grapefruit, resinous, piney, fruity and spicy.

Hops in the Brewing Process

Brewers use hops primarily to get bitterness, flavor and aroma. Hops can be added at several points in the brewing process to enhance one or the other of those things. While most hops are added in the boil kettle, they can be added a various stages prior to and after the boil as well.

- Kettle Hops: Kettle hops is the name given to those hops added to the kettle during the boil. These include early addition hops for bitterness and late addition hops for flavor and aroma.
- Bittering Hops: Bitterness from hops comes from alpha acids found in the lupulin glands of the hop flowers. The main alpha acids are humulone and cohumulone and adhumulone. In order to become bitter these acids must be chemically altered, isomerized, by boiling. Isomerization is a chemical process

in which a compound is changed into another form with the same chemical composition but a different structure. The percentage of the potential alpha acid that is isomerized is referred to as utilization. Because the length of the boil determines degree of utilization, bittering hops are usually added at the beginning of the boil or with at least 60-minutes of boiling time remaining.

- Flavor Hops: Hop flavor and aroma are derived from essential oils found in the lupulin glands. These oils include humulene, myrcene, geraniol, and limonene, among others. The flavors are released as these oils become dissolved into the worst during the boil. However, these oils are highly volatile and are to a large degree lost to evaporation. For this reason flavor hops are added with twenty to forty minutes remaining in the boil. This provides a compromise between isomerization of the alpha acids and loss of essential oils.
- Aroma Hops: Because the aromatic essential oils are highly volatile, aroma hops are added in the last minutes of the boil to minimize their loss to evaporation.
- Other Hop Additions: Hops can be added at other points in the brewing process to enhance the flavor and aromatic qualities of beer.
- Dry Hopping: Perhaps the most common non-boil use of hops is dry hopping. In this process, hops are added to beer in the conditioning tank after fermentation is complete. The hops are left in the beer for a week or two allowing the essential oils to dissolve. Dry hopping provides a very bright and fresh hop aroma with slight enhancement of flavor.
- Hop Back: Another process for increasing hop aroma is to use a hop back. A hop back is a small tank that is placed between the kettle and the chiller in a brewing system. The hop back is filled with hops and the hot wort is run through it on the way to the chiller.
- First Wort Hopping: First wort hopping is a pre-boil addition of hops to the hot wort as it runs into the kettle from the mash/lauter tun. This is said to give a smoother hop aroma and flavor without significantly increasing bitterness.
- Mash Hopping: Mash hopping is the addition of hops in the mash tun. This is a controversial practice said to increase hop flavor without significantly affecting bitterness.
- Randall: A few years ago the Dogfish Head brewery in Maryland was looking for a way to inject their beers with more hop flavor and aroma. They invented Randall the Enamel Animal, an "organoleptic hop transducer module". Basically a Randall is a plastic filter housing that is filled with hops and inserted in the draft line coming from the keg. As the beer passes through the Randall on its way to the tap faucet, the alcohol dissolves the essential oils providing a fresh burst of hop character.

Hops Vocabulary

- **Alpha Acids:** The chemical compounds in hops that, when isomerized by boiling, give bitterness to beer.
- **Essential Oils:** The volatile compounds in hops that, when dissolved into beer, provide flavors and aromas.
- **Gruit:** A beer that is bittered with a mixture of herbs and spices. Also refers to the spice mix.

- **Hop Back:** A vessel filled with hops that acts as a filter, removing hot break material from wort on the way to the chiller.
- **International Bittering Units (IBU):** A chemical measurement of the actual bitterness in beer. An IBU is defined as one milligram of isomerized alpha acid per liter of beer. May be different from perceived bitterness.
- **Isomerization:** A chemical process in which a compound is changed into another form with the same chemical composition but a different structure.
- **Lupulin Glands:** Small, bright yellow nodes at the base of each hop petal that contains the alpha acids and essential oils utilized by brewers.
- **Randall:** A hop-filled vessel that is placed in the draft line between the keg and the faucet.

Hops for Decoration

Traditionally, garlands of hops were hung afresh every year - for good luck - in the pubs and farmhouses of the hop-growing areas of the UK (Kent, Herefordshire and Worcestershire) but few people outside of these areas appreciated the decorative potential of a full-flowered hop bine until the Hop Shop started, in 1986, growing and marketing them nationwide specifically for interior use. To achieve top decorative quality, our hops are grown at extra-wide spacing to encourage flowering along the full length of the bine. (This means that they are bigger, fuller bines and more consistent in their flowering than hops produced from closely-spaced brewing hops which are always competing for sunlight). The fully-grown bines are harvested from mid-August to mid-September when they are in their prime and have their freshest green color. They are either sold as fresh-cut bines for immediate decorative use or dried in the dark in temperature- and humidity-controlled sheds to hold their color. They are then boxed and stored in insulated, dehumidified stores for sale throughout the year. The decorative bines are approximately 3m (10 ft) in length. Now, dried hop bines can be seen throughout the UK, over the bars in pubs, trailed along the top of kitchen units, twisted around wedding marquee poles or adorning the beams of old barns.

Fresh hop bines can be purchased (cut to order) from mid-August to mid-September and either collected direct from the shop or despatched by 24-hour courier to most. Dried hop bines are available throughout the year for purchase direct from the shop or for despatch by Royal Mail or 48-hour courier throughout the UK and Northern Ireland.

Hops for Sleep

Read old books on herbal remedies and you will always find reference to both hops and lavender being good for sleep and for many years customers have been asking us for hop flowers to make sleep pillows and lavender oils to aid relaxation.

It was therefore a logical step to combine the soporific and therapeutic qualities of hops and lavender into a unique Sleepy Scent, a Sleepy Tea and a Pillow Mix – all for people who don't want to take conventional sleeping pills. The BBC2 program by James Wong, first broadcast in March 2009, recommended the use of hop and lavender flowers to make hop pillows and The Hop Shop was instantly inundated with orders and enquiries. The response from users was overwhelmingly and consistently positive to the entire product range, with many recommendations and repeat orders. As the result of such a powerful vote of confidence, The Hop Shop is now looking to conduct quantifiable research into the perceived benefits. We have therefore devised a 2-part questionnaire: the first part asks you to assess your current sleep patterns and the factors that you think influence the quality of your sleep. The second part, to be completed after using the Natural Sleep products for at least a week, is designed to assess any changes. We hope that if enough people complete the questionnaire, which several doctors have helped us to write, we will be able to take the project further.

There are several different products in Natural Sleep range, from simple hop flowers to the subtle and complex formula of our Hop and Lavender Sleepy Scent:

- **Sleepy Scent**: A complex and totally calming scent using 4 essential oils. It's a very concentrated scent so you only need a few drops on a handkerchief next to your pillow every night. Keep it on a bedside table and take it with you when travelling (especially on overnight flights).
- **Sleep Balm:** A gentler scent made from the same Sleepy Scent compound, this balm can be massaged into the temples or the upper lip below the nose.
- **Sleepy Tea**: A delicate calming herbal mix of chamomile, lavender, rose petals and hops.
- **Sleep Pillow Mix**: A balanced combination of hops and sweet-scented *Lavandula angustifolia*, there is enough here to make a thin pad to put on top of your usual pillow. It can be supplemented with Sleepy Scent or Sleepy Balm to balance the fragrance. With regular use, the natural fragrance of the hops and lavender will fade or change as the aromatic oils oxidize, so customers need to judge for themselves when they think that the effectiveness of the aroma is reducing and replenish the pillow with a new batch.
- **Hop Flowers**: Whole and unpressed, for sleep pillows and brewing.

Hops in Beer

The use of hops in beer most likely began when some ancient cave brewer, in an effort to gain a competitive edge, started experimenting with "additives" to his product. The hops grew wild, as did the brewer, the barley and the yeast. Some degree of variability in the product was no doubt acceptable.

The use of hops probably started before recorded history. It is known that the Babylon and Egyptian people used hops and other aromatic and spicy plants to improve the palatability of their brewing efforts.

Germans are often identified with hops and beer, but from a historical perspective, this is of recent practice. The first documented evidence of hop yards in Germany dates back to the year 736, to a monastery in Bavaria.

The early brewers, especially those on the cutting edge of technology, discovered that the beer containing hops had better keeping qualities than their unhopped products. The practice then began of adding greater quantities of hops to beer depending on the season of year and expected storage time. More hops equaled greater storage life. The reason for this was not known and not important; the results were important.

Hop production in America followed closely the settlement of the first colonies in the New England areas. Early American brewers used wild hops, but the cultivation of hops in the old world had progressed to "industry status" and soon moved to the new world. After growing hops in New England and Virginia, the center of hop production moved to New York State by the middle 1800s. Problems with powdery mildew practically wiped out the production of hops in New York about 1909. The region revived again around 1920 with the discovery of sulfur-based fungicides only to be devastated again in the late 1920s by downy mildew.

Starting about 1850 the hop industry in the Western States of Washington, Oregon and California began to develop and eventually became one of the major regions of the world. In recent years, California and Western Washington hop production has ceased. Oregon and Idaho still account for 25–30% of US production while the Yakima Valley of Washington totals 70–75%. The total US production accounts for nearly 30% of the world hop crop.

Brewers no longer rely on the antiseptic properties of hops for microbiological control and, in general, the modern consumer prefers a lighter and lesser hopped beer. The growing and processing of hops has become a highly scientific endeavor as has the brewing of beer. Hop usage in beer is deeply ingrained and is considered one of the more vital ingredients. Beer without hops is unthinkable. Or, for that matter, so are hops without beer!

Advantages of Hopped Beer

Beer was the one drink that had been sterilized and was safe to drink. Prior to hops, the stronger (more alcoholic) beer was, the longer it kept. The addition of hops is a preservative, thus allowing beer to be weaker and still keep longer.

Hops allowed you to produce more beer from the same amount of malt. Reynold Scot, in A Perfite Platforme for a Hoppe Garden, states *"whereas you cannot ake above 8–9 gallons of a very indifferent ale from a bushel of malt, you may draw 18–20 gallons of very good beer"*.

Important Advice on Handling Hop Bines

A hop bine is composed of two or three stems that have grown and twisted up a long central string. Fresh hop bines are supple and can be easily draped and twined into position and left to dry out naturally. Hanging the cut bines is easy—simply hook the stems or string over a nail. The bines are very light when dry so weight is not a problem. Dried bines have to be stored at low humidity in order to preserve their color and condition and can therefore be quite brittle to handle. We strongly recommend that 24 hours before they are to be hung, the boxes are opened and left in a damp atmosphere such as a shed, cellar or garage (not outside). Damp air will be absorbed into the flowers and foliage, softening them and making them easier to handle. An alternative is to use a fine mist spray and leave it for a short while to be absorbed.

Hops should always be hung in a position where they will not be knocked by people or disturbed by draughts as the flowers may disintegrate if damaged. The greenness of the flowers will be retained longer if the hops are not exposed to direct sunlight. Please note: Hop flowers contain a yellow pollen-like substance that contains the plant's essential oils. This can stain fabrics and furnishings, so dust-sheets should always be used to protect interiors whilst hops are being handled. Occasionally there may be small insects or aphids hidden in the foliage or flowers of fresh hops, feeding off the sap. These will emerge as soon as the hops start to dry and will die off very quickly within a couple of days. We inspect all bines before despatch and reject any that have an obvious problem—but detecting small infestations is very difficult, so please be patient!

The fresh bines have a rough, slightly barbed surface to the stems and underside of the leaves. This can scratch the skin and cause short-term irritation so we recommend the wearing of thin gloves and long sleeves while handling the fresh bines.

WORLD

Hops Production

Day length during the growing season has a major effect on yield. For this reason the majority of the world's commercial hop production occurs between latitudes 35° and 55°, either north or south of the equator. The largest producers of hops are Germany, the United States, China, and the Czech Republic. Other important growing regions include England, New Zealand, and increasingly Argentina. Climate and soil conditions have a major effect on hops. Varieties developed in one region will have different flavor and aroma profiles when grown in another. Hop plants sprout in the spring and die back to a cold-hardy rhizome in the fall. During peak growing season they grow very rapidly, up to twenty inches per week. Commercial hop growers cultivate hop bines on V-shaped, wire and twine trellises that are up to 20 feet tall. In spring, at the start of the growing season, two to three young shoots are trained in a clockwise direction around each horizontal length of twine. The harvest season begins in August and continues into October with different varieties of hops coming ready at different times. Harvesting machines cut the bines and twine at the top and bottom and load them onto trucks. They then pass through a series of sorters to separate the cones from the stems and leaves. The cones are placed in a kiln where 140° air is circulated, drying the cones to about 30% of their green weight. After cooling the cones are compressed into bales or further processed into pellets or extracts.

Acreage and Production

Hops are grown in approximately 30 countries worldwide, the majority of which are in the Northern Hemisphere. World production is dominated by two countries, Germany and the USA, who jointly represent more than half of the world hops production (59.2% in 2009). In 2008, global hops area amounted to almost 54,000 hectares, of which the EU-27 accounted for about 55%, the United States for 30% and China for more than 10%. In the US, the bulk of production is provided by Washington State (Yakima area) whilst other important areas can be found in Idaho and Oregon.

The global area under hops declined from 57,967 hectare in 2001 to 53,865 in 2008 (–6%). On the other hand, world production in tons has increased from 98,705 tons in 2001 to 111,140 tons in 2008, a rise of 13%. The 2008 harvest was exceptionally high due to the choice of varieties and to exceptionally good weather. The increase in acreage of about 4,000 hectare from the previous year, mainly in the US, Germany and China, was also important and shows a change in the tendency toward a reduction in acreage. In all other countries, changes in acreage were (less than) zero or not relevant. The following table shows the global development of hops area and yield (Table 4.1).

Table 4.1: Development of surface and yields of hops worldwide

		2001	2002	2003	2004	2005	2006	2007	2008
Acreage (aroma varieties)	Ha	28,069	27,000	25,595	25,903	25,879	25,862	25,583	27,105
Acreage (bitter varieties)	Ha	27,460	25,725	25,064	24,197	22,565	20,212	23,940	26,759
Total acreage	Ha	57,967	55,348	52,203	51,408	48,995	46,095	49,523	53,865
% bitter varieties	%	47.4	46.5	48.0	47.1	46.1	43.8	48.3	49.7
Acreage (new)	Ha	2,438	2,623	1,544	1362	586	844	1,551	5,420
Yield (aroma varieties)	Kg/ha	1,361	1,448	1,233	1,486	1,636	1,338	1,559	1,706
Yield (bitter varieties)	Kg/ha	2,203	2,911	2,116	2,238	2,265	1,846	2,171	2,426
Yield (all varieties)	Kg/ha	1,703	2,059	1,812	1,802	1,907	1,766	1,815	2,063
Yield of alpha acid	Kg/ha	149	155	135	164	167	151	165	194
% alpha acid	%	8.8	7.5	7.4	9.1	8.7	8.5	9.1	9.4
Production (aroma varieties)	Tons	38,212	39,090	31,566	38,504	42336	34,594	39,893	46,228
Production (bitter varieties)	Tons	60,494	74,892	53,024	54160	51,106	37,306	51,974	64,912
Total production	Tons	98,705	113,983	94,590	92,655	93,445	81,401	89,866	111,140
Total production of alpha acid	Tons	8,639	8,596	7,023	8,452	8,158	6,956	8,161	10,468

Source: IHGC, adaptation LEI.

The ratio between aroma varieties and bitter varieties has changed over the years. Since 2001 the share of bitter varieties in the total acreage has been approximately 48%. The share of bitter varieties increased over the decade to 2001 from a share of 37% in 1991. Table 4.2 shows the production of alpha acid by continent. Europe is the largest producer with a share of 50%, closely followed by America with a share of 40%. Asia produces only 8% of world production with Oceania contributing 2% and Africa only 1% (Table 4.2A).

Table 4.2: Production of alpha acid by continent

(In tons)

	2001	*2002*	*2003*	*2004*	*2005*	*2006*	*2007*	*2008*
Europe	3,672	4,064	2,847	4,469	4,562	3,191	3,847	5,187
America	3,450	3,140	2,900	2,900	2,584	2,929	3,280	4,150
Asia	907	862	921	727	644	550	717	860
Africa	90	118	111	134	127	95	121	79
Oceania	370	412	244	222	241	192	196	192
World	8,489	8,596	7,023	8,452	8,158	6,956	8,161	10,468

Source: IHGC, adaptation LEI.

The Farm Structure

The number of holdings growing hops has declined significantly during the 2000-2008 period in the main producing countries where comparable data are available. In the most important producing countries, the reduction ranges between 10.92% in Poland to 37.69% in Spain. In Germany holdings have decreased by 22.95% with the loss of 446 holdings (Table 4.3).

While the number of holdings has decreased, the average area per holding has increased in all the listed countries (but the UK) from +2.50% in the Czech Republic to +31.58% in Germany. These data series show a large variability in average area across Member States. The largest holdings are in the Czech Republic (40.7 hectare per holding in 2008) when the smallest are in Spain and Poland (around 2 hectare per holding).

The World Market for Hops

Demand

The majority of the hops produced is used in the beer brewing industry and therefore the demand for hops worldwide is dependent on beer consumption. The beer market is changing. In East Asian countries beer consumption is increasing, but it is falling in Europe (especially in western countries), America and Africa. Beer production in 2009 reached 1,817 million hectoliters, an increase of 396 million hectoliters since 2001 (Table 4.4). With the beer market stagnating in several important markets, competition between brewers actors is increasing (Table 4.5).

It has to be highlighted that the hops downstream market is today extremely concentrated as the number of traders and the number of brewers have significantly decreased over the last 20 years. Some niche players remain, often local suppliers, but they have a tiny impact on demand. The top three global brewers produce over 50% of the world's beer and have a 70–80% market share in developed countries.

Table 4.2A: Share of hopes production in different countries

Rank	2001		2003		2005		2007		2008	
	Country	Production (MT)	Country	Production (MT)	Country	Production (MT)	Country	Production (MT)	Country	Production (MT)
1	Germany	31742	Germany	25355	Germany	34456	Germany	32100	Germany	39700
2	United States of America	30315	Ethiopia	24920	United States of America	24002	United States of America	27330	United States of America	36573
3	Ethiopia	24000	United States of America	24750	Ethiopia	22780	Ethiopia	25000	Ethiopia	32361
4	China	12500	China	14927	China	9772	China	10000	China	10000
5	Czech Republic	6622	Czech Republic	5527	Czech Republic	7831	Czech Republic	5631	Czech Republic	6753
6	United Kingdom	2500	Poland	3057	Poland	3414	Poland	3392	Poland	3491
7	Poland	2382	Democratic People's Republic of Korea	2300	Slovenia	2501	Slovenia	2157	Slovenia	2400
8	Democratic People's Republic of Korea	2300	United Kingdom People's Republic of Korea	1950	Democratic People's Republic of Korea	2300	Democratic	1900	Democratic People's Republic of Korea	1900
9	Slovenia	2158	Slovenia	1422	United Kingdom	2110	United Kingdom	1500	United Kingdom	1500
10	Australia	2000	France	1395	France	1374	France	1493	France	1469
11	Spain	1399	Spain	1312	Spain	1303	Albania	1000	Albania	1000
12	France	1230	Australia	1086	Australia	1111	Spain	948	Ukraine	910
13	Serbia and Montenegro	878	New Zealand	885	Albania	800	Australia	859	Spain	900
14	New Zealand	830	Albania	700	New Zealand	790	New Zealand	800	Australia	859
15	Japan	692	Japan	700	Japan	700	Japan	715	New Zealand	800

Table 4.2A: Share of hopes production in different countries *(Contd.)*

	2001		*2003*		*2005*		*2007*		*2008*	
Rank	*Country*	*Production (MT)*	*Country*	*Production (MT)*	*Country*	*Production (MT)*	*Country*	*Production (MT)*	*Country*	*Production (MT)*
16	Ukraine	688	Ukraine	547	Ukraine	640	Ukraine	700	Japan	715
17	Russian Federation	600	Russian Federation	520	Belgium	435	Bulgaria	647	Argentina	450
18	Belgium	500	Belgium	451	Slovakia	426	Argentina	450	Austria	384
19	South Africa	350	Serbia and Montenegro	380	Russian Federation	390	Belgium	384	Bulgaria	384
20	Austria	310	South Africa	350	Serbia and Montenegro	386	Romania	374	South Africa	360
* :	Unofficial figure		Unofficial figure		Unofficial figure		Unofficial figure		Unofficial figure	
[ ]:	Official data		Official data		Official data		Official data		Official data	
F :	FAO estimate		FAO estimate		FAO estimate		FAO estimate		FAO estimate	

Table 4.3: Evolution of number of holdings and average acreage per holding in major hops producing countries (2002-2008)

Country	*Indicators*	*2002*	*2003*	*2004*	*2005*	*2006*	*2007*	*2008*	*2000/2008 change (in %)*
Germany	Nb of holdings	1,943	1,710	1,698	1,611	1,554	1,510	1,497	–22.95
	Average acreage/holding	9.5	9.7	10.3	10.7	11.1	11.7	12.5	31.58
Czech Republic	Nb of holdings	185	165.0	162.0	145.0	145.0	139.0	131.0	–29.19
	Average acreage/holding	40	36.0	36.0	39.0	37.0	39.0	41.0	2.50
Poland	Nb of holdings	1191	1129	1121	1144	1113	1066	1061	–10.92
	Average acreage/holding	1.9	1.9	2.0	2.0	2.0	2.0	2.1	10.53
Slovenia	Nb of holdings	189	186.0	176.0	176.0	150.0	140.0	140.0	–25.93
	Average acreage/holding	9.6	8.9	8.8	8.8	10.1	11.0	11.0	14.58
UK	Nb of holdings	85	76.0	60.0	60.0	60.0	60.0	58.0	–31.76
	Average acreage/holding	21.4	19.0	22.6	17.9	17.4	17.7	18.5	–13.55
France	Nb of holdings	111	100.0	96.0	96.0	96.0	90.0	89.0	–19.82
	Average acreage/holding	7.4	8.2	8.2	8.4	8.3	8.8	9.3	25.68
Spain	Nb of holdings	398	400.0	395.0	353.0	325.0	248.0	248.0	–37.69
	Average acreage/holding	1.7	1.7	1.7	1.9	1.9	2.0	2.0	17.65
Belgium	Nb of holdings	52	49	47	45	44	42	29	–44.23
	Average acreage/holding	4.8	4.7	4.4	4.6	4.5	4.4	5.8	20.73
Portugal	Nb of holdings	14	12	12	12	7	4	4	–71.43
	Average acreage/holding	2.6	3.1	3.1	3.3	2.6	5.3	5.0	89.19
Austria	Nb of holdings	72.0	73.0	70.0	70.0	67.0	65.0	63.0	–12.50
	Average acreage/holding	3.1	3.0	3.0	3.0	3.0	3.1	3.3	9.61
USA	Nb of holdings	n.a.	n.a.	52	52	56	62	74	
	Average acreage/holding	n.a.	n.a.	195.0	200.0	200.0	200.0	224.0	

Source: Barth report.

Table 4.4: World beer production 2001-2009

		2001	*2002*	*2003*	*2004*	*2005*	*2006*	*2007*	*2008*	*2009*
Germany	Mio hl	109	108	106	106	105	107	104	101	100
	% of world Production	7.7	7.5	7.0	6.8	6.5	6.3	5.8	5.6	5.5
Rest of Europe	Mio hl	384	389	411	426	439	466	485	495	500
	% of world Production	27.0	27.4	27.4	27.4	27.3	27.3	27.2	27.0	28.0
North America	Mio hl	254	255	263	258	25	255	257	260	270
	% of world Production	17.9	17.6	19.9	16.6	15.8	15.0	14.5	14.5	14.9
South America	Mio hl	221	225	226	226	243	263	273	278	280
	% of world Production	15.6	15.5	15.1	14.6	15.1	15.5	15.4	15.4	15.4
Asia	Mio hl	369	380	415	449	475	514	558	560	562
	% of world Production	26.0	26.2	27.7	28.9	29.5	30.1	31.4	31.1	30.9
Africa	Mio hl	63	64	65	67	73	79	78	82	83
	% of world Production	4.4	4.4	4.3	4.3	4.5	4.6	4.4	4.5	4.6
Australia	Mio hl	21	22	21	21	21	21	22	22	22
	% of world Production	1.5	1.5	1.4	1.4	1.3	1.3	1.2	1.2	1.2
Total	Mio hl	1421	1451	1497	1552	1611	1704	1779	1799	1817
Evolution (100 in 2001)		100.0	102.1	103.2	103.9	104.2	106.5	105.3	101.4	101.3

Source: 2008 Hopsteiner, Guidelines for hops buying.

Table 4.5: Main brewers market shares based on 2007/2008 volumes estimates

	World share
ABI	26
Miller/Coors	17
Heineken	10
Top 3 share	51

Source: Beer Institute.

Additionally, due to changing consumer preference, hopping rates are falling year after year: the figure calculated for 2008 is 4.6 gram of alpha acid per hectoliter, a decline from 5.5 gram alpha acid per hectoliter in 2001. Consumer taste is moving towards less bitter beers requiring lower hops content. This is another factor explaining the decrease in the demand for hops. It is interesting to note that hops accounts for about 0.3% of beer production costs, taxes excluded (Table 4.6).

Table 4.6: Average hopping rate (gram alpha acid/hectoliter)

	2001	*2002*	*2003*	*2004*	*2005*	*2006*	*2007*	*2008*
Hopping rate	5.5	5.3	5.2	5.1	5.0	4.9	4.8	4.6

Source: The Barth report, 2007-2008.

The demand for hops exceeded the available supply in 2005–2007 resulting in a reduction of stocks held by brewers. The shortage was mainly due to bad climatic conditions. As stocks were insufficient to fully meet demand, spot prices (non-contracted) for hops reached extremely high prices—even three times higher than contracted hops (Fig. 4.1). But after the good global hops harvest in 2008, in 2009

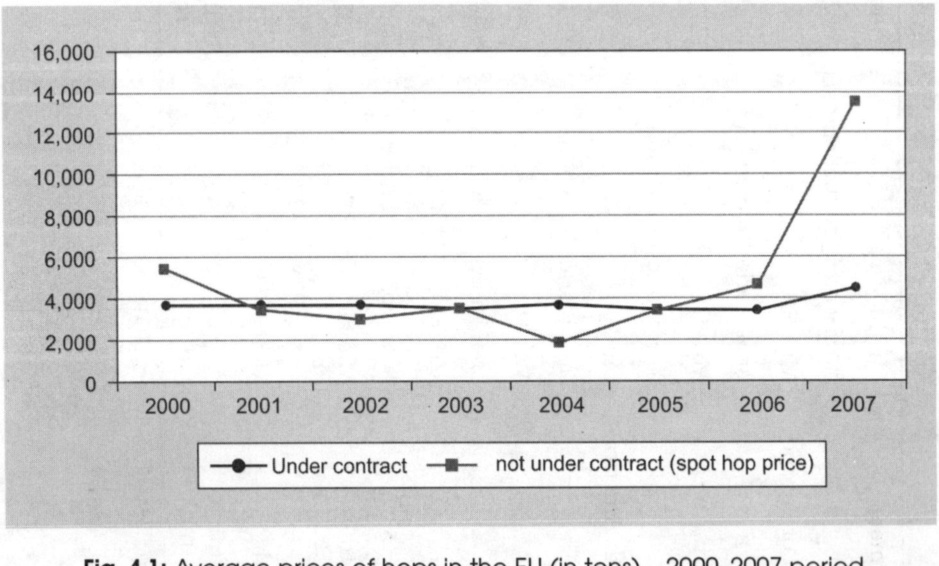

Fig. 4.1: Average prices of hops in the EU (in tons) – 2000–2007 period
Source: DG AGRI.

there is likely to be another surplus of alpha acids. This is evidenced by spot market demand (Fig. 4.2), where compared with years 2007/08 the spot prices of hops from autumn 2008 are much lower than contracted ones. A preliminary estimate for the 2009 brewing year shows that the alpha acid production of 2008 exceeds the needs of the brewing industry by at least 1,500 tons as a result of a very good harvest and a global increase in area. Thus, global stocks are likely to be increased (Table 4.7).

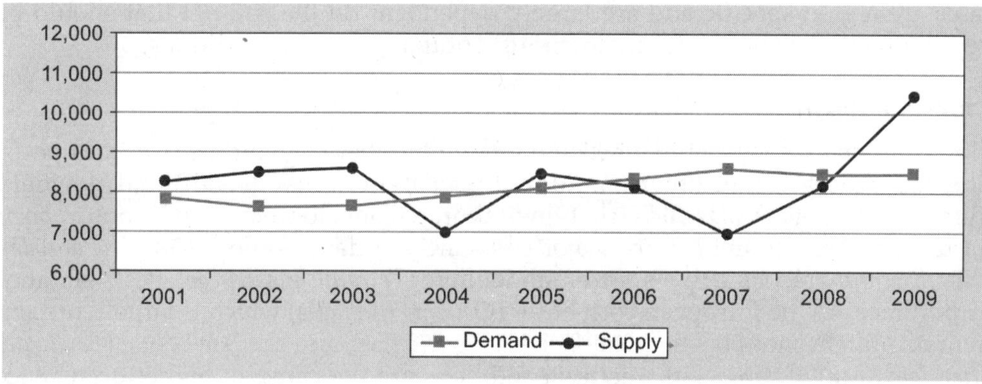

Fig. 4.2: Worldwide demand and supply of alpha acid in the latest brewing years (in tons)
Sources: IHGC, adaptation LEI (supply), the Barth Report (demand).

Table 4.7: Estimation of the evolution of the demand for alpha acids

(1,000 ton)

	2001	*2002*	*2003*	*2004*	*2005*	*2006*	*2007*	*2008*
Europe	2,627	2,621	2,644	2,647	2,640	2,669	2,705	n.a.
America	2,555	2,506	2,458	2,489	2,507	2,426	2,402	n.a.
Asia	1,911	1,913	1,962	2,163	2,223	2,392	2,352	n.a.
Africa	346	363	380	391	401	372	371	n.a.
Oceania	118	115	112	108	109	106	106	n.a.
World	7,557	7,518	7,556	7,799	7,880	7,965	7,936	7,450
Barth report	7,834	7,649	7,664	7,916	8,103	8,313	8,580	8,500

Source: FAO; adoption LEI and the Barth Report 2007-2008.

FERTILIZING

Fertilizing hops improves yield and quality by supplying the crops with adequate nutrient in advance of demand. The yield of hops cones depends on production system and weather conditions, especially in terms of nutrient supply. Mineral nitrogen (N) fertilizing is one of the treatments that can influence yield. Hops require about 180 to 200 Units of N per hectare with applications starting in the spring as most of the N uptake takes place in the early summer (June). A large variation is observed throughout the EU. Taking into account the differences in climatic conditions and production system, in Germany 270 kg N/hectare in more than one split dose is recommended (Rossbauer and Zwack, 1983), in the Czech Republic 65 to 135 kg N/hectare, in the UK 150-225 kg N/hectare and far less in the USA with

160 kg N / hectare (Neve, 1991). In general, calcium-ammonium nitrates (partly slow releaze fertilizer) are used at the beginning of vegetation, when urea that is directly available for the plants is used during the vegetative period.

The hops plant phosphorus (P) requirement is small when compared to the plant's need for N and potassium (K). Phosphorous and potassium rates amount to about 100–150 kg P_2O_5 / hectare and 200 kg K_2O / hectare. Additional nutrients, e.g. calcium (Ca), magnesium (Mg), manganese (Mn) are required in low quantities. Application rates are region specific and are largely dependent on the soil pH that should be kept between 5.0 and 7.0 for maintaining optimal growing conditions.

Crop Protection

Hops gardens are subject to attacks of a large number of plant diseases and pests. The main diseases are downy mildew (*Pseudoperonospora humuli*) and powdery mildew (*Podosphaera macularis*) that find favorable development conditions in hops gardens during summer time. Major pests are the damson-hops aphid (*Phorodon humuli Schrank*) and the two-spotted spider mite (*Tetranychus urticae*). Pests of minor importance are the European corn borer (*Ostrinia nubilalis*) which is largely present in maize, alfafa snout beetle (*Otiorhynchus ligustici* L.), and the flea beetle (*Psylliodes attenuate Koch*). Changes in weather conditions are the cause of higher occurrence of these pests in Central Europe. In some specific areas, some diseases are of key importance, but with a limited spread, e.g. verticilium wilt in the UK.

Crops are protected by systemic fungicides, e.g. azoxystrobin, fosetyl-al, etalaxyl M, and a combination of active substances, e.g. metalaxyl M associated with folpet. Previously, copper fungicides were used in preventive spraying. organophosphates, carbamates, and pyretroids are the most popular insecticides in use. Since 1993, some resistance to imidachloprid has appeared. New, efficient insecticides, with improved environmental profiles, are now available for farmers, e.g. flonicamid (novel systemic insecticide with selective activity against as aphids and whitefly), and spirotetramat (efficient against a broad spectrum of sucking insects). The two-spotted spider mite is commonly controlled using several miticides, although their use is quite limited (e.g. restriction of fenpyroximate in Germany in 2008). New miticides are undergoing the registration process (acequinocyle, bifenazate, etoxazole).These new active substances are leading to the registration of plant protection products that are more environmentally-friendly and better for the growers. In terms of weed management, few herbicides are available for hops, and weed control is largely carried out through cultivation. Integrated Pest Management (IPM) is also under development in hops gardens. As examples, releases of ladybird Harmonia axyridis succeeded in controlling damson hops aphid in Alsace several years ago and new techniques are under development; quessia extracts have been rediscovered to protect hops plants against pests. These solutions should be considered as alternatives to chemicals, but they cannot be used alone.

Breeding efforts are devoted to developing new cultivars with improved resistance against diseases, e.g. Verticilium wilt. Moreover, a precise typing of hops pathogens is necessary to select the right and appropriate control strategy for use within an IPM approach. Finally, it should be noted that in the USA, the hops industry has received a Pesticide Environmental Stewardship Program (PESP) grant from the Environmental Protection Agency (EPA) and is in the process of collecting information for the purposes of building an industry-wide IPM program.

Hop Cultivation in the Yakima Valley

One of the first, Charles Carpenter, is said to have begun hop farming in the Yakima Valley in 1872. Carpenter's father, a settler in Constable, New York, supplied the cuttings. In 1876 Yakima sent 80 bales of hops West. At the beginning of 1890, hop farming spread in a southeasterly direction. Yakima County had become the most important hop producer in Washington State. As in all US Hop regions, the period between 1920 and 1940, marked by Prohibition and Depression and a consequent overproduction, threatened the very existence of the planters in Washington State. Even so, the farmers of the Yakima Valley were able to produce hops at a lower cost than anywhere else in the world. Thanks to their open-mindedness they had converted to seedless hops at an early stage and had improved the quality of hop picking. By doing this they established the basis for the good reputation of "Yakima Hops". These hops were exported throughout the world, particularly in the years 1939–1950.

The Yakima region has one further notable advantage: it is the only region in the world in which a farmer can plant cuttings in the spring and expect a full harvest in autumn. Because of this the farmers in the region can react more quickly to changes in the marketplace.

Yakima Valley Hop Region Today

The Yakima Valley contains approximately 75% of the total United States hop acreage, with an average farm size of 450 acres (182 hectares) accounting for over 77% of the total United States hop crop. Many hop farms in Washington are third or fourth generation family operations. Most growers also grow fruit, but some grow mint, grapes and even row crops. Typically, a Washington hop grower will raise a combination of both aroma and alpha variety hops. The majority of the hops produced in Washington however is alpha and super alpha varieties. Important Washington aroma varieties include Willamette, Cascade and Mt. Hood. Alpha varieties include Columbus/Tomahawk, Zeus, Nugget and Galena, which when combined account for over half of the total Washington hop acreage.

In the State of Washington, hops are only grown commercially in the Yakima Valley. However, within this valley there are three distinct growing areas, the Moxee Valley, the Yakama Indian Reservation, and the Lower Yakima Valley. Each of these areas, while no more than 50 miles (80 kilometers) apart, possess unique growing conditions. The Lower Yakima Valley, with its slightly warmer climate, can produce outstanding yields during first year (baby) hop plantings. Many other crops grow in the lower Yakima Valley enabling growers to easily diversify. The Yakama Indian Reservation, located in the center of the Yakima Valley, is most noted for its vast open spaces and its ability to produce superior alpha levels.

The Yakima Valley of Washington State is one of the most important hop growing regions in the world. Approximately two-thirds of the hops produced in the Yakima Valley are exported to countries all over the globe. Sophisticated, environmentally friendly, irrigation techniques, combined with ideal growing conditions enable the Yakima Valley to consistently produce the finest hops in the world.

Trade

The import figures in Africa are very variable. The net exports in Table 4.8 show in most years a general trend in hops movements from Europe and Oceania to Asia and America. Of course net exports worldwide should add up to zero, but unfortunately the FAO statistics are not quite consistent and a statistical correction has been made.

The FAO provides import and export data of hops worldwide until 2006. The total trade between countries is about 40,000 tons, or about 40% of annual production. Europe exports far more hops than it imports with a share of about 80% of world exports (Tables 4.9 and 4.10), although this figure does include intra-EU trade. The second largest exporter is America, while exports from Asia, Africa and Oceania are of minor importance.

Table 4.8: Export of hops (in tons)

	2001	*2002*	*2003*	*2004*	*2005*	*2006*
Europe	27,821	27,723	27,298	27,156	29,268	28,715
America	6,712	5,143	6,551	6,895	5,784	6,071
Asia	1,170	1,258	1,070	200	500	738
Africa	189	721	1,025	771	205	297
Oceania	1,820	1,538	935	789	923	486
World	**37,712**	**36,383**	**36,879**	**35,811**	**36,680**	**36,307**

Source: FAO.

Table 4.9: Import of hops (in tons)

	2001	*2002*	*2003*	*2004*	*2005*	*2006*
Europe	20,638	30,929	21,527	20,657	20,920	20,083
America	8,704	7,236	8,837	7,333	7,092	8,446
Asia	8,096	8,565	6,685	6,257	8,217	9,167
Africa	910	792	1,640	805	4,053	2,363
Oceania	53	92	209	64	107	150
World	**38,401**	**47,614**	**38,898**	**35,116**	**40,389**	**40,209**

Source: FAO.

Table 4.10: Net export of hops (in tons)

	2001	*2002*	*2003*	*2004*	*2005*	*2006*
Europe	7,183	–3,206	5,771	6,499	8,348	8,632
America	–1,992	–2,093	–2,286	–438	–1,308	–2,375
Asia	–6,926	–7,307	–5,615	–6,057	–7,717	–8,429
Africa	–721	–71	–615	–34	–3,848	–2,066
Oceania	1,767	1446	726	725	816	336
Statistical correction	689	11,231	2,019	–695	3,709	3,902
World	**0**	**0**	**0**	**0**	**0**	**0**

Source: FAO.

Stocks

It is very difficult to obtain robust data on present stocks as this is considered commercially sensitive by brewers because stocks contribute to spot price formation and as a result are not normally disclosed. We therefore present an estimation of the changes in stock following the demand/supply trend.

Table 4.11 shows the stock changes of alpha acid over the last 9 years. Demand figures are based on the Barth Report while supply figures are based on IHGC data under the assumption that the harvest of the former year is available for the current brewing year. The supply is not easy to calculate for several reasons. First, the alpha acid content in hops is not stable; during storage it is vulnerable to oxidation, despite measures such as refrigerated and frozen storage. Approximately 10% of the alpha content disappears during storage, but this percentage is only a best guess. Another uncertainty is the amount of hops used for other purposes. The Barth Report mentions that around 200 tons of alpha acid is not used for brewing annually. This amount is not included in the Table 4.11. A third aspect worth mentioning is a fire in an American warehouse in 2006, which destroyed about 200 tons of alpha acid. This is also excluded. For these reasons, the estimations of stock changes are probably optimistic.

Table 4.11: Estimation of the world demand and supply of alpha acid

(In tons)

Brewing year	2001	2002	2003	2004	2005	2006	2007	2008	2009
Crop year	2000	2001	2002	2003	2004	2005	2006	2007	2008
Demand	7,834	7,649	7,664	7,916	8,103	8,313	8,580	8,469	8,500
Supply	8,250	8,489	8,596	7,023	8,452	8,158	6,956	8,161	10,468
Stock changes	416	840	932	–893	349	–	–	–	1,968

Sources: IHGC, adaptation LEI (supply), the Barth Report (demand).

Stocks increased significantly in the years 2001, 2002 and 2003, but then fell rapidly between 2004 and 2008. Because of the extremely high production in 2008 a substantial increase in stocks is expected for 2009. Figure 4.2 presents supply and demand graphically.

THE MAIN EU HOPS PRODUCTION SYSTEMS

A peculiar aspect of hops growing is the necessity to offer the plant the possibility to vine. For this purpose, a trellis system is built. A hops planting follows the rows with a planting distance of about 1.5 meters, depending on farmers' equipment, and a density about 2,600 plants/hectare. Pruning is an annual spring cultural practice which holds back the vigorous new growth until the proper training date for the variety. This cultural practice also removes early hops shoots that may be infected with overwintering diseases and limits the use of fungicide during the growing season. In May, the three most developed sprouts from each hops stump are wound around the leading wire; the other sprouts are cut off. Harvest takes place from the end of August through September. The hops vines are cut at the bottom and the top, together with the leading wires. The vines are brought to the farm to reap, clean, dry and store the hops cones. The cones are dried soon after the harvest to prevent loss of valuable components.

The European Union Hop Sector

The European Union is the main player in the world hops market. Total production was about 57,000 tons in 2008, a share of over 50% of world hops production. The largest producer within the EU is Germany. The area sown to hops is decreasing steadily in the EU, with a reduction of 16% since 2001. About one-third of the area is grown with bitter varieties. This percentage has been constant throughout the last 8 years (Table 4.12).

Table 4.12: Development of surface of hops in European Union (EU-7)

		2001	2002	2003	2004	2005	2006	2007	2008
Acreage (aroma varieties)	Ha	21,554	20,817	19,462	20,172	19,711	19,603	19,579	19,756
Acreage (bitter varieties)	Ha	11,015	11,215	11,075	11,027	10,208	9,525	9,317	9,949
Total acreage	Ha	32,569	32,032	30,537	31,199	29,919	29,128	28,896	29,705

Source: IHGC.

The increase in new hops area decreased year on year over the 2001–2005 period before establishing in 2006. The trend was upward in 2007 and 2008. Preliminary data published by IHGC in August 2009 indicate that fewer new hectares have been planted in 2009 in Germany (706 hectares in 2009 compared to 1,135 hectares in 2008) (Table 4.13).

Table 4.13: Evolution of new hops hectares in the European Union (EU-27)

		2001	2002	2003	2004	2005	2006	2007	2008
Acreage (new)	Ha	1,845	1,455	1,241	1,113	550	724	1,271	1,594

Yield, and in particular alpha acid content, shows a large increase over the 2001–2008 period. The average yield was 1,630 kg hops per hectare with an alpha acid content of 7.8% during these years. The average alpha acid yield was 127 kg/hectare. However, only 87 kg of alpha acid per hectare was harvested in 2003 as a result of very low alpha acid contents. In contrast, 2008 was a very good year with an average yield of 173 kg of alpha acid per hectare. This trend is the consequence of an increase in yield from bitter varieties (Table 4.14) and the planting of new bitter varieties with higher alpha acid content.

Hops are produced by fourteen EU Member States although together Germany and the Czech Republic account for over 80% of total EU production by volume. Poland is the only other Member States to account for more than 5% of total EU production (3,256 tons in 2008). Traditional hops production areas can be found within each producing Member State including Bavaria, Saxony and Bitburg in Germany, Bohemia in Czech Republic, Lublin in Eastern Poland, Kent in the United Kingdom, León in Spain and Alsace in France (Table 4.15).

Table 4.14: Evolution of hops yield and alpha-acid content in the European Union (EU-27)

		2001	2002	2003	2004	2005	2006	2007	2008
Yield (aroma varieties)	Kg/ha	1,373	1,46	1,14	1,466	1,68	1,341	1,545	1,74
Yield (bitter varieties)	Kg/ha	1,852	1,784	1,734	2,011	2,106	1,786	1,934	2,291
Yield (all varieties)	Kg/ha	1,453	1,505	1,617	1,604	1,792	1,485	1,67	1,924
Yield of alpha acid	Kg/ha	109	120	87	136	148	107	132	173
Alpha acid content	%	7.5	8.0	5.4	8.5	8.2	7.2	7.9	9.0

Source: IHGC.

Most of hops acreage is sold by forward contracts by the merchants (95% in Germany1 in 2009). The remainder is sold on the spot market. The forward contract rates in the EU-27 for the coming four years are well below 50% with the exception of Poland and Slovenia. Prices are significantly different for these two markets with the forward contract price quite stable over time and the spot price more volatile and generally higher.

The hops processing and transformation industries act at the international level. The hops supply chain is characterized by a small number of large merchants that own the majority of the world's pelletizing and extract machines. There has been significant consolidation in the industry over the past four decades with many hops trading companies going out of business; in the 1960s there were more than 90 companies in Germany alone. The four largest merchants today are German or American conglomerates (John Barth and Sohn, SS Steiner, Hops Union, and Lupotresh). There are two other international hops merchants, Magma from the Czech Republic and Morris Harbury Jackson and E May from United Kingdom. Other operators exist, but they do not sell significant volumes of hops. The transnational merchants currently hold about 90% of forward contracts with breweries. However, opportunities exist for niche markets to be exploited.

Table 4.15: Trend in area and production volumes in EU hops producing MS (2001–2008)

	2001				*2008*				*2001–2008 change*		
	Acreage	*Production*	*Alpha acid content*		*Acreage*	*Production*	*Alpha acid content*		*Acreage*	*Production*	*Alpha acid volumes*
	in hectare	*in tons*	*in %*	*in tons*	*in hectare*	*in tons*	*in %*	*in tons*	*in %*	*in %*	*in %*
Austria	220	337	6.10	23	210	382	8.00	31	–4.55	13.35	34.78
Belgium	250	416	9.30	39	186	325	8.30	27	–25.60	–21.88	–30.77
Bulgaria	380	295	9.60	31	221	342	9.50	33	–41.84	15.93	6.45
Czech Republic	6,075	6,621	4.00	213	5,125	6,700	4.20	300	–15.64	1.19	40.85
France	816	1,212	2.70	30	773	1,469	2.50	39	–5.27	21.20	30.00
Germany	19,021	31,739	8.40	2,726	17,510	39,510	10.00	4,100	–7.94	24.48	50.40
Hungary	34	34	5.00	2	23	35	9.40	3	–32.35	2.06	50.00
Poland	2,250	2,200	5.50	122	2,141	3,256	7.40	256	–4.84	48.00	109.84
Portugal	38	52	10.20	5	37	57	10.60	6	–2.63	9.62	20.00
Romania	100	50	5.00	3	278	246	6.90	17	178.00	392.00	466.67
Slovakia	350	300	3.40	10	261	328	3.90	13	–25.43	9.33	30.00
Slovenia	1,657	2,149	7.20	129	1,652	2,430	7.00	138	–0.30	13.08	6.98
Spain	730	1,668	11.90	167	465	810	12.60	109	–36.30	–51.44	–34.73
UK	1,997	2,518	9.10	209	1,100	1,350	6.60	89	–44.92	–46.39	–57.42
Total EU	33,918	49,591		3,709	29,982	57,240		5,161	–13	15.42	39.15

Source: IHGC annual reports

5

Lac

INTRODUCTION

Lac is a resinous exudation from the body of female scale insect. Since Vedic period, it has been in use in India. Its earliest reference is found in Atherva Veda. The insect is termed as "Laksha", and its habit and behavior are described. The great Indian epic "Mahabharata" also mentions a "Laksha Griha", an inflammable house of lac, cunningly constructed by "Kauravas" through their architect "Purocha" for the purpose of burning their great enemy "Pandavas" alive. The English word lac synonyms Lakh in Hindi which itself is derivative of Sanskrit word Laksh meaning a lakh or hundred thousand. It would appear that Vedic people knew that the lac is obtained from numerous insects and must also know the biological and commercial aspects of lac industry. It is also worth to mention that a laksh griha would need a lot of lac which could only come from a flourishing lac industry in that period. Since ancient times, Greeks and Romans were familiar with the use of lac. The cultivation of lac insects has a long history in Asia, with some suggestion that it is as old as 4,000 years in China where its cultivation accompanied the development of the silk industry. Lac is Nature's gift to mankind and the only known commercial resin of animal origin. It is the hardened resin secreted by tiny lac insects belonging to a bug family. To produce 1 kg of lac resin, around 300,000 insects lose their life. The lac insects yields resin, lac dye and lac wax. Application of these products has been changing with time. Lac resin, dye, etc still find extensive use in Ayurveda and Siddha systems of medicine.

Lac is the name given to the resinous secretion of the tiny lac insect *(Laccifer lacca)* which is parasitic on certain trees in Asia, particularly India and Thailand. This insect secretion is cultivated and refined because of the commercial value of the finished product known as shellac. The term shellac is derived from shell-lac (the word for the refined lac in flake form), but has come to refer to all refined lac whether in dry or suspended in an alcohol-based solvent.

Lac has been cultivated for three centuries. For most of that time, the lac bug secretions were valued for the purple-red dye derived from being soaked in water. This dye was used to color silk, leather, and cosmetics and was cultivated primarily for this purpose until the 1870s. Then, aniline or chemical dyes began to supplant these and other natural dyes.

As early as the 16th century, references were made to the usefulness of the lac bug secretions as a decorative lacquer for furniture and fine musical instruments. Natives of the Far East had laboriously cultivated and processed the shellac by hand, scraping the branches encrusted with the lac bug secretions, forcing the secretions into muslin, and holding long muslin bags of the secretions over the fire to liquefy and purify it. They pulled it by hand into huge sheets and then broke the sheets into flakes for re-moisturizing later.

Hand processes were partially replaced by the mid-19th century. Just as the lac derived dye was about to fade in popularity, industrial plants began processing the lac secretions for use as a wood sealer and finish. In 1849, William Zinsser founded Wm. Zinsser and Company in New York. Zinsser's shellacs were soluble in ethyl alcohol and were the first quick-drying, tough, colorless finishes available in the United States. Shellac was particularly popular late in the nineteenth century and in the early 20th century when houses were being quickly built in early subdivisions at break-neck speed—shellac was an ideal wood finisher because it was so fast to dry and several coats could be applied in a single day. A shellac known as buttonlac, a very dark shellac, imparted a very deep walnut color to inexpensive woodwork that people then found very desirable.

Shellac is primarily used as a wood sealer and finisher today. It has the great advantage of being soluble in ethyl or denatured alcohol, an environmentally-safe solvent. Alcohol solvents also render shellac a quick dry—shellac coatings on wood generally dry in about 45 minutes, as opposed to oil finishes which take many hours to dry. In addition, shellac does not fade in sunlight or oxidize over time. However, shellac has a limited shelf-life and may not dry properly if it has exceeded the shelf-life recommended by the manufacturer. This shelf life may be as short as 6 months or as long as 3 years depending on the manufacturer's additives.

Industrial uses for shellac include floor polishes, inks, grinding wheels, electrical insulations, and leather dressings. This natural, resinous sealer is nontoxic and is Food and Drug Administration (FDA) approved for use to coat candies, pharmaceuticals, fruit, and baby and children's furniture.

With increasing universal environment awareness, the importance of lac has assumed special relevance in the present age, being an eco-friendly, biodegradable and self-sustaining natural material. Since lac insects are cultured on host trees which are growing primarily in wasteland areas, promotion of lac and its culture can help in ecosystem development as well as reasonably high economic returns. It is a source of livelihood of tribal and poor inhabiting forest and subforest areas.

LAC INSECT TAXONOMY

The first scientific account of the lac insect was given by J Kerr in 1782 which was published in Philosophical Transaction of Royal Society of London. The first scientific name given to it was *Tachardia lacca* following the name of French Missionary Father "Tachardia". It was later changed to *Laccifer lacca Kerr*. The other name given to it has been Kerria Lac Kerr.

Phylum – *Arthropoda*, Class – *Insecta*, Order – *Hemiptera*, Suborder – *Homoptera*, Super family – *Coccoidea*, Family – *Lacciferidae*, Genus – *Laccifer*, and Species – *lacca*.

Lac insect belongs to super-family *Coccoidea* which includes all scale insects. Scale insect is a common name for about 2,000 insect species found all over the world. Scale insects range from almost microscopic size to more than 2.5 cm. These insects attach themselves in great numbers to plants. The mouth part of these insects is piercing and sucking type. They can be very destructive to tree-stunting or killing twigs and branches by draining the sap.

There are six genera of lac insects, out of which only five secrete lac, and only one, i.e. Laccifer secretes recoverable or commercial lac. The most common and most widely occurring species of lac insect in India is *Laccifer lacca* (Kerr) which produces the bulk of commercial lac. Lac insect of South-East Asia is referred to as *Kerria chinensis*.

DISTRIBUTION

Since the lac insects thrive and feed on certain species of the tropical trees, it is found distributed in South-East Asian countries. Lac is currently produced in India, Myanmar, Thailand, Malaya, Lao and Yuan province of China. India and Thailand are main areas in the world while India has prime position in relation to lac production. Lac cultivation is introduced into Thailand from India. Over 90% of Indian lac produced comes from the states of Bihar, Jharkhand, West Bengal, Madhya Pradesh, Chattisgarh, Eastern Maharashtra and Northern Orissa. Some pockets of lac cultivation also exist in Andhra Pradesh, Punjab, Rajasthan, Mysore, Gujarat, and Mirzapur and Sonebhdra districts of Uttar Pradesh.

LIFE CYCLE

Lac insect is a minute crawling scale insect which inserts its suctorial proboscis into plant tissue, sucks juices, grows and secretes resinous lac from the body. Its own body ultimately gets covered with lac in the so called "CELL". Lac is secreted by insects for protection from predators. Male is red in color and measures 1.2–1.5 mm in length. It has reduced eyes and antennae. Thorax bears a pair of hyaline wings. Female is larger than male, measures 4–5 mm in length and has a pyriform body. The head, thorax and abdomen are not clearly distinct. The antennae and legs are in degenerated form, and wings are absent. The life cycle of lac insect takes about 6 months and consists of stages: egg, nymph instars, pupa and adult. The lac insects have an ovoviviparous mode of reproduction. Female lays 200–500 ready to hatch eggs, i.e. the embryos are already fully developed in eggs when these are laid. Eggs hatch within a few hours of laying and a crimson-red first instar nymph called crawlers come out. The crawler measures 0.6 × .25 mm in size. The emergence of nymph is called swarming, and it may continue for 5 weeks. The nymphs crawl about on branches. On reaching soft succulent twigs, the nymphs settle down close together at rate of 200–300 insects per square inch. At this stage, both male and female nymphs live on the sap of the trees. They insert their suctorial proboscis into plant tissue and suck the sap. After a day or so of settling, the nymphs start secreting resin from the glands distributed under the cuticle throughout the body, except mouth parts, breathing spiracles and anus. The resin secreted is semi-solid which hardens on exposure to air into a protective covering. The nymphs molt thrice inside the cells before reaching maturity. The duration of each instar is dependent on several factors, viz. temperature, humidity and host plant. After the first moult, both male and female nymphs lose their appendages, eye and become degenerate. While still inside their cells, the nymphs cast off their second and third moult and mature into adult. Both the male and female larvae become sexually mature in about 8 weeks.

Only the male one undergoes a complete metamorphosis or transformation into another form; it loses its proboscis and develops antennae, legs and a single pair of wings. It is contained in a brood cell somewhat slipper like with a round trap door (operculum) through which it emerges. The adult male is winged and walks over the females to fertilize them. The female brood cell is larger and globular in shape and remains fixed to the twig. The female retains her mouth parts but fails to develop any wings, eyes or appendages. While developing, it really becomes an immobile organism with little resemblance to an insect. Females become little more than egg producing organisms.

The female increases in size to accommodate her growing number of eggs. Lac resin is secreted at a faster rate, and a continuous layer coalesces or grows into one body. After fourteen weeks, the female shrinks in size allowing light to pass into the cell and the space for the eggs. About this time, two yellow spots appear at the rear end of the cell. The spots enlarge and become orange colored. When this happens, the female has oviposit a large number of eggs in the space called "Ovisac". The ovisac appears orange due to crimson fluid called lac dye which resembles cochineal. It indicates that the eggs will hatch in a week time. When the eggs hatch, larvae emerge and the whole process begins all over again. After the cycle has been completed and around the time when the next generation begin to emerge, the resin encrusted branches are harvested. They are scraped off, dried and processed for various lac products. A portion of brood lac is retained from the previous crop for the purpose of inoculation to new trees.

HOST PLANTS

Lac insects thrive on twigs of certain plant species, suck the plant sap, and grow all the while secreting lac resin from their bodies. These plants are called host plants. Although lac insect is natural pest on host plant, these insects enjoy the privileged position not being treated as pest. This is because: (i) they yield a useful product, (ii) the host plants are economically not so important and (iii) the insects cause only temporary and recoverable damage to the host plants. About 113 varieties of host plants are mentioned as lac host plant. Out of which the followings are very common in India:

1. *Butea monosperma* (Vern. Palas)
2. *Zizyphus spp* (vern. Ber)
3. *Schleichera oleosa* (Vern. Kusum)
4. *Acacia catechu* (Vern. Khair)
5. *Acacia arabica* (Vern. Babul)
6. *Acacia auriculiformis* (Vern. Akashmani)
7. *Zizyphus xylopyrus* (Vern. Khatber-grown in part of MP and UP)
8. *Shorea talura* (Vern. Sal grown in mysore)
9. *Cajanus cajan* (Vern. Pigeon-pea or Arhar)
10. *Grewia teliaefolia* (Vern. Dhaman preferred in Assam)
11. *Albizzia lebbek* (Vern. Siris/Gulwang)
12. *Flemingia macrophylla* (Vern. Bholia)
13. *Ficus benghalensis* (Vern. Bargad)
14. *Ficus religiosa* (Vern. Peepal).

Of these host plants, palas, kusum, ber and khair are of major importance, while others are of regional and minor importance. It is also important to mention that the quality of lac is directly related to the host plant and to the strain of lac insects. Based on industrial parameters, kusumi lac is better and fetches higher price in market. In this respect, ber tree as a potential kusumi lac host is already getting momentum. This host species is available in plenty and can supplement and fulfill the kusmi brood lac requirement in many areas. Similarly, siris (*Albizzia* sp.) has also been identified as good host for kusumi brood lac. The trees can be raised and utilized within a period of 5–6 years of plantation in comparison to around 15 years for kusum. Flemingia semialata is a bushy host plant and has also been identified as well as established as a good kusumi lac host on plantation basis. Thus, these three hosts viz., ber, siris, semialata and lately *Prosopis juliflora* (in Gujarat areas) are expected to enhance kusumi lac cultivation. Adoption of this activity may enhance lac production to the tune of 3–4%.

STRAINS OF LAC INSECT

In India, lac insect is known to have two distinct strains: kusumi and rangeeni. The kusumi strain is grown on kusum or on other host plants using kusumi brood. The rageeni strain thrives on host plants other than kusum. The life cycle of lac insects take about 6 months, hence, two crops a year can be obtained. In case of kusumi strain, two crops are: (i) Jethwi (June/July) and (ii) Aghani (Jan/Feb). In case of rangeeni, tow crops are: (i). Karrtiki (Oct/Nov) and (ii) Baisakhi (May/June). The crops have been named after Hindi months during which these are harvested. The lac of rangeeni crops is harvested while it is still immature. Aghani and baisakhi of rangeeni strain are the main corps contributing about 90% of lac production, remaining 10% is contributed by kusumi crops.

However, the kusumi crop lac is considered superior resin, because of the lighter color of resin, and it fetches better price.

RAW MATERIALS

Shellac is generally made from two ingredients: (1) raw seed lac and (2) ethyl alcohol. In fact, most companies want to purify shellac as completely as possible—impurities from the bug, the cocoon, etc are removed, as are natural waxes. Shellac is generally shipped in dry or flaked form and is re-moisturized with an alcohol solvent, generally denatured alcohol. Some companies add ingredients to lengthen the shelf life of their product but will not reveal these proprietary additives. Shellac that is bleached (or made into clear shellac) are dissolved in sodium carbonate and centrifuge to remove insolubles and then bleached with sodium hypochlorite.

LAC CULTIVATION

Lac cultivation is done by putting brood lac on suitably prepared specific host plants. The brood lac contains gravid females which are about to lay eggs to give birth to young larvae. After emergence from mother cells, the young larvae settle on fresh twigs of host plants, suck the plant sap and grow to form encrustations.

RESEARCH

Thanks to the groundbreaking research by the Indian Institute of Natural Resins and Gums (IINRG) in Ranchi, Jharkhand, many tribal farmers like Horo have returned to lac. The scientists have found a way to produce lac on smaller plants. "We were worried about the back-breaking labor required for cultivation. Production was also dipping because host trees took nearly 15 years to grow", says KK Sharma, head of lac production division at IINRG. In 2010–2011, lac production in Jharkhand, one of the major producers, dwindled by 42% compared to last year. Lac is used in ammunition, airplanes, furniture polish and perfumes, and in making bangles, imitation fruits and flowers.

EXPORT OF LAC

Year	*Production (tons)*	*Income (Rs lakh)*
2007–08	7,906	12,426
2008–09	6,968	12,414
2009–10	6,422	11,002

The scientists' motive was to give lac farmers a host plant that grows faster and reduces tree-based farming. Ninety percent of lac is produced on palash, ber and kusum trees. "We started experimenting on the semialata plant and laboratory tests gave positive results", says Sharma. A native plant of Jharkhand, semialata grows up to one and a half meters in 6 months. Farmers tie a host shoot of lac insects around the main stem of semialata plant. The lac insects start breeding on their own and require little attention.

IINRG scientists have added a few modern farming techniques that ensure better production on semialata plants (*see* "Using semialata for lac production"). In the traditional method, farmers use half of the palash, ber or kusum tree as host. "Using the entire tree would weaken it", says Sharma. As per estimates by IINRG, a farmer using semialata plant can earn a profit of Rs 25,000 per hectare in the first year, which increases to Rs 187,000 from second year (*see* "Profit after cultivation"). Using the traditional method, farmers earned a profit of Rs 15,000–20,000 per hectare.

In February 2012, Horo cultivated semialata plant on his 0.3 hectare. A year later, his land produced 100 kg of kusumi lac, a variety that fetches the highest price in the market (Rs 800 per kg). Horo earned a profit of Rs 60,000.

USING SEMIALATA FOR LAC PRODUCTION

To further boost lac production in Jharkhand, IINRG has collaborated with Indian Council of Agricultural Research, Ranchi. It is experimenting with planting semialata plant between mango trees. Semialata plant root goes barely 0.3 meter deep into the soil.

1. Local Practice

Lac cultivation is simple, does not need any large investment and requires only part-time attention. In India, lac cultivation is carried out casually, and the cultivator

Initial farming expense

Activities	*Quantity*	*Expenditure (Rs)*
Fencing of land	1 hectare	50,000
Fertilizer and manure	246 kg urea, 328 kg SSP, 164 kg MOP, 50 tons farmyard manure	55,000
Seedling and plantation raising	200 man-days (Rs 100 and) 500 g seeds (Rs 2,000/kg)	21,000
Farm implements	25 secateurs, 10 tree pruners, one foot sprayer, buckets and baskets	15,000
Miscellaneous expenditure	–	4,000
Total	–	**1,45,000**
Income from vegetables during plantation establishment	–	20,000
Grand total	–	**1,25,000**

Profit after cultivation

Items required	*Quantity*	*Amount (Rs)*
Expenditure		
Broodlac (20 g)	164 kg (Rs 120/kg)	19,680
Nylon *sutli* and pesticides	5 kg sutli, 3 liters endosulfan, 3 liters dichlorvos, 4 liters ethofenprox, 6 kg carbendazim	5,500
Labor	300 mandays (Rs 100)	30,000
Refund of principal and interest (10% per annum) in five installments	–	27,500
Total		**82,680**
Income		
Broodlac	820–246 = 574 kg	68,880
Sticklac including *phunk*)	150 kg	15,000
Fuel wood (stick)	4,000 kg	4,000
Income from growing vegetables	–	20,000
Gross income	–	1,07,880
Less expenditure	–	82,680
Net profit	–	25,200

is satisfied with what he gets, as it is being regarded as subsidiary crop. The local practices in lac cultivation has some disadvantages like:

i. The same host plants are continuously exploited without giving rest for recoupment.
ii. Only natural inoculation occurs.
iii. Partial harvest is done leaving few branches untouched for auto inoculation of next crop and no pruning is done.

As a result of the defective local practices, host trees loss the vigour and unable to throw out new succulent shoots, and in course of time, the trees become weak and die. The self inoculation leads to heterogeneous infestation of nymphs, which results in wholesome mortality of brood in seasons of extreme heat, and thereby, the cultivator is forced to abandon lac cultivation.

2. Improved Practice

Sustained production of lac and steady returns can be achieved by adopting improved method of cultivation. The underlying principle in improved method of lac cultivation is to provide much needed rest to the host plants after a harvest has been taken. For this purpose, coupe system of lac cultivation is adopted. As the term coupe means a chamber, the host plant trees are divided into coupes, i.e. groups that consist of certain number of trees. In practice, only few numbers of trees in a coupe are inoculated. Following harvest, these trees are made to rest and recoup the lost vigour while other trees (which have till now been restring) are ready with succulent twigs for inoculation. Thus, in a coupe system, alternate groups of trees are put to lac cultivation. Full inoculation and full cropping is the rule under this system. In addition, the following considerations are desirable in improved lac cultivation.

The mean lac productivity (per tree and per unit area) of 2, 5 and 15 kg per tree or 3, 4 and 5 q/hectare for palas, ber and kusum respectively in traditional lac culture is very low. This is all due to poor sustainability, continuous exploitation and increased threat from pests. So, the technology of improved scientific method of lac cultivation should be adopted, that includes superior breeds of lac insect, providing proper rest to host plants, use of good quality brood lac in appropriate quantity, post harvest management of lac crop, host plant management and lac pest management.

- As the lac cultivation is mainly practiced by the forest and forest fringe dwellers, their involvement in the Joint Forest Management (JFM) programs in different lac growing states is likely to enhance the lac production. Lac host trees under the custody of state forest department are out of reach of the forest dwellers and interested lac growers and are not being utilized for lac cultivation. If these are jointly managed by forest department and forest dwellers and they work in close association, it will be a boon for lac cultivation and production.
- Timely availability of pest free and quality brood lac is the most important input for lac cultivation. Quality brood lac ensures high fecundity of insects and fewer requirements of inoculums. Timely harvesting of mature crop and proper inoculation will reduce the risk of loss of lac insect to a large extent.

PROPAGATION OF LAC INSECTS

Propagation means the spread of lac insects on the same or different host plants. This is done by inoculation of newly hatched (Brood) nymphs. Inoculation is of two types:

i. *Natural self/auto inoculation*: This type of inoculation occurs naturally. It is very simple and common process, when the swarmed nymphs infect the same host plant again. Natural inoculation, being repeated on the same host, makes in host plant weak, and thereby, nymphs do not get proper nutrition. Also in natural inoculation, it is not sure that uniform sequence of inoculation take place. Therefore, natural inoculation should be discouraged.

ii. *Artificial inoculation*: Artificial inoculation is brought about by the agency of man. The main idea behind the artificial inoculation is to check the drawbacks of natural inoculation. In this method, the host plants are first of all pruned in Jan. or June. Pruning means cutting away old, weak and diseased twigs. It induces host plants to throw out new succulent twigs and is as important in lac culture as ploughing is for seed sowing in agriculture. Pruning should be done with a sharp instrument (scateur, pruning shaw and pruning knife) to give a sharp and neat cut. Only light pruning should be carried out. In artificial inoculation, brood twigs are cut in size 20–30 cm in length. Then, the cut pieces of brood twig are tied to fresh tree twigs in such a way that each stick touches the tender branches of trees at several places. The nymphs swarm from brood and migrate to tender and succulent twigs and infest them. Following swarming, the brood twigs should be removed from the host plant, as this would decrease the chance of pest infestation.

Following precautions are desirable is artificial inoculation:

1. Fully mature and healthy brood free from pest infestations should be taken.
2. Brood meant for inoculation should not be kept for long and used immediately after crop cutting.
3. Tying of the brood lac stick should be done securely on the upper surface of branches. This will prevent falling of twigs and provide full contact for quick and easy crawling of the nymphs. One should keep a watch on the brood lac dropping down.
4. Some times due to bad weather, swarming of nymphs from brood is prevented. Hence, the room storing brood lac sticks is moderately heated to 200°C to induce swarming, and then sticks are tied.
5. Generally, cultivation of kusumi in rangeeni area and vice versa should be avoided.

Brood lac from a particular host used year after year is likely to deteriorate in quality. Therefore, alternation of brood and host give production of a better quality of brood lac.

Inoculation Period

As discussed above, each strain of lac insects (Kusumi and Rangeeni) yield two crops a year: jethwi and aghani in case of kusumi strain, and kartiki and baisakhi in case of rangeeni. The inoculation period of all the four types of crops is different: for kartiki, June/July; for baisakhi, Oct./Nov. for agahani, June/July; for jethwi, Jan./Feb.

HARVESTING OF LAC

Harvesting is the process of collection of ready lac from host trees. It is done by cutting the lac encrusted twigs when is crop is mature. It may be of two types:

1. In Immature harvesting, lac is collected before swarming, and lac thus obtained is known as "ARI LAC". The immature harvesting has drawbacks, as the lac insects may be damaged at the time of harvesting. However, incase of palas lac (Rangeeni lac), it is found that ARI Lac gives better production. Hence, ARI lac harvesting is recommended in case of palas only.
2. In mature harvesting, lac is collected after swarming. The lac obtained is known as mature Lac. To know the exact date emergence and swarming of nymph, a simple visual method is adopted. A yellow spot develops on the posterior side of lac cell towards crop maturity. This spot spread forwards until it covers half of the cell. Cutting of twigs for harvest can be done at any time between the stages while yellow spot occupies one third to one half of the cell area. It is sometimes desirable to wait till the emergence of the first few nymphs. The harvesting periods of different crops are different. The kartiki crop is harvested in Oct/Nov; baisakhi, in May/June; aghani in Jan/Feb.; and jethwi, in June/July.

When the nymphs have escaped from the brood lac, what is left is the stick lac or phunki lac. These sticks should be tied in bundles and immersed in water, preferably running water for 3–4 days, keeping them well under waters with help of heavy stones. The stick lac should then be kept in shade for drying. The raw lac should be scraped while sticks are still moist. Following consideration are recommended for harvesting:

- Lac crop should be harvested only when mature. Immature or ARI lac cutting should be avoided though it is recommended in case of palas.
- A mature crop is said to be the one from which nymphs will emerge in 7–10 days. So, the crop should be harvested within the above said days prior to nymphal emergence. If cut earlier, there is a chance of nymphs dying. If cut later, the nymphs may already have emerged before inoculation is adopted.
- Attempt should be made to reap the entire crop, if self inoculation is not required.
- In the case of rangeeni crop, only lac encrusted twigs are cut, while in the case of kusumi one, reaping should combine with pruning.
- The brood sticks harvested should be utilized for inoculation as soon as possible. If storage is needed, these have to be stored in a well-ventilated room or under shade in open prevented from rain and heat.
- Harvesting of lac crop at maturity can solve the crisis of brood lac dearth to a large extent without affecting the quality of lac obtained as phunki lac. This will also reduce the loss of brood lac and enhance the yield.

COMPOSITION OF LAC

The major constituent of lac is the resin. Lac resin is a polyester complex of straight-chain hydroxy fatty acids of C14–C18 carbon chain (such as aleuritic acid, butolic acids), mono- and di- hydroxy acids along with hydroxy terpenic acids. Other constituents present are: dye, wax, sugar, proteins, soluble salts, sand, woody matter, insect body debris, etc. Lac wax is a mixture of anthroquinoid derivatives. Percent-wise composition of lac given below (adopted from ILRI data):

Constituent	*Percentage*
Lac resin	68
Lac wax	6
Lac dye	1-2
Others	25

Byproducts/Waste

The denatured ethyl alcohol used in the process of manufacturing shellac is a strictly regulated by product and is known as a volatile organic substance (VOC). The most dangerous or hazardous part, perhaps the most polluting, are the insolubles that are refined out of the sticklac and grainlac such as twigs, cocoons, leaves, bug bodies, etc. saturated with alcohol. The shellac industry is working on building huge evaporators, which will suck all the alcohol out of these insolubles so the volatility will not be an issue. Shellac flakes are all natural and nontoxic. It is the alcohol solvents that are regulated.

LAC PROCESSING

The Manufacturing Process

The Role of the Lac Bug

Shellac is produced by a tiny red insect. Swarms of the insects feed on certain Trees, primarily in India and Thailand, known informally as lac trees. The lac bugs' life cycle is only 6 months, in which time they eat, propagate, and secrete the resin they've taken in from the tree to produce shellac. In certain seasons of the year, these insects swarm in huge numbers on the trees, settle on branches, and project protrusions into the tree to penetrate the bark. They suck up the sap and absorb it until they feed themselves to death (called the feast of death amongst the indigenous peoples). At this same time, propagation continues, with each female lac bug laying about 1,000 eggs before dying.

The sap is chemically altered in the lac bug's body and is then exuded onto the tree branch. On contact with the air, the excretion forms a hard shell-like covering over the entire swarm. This covering forms a crust over the twig and insects. As the female lac, bug is exuding the ingested sap she is preparing to die and is providing a fluid in which her eggs will mature under protection. The males' role is to fertilize the female, and it is after fertilization that the females' lac output is vastly increased. The adult males and females become inactive, and the young start to break through the crust and swarm out.

Lac Makes It Count

Lac is produced mainly in India, which contributes up to 80% of total global production, as also in countries like Thailand, Indonesia, Myanmar, Philippines,

China, Vietnam and Combodia. India produced 16,495 tons of lac in 2009–10 with Jharkhand producing about 42% followed by Chhattisgarh (30 tons), Madhya Pradesh (15), West Bengal (5) and Maharashtra (3). Simdega (Jharkhand) district alone produced 3,145 tons. Lac production in India has been steadily going down from 23,229 tons in 2006–07 to 16,495 tons in 2009–10. While India exports lac worth Rs 12 crore, it also imports non-Indian varieties of lac worth nearly Rs 16 crore.

USES

Lac is harvested as sticklac, which is then processed to produce commercial grades called shellac, button lac, seedlac, bleached lac and lac dye. There are about 200 such units in India, 138 of them in West Bengal. The shellac variety has application in a number of industries such as wood finishing, printing ink, electric products, leather and footwear, pharmaceuticals, confectionary, fruit coating, cosmetics, paper varnish, photography, rubber, paint, grinding wheels, automobile, dentistry, waxes and dyes.

With a new scientific method of cultivation prescribed by the Indian Institute of Natural Resins and Gums (IINRG), formerly Indian Lac Research Institute, Ranchi—the only of its kind in the world—farmers are handsomely supplementing their income along with growing paddy as the main crop. The KVKs, units promoted by Indian Council of Agriculture research (ICAR), have been painstakingly at work for quite some time in the Vidarbha region: spreading awareness about IINRG's method of lac cultivation, training and field assistance, and also guiding farmers in marketing their produce in select districts. KVK forayed into Gondia district only last year in coordination with the Forest Department.

India is the largest producer (16,495 tons in 2009–10) and exporter (6,700 tons worth Rs 12 crore) of lac in the world. Gondia, incidentally, is also the only lac-producing district in Maharashtra producing 400 tons per year. The two seasons fall in June–July and October–November. Lac is also easy to cultivate. All that a farmer has to do is infest the host trees like palas, berry and kusum with lac insects, Kerria lacca. Thousands of lac insects colonise branches of the trees and secrete the resinous pigment. The coated branches of the host trees are cut and harvested as sticklac.

The scientific intervention has been in many ways. "Earlier, farmers would not prune the tree branches enough number of times. Now, we have given them equipment for extensive pruning that helps in formation of fresh branches. This helps in more lac formation. Earlier, the farmers would simply put branches with lac insects on trees in the next season for fresh growth. Winds would often bring the branches down. We now provide them with branches covered with nets developed by IINRG. The nets lets only the lac insect come out while the enemy pest, crysopa, remains stuck inside". The IINRG has also been promoting a new foreign-origin tree called Flemingia semialta—over the past few years. While it would take up to 7 years for a farmer to grow lac on these trees, production starts within 2 years.

LAC COMPOSITION

Lac, a natural resin, is a hydrocarbon secretion of many plants, particularly coniferous trees. It is valued for its chemical properties and associated uses such as production of varnishes, dyes, wax and adhesives and food-glazing agents. It is also an important source of raw materials for organic synthesis and a constituent of incenses and perfumes. There are two main colors of lac—red and white. The latter is considered premium variety.

1. Stick Lac

Following harvest, lac encrustations are removed from the twigs of host plant by scraping. The raw lac thus obtained is known as raw or crude lac or scraped lac or stick lac. This crude lack consists of resin, encrusted insect body, lac dye, sand and twig debris. The freshly scraped lac contains a lot of moisture and usually left to dry. The quality and value of stick lac depend very much upon variety of factors, viz. host tree, climate, whether the crop is harvested before or after emergence of larvae, and the method of drying and storage. The stick lac cannot be stored for longer duration, as the lac has tendency to form lump, and there is loss in quality of lac. High moisture content is responsible for lump formation. The optimum moisture content has been identified to be 4% for storage of stick lac to avoid lump formation. It is recommended to store the stick lac on floor in layers less than 30 cm in height and racked frequently. If stick lac is converted into seed lac, it can be stored for longer duration like food grains. Establishment of small scale lac processing unit in lac grower villages will help in overcoming this problem.

2. Seed Lac

The primary processing to seed lac soon after harvesting is necessary, because the storage of stick lac is more congenial for lump formation and breeding of storage pests, and thereby causing substantial loses and deterioration in quality of desired industrial parameters. The stick lac is crushed and sieved to remove sand and dust. It is then washed in large vats again and again to break open the encrusted insect bodies, to wash out the lac dye and twig debris. Decaying bug bodies turn the water a deep red that is processed further to get the byproduct lac dye. The remaining resin is dried, winnowed and sieved to get the semi-refined commercial variety product called seed lac. The dusty lac eliminated by sieving is refuse lac known as molamma. The seed lac is in form of grain of 10 mesh or smaller and yellow or reddish brown in color in general appearance. Adhering impurities on the grains of seed lac may be to 3–8% (average 5%).

Following grades of hand made seed lac are commonly available in the market:

- Ordinary / genuine bysakhi
- Fine bysakhi
- Golden bysakhi
- Golden kusumi
- Golden bysakhi – bold grain
- Golden kusumi – bold grain
- Golden kusumi seedlac – medium
- Manbhum fine seedlac.

(In lac trade, baisakhi crop is commonly referred to as bysakhi or bysacki).

3. Shellac

The shellac is the name of finished product and is commonly used across the world. Seed lac is processed into shellac by any of the three methods: (1) handmade country process, (2) heat process and (3) solvent process.

3.1. Handmade Process

Traditionally seed lac is processed by hand. The seed lac is filled into long sausage shaped cloth bag of about 2 inch diameter and 30 feet long. The long bag is passed gradually in front of a charcoal-fired hearth hot enough to melt the lac. By twisting the bag, molten lac is squeezed out through cloth. The residue left inside cloth bag is another variety of refuse lac known as kirilac. The molten filtered mass is stretched into sheets approximately 0.5 cm thick and thinner by skilled work man with the help of glazed ceramic cylinder. Alternatively, the molten mass is allowed to solidify in form of disks, and then it is called as "button lac". The following grades of hand made shellac are commercially available.

- Lemon one shellac
- Lemon tow shellac
- Standard one shellac
- Superior shellac
- Superior kusumi lemon
- Kusumi button lac
- Superior kusumi button lac
- Light pure button lac
- Pure one button lac.

3.2. Heat Process

In this process of manufacturing of shellac, the seed lac is melted by steam heat. The molten soft lac is squeezed through filter by means of hydraulic pressure. The filtered molten lac is drawn into long and continuous sheets with help of roller. The sheet is then broken into pieces called flakes. Following grades of machine made shellac are commercially available:

- Orange shellac
- Lemon one shellac
- Lemon two shellac
- Standard one shellac
- Black T.N. shellac
- Kusumi lemon shellac
- Orange fine shellac.

3.3. Solvent Processes

If the solvent process is used to purify the semi-refined lac, dewaxed and decolorized shellac can be obtained as end-product. The normally amber color resin can also be bleached to get bleached shellac.

Seed lac is dissolved in a refrigerated alcohol and filter through filter press to remove wax and impurities. The color may be removed to any required standard by charging with the activated carbon and then alcohol is recovered. The molten shellac is stretched with a roller. The solvent process of lac manufacture yields the following grades:

- Dewaxed platina dewaxed blonde
- Dewaxed super blonde
- Dewaxed lemon

- Dewaxed orange
- Dewaxed garnet.

(Actually above Roman culture is based on the color of and product. For instance, the color index of platina is about 0.6, of garnet is 35 and of other varieties fall in between) In manufacturing bleached shellac, the basic procedure consists of (i) dissolving seed lac in aqueous sodium carbonate solution at 90–1000°C, (ii) stirring off solution with sodium hypochlorite and (iii) filtering after cooling. The bleached shellac is reclaimed from the filtered solution with sulphuric acid. The reclaimed bleached shellac is then filtered, washed with water for removal of acid and dried. Bleached lac is white in color. It has specialized demand and manufactured commercially in two grades:

a. Dewaxed bleached shellac
b. Waxy bleached shellac.

Aleuritic acid (shellac aleuritic powder) is also isolated further by saponification from resin lac.

LAC PRODUCTS AND THEIR USE

1. Lac Dye

Lac dye is a mixture of anthroquinoid derivatives. It is traditionally used to color wool and silk. Its color varies between purple red, brown and orange often depending upon the mordant used. It is used in food and beverages industry for coloring. In recent past, lac dye has been replaced by synthetic dye. But, nowadays with increasing stress and awareness on use of ecofriendly and safe material particularly associated with human contact and consumption has made revival of great demand of lac dye as a coloring material.

2. Lac Wax

Lac wax is a mixture of higher alcohols, acids and their esters. It is used in:

- Polishes applied on shoes, floor, automobiles, etc.
- Food and confectionary, and drug tablet finishing
- Lipsticks
- Crayons.

3. Shellac

Shellac is a natural gum resin, a nature's gift to the mankind and is used in over 100 industries. It is natural, non toxic, physiologically harmless and edible resin. Shellac is a hard, tough, amorphous, and brittle resin containing small amount of wax and a substance responsible for its characteristic pleasant odor. The lac resin is not a single chemical compound, but an intimate mixture of several components. Shellac is slightly heavier than water. Its natural color varies from dark-red to light yellow. When slowly heated, it softens at 65–70°C and melts at 84–90°C. Shellac is insoluble in water, glycerol, hydrocarbon solvents and esters, but dissolves readily in alcohols and organic acids. Usually, the milder alkalis, ammonia, borax and sodium carbonate can also be employed to prepare aqueous solutions. Shellac is acidic in character. Acid value is 70. It is an ester. Saponification value 230. It has free five hydroxyl groups and has hydroxyl number 260. It has unsaturation indicated by iodine value of 18. Free aldehydic group also has been indicated by carboxyl value of 18. Its average molecular weight is 1,000. Normal wax content of shellac is 5% which is insoluble in alcohol. It is soluble in n-hexane, pure terpentine, and other hydrocarbon oils. It is hard and having melting point 84°C. It has the following extra ordinary properties:

i. It is thermoplastic.
ii. It is approved for various applications in the food industry.
iii. It is UV-resistant.
iv. It has excellent dielectric properties, dielectric strength, a low dielectric consent, good tracking resistance, etc.
v. It has excellent film forming properties. Its film shows excellent adhesion to wide variety of surfaces and possess high gloss, hardness and strength.
vi. Shellac is a powerful bonding material with low thermal conductivity and a small coefficient of expansion. Its thermal plasticity and capacity of absorbing large amounts of fillers is noteworthy.
vii. Shellac under tropical conditions of storage, may soften and form a solid block, without adverse effects on its properties. Long storage under adverse conditions, however, may lead to deterioration in properties.
viii. When shellac is heated for a long time above its melting point, it gradually loses its fluidity and passes through a rubbery stage to hard, horn-like and infusible.

Uses:

- It is used in fruit coatings, e.g. for citrus fruits and apples, parting and glazing agents for sweets, marzipan, chocolate, etc. Also used as binder for foodstuff stamp inks, e.g. for cheese and eggs.
- It is used as binder for mascara, nail varnish additive conditioning shampoo, film forming agent for hair spray, micro-encapsulation for perfumes.
- It is used for enteric (i.e. digestive juice-resistant) coatings for tablets and as odor barrier for dragées.
- It is used in manufacturing of photographic material, lithographic ink and for stiffening felt and hat material.
- It is utilized in preparation of gramophone records.
- Jewelers and goldsmiths use lac as a filling material in the hollows in ornaments.
- It is also used in preparation of toys, buttons, pottery and artificial leather.
- It is also used commonly as sealing wax.

With increasing environmental awareness of consumers, this natural and renewable raw material is being used increasingly in the development of new products apart from the conventional user industries. Few to name:

- Leather: Seasoning, leather care products.
- Printing inks: As binder for flexographic printing inks for nontoxic printing of food packaging.
- Wood treatment: Primers, polishes, matt finishes.
- Textiles: As stiffeners.
- Electrical: Insulation, capping, lamination.
- Abrasives: Binder for grinding wheels.
- Others: Binder for inks and water colors, microencapsulation for dyes.

4. Bleached Shellac

Bleached shellac is nontoxic, physiologically harmless (edible), and is widely used in the food industries, food packaging and allied industries. Apart from the above, bleached shellac is also used for its qualities, i.e. binding, adhesive, hardening, gloss, odorless, fast drying, and extending shelf life (in absence of refrigeration), etc. Clear and transparent or very light colored alcoholic or water-alkali solutions can be obtained from bleached shellac.

Uses: Bleached shellac is widely used in the following industry:

- Paints (primer for plastic parts and plastic film)
- Aluminum industry (primer for aluminum and aluminum foils)
- Flexographic printing inks
- Pharmaceuticals (for coating of pills, tables and gel caps and coating for controlled release preparation)
- Confectionery (in coating of confections, chewing gums, marzipan chocolates, nutties, jelly- and coffee-beans, etc)
- Binder for food marking and stamping inks and Binder for egg coating
- Barrier coating for processed food, vegetables, fruits and dry flowers
- Textiles (used as textile auxiliaries and felt hat stiffening agents)
- Cosmetics (used in hair spray, hair and lacquers, hair shampoos, and binder for mascara)
- Wood finishing (as binder for wood coatings and wood stains and as filler/ sealer for porous surfaces and cracks)
- Antique frames for paintings and Wood polish (French polish)
- Fireworks and pyrotechnics (as binder for fireworks, matches, etc and used in coating of magnesia
- Electric (as binder for lamp cements)
- Electronics (it is binder for insulation materials, serves as additive to molding compounds. Mass coating for print-plates and is adhesive for si-cells.)
- Grinding wheels (it is binder for additive of grinding wheels)
- Plastic (it is primer for plastic parts and films)
- Rubber (it is additive to natural rubber)
- Leather (in leather auxiliaries).

5. Dewaxed Bleached Shellac

Dewaxed white shellac is used in the same way as any other grade of shellac. The major difference between this shellac and the others is that it is a bit harder, shines a bit brighter, is completely free from wax. Bleached lac has super characteristics and qualities, i.e. adhesive, binding, hardening, gloss, odorless. It has good film forming properties, a high gloss and excellent adhesion to various substrates including the human hair. It is nontoxic and physiologically harmless. Good solution can be obtained in ethanol and lower alcohols. It can also be dissolved in water by adding an alkali like Ammonia. It is compatible with many other resins, raw materials and additives used in cosmetics, pharmaceuticals and food formulations.

Uses:

i. Coating of fruits and vegetables
ii. Coating in tablets and capsules

iii. Coating in confectionary
iv. Coating in aluminum foil, paper
v. Coating in cosmetic industry
vi. In cosmetics, it is used in hair sprays (pump sprays or aerosol sprays, hair setting lotions, hair shampoos, mascara, eyeliners, nail polishes, lipsticks, microencapsulation by coacervation of fragrances and perfume oils.
vii. In food, it is used for coating of confections, chewing gum, candles, cakes, eggs, citrus fruits and apples, and printing inks for eggs and cheese.

LAC PESTS

The insects are serious and damaging pests to the lac crop also, like the other agricultural crops. These insect pests destroy 30–40% of lac. The insects damage the lac crop is two ways:

i. As parasites: Lac insects are parasitized by small winged eight species of insect belonging to family chalcidae order Hymenoptera. These insect pests lay eggs in lac cells. Their grubs on hatching feed on lac insects within the cells. Loss due these parasites is 5–10%.
ii. As predators: The predators account major damage (up to 35%) of lac crop.

There are three main insect predators on lac:

a. *Eublemma amabilis moori*: Commonly known as white lac moth, order Lepidoptera
b. *Holocerca pulverea meyr*: Commonly known as black lac moth, order lepidoptera
c. *Chrysopa spp*.: Commonly known as lac wing fly, order Diptera

These predators moths and fly lay their eggs on the lac encrusted twigs. On hatching, their larvae make their way inside the lac encrustation and feed on the lac insects as well as on lac encrustations. The white lac moth is more destructive on trees; while black lac moth, on the stored lac. In addition to insect pests, squirrels and monkeys also damage lac. The rodents could damage greatly. These pests gnaw the mature lac encrustations on the trees or brood lac sticks tied for inoculation, and thus, consuming gravid females. The brood lac can be made to fall on the ground by these animals preventing inoculation. Forest fires too often break out in deciduous forests in summer season and destroy both lac insects and their host plants.

Following precaution should be taken to prevent the damage caused by insect pests:

i. Only healthy pest-free brood lac should be used for inoculation. The twigs for inoculation should be cut just before swarming to get healthy brood.
ii. Entire crop should be harvested, as left over may attract the pests.
iii. The stick or phunki lac should be fumigated or immersed in water to kill the pest if any.
iv. Scrapping of encrusted lac from twigs should be done as soon as possible, and lac, thus obtained should be immediately converted into seed lac and not left near the inoculated lac hosts.
v. Infected stick lac should be destroyed along with predators and pests.

POTENTIAL OF INDIA IN LAC PRODUCTION

Nowadays, there is increased stress on the use of eco-friendly and safe material particularly associated with human contact and consumption. Lac is natural, renewable, biodegradable, versatile and nontoxic resin. Thus, a very good increase in demand for lac worldwide is envisaged. The envisaged objective of enhancing lac production has relevance and importance. It is a source of livelihood of tribal and poor inhabiting forest and subforest areas. India is the principal lac producing country of the world, producing approximately 18,000 metric tones of unrefined raw lac annually. About 85% of the country's production is exported to various countries. The USA, Germany and Egypt are some of the major lac importing countries of the world. Export of lac from India is in the form of shellac/button lac, seed lac, dewaxed lac, bleached lac and aleuritic acid. India has great potential for lac culture. The areas for lac cultivation can be broadly classified into three categories: (a) regular lac cultivation areas – at present, only 20–25% of the total available trees are being utilized, (b) moderate lac cultivation areas – around 10-15% available trees are being utilized and (c) lac host trees are available but due to lack of knowledge and awareness, none of the trees are utilized for lac cultivation. Thus, on an average, only 15% of the available lac host trees owned by farmers are being utilized for lac cultivation presently. There are vast untapped areas, which are ecologically favorable for lac production in the country. These areas possess the potential lac host plants which if exploited properly in scientific and systematic manner is liable to enhance the lac production. Enhancing the exploitation of the idle or unexploited lac host plants in favorable lac growing areas can also enhance the lac production. Indian Lac Research Institute (ICAR), Namkum, Ranchi established in 1924 is actively engaged in addressing the objective of enhancing lac productivity and production through transfer and adoption of proven technologies by interfacing research, development and extension. The Institute has developed various technologies and cultivation packages. By implementing and adopting the scientific method of cultivation, proper host plant management, integrated pest management, enhancing exploitation of unexploited host plants, and cultivation through "Joint Forest Management" program, the lac production can be enhanced in future.

While enhancing production quality needs equal emphasis to meet the National and International demand. The quality of lac suffers due to following reasons like untimely harvesting, lack of appropriate storage, primary processing soon after harvesting and lack of appropriate processing machines for quality and recovery. These problems may be addressed by adopting recommended technologies developed by the Institute.

LAC IN INDIA

Biggest producer Jharkhand worst hit—and clueless Jharkhand has the reputation of being India's biggest producer of lac. The state accounts for more than 50% of the country's lac produce. In 2004–05, Jharkhand produced 10,780 tons of lac. This season (2010) from March to October, traders were expecting 2,500–3,000 tons. Much of the demand for lac comes from the defence industry, for making ammunitions. It is also used in airplanes, furniture polish and perfumes, and in making bangles, imitation fruits and flowers.

FARMERS AND TRADERS HELPLESS

Lac production is declining in all the states as well, including Chhattisgarh, Madhya Pradesh, Maharashtra and West Bengal. The situation is so grave that India has to turn to Thailand—its biggest competitor in the global market—to import broods of lac insects, and lac in the form of final product.

Since 2008, entire colonies of lac insect, Kerria lacca, have been dying during the reproductory period. The reason for the mass deaths is uncertain. Some say it is change in climatic conditions, others blame a parasite or even weather changes responsible for the reduced lac production. According to this school of thought if the weather is not favorable there may not be enough insects to infest the next crop. "During March and April, the heat is unbearable. This excessive heat makes the resin melt, killing the newly produced baby insects. It is believed that an internal parasite is eating the insect". The parasite has always lived inside the insect and that is why it was never perceived as a threat. It is destroying colonies of the insect at the time they reproduce. So far the parasite, *Afrosticus purpurious,* accounted for 8% of the damage, but now it has gone up to 50%. Since it grows within the lac insect, insecticides cannot be used because they will kill the parasite along with its host, Mishra added. The rate at which lac insects are dying is high which makes it difficult for poor farmers to continue investing in broods to infest trees. So, they give up lac cultivation.

Despite rural people's dependence on lac, the government does not have a support price. This leaves producers at the mercy of traders. The number of host trees in Jharkhand can produce 100,000 tons of lac and the state alone can meet the whole country's demand for lac.

In India, two strains of the lac insect, rangeeni and kusmi, contribute to the production. The Rangeeni strain is the one getting destroyed. To revive cultivation of the insects, the National Bank for Agriculture and Rural Development a trying to experiment with the Kusumi strain though Rangeeni is more popular. The government is yet to respond.

LAC PRODUCTION IN INDIA

Year-wise production of raw lac (tons)

State	*2003-04*	*2004-05*	*2005-06*	*2006-07*	*2007-08*	*2008-09*	*2009-10*	*Mean*
Jharkhand	9,860	10,780	6,414	7,490	6,385	4,000	6,925	9,831,50
Chhattisgarh	5,140	4,270	6,015	8,875	7,160	7,198	4,995	6,236,14
Madhya Pradesh	1,905	2,870	2,515	3,164	3,755	2,970	2,390	2,795,57
Maharashtra	633	875	1,160	1,300	1,070	1,050	520	944,00
West Bengal	1,270	1,395	926	1,240	1,140	830	855	1,093,71
Total	18,808	20,190	17,030	22,069	19,510	16,048	15,685	

Source: Down to Earth, November 16-30, 2010.

LAKHS IN LAC

Despite a drop in production in the past 5 years, India remains the global leader in lac export (*see* "Export of lac"). The US is the largest consumer of lac with an annual demand of 6,000 tons, according to the Forest Products Export Promotion Council. IINRG scientists say lac has the capability of turning around economic conditions of farmers. Demand for natural products in Western countries coupled with declining lac production has increased its price, they say. The scientists, however, point out that many importers are using synthetic or artificial lac owing to the rising costs. "We need to start a mission jointly with the forest and agriculture departments, and NGOs to boost lac production in Jharkhand, Chhattisgarh and West Bengal", says R Ramani, director of IINRG. As for the method they have developed to produce lac, he says, "We are a research institute. We can make breakthroughs in lac production but it is the government and nonprofits that can spread the new method of lac farming".

To further boost lac production in Jharkhand, INRG has collaborated with Indian Council of Agricultural Research, Ranchi. It is experimenting with planting semialata plant between mango trees. Semialata plant rot goes barely 0.3 meter deep into the soil.

- **Hop Back:** A vessel filled with hops that acts as a filter, removing hot break material from wort on the way to the chiller.
- **International Bittering Units (IBU):** A chemical measurement of the actual bitterness in beer. An IBU is defined as one milligram of isomerized alpha acid per liter of beer. May be different from perceived bitterness.
- **Isomerization:** A chemical process in which a compound is changed into another form with the same chemical composition but a different structure.
- **Lupulin Glands:** Small, bright yellow nodes at the base of each hop petal that contains the alpha acids and essential oils utilized by brewers.
- **Randall:** A hop-filled vessel that is placed in the draft line between the keg and the faucet.

Hops for Decoration

Traditionally, garlands of hops were hung afresh every year - for good luck - in the pubs and farmhouses of the hop-growing areas of the UK (Kent, Herefordshire and Worcestershire) but few people outside of these areas appreciated the decorative potential of a full-flowered hop bine until the Hop Shop started, in 1986, growing and marketing them nationwide specifically for interior use. To achieve top decorative quality, our hops are grown at extra-wide spacing to encourage flowering along the full length of the bine. (This means that they are bigger, fuller bines and more consistent in their flowering than hops produced from closely-spaced brewing hops which are always competing for sunlight). The fully-grown bines are harvested from mid-August to mid-September when they are in their prime and have their freshest green color. They are either sold as fresh-cut bines for immediate decorative use or dried in the dark in temperature- and humidity-controlled sheds to hold their color. They are then boxed and stored in insulated, dehumidified stores for sale throughout the year. The decorative bines are approximately 3m (10 ft) in length. Now, dried hop bines can be seen throughout the UK, over the bars in pubs, trailed along the top of kitchen units, twisted around wedding marquee poles or adorning the beams of old barns.

Fresh hop bines can be purchased (cut to order) from mid-August to mid-September and either collected direct from the shop or despatched by 24-hour courier to most. Dried hop bines are available throughout the year for purchase direct from the shop or for despatch by Royal Mail or 48-hour courier throughout the UK and Northern Ireland.

Hops for Sleep

Read old books on herbal remedies and you will always find reference to both hops and lavender being good for sleep and for many years customers have been asking us for hop flowers to make sleep pillows and lavender oils to aid relaxation.

It was therefore a logical step to combine the soporific and therapeutic qualities of hops and lavender into a unique Sleepy Scent, a Sleepy Tea and a Pillow Mix – all for people who don't want to take conventional sleeping pills. The BBC2 program by James Wong, first broadcast in March 2009, recommended the use of hop and lavender flowers to make hop pillows and The Hop Shop was instantly inundated with orders and enquiries. The response from users was overwhelmingly and consistently positive to the entire product range, with many recommendations and

Index

R

S

T

W

Y

Table 4.1: Development of surface and yields of hops worldwide

		2001	2002	2003	2004	2005	2006	2007	2008
Acreage (aroma varieties)	Ha	28,069	27,000	25,595	25,903	25,879	25,862	25,583	27,105
Acreage (bitter varieties)	Ha	27,460	25,725	25,064	24,197	22,565	20,212	23,940	26,759
Total acreage	Ha	57,967	55,348	52,203	51,408	48,995	46,095	49,523	53,865
% bitter varieties	%	47.4	46.5	48.0	47.1	46.1	43.8	48.3	49.7
Acreage (new)	Ha	2,438	2,623	1,544	1,362	586	844	1,551	5,420
Yield (aroma varieties)	Kg/ha	1,361	1,448	1,233	1,486	1,636	1,338	1,559	1,706
Yield (bitter varieties)	Kg/ha	2,203	2,911	2,116	2,238	2,265	1,846	2,171	2,426
Yield (all varieties)	Kg/ha	1,703	2,059	1,812	1,802	1,907	1,766	1,815	2,063
Yield of alpha acid	Kg/ha	149	155	135	164	167	151	165	194
% alpha acid	%	8.8	7.5	7.4	9.1	8.7	8.5	9.1	9.4
Production (aroma varieties)	Tons	38,212	39,090	31,566	38,504	42,336	34,594	39,893	46,228
Production (bitter varieties)	Tons	60,494	74,892	53,024	54,160	51,106	37,306	51,974	64,912
Total production	Tons	98,705	113,983	84,590	92,655	93,445	81,401	89,866	111,140
Total production of alpha acid	Tons	8,639	8,596	7,023	8,452	8,158	6,956	8,161	10,468

Source: IHGC, adaptation LEI.